Genre Talks for Teens

Booktalks and More for Every Teen Reading Interest

Lucy Schall

LIBRARIES UNLIMITED

A Member of the Greenwood Publishing Group

Westport, Connecticut • London

Library of Congress Cataloging-in-Publication Data

Schall, Lucy.
    Genre talks for teens : booktalks and more for every teen reading
interest / Lucy Schall.
        p. cm.
    Includes bibliographical references and index.
    ISBN 978–1–59158–743–9 (alk. paper)
        1. Teenagers—Books and reading—United States.   2. Book talks—United States.
3. Young adult literature—Bibliography.   4. Fiction genres—Bibliography.   I. Title.
Z1037.A1S272   2009
028.5'5—dc22   2008054984

British Library Cataloguing in Publication Data is available.

Library of Congress Catalog Card Number: 2008054984
ISBN: 978–1–59158–743–9

First published in 2009

Libraries Unlimited, 88 Post Road West, Westport, CT 06881
A Member of the Greenwood Publishing Group, Inc.
www.lu.com

Printed in the United States of America

The paper used in this book complies with the
Permanent Paper Standard issued by the National
Information Standards Organization (Z39.48–1984).

10 9 8 7 6 5 4 3 2 1

*To my sister, Kathleen Smith, and
my brother, James Flynn, whose enthusiasm for reading
has led me to many good books for teens.*

Contents

Acknowledgments

I wish to thank Barbara Ittner, my editor, for her insight, encouragement, and patience; Linda Benson, from VOYA, for the generous sharing of her expertise; and Diana Tixier Herald for my organizational model.

The staffs of the following libraries and media centers have provided me with resources and support: St. Petersburg Public Libraries in St. Petersburg, Florida; the growing teen section in the Meadville Public Library; and the Meadville Middle School and High School Media Center in Meadville, Pennsylvania.

Introduction

Like my other booktalk guides, *Genre Talks for Teens* suggests high-quality books for booktalks, reading aloud, discussion, research projects, creativity, coordinated displays, book club programs, lesson plans, and just enjoyment and involvement. Families and professionals who live and work with teens will find a wide range of reading choices that encourage teenagers to think about and explore their interests, and discover a few new ones. These selections should prepare readers for classics, more difficult writing styles, and thoughtful conversation. The seven chapter titles are based on popular genres, the same as those in *Booktalks and Beyond: Promoting Great Genre Reads to Teens:* Issues, Contemporary, Adventure/Survival, Mystery/Suspense, Fantasy/Science Fiction/Paranormal, History, and Multiple Cultures. More specific topics and themes divide each chapter.

The bibliography information for featured books and "Related Works" includes the author name, book title, publisher and date of publication, number of pages, price and ISBN, as well as a bracketed fiction, nonfiction, graphic novel [graphic], or reference [reference] designation, and a reading level suggestion (see below). After reading Rollie James Welch's challenging book, *The Guy-Friendly YA Library* (2007), I added a gender designation. These designations are coded as follows:

C	=	children
M	=	middle school
J	=	junior high
S	=	senior high
A	=	adult
G	=	girls
B	=	boys
CG	=	cross gender

In addition, cross gender designations may also include the phrases "with high interest for boys" or "with high interest for girls." The abbreviation "pa." indicates paperback.

Remember! Because teen readers, like adults, have a broad range of purpose and preference in their reading, these reading level and gender designations are only *suggestions*. They are intended to help a reading guide reach his or her customer more quickly, not limit reader choices. I hope that the designations and suggestions for these books that were published primarily between 2005 and 2008, as well as the theme/topic listings and book summaries, will aid professionals and nonprofessionals working with young people to match books and readers.

Following the theme/topic designations and summary, each selection includes a "Read Aloud/Reader Response" section. At least five specific passages are designated for sharing aloud, reflecting for discussion or writing, or preparing dramatic readings or performances. The "Read Aloud/Reader Response" entries include a chapter, section, or division where possible, as well as a page designation, a beginning and ending phrase to locate the passage, and a brief comment on the content. In some cases, an entire chapter is utilized. If a book has no chapter headings, the passages are designated by page numbers only. (For example, the graphic novel, *Mouse Guard: Fall 1152*, has no page numbers.) Sections of special interest are indicated by chapter placement. Some "Read Aloud/Reader Response" passages can be used as attention-getting statements for classroom or book display posters. Others are natural springboards for discussions or provide ready-made booktalks.

Booktalks advertise both the book and the library. Teachers supplementing textbook information may find that booktalking makes that supplemental reading list a personalized reference document as students note their preferences during the presentation. Booktalks in this volume can be considered either "ready-mades" or springboards for writing another booktalk according to your personal style or purpose. Presenter directions for some of the booktalks are in italics. Because they are short enough to hold a teen audience's attention, several booktalks from different genres can be included in one standard forty-five-minute program. Individual booktalks might introduce or conclude a class period or library program. Easily adapted for a school's morning announcements or the school newspaper, the booktalks are also appropriate for local public service announcements, newsletters, or Web sites. Nonprofit use is permitted and encouraged.

Every booktalker has a distinct style and favorite methods. The following are some suggestions I can pass on from my own experience. Read every book you booktalk. Booktalk only the books you respect.

Include books from several genres. Tell your audience how a book from one genre relates to a book in another. If you are planning a full program of booktalks, invite your audience to select the books they want to hear about from the books that you bring. Display the books so that the covers hold the audience's attention. Hand out an annotated list at the beginning of the program for the audience to refer to and visit later. In any booktalk situation, keep the booktalk short. Hold the book while you speak. Have extra copies so that (if you are lucky) you have a replacement for the one snatched by an eager reader. Involve your audience, if only with a rhetorical question, at least every five minutes. Refer to another publication from Libraries Unlimited, *The Booktalker's Bible: How to Talk about the Books You Love to Any Audience* (2003) by Chapple Langemack. Keep in mind that in this age of fragmented scheduling, forty-five-minute presentations by one speaker may not be possible, and adapt as needed. Remember to involve the technology and the teen customers who use it. They will undoubtedly have some ideas for booktalk delivery too. *The Tech-Savvy Booktalker: A Guide for 21st-Century Educators* (2009) by Nancy J. Keane and Terence W. Cavanaugh is a strong resource for expanding booktalk delivery within a shrinking time frame and budget if you have willing and skilled volunteers to help.

The format of the "Get Involved" sections was influenced by Bonnie Kunzel's and Constance Hardesty's *The Teen-Centered Book Club: Readers into Leaders* (2006). The sections include primarily six different types of activities for book groups and individuals. "Research" suggestions require that a member of a discussion group prepare before the book discussion. His or her job will be to find background or related information that will enrich the discussion and to interject that information as the discussion develops. "React" and "Discuss" designate questions or directions that require readers to give a personal opinion and then support that opinion and compare it with others. "Create" activities call for artistic, writing, or dramatic responses to particular books. "Compare" designations refer to additional reading or works. "Follow-up" suggestions take the reader and the group beyond the book, and sometimes into their community. Many activities in the "Get Involved" section may provide a basis for independent studies, portfolios, or senior projects, and some can supplement the traditional classroom questions and activities often marketed with a teen book.

"Related Works" include sources for expanded learning, further reading, and inter-genre relationships. The listings include books as well as graphic novels, short stories, plays, poems, reference books, and Web sites. These sections will help build book displays, book programs, and units of study. Including graphic novels with traditional books, some from other genres, may surprise readers and expand their reading interest. "Related Works" can also guide instructors, librarians, and parents to additional reading or information sources. The index includes authors, titles, and topics for a quick overview of a work's relationships to others mentioned in this volume.

As for the selection of titles found in this guide, the professional recommendations from *VOYA, Booklist, School Library Journal,* the *ALAN Review,* as well as award lists and YALSA's "best" booklists are a must for me. Personal reactions from my reading family, friends, and audiences influence my final choices, too.

It is my hope that this volume gives you useful tools for advertising the great collections you have, motivating more readers to explore recent texts, and encouraging your "customers" to show or tell their own stories.

Issues

Issues books confront serious topics such as identity, abuse, dependency, dysfunctional families, and disease. Selections with high interest for boys tend to have more action and unusual situations, but all have resolutions that either give hope for the future or challenge readers to find hope and meaning in their own lives. The books in "Coping with Others' Choices" confront problems that come to us from others. "Facing Our Own Choices" books deal with problems or situations that we initiate.

Coping with Others' Choices

Anderson, Laurie Halse. **Twisted.**
New York: Viking Press, 2007. 250p. $16.99.
ISBN-13: 978 0 670 06101 3. [fiction] JS, CG

Themes/Topics: family problems, friendship, high school, coming of age, bullies

Summary/Description

Senior Tyler Miller builds muscles and catches the attention of the most popular girl in school after he is arrested for graffiti and required to work outdoors to pay for the damage. The girl is the sister of the boy who bullies him and the daughter of his father's boss. During a wild party, she is photographed nude, and the pictures are sent over the Internet. Tyler, because of the graffiti incident, is accused, and because he refused to have sex with her when she was drunk, the girl turns against him. The resulting turmoil removes Tyler temporarily from classes, disrupts the already fragile marriage of Tyler's upwardly mobile parents, and threatens the job of Tyler's father. Eventually, Tyler takes a stand against both the school and his father. He insists on attending class, signs up for the courses he wants rather than the ones his parents want, sees the popular girl for what she is, and confronts his father about bullying the family.

Read Aloud/Reader Response

1. Chapter 8, page 21, beginning "See, that was why..." and ending "...after the game." Describing why he is a bad son, Tyler reveals the unrealistic standards of his father and grandfather.
2. Chapter 18, page 56. This chapter illustrates the excuses the mother makes for the father's behavior and Tyler's reaction to them.
3. Chapter 22, pages 61 to 62. The chapter describes the popular dress of the high school girls and why that behavior disturbs the school.
4. Chapter 39, pages 104 to 106, beginning "Level Thirty-Six in Tophet..." and ending "...the bond market?" Tyler realizes that his father suffers from his job and values.
5. Chapter 65, pages 196 to 197, beginning "A cracking metal sound..." and ending "'...live your own life.'" The janitor tells Tyler to stop being a victim.

Booktalk

Senior Tyler Miller used to be a loser nobody noticed. In his junior year, he did a graffiti number, got caught, and spent his summer working outside to pay for the damage. School is about to start. According to the high school population, the new Tyler is a dangerous rebel with muscles all over his six-foot-three, one-hundred-and-ninety-five-pound frame. The high school crowd notices him now, especially the school's glamour goddess. One of Tyler's problems is that the glamour goddess's brother loves to make Tyler's life miserable. Another problem is that her father is his dad's boss. Should he get close to her? She seems to want to. But Tyler's parents aren't impressed with his new muscles or his romantic questions. All they want are high grades. They sign him up for courses more advanced than he can handle. Then they ignore the manual labor that gave him his new look. They want him to study, study, study, stick to the straight and narrow, get into a great school, and make them proud. But Tyler isn't ready to get with their program. He knows that the success path brought them fighting, therapy, high blood pressure, and too much liquor. To him, the road to success doesn't look either straight or narrow. To him, it just all looks *Twisted*.

Get Involved

1. (Research) Using your library resources read about *Paradise Lost* and *Faustus*. Act as a resource person for the discussion, and based on the information you find, discuss how those allusions add to the story.
2. (Research) Using your library resources research the definitions for motif, symbol, and theme. Share the definitions with the group and discuss if the definitions apply to *Twisted*.
3. (Compare) Parties are crucial in *Speak* (Related Work 2), *Prom* (Related Work 1), and *Twisted*. Read all three or organize a discussion group in which the members have read at least one of the three. Discuss how Anderson uses the party setting in each novel.
4. (React) Do you agree with Anderson's portrayal of high school life? Support your opinion with specifics from the novel.
5. (React) Is the ending of *Twisted* realistic for you? Support your answer with specifics from the text.

Related Works

1. Anderson, Laurie Halse. **Prom.** New York: Viking Press, 2005. 215p. $16.99. ISBN 0 670 05974 9. [fiction] JS, G (See full booktalk in *Booktalks and Beyond,* 2007, pages 56 to 58.) Eighteen-year-old Ashley Hannigan, the oldest of four in a dysfunctional family, decides to help with the prom and discovers her leadership abilities and her mistakes in choosing her boyfriend and neglecting school.
2. Anderson, Laurie Halse. **Speak.** New York: Farrar, Straus and Giroux, 1999. 198p. $16.00. ISBN 0 374 37152 0. [fiction] JS, G (See full booktalk in *Booktalks and More,* 2003, pages 75 to 77.) Melinda Sordino, the daughter of upwardly mobile parents, is raped by a football player and waits a full school year to tell her story.
3. Korman, Gordon. **Jake, Reinvented.** New York: Hyperion, 2003. 213p. $15.99. ISBN 0 786 81957 X. [fiction] JS, CG with high interest for boys. Through the narrator Rick, the reader learns about Jake, a brainy social outsider who manufactures a new persona to capture the cold, popular girl he adores.
4. Nelson, Blake. **The New Rules of High School.** New York: Viking Press, 2003. 227p. $16.99. ISBN 0 670 03644 7. [fiction] JS, CG Seventeen-year-old Max Caldwell decides, in his senior year, that he will build a life based on his own feelings and ambitions rather than his parents' expectations.
5. Simmons, Michael. **Pool Boy.** Brookfield, CT: Roaring Brook Press/ A Neal Porter Book, 2003. 164p. $23.90. ISBN 0 7613 1914 2.

[fiction] JS, CG with high interest for boys. (See full booktalk in *Booktalks and Beyond,* 2007, pages 55 to 56.) After his father is convicted of insider trading, fifteen-year-old Brett works for the family's former pool man and learns the satisfaction of hard work and good personal relationships.

ლჯ'ঌ

Brooks, Martha. **Mistik Lake.**

New York: Farrar, Straus and Giroux/Melanie Kroupa Books, 2007. 207p. $16.00.
ISBN-13: 978 0 374 34985 1. [fiction] S, G

Themes/Topics: secrets, interpersonal relations, mothers, conduct of life, choices in love, Manitoba (Canada), Icelanders

Summary/Description

In the small town of Mistik Lake, the family's summer retreat, seventeen-year-old Odella slowly unravels the web of secrets that grips her family and discovers her own love in the process. Odella's mother dies in a climbing accident in Iceland after running off to Iceland with her film teacher. Odella's great-aunt Gloria comes to help heal the family but then leaves and stays away. Odella's father keeps the family functioning day to day but ignores the critical issues that they face. As Odella tries to draw the family together and understand how an automobile accident for which her mother felt responsible warps her mother's and her family's lives, she discovers that her glamorous aunt is a lesbian afraid to introduce her partner to her nieces, that her mother had another baby after abandoning the family, that her biological father is a man her mother dated while engaged to be married, and that the man Odella considered her father knew that she was not his child. In her healing process, she enters a love affair with the grandson of the man her aunt refused to marry, accepts her new baby sister, and resolves to allow her heart, rather than other people's opinions, direct her life. The content requires a mature audience and may be considered controversial.

Read Aloud/Reader Response

1. "Prologue," pages 1 and 2. The prologue explains the mother's accident on the ice and the setting of family and Mistik Lake.
2. Part I, "At Fifteen," pages 21 to 22, beginning "Later, in bed, as all of this..." and ending with "...missing tooth." Odella reflects on the pain of her mother leaving.

3.   Part I, "From Bad to Worse," pages 74 to 75, beginning "Around the end…" and ending with the chapter. Odella begins to find her solace in her dreams of Mistik Lake and Jimmy.
4.   Part II, "Family Secrets," page 97, beginning "I finally answer…" and ending "…why I called her." Odella expresses her regret over her last visit with her mother.
5.   Part II, "Getting to Know Mr. Isfeld," pages 176 to 178, beginning "On Wednesday,…" and ending "But he doesn't." Mr. Isfeld initiates a private conversation with Odella before she learns he is her biological father.

Booktalk

Seventeen-year-old Odella wonders why her mother ran away to Iceland, why her aunt never comes to visit the family anymore, and why her father just buries himself in work. Are Odella and her sisters that difficult to be around? Then she begins to unravel a web of secrets—accidents, betrayals, lies, and lovers that no one wants to talk about. And slowly, Odella decides to make her own secrets with a new boy in her life, a boy named Jimmy whose family's lives intertwine with her family's lies. A boy who shares and understands the mistakes that all families make. A boy who understands what it means to live, like Odella, with things not talked about and problems not solved. A boy who knows the private lives and prying eyes of the small town called *Mistik Lake.*

Get Involved

1.   (Research) Find out as much as possible about Martha Brooks and her works. During the discussion, act as a resource person for the group.
2.   (Compare) After reading *Mistik Lake,* read *Being with Henry, Bone Dance,* and *True Confessions of a Heartless Girl* (Related Works 1, 2, 3), discuss the themes, characters, settings, and organization that these four works share.
3.   (React) Do you agree with the title choice?
4.   (Discuss) Do you think that Odella is headed for a better and happier life than her aunt and mother? Support your opinion with specific details from the text.
5.   (React) Odella uncovers many family secrets. Which do you feel is the most important? Support your choice with specifics from the story.
6.   (Follow-up) Explain how secrets have affected you and your relationship with others.

Related Works

1. Brooks, Martha. **Being with Henry.** New York: DK Ink/Melanie Kroupa Books, 2000. 216p. $17.95. ISBN 0 7894 2588 2. [fiction] JS, CG Sixteen-year-old Lake Wyatt finds a home with an older, lonely man, and eventually, with the man's help, uncovers the family secrets that have haunted him.
2. Brooks, Martha. **Bone Dance.** New York: Laurel-Leaf Books, 1997. 179p. $4.50pa. ISBN 0 440 22791 7. [fiction] JS, G (See full book-talk in *Booktalks and More,* 2003, pages 70 to 72.) A piece of land, and mysterious dreams, bring together two teenagers and help them understand their personal and family histories.
3. Brooks, Martha. **True Confessions of a Heartless Girl.** New York: Farrar, Straus and Giroux/Melanie Kroupa Books, 2003. 181p. $16.00. ISBN 0 374 37806 1. [fiction] JS, G (See full booktalk in *Booktalks and Beyond,* 2007, pages 47 to 50.) The mistakes of a pregnant teenage runaway help a small town come to terms with the mistakes and secrets of their own lives and help her understand responsibility.
4. Nolan, Han. **Dancing on the Edge.** New York: Puffin Books, 1997. 244p. $4.99pa. ISBN 0 14 130203 8. [fiction] S, G (See full booktalk in *Booktalks and More,* 2003, pages 26 to 28.) A family's secrets, lies, and distortions drive sixteen-year-old Miracle McCloy to the edge of mental illness.
5. Woodson, Jacqueline. **Miracle's Boys.** New York: G. P. Putnam's Sons, 2000. 131p. $15.99. ISBN 0 399 23113 7. [fiction] MJS, CG (See full booktalk in *Teen Genre Connections,* 2005, pages 28 to 30.) Three brothers sort out their guilt and family history after their parents' deaths.

௸௸

Cooney, Caroline B. A Friend at Midnight.

Colorado Springs, CO: Waterbrook Press, 2006. 183p. $15.95. ISBN 1 4000 7208 5.

[fiction] J, CG with high interest for girls

Themes/Topics: brothers and sisters, blended family, Christian life, love and trust

Summary/Description

When eight-year-old Michael is abandoned by his father at the airport without money, ticket, food, or a way to get home, he calls his fifteen-year-old sister Lily who buys a plane ticket, packs up her twenty-two-month-old stepbrother, rescues Michael at the airport, and brings him back home. Neither Lily nor Michael, at Michael's insistence, tells their older sister, mother, or step-father what happened. Michael's biological father makes no contact with the family for a year except to say that he will stop paying child support. The older sister arrives home on a surprise visit, announces her engagement, and plans a wedding to occur in six weeks. Her biological father will give her away, and she announces that their biological father blames Lily, who refuses to be in the wedding if he is there, for his estrangement from the family. Michael remains silent while the sisters fight. Lily feels betrayed by both her brother and sister and blames God for allowing the injustice. Upset by the conflict, their stepbrother, now three, wanders to the house of Lily's friend. Michael realizes that arguing occurred because he did not tell what happened. He explains, and their underrated and underappreciated step-father decides how the family can reconcile with the biological father by keeping love but withholding trust.

Read Aloud/Reader Response

1. Chapter 3, page 44, beginning "Kells had said…" and ending "… about themselves." Kells reflects on the natural instinct of most people to be selfish.
2. Chapter 6, pages 68 to 69, beginning "Dr. Bordon read…" and ending "…with you, too." Dr. Bordon explains the Bible passage keyed to the title, and Lily applies it to Michael's situation. Join with this passage, Amanda's interpretation of the same text. (Chapter 15, pages 182 to 183, beginning "I'm giving a pool…" and ending with the novel.)
3. Chapter 8, pages 84 to 87, beginning with the chapter and ending "Make him suffer." Dr. Bordon explains a Biblical passage dealing with forgiveness and Lily reacts.
4. Chapter 10, page 114, beginning "Mom had said…" and ending "…us to be different." Lily explains why Reb stays with Freddie's family more than theirs.
5. Chapter 11, pages 122 and 123, beginning "So many parents…" and ending "…who practiced Mozart." The passage reflects on children not meeting parents' expectations.

Booktalk

A closed car door and one sentence from the driver produce enough turmoil to destroy a family. Eight-year-old Michael is dropped off at the airport by his father. The father goes back to his own house without Michael. Michael has no food, money, or airplane ticket. How will he get back to his mother's house? Why did his father just dump him out of the car like that? How will Michael hide from airport security while he figures it all out? And how can he keep the world from finding out what his father did? There is only one person who he thinks can even start to answer those questions, and he calls her. Lily, his fifteen-year-old sister. Lily has some questions herself. How can she get to the airport to pick Michael up when she doesn't have a plane ticket or a driver's license? How can she deliver a slow and agonizing death to her father? But most important, how could God, also a father, ever let it happen? Neither the brother nor the sister can answer all their questions or each other's on their own. The most that they can hope for is a little help from *A Friend at Midnight*.

Get Involved

1. (Research) Using your library resources, learn more about the role of forgiveness in people's lives. Act as a resource person for the group during discussion.
2. (Discuss) Write down how you think each character in the novel would deal with forgiveness. Support your answer with specifics from the text.
3. (Discuss) Should Lily have kept her promise to Michael?
4. (Discuss) What do you think are the roles of Kells and Amanda in the novel?
5. (React) Would you forgive Dennis Rosetti? Explain your answer.
6. (Discuss) List what you learned about Christian values by reading the novel. Compare your list with those written by others in the group.

Related Works

1. Cooney, Caroline B. **Hush Little Baby.** New York: Scholastic Press, 1999. 258p. $4.99pa. ISBN 0 590 81974 7. [fiction] MJ, G (See full booktalk in *Booktalks Plus*, 2001, pages 168 to 169.) Kit Innes finds herself in the middle of a baby selling scheme and discovers that asking for adult help is better than trying to solve the problem entirely on her own.
2. Covey, Sean. **The 6 Most Important Decisions You'll Ever Make: A Guide for Teens.** New York: Simon & Schuster/Fireside Books, 2006. 319p. $15.95. ISBN-13: 978 0 7432 6504 1. [nonfiction] JS, CG Using the 7 habits philosophy, Covey addresses the issues of school, friends, parents, dating and sex, addictions, and self-worth. Each chapter concludes with a "Baby Steps" application section for reader application. "Help Desk," at the end of the book, lists applicable Web sites for each chapter. A bibliography lists the references for each chapter.

3. Garfinkle, D. L. **Storky: How I Lost My Nickname and Won the Girl.** New York: G. P. Putnam's Sons, 2005. 184p. $16.99. ISBN 0 399 24284 8. [fiction] MJ, CG (See full booktalk in *Booktalks and Beyond,* 2007, pages 63 to 65.) High school freshman Michael "Storky" Pomerantz seeks approval from his cold and self-centered father but finds a more positive relationship that includes attention and respect from his new step-father.

4. Quarles, Heather. **A Door Near Here.** New York: Delacorte Press, 1998. 231p. $13.95. ISBN 0 385 32595 9. [fiction] MJ, G (See full booktalk in *Booktalks Plus,* 2001, pages 54 to 56.) Fifteen-year-old Katherine tells the story of her family's disintegration and rebirth as they deal with their alcoholic mother and a father who has abandoned the family.

5. Yancey, Philip, and Tim Stafford (notes). **Student Bible: New International Version.** Grand Rapids, MI: Zondervan, 2002. 1440p. $32.99. ISBN 0 310 92784 6. [religion] JS, CG This user-friendly version includes "Insights" (background information), "Guided Tour" (essays providing "bird's eye view") and "100 People You Should Get to Know."

ᏟᏃᏋᎯ

Davis, Deborah. Not Like You.

New York: Clarion Books, 2007. 268p. $16.00.
ISBN-13: 978 0 618 72093 4. [fiction] JS, G

Themes/Topics: mothers and daughters, alcoholism, single-parent families, conduct of life

Summary/Description

Fifteen-year-old Kayla and her mother move frequently because her mother drinks, loses jobs, and builds debt. Their latest home is a dilapidated trailer court. Trying to reform, the mother joins a support group but relapses under Kayla's critical eye. Kayla pays their bills with a dog walking/training business. An older man tells Kayla he loves her but exploits her for money just as her previous boyfriends exploited her for sex. After her mother binges again, Kayla steals money from a customer and follows the man to Denver. She realizes how self-centered he is and how loving her mother has tried to be. Kayla returns home, confesses to the robbery, vows to pay back the money, and concludes that loving means accepting the whole person, both strengths and flaws. Content and language could be considered controversial.

Read Aloud/Reader Response

1. Chapter 12, page 81, beginning "I lay on my bed…" and ending with the chapter. Kayla decides that Remy can make her successful.
2. Chapter 19, page 132, beginning "She ran the engine…" and ending "…*I* want to be?" Kayla questions who will run her life.
3. Chapter 25, pages 182 to 185, beginning "Seriously, Kayla…" and ending with the chapter. Luz cross examines Kalya and questions Remy's motives.
4. Chapter 26, page 188, beginning "Sometimes,…" and ending with the sentence. Sherrie challenges Kayla to share her good fortune with her mother.
5. Chapter 35, page 268, Kayla's poem, "What You Want." Kayla reveals what she learned about love and self-reliance.

Booktalk

Fifteen-year-old Kayla knows how to get boys. She does anything they want. She figures that she has to be fast and easy because her mother and she never stay too long in one town to make friends, let alone start long-term relationships. Her mother just stays long enough to get a job, some liquor, a boyfriend, and some deep debt. Then it's time to start over. Their latest move is the pits. A guy named Redbone rents them a rundown trailer in what looks like a junkyard. Everything old is new again. The boyfriends, the booze, no money, and Mom's empty promises. But Kayla is strong. She starts her own dog walking business. When she makes money, she knows how to handle it. When she meets a guy, she is sure, well she is almost sure, that he is the real thing. Unlike her mother, she isn't meeting them in bars. She knows that someday she will make something of herself, and if her mom ever sobers up long enough to ask what that will be, Kayla's answer will be *Not Like You.*

Get Involved

1. (Research) Using your library resources, learn more about alcoholism and available support groups. Act as a resource person during the discussion.
2. (Research) Using your library resources, research support groups for women starting over from domestic violence. Act as a resource person during the discussion.
3. (React) Who do you think are the two most important supporting characters? Support your opinion with specifics from the story.
4. (Discuss) Is Kayla like her mother? Use specifics from the story to support your opinion.

5. (Create) Write the letter that Kayla might write to her mother in five years. Compare your response with the responses of others in the group.

Related Works

1. Acheson, Alison. **Mud Girl.** Regina, Saskatchewan: Coteau Books, 2006. 319p. $10.95. ISBN-13: 978 1 55050 3548. [fiction] JS, G Sixteen-year-old Aba Zytka Jones, who lives with her clinically depressed father, decides to enter foster care with her irresponsible boyfriend's little boy after she sees how good a child's life can be with the help of responsible adults.
2. Clinton, Cathryn. **The Eyes of Van Gogh.** Cambridge, MA: Candlewick Press, 2007. 216p. $16.99. ISBN-13: 978 0 7636 2245 9. [fiction] JS, G Living a rootless life with her alcoholic mother, seventeen-year-old Jude identifies with Vincent van Gogh's insanity and fantasizes about love and family. When her dreams crash, she decides to commit suicide, but changes her life's directions with the help of a concerned teacher and new friends.
3. Flake, Sharon G. **Who Am I without Him?: Short Stories about Girls and the Boys in Their Lives.** New York: Hyperion Books for Children/Jump at the Sun, 2004. 168p. $15.99. ISBN 078680693 1. [fiction, short stories] JS, G (See full booktalk in *Booktalks and Beyond,* 2007, pages 19 to 21.) Ten short stories explore the female/male relationship and emphasize that a girl must find strength in herself before she finds it in a boyfriend.
4. Pearson, Mary E. **A Room on Lorlelei Street.** New York: Henry Holt and Company, 2005. 266p. $16.95. ISBN 0 8050 7667 0. [fiction] JS, G A young girl believes that she can escape her dysfunctional family by renting a room of her own, but the dream goes sour when she prostitutes herself to pay the rent.

☙❧

Flake, Sharon G. Bang!

New York: Hyperion Books for Children/Jump at the Sun, 2005. 298p. $16.99. ISBN 078681844 1. [fiction] MJS, CG with high interest for boys

Themes/Topics: grief, families, self-reliance, conduct of life

Summary/Description

Thirteen-year-old Mann's brother dies in a shooting. Mann feels that the seven-year-old would still be alive if he had stayed with him that day. The father decides that Mann needs to toughen up or die also. First, he deserts Mann and his friend Kee-lee in a campground. They find their own way home, a walk that requires about two weeks. Enduring hunger, danger, and abuse, the boys finally arrive, but Mann's father throws him out again and demands that he survive alone in the city. The two boys live with and work for Kee-lee's aunt who runs several illegal businesses. Kee-lee is killed on one of the jobs but kills the shooter. Mann knows he will be accused of both deaths. He runs away, and lives in a deserted horse barn where his father once took him and his brother. Eventually, the father finds Mann. Caring for the abandoned horses, they reconcile.

Read Aloud/Reader Response

1. Introductory poem "Boys Ain't Men...Yet." On the page before page 1, Flake uses a poem to introduce her main point, that boys need responsible role models to become responsible men.
2. Chapter 2, pages 7 to 9. In this chapter, Mann explains how Jason's death has affected his relationship with his father.
3. Chapter 8, pages 34 to 36, beginning with the chapter and ending with "...all be over." Mann explains the growing effect of death on him.
4. Chapter 20, pages 98 to 103. In this chapter, Mann's father resolves to make his son a man so that he will survive.
5. Chapter 36, pages 187 to 189, beginning "I shouldn't have let him..." and ending with the chapter. Mann begins with negatives in his search for becoming a man.
6. Chapter 59, pages 294 to 295, beginning "I push him away..." and ending "...don't let it burn." Mann and his father begin to reconcile as they define manhood.

Booktalk

Ask if someone in the group can define what it means to be a man. Discuss the answers.

Thirteen-year-old Mann can't really tell anyone what it means to be a man, but he is about to find out. Mann lives in a world of random shootings. His seven-year-old brother Jason was killed in one, and Mann was too busy to watch him, to keep him from getting killed. He lives with that guilt all the time, but Mann's father is too much of a man to talk about the death. The shootings are increasing, and his father has an idea. African boys are turned out into the jungle. They learn to survive and become men. Mann's father thinks that if he turns Mann out into the modern world, he will learn to survive too. He will become a man. So he throws him out—twice. What is out in this jungle is more dangerous than lions or snakes. Mann finds it all. He confronts it all, and once again, before he can become a man, his whole world changes with a *Bang!*

Get Involved

1. (Research) Using your library resources, find more information about urban crime that involves guns. Act as a resource person for the group during discussion.
2. (Research) Mann's father talks about African rites of passage. Using your library resources, research those customs. Act as a resource person for the group during discussion. Discuss how this information supports or fails to support the father's decision to throw his son out.
3. (Create) Write your own definition of a man. Share your definition with others in the group who also wrote a definition.
4. (Create) After reading another book by Flake, *Who Am I without Him?: Short Stories about Girls and the Boys in Their Lives* (Related Work 3), write a definition of a woman.
5. (Discuss) How are the definitions written in 3 and 4 of Get Involved the same and different? How do they apply to the men and women in *Bang!*?
6. (Follow-up) Invite a grief counselor to speak to the group. Ask the speaker to explain the stages of grief and how to deal with grief.

Related Works

1. Booth, Coe. **Tyrell.** New York: Scholastic Inc./Push, 2006. 320p. $16.99. ISBN 0 439 83879 7. [fiction] JS, CG with high interest for boys. In this painfully realistic account, fifteen-year-old Tyrell, who has grown up in the projects, unsuccessfully tries to hold his family and his love life together even though his father is in jail and his mother is self-centered and dysfunctional. The language and subject matter require a mature reader.
2. Flake, Sharon G. **Money Hungry.** New York: Hyperion Books for Children/Jump at the Sun, 2001. 187p. $15.99. ISBN 0 786 80548 X. [fiction] MJS, G (See full booktalk in *Teen Genre Connections*, 2005, pages 285 to 286.) Thirteen-year-old Raspberry Hill, living in the projects with her mother, constantly tries to make money because she fears living, as she and her mother used to, on the streets.
3. Flake, Sharon G. **Who Am I without Him?: Short Stories about Girls and the Boys in Their Lives.** New York: Hyperion Books for Children/Jump at the Sun, 2004. 168p. $15.99. ISBN 078680693 1. [fiction, short stories] JS, G (See full booktalk in *Booktalks and Beyond*, pages 19 to 21.) Ten short stories explore the female/male relationship.

4.   Lekuton, Joseph Lemasolai. **Facing the Lion: Growing up Maasai on the African Savanna.** Washington, DC: National Geographic, 2003. 123p. $15.95. ISBN 0 7922 5125 3. [nonfiction] MJS, CG with high interest for boys. (See full booktalk in *Booktalks and Beyond,* 2007, pages 234 to 236.) Joseph Lekuton describes his life as a Maasai. In Chapter 1, he relates an unsuccessful lion encounter that teaches him to confront the other "lions" in his life.

5.   Woodson, Jacqueline. **Miracle's Boys.** New York: G. P. Putnam's Sons, 2000. 131p. $15.99. ISBN 0 399 23113 7. [fiction] MJS, CG with high interest for boys (See full booktalk in *Teen Genre Connections,* 2005, pages 28 to 30.) Three brothers work through their grief and guilt over their parents' death as they try to survive in the city.

ርያ'ይጋ

Friend, Natasha. Lush.

New York: Scholastic Press, 2006. 178p. $16.99. ISBN 0 439 85346 X. [fiction] MJ, G

Themes/Topics: alcoholism, father/daughter relationships, friendship, trust, family

Summary/Description

Eighth-grader Samantha Gwynn lives with her mother, four-year-old brother, and alcoholic father. The father, a successful architect, is an abusive alcoholic. When Samantha goes to the library, she writes notes about her problems to a girl she sees there often. The person who receives the notes, however, is a new boy in town who stacks the shelves and who has problems with his family because he is gay. When Samantha's father hits his son in the face with a liquor bottle, the family finally confronts the father's disease, and he leaves for rehabilitation. As Samantha works through her anger with her family, she also lives through her own poor judgments with boyfriends, drinking, peer pressure, and friends. The boy who receives her notes and her other friends support her, and she matures. By the end of the novel, the family reunites. Even though Sam is happy, she is working with the reconciliation one day at a time.

Read Aloud/Reader Response

1.   Chapter 1, pages 1 and 2, beginning with the chapter and ending with "...won't remember a thing." Sam describes a regular occurrence with her father's drinking.

2.   Chapter 4, page 22, beginning "If you want my advice..." and ending "...off you'll be." AJK advises Sam to stop trying to change her parents.

3. Chapter 16, pages 100 to 101, beginning "I wait for her..." and ending "...being in high school yet." Mrs. Howe reveals her own frustration with her life.
4. Chapter 17, pages 106 to 108, beginning "I have to give my mother..." and ending with the chapter. Both the mother and Sam confront the father's disease.
5. Chapter 24, pages 164 to 165, beginning "I look down..." and ending with the chapter. Sam wonders if she will be like her father, and her mother tells her about the father's admirable traits.

Booktalk

Samantha Gwynn is in eighth grade. She has friends whom she trusts and some former friends she doesn't. Her dad is a successful architect. Her mother stays home and devotes all her time to taking care of Sam and Luke, Sam's four-year-old brother. Sam's life should be pretty nice, even if the school snob keeps picking on her. But Sam has bigger problems than making the school social scene. Sam's dad is an alcoholic. He falls down, breaks things, hits people, and sometimes disappears. He never remembers what he does, and her mother doesn't seem to either. Mom just picks up the pieces and rushes off to yoga classes. Sam can't talk to Mom or Dad, and she sure doesn't want her friends to know. So Sam makes a leap of faith. She sees a high school girl in the library, and decides to do a Dear Abby. Sam will write to this older girl who seems to have her life under control and get some advice. Problem? Someone else picks up the note. Just when Sam thought she could get it all together, life flies apart. So what's new? That's the way things usually happen when you are living with a *Lush*.

Get Involved

1. (Research) Using your library resources, learn as much as possible about alcoholism and Alcoholics Anonymous. Act as a resource person for the group during discussion.
2. (Discuss) Ask each person in the group to describe the role of one adult in the story. Decide what contribution each one makes to Sam's life.
3. (Discuss and React) What personal mistakes does Sam make? How does she try to rectify them? Do you feel that the result is realistic?
4. (Discuss) AJK tells Sam not to try to change her parents but then takes her to see her father in rehabilitation. Are his actions consistent or inconsistent with his advice?
5. (Follow-up) Sam hopes for a "normal, happy family." Using your library resources, research the family today in the United States. Then define what makes up a "normal, happy family."

Related Works

1. Covey, Sean. **The 6 Most Important Decisions You'll Ever Make: A Guide for Teens.** New York: Simon & Schuster/Fireside Books, 2006. 319p. $15.95. ISBN-13: 978 0 7432 6504 1. [nonfiction] JS, CG. Using the 7 habits philosophy, Covey addresses the issues of school, friends, parents, dating and sex, addictions, and self-worth. Each chapter concludes with a "Baby Steps" application section for reader application. "Help Desk," at the end of the book, lists applicable Web sites for each chapter. A bibliography lists the references for each chapter.

2. Jennings, Patrick. **Outstanding in My Field.** New York: Scholastic Press, 2005. 176p. $16.95. ISBN 0 439 46581 8. [fiction] M, CG with high interest for boys. Dominated by his alcoholic father, eleven-year-old Ty decides to stand up and free himself from emotional turmoil.

3. Monthei, Betty. **Looking for Normal.** New York: HarperCollins Publishers, 2005. 185p. $15.99. ISBN 0 06 072505 2. [fiction] JS, G After their father kills their mother and himself, twelve-year-old Annie and eight-year-old Ted move in with their upper-class maternal grandparents, who have marital problems related to the grandmother's alcoholism.

4. Philbrick, Rodman. **The Young Man and the Sea.** New York: The Blue Sky Press, 2004. 142p. $16.95. ISBN 0 439 36829 4. [fiction] MJ, CG with high interest for boys. (See full booktalk in *Booktalks and Beyond,* 2007, pages 93 to 95.) Twelve-year-old Skiff Beaman wants to keep the family boat, the *Mary Rose,* and his family afloat but must cope with his mother's death, his father's alcoholism, and the school bullies.

5. Ryan, Pam Muñoz. **Becoming Naomi León.** New York: Scholastic Press, 2004. 256p. $16.95. ISBN 0 439 26969 5. [fiction] MJS, CG (See full booktalk in *Booktalks and Beyond,* 2007, pages 249 to 251.) Naomi and her physically challenged brother Owen live with their grandmother because they were abandoned and abused by their alcoholic mother who is returning to their lives.

ᘜᘞ

Prose, Francine. **Bullyville.**

New York: HarperTeen, 2007. 260p. $16.99. ISBN-13: 975 0 06 057497 0. [fiction]
MJ, CG with high interest for boys

Themes/Topics: death, grief, bullies, preparatory schools,
Twin Towers attack

Summary/Description

After his father is killed in the Twin Towers terrorist attack, thirteen-year-old Bart Rangely receives a scholarship to an exclusive boys' school in his New Jersey town. His mentor or big brother and junior Tyro Bergen leads a bullying campaign against him that Bart hides from his grieving mother. Bart retaliates by vandalizing the boy's Escalade. In a parent conference that focuses on the bullying and vandalism, Mr. Bergen suggests that both boys participate in a Reach Out program to make them more compassionate. Bart is assigned to a children's hospital ward where he meets and bonds with ten-year-old terminally ill Nola. When she dies, Bart discovers that Nola is Tyro's sister. The parents thank Bart for helping Nola, but Tyro confronts him in the school hall and starts a fight. Bart pours all his grief and anger into the fight, and is dismissed from the school. He reasons that, like the Twin Tower victims, he was in the wrong place at the wrong time.

Read Aloud/Reader Response

1. Chapter 2, pages 18 to 34, beginning with the chapter and ending with "...deep dark secret?" Bart reflects on the terrorist attack and the aftermath.
2. Chapter 3, page 45, beginning "I suppose..." and ending "'...something bad.'" Bart's mother reflects on the attitude that something good always comes from a seemingly bad event.
3. Chapter 4, page 58, beginning "Later, I couldn't..." and ending "...tennis courts." Bart reflects on the public versus private personas of the prep school students.
4. Chapter 6, pages 114 to 120, beginning with the chapter and ending "...don't know what happened." Bart is stuffed into a locker.
5. Chapter 14, pages 254 to 256, beginning "All the time..." and ending "...it was over." Bart fights Tyro.

Booktalk

Thirteen-year-old Bart Rangely gets the flu and saves his mother's life. How? Mom stays home to take care of Bart on the day that terrorists crash into the Twin Towers. His mom worked in the Towers. So did Bart's father. Bart's father wasn't as lucky. He died in the flames. Bart is called the Miracle Boy for saving his mother's life. And even though Bart grieves for his father, he is hoping that no one finds out that Dad left the family six months before the attack. His parents' split stays a secret. Bart and his mother receive more sympathy gifts than they can count. Bart wishes that one of those gifts would disappear. Baileywell Preparatory Academy offers Bart a full scholarship. His mother loves the idea. She believes that Baileywell will open the doors to the best colleges in the United States. But Bart knows the school's other reputation. According to the town rumors, bullying at Baileywell is a blood sport. Bart believes he is facing the worst year of his life. And he is right. This school is so exclusive that Bart has his own personal terrorist. Welcome, Bart, to *Bullyville.*

Get Involved

1. (Research) Using your library resources, find out as much as possible about bullying. Act as a resource person during the discussion.
2. (React) React to the final fight between Tyro and Bart. Be sure to comment on what you think caused the fight.
3. (Discuss) What roles does coincidence play in the novel and is it believable?
4. (Create) Write a letter to the Bergen family about Bart's dismissal. In it, explain what the two families may have in common.
5. (Follow-up) Investigate the issue of bullying in your own community or school. Find out as much as possible about what is being done and what can be done to combat it.

Related Works

1. Beard, Philip. **Dear Zoe.** New York: Viking Press, 2005. 196p. $21.95. ISBN 0 670 03401 0. [fiction] JS, G (See full booktalk in *Booktalks and Beyond,* 2007, pages 14 to 16.) Fifteen-year-old Tess feels responsible for the death of her stepsister who dies on September 11, 2001. As she works through her grief, she chooses between her stable blended family and the home of her permissive, drug dealer father.
2. Flinn, Alex. **Breaking Point.** New York: HarperTempest, 2002. 240p. $6.99pa. ISBN 0 06 447371 6. [fiction] JS, CG with high interest for boys (See full booktalk in *Booktalks and Beyond,* 2007, pages 12 to 14.) Eighteen-year-old Paul Richmond reflects on his experience in an exclusive boys' school where a charismatic student befriended him and then set him up for a felony.
3. Korman, Gordon. **Jake, Reinvented.** New York: Hyperion, 2003. 213p. $15.99. ISBN 0 786 81957 X. [fiction] JS, CG with high interest for boys. Through Rick, the reader learns about Jake, a brainy, social outsider who manufactures a new persona to capture the cold, popular girl he adores.
4. Myers, Walter Dean. **Shooter.** New York: HarperTempest, 2004. 223p. $16.89. ISBN 0 06 029520 1. [fiction] JS, CG with high interest for boys. A friendship among three outcasts and unchecked bullying lead to a fatal school shooting.

5. Strasser, Todd. **Give a Boy a Gun.** New York: Simon & Schuster, 2000. 146p. $16.00. ISBN 0 689 81112 8. [fiction] MJS, CG with high interest for boys. (See full booktalk in *Booktalks and More*, 2003, pages 116 to 118.) Two boys, bullied and teased by the school jocks, plan and execute a terrorist act in their school.

Facing Our Own Choices

Cameron, Peter. **Someday This Pain Will Be Useful to You.**

New York: Farrar, Straus and Giroux/Frances Foster Books, 2007. 229p. $16.00. ISBN-13: 978 0 374 30989 3. [fiction] S, CG

Themes/Topics: conduct of life, interpersonal relations, self-perception, dysfunctional families, sexual orientation

Summary/Description

Charming, intelligent, and analytical eighteen-year-old James Sveck decides to forgo college and buy a house in the Midwest after his emotional meltdown at a summer political conference convinces him that he can't live with his peers. His self-absorbed parents direct him to a psychiatrist who helps him discover his fears of adulthood and his homosexuality. With his grandmother's support, he accepts his feelings, decides to enter Brown University after all, and really prepare for the rest of his life.

Read Aloud/Reader Response

1. Chapter 1, pages 11 and 12, beginning "Right outside of our..." and ending "...well enough alone." James demonstrates his love of old buildings and neighborhoods as he describes the memorial to the block president.
2. Chapter 6, page 80, beginning "I didn't answer..." and ending "...hate." James realizes that he doesn't want to move on because he is so comfortable in his life.
3. Chapter 10, pages 123 to 133. In this chapter, James tells about his meltdown.
4. Chapter 12, page 158, beginning "A young man..." and ending "...did not know it." James observes a young man and woman on the street and sees their lives getting worse.
5. Chapter 13, pages 178 to 179, beginning *"How is..."* and ending "...'easier to control than behavior.'" Trying to change the

topic while talking with the psychiatrist, James stumbles on a self-revelation.

6.   Chapter 15, page 211, beginning "And if college..." and ending "...gift nonetheless." James's grandmother counsels him on the importance of negative experiences.

Booktalk

Charming and intelligent James Sveck is eighteen. He lives in New York, and he isn't sure that he wants to make it to nineteen. Next year, he will go on to college. If college is anything like last summer's experience in a teen leadership conference, he *is* sure that he doesn't want to spend four years with people his own age. He would feel much better if his parents gave him half of that college tuition and let him buy a house in the Midwest. He loves old houses so much that he would even walk there and save the plane fare. Since 9/11, James isn't too excited about flying anyway. But he can't seem to get enough time to talk about his brilliant self-education plan. Mom is busy divorcing her third husband. Dad is worried about his plastic surgery, and James's older sister is trying to keep her married professor boyfriend. The only two people James wants to talk to are his grandmother and the young man who runs his mother's art gallery. Is there anything wrong with that? Well, maybe. His parents seem to think that he should be talking to a psychiatrist first. As far as James is concerned, he is walking into one more parental plan whose motto is *Someday This Pain Will Be Useful to You.*

Get Involved

1.   (Research) Using your library resources, find the most and least expensive places to live in the United States. Research the reasons for the difference in pricing. Act as a resource person in your group.
2.   (React) James describes several scenes in which he observes people. Choose your favorite. Read it out loud and explain your choice.
3.   (React) List five possessions that you feel you will need in your life. Explain your choices to the group.
4.   (Discuss) James describes settings in detail. Contrast the settings of his grandmother's house and the psychiatrist's office. Why do you think that Cameron took time to establish these two settings?
5.   (Discuss) Does Cameron stereotype his characters?

Related Works

1.   Earls, Nick. **48 Shades of Brown.** New York: Houghton Mifflin Company, 1999, 2004. 288p. $6.99pa. ISBN 0 618 45295 8. [fiction] S, CG with high interest for girls. (See full booktalk in *Teen Genre*

Connections, 2003, pages 75 to 77.) Naïve and intellectual sixteen-year-old Dan spends a year with his twenty-something aunt, and experiences his identity and sexual awakening.

2. Ferris, Jean. **Eight Seconds.** New York: Harcourt Brace and Company, 2000. 186p. $17.00. ISBN 0 15 202367 4. [fiction] JS, CG (See full booktalk in *Booktalks and More,* 2003, pages 221 to 223.) A young man, frightened by the idea that he is gay, refuses to defend a gay young man and loses a good friend.

3. Freymann-Weyr, Garret. **My Heartbeat.** Boston, MA: Houghton Mifflin Company, 2002. 154p. $15.00. ISBN 0 618 14181 2. [fiction] JS, G (See full booktalk in *Teen Genre Connections,* 2003, pages 21 to 23.) Raised in an upper-class, intellectual world by yuppie parents, Ellen McConnell, the narrator, tells about the love triangle among her brother, his friend, and herself from the twelfth to fifteenth year. Eventually, through therapy, both young men learn the roots of their fears and feelings about family, achievement, and sexual identity.

4. Green, John. **Looking for Alaska.** New York: Dutton Books, 2005. 224p. $15.99. ISBN 0 525 47506 0. [fiction] S, CG (See full booktalk in *Booktalks and Beyond,* 2007, pages 37 to 40.) Sixteen-year-old Miles Halter enters his father's alma mater and discovers a social world of pranks and status as well as two loyal friends who teach him the responsibility involved in caring for others.

5. Salinger, J. D. **The Catcher in the Rye.** Boston, MA: Little, Brown & Company, 1991. 224p. $6.99pa. ISBN 0 316 76948 7. [fiction] S/A, CG Set in 1949 and first published in 1951, the book is about a young man who tells his psychiatrist about his alienation from the world.

ℭℌ

Cushman, Karen. **The Loud Silence of Francine Green.**

New York: Clarion Books, 2006. 225p. $16.00.
ISBN-13: 978 0 618 50455 8. [fiction] MJ, G

Themes/Topics: conformity, Catholic schools, friendship, conduct of life, California, twentieth century, Communism, Cold War, weapon escalation

Summary/Description

Thirteen-year-old Francine Green, a conformist from a conformist family, attends a Catholic school in California. In the 1949-1950 school year, Sophie Bowman, a new girl expelled from public school, enrolls in Francine's class. Sophie, justifying her endless confrontations under the right of free speech, infuriates the rigid eighth-grade teacher and principal, Sister Basil the Great, who tries to humiliate her. Sophie perseveres, and her father, a Hollywood screen writer, encourages Francine to express and stand up for what she believes. At this time, McCarthyism, fueled by the fear of the atom bomb, is intimidating anyone suspected of being a Communist or a Communist sympathizer. When one of the Bowmans' friends, a blacklisted lovable actor, commits suicide, Francine begins to question the Red Threat. Then Sophie's father loses his job, and the Bowmans leave town. Francine, counseled by her father to avoid the Bowmans, finally decides to take a stand and confront the bullies in her life. She starts with Sister Basil the Great. An "Author's Note" explains the story's social and historical context, and a resource list provides additional sources about the early 1950s.

Read Aloud/Reader Response

1. Chapter 2, pages 9 to 15. In this chapter, Sophie makes "trouble" the first day of school, and Francine imagines how she might have defended her.
2. Chapter 9, pages 52 to 60. In this chapter, Sophie delivers a prize-winning speech on the topic "What Today's Youth Can Learn from Yesterday's Saints," and gains Francine's respect.
3. Chapter 13, pages 83 to 85, beginning "Acting you know..." and ending with the chapter. Mr. Mandelbaum's comparison between acting and baseball also applies to life.
4. Chapter 25, pages 154 to 156, beginning "Mr. Mandelbaum came in..." and ending with the chapter. Mr. Mandelbaum expresses his fears about being called in by the FBI, and Mr. Bowman explains the dangers of being different.
5. Chapter 33, pages 207 to 208, beginning "Holy Father..." and ending "...we are all dead?" Francine practices her phone call to the Pope.

Booktalk

Thirteen-year-old Francine Green fears that Communists will drop a bomb on her head. So do lots of other Americans in 1949 who find themselves in a Cold War with Russia. Then a bomb does drop into her life, but this one has a name, Sophie. Sophie is the new girl in the eighth grade of All Saints School for Girls. Before Sophie came, everyone knew that getting along meant agreeing with their teacher, Sister Basil the Great, and all the other adults in their lives. But Sophie thinks that ideas and justice are more important than getting along. Sophie and Sister are on a collision path when Sister makes Sophie stand in the wastebasket the first day. That should teach Sophie, but it doesn't. In fact, Sophie asks even more questions. Francine likes this new girl. She wishes Sophie would calm down. But it is just so much fun to be around her. Sophie makes Francine think that everyone should do something about the atom, free speech, and something called the Communist blacklist, a new and very important document in their Hollywood neighborhood. For Francine, Sophie's outrageous thoughts are appealing, but since Francine is surrounded by adults who constantly tell her "no" and "don't try it," will those thoughts in Francine's head just remain *The Loud Silence of Francine Green?*

Get Involved

1. (Research) Using your library resources and the source list at the end of the "Author's Note," continue to learn about the early 1950s. Share your information with the group during the discussion.
2. (Research) Using your library resources, further research the novel and film *Mr. Roberts.* Share your information with the group during discussion.
3. (React) How does the title affect you?
4. (Discuss) Identify the bullies in the book. How can each be stopped?
5. (Create) The novel ends with Francine about to confront Sister Basil the Great. Using the scripts Francine writes throughout the book as models, write a script of the exchange between the two.
6. (Research and Create) Using your library resources, research the lives of the Saints. Choose one life that you would use for the speech contest "What Today's Youth Can Learn from Yesterday's Saints." Explain your choice, and write the speech.

Related Works

1. Hearn, Julie. **The Minister's Daughter.** New York: Atheneum Books for Young Readers, 2005. 263p. $16.95. ISBN 0 689 87690 4. [fiction] JS, G (See full booktalk in *Booktalks and Beyond,* 2007, pages 136 to 138.) To hide her pregnancy, a minister's daughter makes false accusations against an illegitimate granddaughter of a local midwife.
2. Link, Theodore. **Communism: A Primary Source Analysis.** New York: The Rosen Publishing Group, Inc./Primary Source/ Rosen Central, 2005. 64p. (Primary Sources of Political Systems). $29.25. ISBN 0 8239 4517 0. [nonfiction] MJS, CG Drawing on excerpts from historical documents and pictures, Link traces the

concept of Communism from the Greeks to the twentieth-century violent revolutions and dictatorships that made it a major threat to democracy and resulted in the McCarthy witch hunts of the early fifties, and finally to its failure in Europe and the Soviet Union.

3.   Miller, Arthur. **The Crucible.** New York: Penguin Classics, 2003. 176p. $11.00pa. ISBN 0 14 243733 6. [drama] S/A, CG Written in 1953, as an anti-McCarthyism statement, the play tells the story of the Salem witch trials of 1692.

4.   Smith, Betty. **A Tree Grows in Brooklyn.** New York: Harper Perennial Modern Classics, 2006. 528p. $16.95pa. ISBN-13: 978 0 06 073626 2. [fiction] MJ/A, G First published in 1943 and adapted for a movie in 1945, the story depicts the struggle of the daughter of poor Irish immigrants in the early twentieth century. The tree, determined to grow through the city pavement, symbolizes the difficulty and success of struggle.

5.   Zindel, Paul. **The Gadget.** New York: HarperCollins Publishers, 2001. 184p. $15.99. ISBN 0 06 028255 X. [fiction] MJ, CG with high interest for boys. (See full booktalk in *Teen Genre Connections,* 2005, pages 151 to 154.) Thirteen-year-old Stephen Orr, living in a new and strange Los Alamos home and frustrated by his father's distance and secrecy, unwittingly befriends a Russian spy who seeks information about the atom bomb project.

ʊʓʓʊ

Dessen, Sarah. Just Listen.
New York: Penguin Group/Speak, 2006. 371p. $8.99pa.
ISBN-13: 978 0 14 241097 4. [fiction] JS, G

Themes/Topics: self-actualization, interpersonal relations, models, family conflicts, high school, anger management, eating disorders

Summary/Description

High school model Annabel Greene keeps silent about an attempted rape by her best friend's boyfriend. The "friend," who has demanded her exclusive loyalty, spreads rumors that Annabel seduced the boy. Annabel struggles with her secret while her family focuses on her older sister's eating disorder. Annabel is befriended by Owen Armstrong, another social outcast called the "Angriest Boy in School," who finds a release for his anger by broadcasting an alternative music radio show. Owen teaches her how to express her opinions and trust her choices. A fellow model, also attacked by Annabel's assailant, brings charges against him, and asks Annabel to testify. Annabel reveals her secret to Owen who encourages her to tell her family and the other victim's lawyer. The family accompanies her to court. Owen is grounded for hitting the attacker in the face. Annabel temporarily takes over his show, quits modeling, reunites with her childhood best friend, and begins dating Owen.

Read Aloud/Reader Response

1. Chapter 1, pages 12, beginning "One open..." and ending "...could be so mean." Annabel describes herself in relation to her sisters and mother.
2. Chapter 5, pages 107 to 111, beginning "As we headed..." and ending "...'know your options, right?'" Owen and Annabel discuss lying and anger.
3. Chapter 8, pages 154 to 155, beginning "Owen didn't answer me." and ending "...'I can still relate.'" Owen and Annabel discuss the phrase, "Story of my life."
4. Chapter 11, pages 211 to 212, beginning "I leaned in closer." and ending "The story of my life." Annabel compares the department store commercial to her own life.
5. Chapter 17, pages 337 to 338, beginning "Now, I pushed back..." and ending "...would not leave me." Annabel discusses the importance of the past with her father.

Booktalk

High school student Annabel Greene is "The girl who has everything." Her family has plenty of money. She lives in one of the most beautiful houses in town, and she models for the local department store. She is smart too, and one of the most popular girls in school. That's what her world looks like on the outside. The inside is a little different. She doesn't want to model anymore, but is too afraid to tell Mom. She and her sisters barely talk. The most successful one is trying, slowly, to kill herself, one starving day at a time. Annabel's best friend is trying to make sure that she never has another friend. And then there is the worst thing in Annabel's life, a secret that she can't tell, a secret that no one would believe if she did tell. It all happened at an end-of-school party. It made Annabel the most talked about girl in school and the girl no one would talk to. How can you tell a thing like that, especially if everyone thinks you are perfect? Then Annabel finds another outcast, Owen Armstrong. He is a new oversized kid known as the "Angriest Boy in School." He has his own goofy alternative music show. No one talks to him either, but he doesn't seem to care. What happens when "The girl who has everything" meets "The Angriest Boy in School"? *Just Listen.*

Get Involved

1. (Research) Using your library resources, learn more about anger management. Act as a resource person during the group discussion.
2. (Research) Using your library resources, learn techniques for discussion and listening. Act as a resource person during the group discussion.
3. (Research) Using your library resources, learn more about eating disorders. Act as a resource person during the group discussion.
4. (Discuss) Describe each character. Do you think that Dessen's resolution for each character is logical? Fair?
5. (Create and Follow-up) After researching anger management, and discussion and listening techniques, create a communication manual for your discussion group. Individually revise it after each meeting. Revise it as a group after every fourth session.

Related Works

1. Anderson, Laurie Halse. **Speak.** New York: Farrar, Straus and Giroux, 1999. 198p. $16.00. ISBN 0 374 37152 0. [fiction] JS, G (See full booktalk in *Booktalks and More,* 2003, pages 75 to 77.) Before her ninth-grade year, Melinda Sordino is raped by a football player at a high school party. Because she calls 911, the police bust the party but fail to discover the rape. Melinda becomes a social leper until the truth comes out.
2. Dessen, Sarah. **Dreamland.** New York: Viking Press, 2000. 250p. $15.99. ISBN 0 670 89122 3. [fiction] JS, G (See full booktalk in *Booktalks and More,* 2003, pages 73 to 75.) Caitlin O'Koren is physically and psychologically abused by her boyfriend, whom she allows to control her life.
3. Flinn, Alex. **Breathing Underwater.** New York: HarperCollins Publishers, 2001. 263p. $15.95. ISBN 0 06 029198 2. [fiction] JS, CG (See full booktalk in *Teen Genre Connections,* 2005, pages 19 to 21.) After beating up on his girlfriend, sixteen-year-old Nick Andreas is sentenced to six months of family violence and anger management classes.
4. Kalodner, Cynthia. **Too Fat or Too Thin?: A Reference Guide to Eating Disorders.** Westport, CT: Greenwood Press, 2003. 228p. $51.95. ISBN 0 313 31581 7. [reference] JS, CG Kalodner defines various eating disorders and explains the medical care, health issues,

education, and cultural influences surrounding them. She also explores the means of prevention.

5. Quill, Charlie. **Anger and Anger Management.** New York: Rosen Publishing, 2009. 48p. (Teen Mental Health). $26.50. ISBN-13: 978 1 4042 1800 0. [nonfiction] JS, CG Quill explains anger, good and bad ways to react to it, and how that feeling is related to you and your family. Chapters 5 and 6 explain understanding and anger management. The "For More Information" section lists several sources for further help. Other titles in the series deal with addictive personality, anxiety and panic attacks, depression and mood disorders, meditation, and obsessive-compulsive disorder.

ↄ♄ↄ♄

Hautman, Pete. **Godless.**
New York: Simon & Schuster Books for Young Readers, 2004. 198p. $15.95. ISBN 0 689 86278 4. [fiction] JS, CG

Themes/Topics: belief, religion, mental illness, bullies, peer pressure, conduct of life

Summary/Description

Six-foot-one, two-hundred-and-twenty-four-pound Jason Bock, disillusioned by his parents' religion, decides to start a new one centered on the town water tower. His brilliant but compulsive best friend, a girl he wants to date, a minister's son, and a violent and volatile bully are his disciples. His best friend descends into mental illness while compulsively writing their bible, and the bully injects his own dangerous and controlling personality while attempting a takeover. The first ceremony turns dangerous and almost deadly. The group, after confronting the consequences, dissolves. The bully forms a new branch made up of his delinquent friends, and Jason's best friend, immersed in his "inspirations and visions," ends up in a mental hospital. By the end of the novel, Jason is alone and distinguishes between belief or faith and religion.

Read Aloud/Reader Response

1. Chapter 1, pages 5 to 6, beginning "But I have to explain…" and ending "…as Henry Stagg." Jason describes Henry's character.
2. Chapter 4, pages 24 and 25, beginning "You know, it…" and ending "…talking about." Shin describes his vision of God.
3. Chapter 15, page 90, beginning "So, you ask, how…" and ending "…about my religion." Jason explains how he can worship a false god.

4. Chapter 18, page 112, beginning "Shin must be miserable…" and ending "…in his pathetic life." Jason absolves himself of any responsibility for Shin.
5. Chapter 31, pages 197 and 198, beginning "The middle of the night…" and ending with the novel. Jason reflects on the difference between faith and religion.

Booktalk

Jason Bock doesn't believe in much. His parents go to church, but to Jason they're only going through the motions. Their empty rituals and prayers don't count for anything. And even though Just Al, the leader of Jason's church youth group, tries to make God everybody's buddy, Jason isn't buying the image. Jason has an image of his own, one that he will make the center of his own religion. For Jason and his disciples, god will be the town water tower. Doesn't it all fit? Water? Life? Baptism? Being reborn? It's a natural. But Jason's disciples are creating some images of their own. Shin, a super brain and Jason's best friend, is getting lost in writing the new bible. He is beyond inspired. Henry, the town bully who loves living on the edge, is trying to turn the congregation into some kind of gang complete with moll. So this pope job may not be as easy as it looks, even if or especially if, what started as a laugh out loud religion is *Godless.*

Get Involved

1. (Research) Choose a religious belief such as Judaism, Christianity, Islam, or Buddhism. Using your library resources, research the religion's roots. Act as a resource person during the group discussion.
2. (Research) Using your library resources, distinguish between a religion and a cult. Act as a resource person for the group during the discussion.
3. (Discuss) Jason's family is Catholic, a Christian faith. How would you describe Jason's character in terms of Christian belief?
4. (Discuss) Choose a Chutengodian. Decide whether or not that character seemed believable to you. Be sure to support your opinion with specifics from the novel.
5. (React) Jason has no deity in whom he can believe. Describe a deity in whom you can or could believe.

Related Works

1. Connelly, Neil. **St. Michael's Scales.** New York: Arthur A. Levine Books, 2002. 32p. $16.95. ISBN 0 439 19445 8. [fiction] MJS, CG (See full booktalk in *Teen Genre Connections*, 2005, pages 59 to 61.)

With a punishment and suffering focus in his beliefs, fifteen-year-old Keegan Flannery decides that the only way he can atone for his twin brother's death and his mother's subsequent mental illness is to kill himself.

2. Fraustino, Lisa Rowe (ed.). **Soul Searching: Thirteen Stories about Faith and Belief.** New York: Simon & Schuster Books for Young Readers, 2002. 267p. $17.95. ISBN 0 689 83484 5. [fiction] MJS, CG The stories illustrate the great faith required in all cultures to face life's problems and responsibilities.

3. Koja, Kathe. **Buddha Boy.** New York: Farrar, Straus and Giroux/ Frances Foster Books, 2003. 117p. $16.00. ISBN 0 374 30998 1. [fiction] MJS, CG with high interest for boys (See full booktalk in *Booktalks and Beyond,* 2007, pages 40 to 43.) Jinsen, a new and talented art student, relies on his Buddhist training and beliefs to deal with bullies.

4. Rylant, Cynthia. **God Went to Beauty School.** New York: Harper-Tempest, 2003. 56p. $15.89. ISBN 0 06 009434 6. [poetry] JS, CG (See full booktalk in *Teen Genre Connections,* 2005, pages 84 to 85.) In twenty-three poems, Rylant characterizes God as an almighty being who puts the world in motion and then discovers, when getting involved, the pain and beauty in His creation.

5. Singer, Marilyn (ed.). **I Believe in Water: Twelve Brushes with Religion.** New York: HarperCollins Publishers, 2000. 280p. $24.89. ISBN 0 06 028398 X. [fiction] JS, CG Twelve short stories examine how real life and spiritual beliefs can both complement and collide.

ꛯꛥ

Hautman, Pete. Invisible.

New York: Simon & Schuster Books for Young Readers, 2005. 149p. $15.95. ISBN 0 689 86800 6. [fiction] JS, CG

Themes/Topics: friendship, models and model making, mental illness, grief, fire

Summary/Description

Seventeen-year-old Doug Hanson, a brilliant loner, is best friends with Andy Morrow, a popular football star. Three years ago, Andy was killed in a fire set by the two boys in an abandoned house, but Doug talks to Andy daily. Doug also spies on a beautiful high school girl who calls him a "worm." When the police cannot catch Doug in the act, the football players, her friends, beat him up. To compensate for his grief and rejection, Doug builds elaborate model trains and a match-stick town, in his basement. Expelled from school for calling in a bomb threat and faced with being drugged and restricted in a private boarding school, Doug stages a hazardous cargo accident in his model town with the red phosphorous saved from the matches. In the final chapter, he is living in what he describes as the Madham Hospital Burn Unit where he continues to see Andy.

Read Aloud/Reader Response

1. Chapter 1, pages 1 to 3. In this chapter, Doug explains his love of trains, fear of fire, and Andy's friendship.
2. Chapter 2, pages 6 and 7, beginning "I am connecting…" and ending with the chapter. Doug describes Madham and acknowledges his obsession.
3. Chapter 8, pages 26 to 28. The chapter reveals Doug's fascination with Melissa Haverman and her rejection of him.
4. Chapter 17, pages 63 to 64, beginning with the chapter and ending "…would not be me." Doug observes that beautiful high school people stay together and acknowledges that he is not one of them.
5. Chapter 34, pages 133 to 138. In this chapter, the tour of St. Stephen's Academy, a cold and controlling environment, convinces Doug that he does not want to be there.

Booktalk

Douglas MacArthur Hanson is seventeen and specializes in the unusual and the impossible. For more than two years he has been building a matchstick bridge in his basement. It is a perfect 1:800 scale model of the Golden Gate Bridge, which Doug saw when he was exactly six years and four months old. Doug remembers things like that. If Doug had built it according to regular HO scale, the bridge would be more than one hundred feet long. It will be the spectacular feature of his train set and town. But people don't use words like unusual and impossible to describe Doug. They use words like disturbed and obsessed. Melissa Haverman, the most beautiful girl in school, even uses the word "worm." But Doug knows that one person understands the bridge, the town, and Doug. Andy Morrow is Doug's next door neighbor and best friend. Their friendship is unusual and impossible too. Andy is a star on the football field and the stage. He is busy most of the time and can have any girl he wants. He is good looking and coordinated, everything Doug is not. It does seem unusual, even impossible, but Andy is Doug's best friend. They talk everyday. Doug can tell him anything. Best of all, when Doug is next to Andy, everybody notices Andy. Nobody bothers Doug or calls him names. Doug becomes almost *Invisible.*

Get Involved

1. (Discuss) What part do trains and the bridge play in the story?
2. (Discuss) Hautman could have chosen several disasters, but decided on fire. Discuss why he made the choice.
3. (Discuss) Do you think the title is appropriate?
4. (Discuss) What problems do Doug's parents present for him?
5. (Research and Create) The sigil is central to the story. Using your library resources, continue to research the sigil and create one of your own.
6. (Research and Discuss) Doug is the narrator. Using your library resources, define unreliable narrator. Then discuss Doug's reliability as a narrator.

Related Works

1. Gilbert, Barbara Snow. **Paper Trail.** Asheville, NC: Front Street, 2000. 161p. $8.95pa. ISBN 1 932425 54 3. [fiction] MJ, CG with high interest for boys. Fifteen-year-old Walker Morgan, the son of an undercover FBI agent, sees his mother killed by an extremist group within which his family lived and experiences heroic delusions and flashbacks of his life in the community before he reunites with his father.
2. Hartnett, Sonya. **What the Birds See.** Cambridge, MA: Candlewick Press, 2002. 196p. $15.99. ISBN 0 7636 2092 0. [fiction] JS, G Surrounded by irresponsible adults, nine-year-old Adrian is drawn into a neighbor girl's tragic fantasy.
3. Leavitt, Martine. **Heck Superhero.** Asheville, NC: Front Street, 2004. 144p. $16.95. ISBN 1 886910 94 4. [fiction] MJ, CG with high interest for boys. (See full booktalk in *Booktalks and Beyond,* pages 28 to 30.) Thirteen-year-old Heck, abandoned by his depression-prone mother, deals with survival on the street by moving back and forth between real and comic book worlds, but finally realizes that the coping method is unhealthy and unwise.
4. Nolan, Han. **Dancing on the Edge.** New York: Puffin Books, 1997. 244p. $4.99pa. ISBN 0 14 130203 8. [fiction] JS, G (See full booktalk in *Booktalks and More,* 2003, pages 26 to 28.) Dominated by a grandmother who builds a fantasy world about their dysfunctional family, sixteen-year-old Miracle McCloy descends into mental illness and eventually tries to melt (or burn) herself.

5. Rapp, Adam. **Under the Wolf, Under the Dog.** Cambridge, MA: Candlewick Press, 2004. 310p. $16.99. ISBN 0 7636 1818 7. [fiction] S/A, CG Seventeen-year-old Steve Nugent, writing a journal in a facility that houses drug users and possible suicides, recalls his mother's death from cancer, his brother's drug-induced suicide, and his own personal physical and emotional deterioration in reaction to those events. The situations, language, and graphic sexual descriptions could be considered controversial and require a mature audience.

☙❧

Hyde, Catherine Ryan. Becoming Chloe.
New York: Alfred A. Knopf, 2006. 215p. $17.99. ISBN 0 375 93258 5. [fiction] S, CG with high interest for girls

Themes/Topics: homelessness, journey, friendship, perception

Summary/Description

When seventeen-year-old gay Jordon rescues a fragile, possibly suicidal, street girl from a gang rape, the two become a dedicated team who decide to travel and find the beauty in the world. They support each other in both pleasant and life-threatening road encounters. Jordon, who is homeless because he was thrown out of his house, stops prostituting himself. By the end of the story, he no longer seeks one-night stands but seeks a partner who will accept Chloe also. Chloe, artistic and intuitive, comes to fully trust Jordon enough to tell him everything that happened to her before they met. She decides that beauty and ugliness live side by side. When they achieve their original travel goals, they decide to keep traveling. The story closes with their letters to the doctor who cared for Chloe and their continued commitment to each other.

Read Aloud/Reader Response

1. Chapter 3, pages 53 to 57, beginning "As we're walking up the driveway, ..." and ending "To prove that I could." The passage describes Jordon's homecoming.
2. Chapter 4, pages 83 to 85, beginning "I'm feeling jumpy..." and ending "... part of the equation." In the discussion with Dr. Reynoso, the doctor challenges Jordon to get his own life.
3. Chapter 5, pages 103 to 104, beginning "We're on the deck..." and ending "... and see things, too." Jordon becomes the "... tour guide for beauty."

4. Chapter 5, pages 158 to 159, beginning "The view is spectacular..." and ending "...'with joy.'" Jordon reflects on the meaning of climbing the mountain.
5. Chapter 5, pages 171 to 174, beginning "The copter holds five..." and ending "...that to be amazed." Jordon and Chloe see the Grand Canyon with the obese woman.
6. Pages 211 to 215. The two letters, separate from the chapters, explain to Dr. Reynoso what both Jordon and Chloe have learned from the trip.

Booktalk

Seventeen-year-old Jordon lives on the streets. He is gay, and because of that, his parents don't want him in their house. While he settles for the night in his new basement home, he hears noise. A gang rape is going on outside his window. He stops it. That's how he meets the victim, a teenage girl who has suffered so much abuse that she doesn't expect anything else. Her name is Wanda Johnston. She doesn't like that name, so Jordon gives her a choice of some new names. She picks Chloe. But Chloe needs more than a new name. She needs a new life. They try starting that new life together, but if violence, prostitution, and shoplifting are the only ways they can survive, this new life looks just like the old one. Finally, Chloe decides she would just rather leave life permanently. But Jordon is determined to show Chloe enough good things to make her want to stay alive. They will take a trip, and Jordon with be "a tour guide for beauty." Jordon will create a new person to go with that new name. But he doesn't realize that the total makeover will include him. Who will he become while this strange and wonderful girl is *Becoming Chloe*?

Get Involved

1. (Research) Investigate the origin and history of the name *Chloe*. Share the information with the group, and discuss how it supports the author's purpose.
2. (Discuss) Is the ending happy or sad?
3. (Discuss) Each person that Jordon and Chloe meet on their journey affects them. Choose your favorite encounter. Explain your choice with specifics from the story.
4. (React) Read the letters that Jordon and Chloe write Dr. Reynoso. (See Read Aloud/Reader Response 6). What do you feel they reveal?
5. (Create) On a map, trace the journey that Jordon and Chloe make. Display the map during the discussion.

6. (Create) Plan your own journey. Explain your choices of destination and stops.
7. (Create) Make your own list of beautiful and ugly things. Share and compare your list with others in the group.

Related Works

1. Frost, Helen. **Keesha's House.** New York: Farrar, Straus and Giroux/Frances Foster Books, 2003. 116p. $16.00. ISBN 0 374 34064 1. [poetry] JS, CG with high interest for girls. (See full booktalk in *Booktalks and Beyond*, 2007, pages 21 to 24.) Keesha, seeking refuge from her alcoholic father, moves in with Joe, who was also homeless as a teen, and encourages other troubled teens to join her.
2. Leavitt, Martine. **Heck Superhero.** Asheville, NC: Front Street, 2004. 144p. $16.95. ISBN 1 886910 94 4. [fiction] MJ, CG with high interest for boys. (See full booktalk in *Booktalks and Beyond*, 2007, pages 28 to 30.) Thirteen-year-old Heck, abandoned by his depression-prone mother, searches for her while surviving on the street and dealing with the pain of a badly infected tooth.
3. Nolan, Han. **Born Blue.** New York: Harcourt Brace and Company, 2001. 177p. $17.00. ISBN 0 15 201916 2. [fiction] JS, G (See full booktalk in *Teen Genre Connections*, 2005, pages 13 to 15.) Janie tells about her life from the time she is four years old when she is rescued from drowning to when she is sixteen and decides to leave her illegitimate daughter with a loving and caring family.
4. Nolan, Han. **A Face in Every Window.** New York: Harcourt Brace and Company, 1999. 264p. $16.00. ISBN 0 15 201915 4. [fiction] S, CG with high interest for girls (See full booktalk in *Teen Genre Connections*, 2005, pages 17 to 19.) James Patrick O'Brian's life completely changes when his dominating grandmother dies, his mother wins a house she fills with "weirdos," and he has to rethink his feelings for his mentally challenged father and the new baby his mother has with her doctor.
5. Rapp, Adam. Timothy Basil Ering (illus.). **33 Snowfish.** Cambridge, MA: Candlewick Press, 2003. 179p. $15.99. ISBN 0 7636 1874 8. [fiction] S, CG (See full booktalk in *Booktalks and Beyond*, 2007, pages 30 to 33.) Custis, who is about ten, runs from his abusive "owner" and the law with a fifteen-year-old prostitute and a seventeen-year-old boy who murdered his parents and plans to sell his baby brother. Eventually, he finds Seldom who offers him a new life that Custis struggles to understand and accept.

✿✿

Jenkins, A. M. Repossessed.
New York: HarperCollins/HarperTeen, 2007. 218p. $15.99.
ISBN-13: 978 0 06 083568 2. [fiction] JS, CG

Themes/Topics: fallen angels, hell, heaven, Seven Deadly Sins, human experience, brothers, conduct of life

Summary/Description

Kiriel, a fallen angel, enters the body of teenage Shaun to take a vacation from hell and experience the human Seven Deadly Sins. Instead, he appreciates God's creation and becomes emotionally involved with his new family and friends. He cleans his room, helps his single mother, supports and includes his hyper-active brother, faces down the school bully, and persuades the girl with a secret crush on Shaun that she is beautiful. He realizes that he will be forced to return to his job in hell, that Shaun must complete his life, and that the difference between him and the angels who have not fallen is that he asks questions and challenges the Creator's plan. He decides that he is in hell through his personal choice. The content could be considered controversial.

Read Aloud/Reader Response

1. Chapter 1, pages 1 to 3, beginning with the chapter and ending with "...to Hell, ha ha?" Kiriel explains why he chose Shaun.
2. Chapter 5, page 34, beginning with the chapter and ending "...that witness." Kiriel explains his job in Hell.
3. Chapter 6, page 44, beginning "The cat knew..." and ending with the chapter. Kiriel questions why God created the imperfect and then rejected them for that imperfection.
4. Chapter 12, pages 75 to 86, beginning "I hadn't thought..." and ending with the chapter. Kiriel compares Shaun and Bailey.
5. Chapter 23, pages 206 to 207, beginning "*It's the glitches and...*" and ending "...perfection is *dull.*" Kiriel decides that he prefers the imperfect world.

Booktalk

Ask how many in the group know the Seven Deadly Sins: sloth, envy, pride, greed, gluttony, wrath, and lust.

Now I would like to introduce you to the character who wants to experience them. (*Read pages 1 and 2.*) The lucky teenager is Shaun, and in a few seconds Kiriel, from Hell, is sure that Shaun will step in front of a truck and die. What would be the harm in taking that body? Neither the Boss nor the Creator could get too excited about that, and Kiriel needs a change, a little excitement. In Hell, Kiriel spends all his time listening to everyone's regrets and complaints. He figures he needs a break. He figures that it's his turn to try out the Seven Deadly Sins on earth. What Kiriel should know is that when somebody messes with the Plan, things don't work out the way they anticipated. The question is how much fun can Kiriel have and how much damage can he do before he is simply *Repossessed?*

Get Involved

1. (Research) Using your library resources read about the fall of the angels. Refer to religious commentaries as well as the Bible. Act as a resource person during the discussion.
2. (Research) Using your library resources, investigate Kiriel's belief that the Creator "wound the watch up, set the hands, and let it start ticking." Act as a resource person during the discussion.
3. (React) Is Kiriel the evil being that you pictured coming from Hell?
4. (Discuss) Should Kiriel run the universe?
5. (Create) List all the things that Shaun might be regretting if he did not have the chance to come back to earth. Try to develop that list into suggestions for living.
6. (Research) Invite ministers or religious studies professionals to read the book also and participate in the discussion group.

Related Works

1. Albom, Mitch. **The Five People You Meet in Heaven.** New York: Hyperion, 2003. 196p. $19.95. ISBN 0 7868 6871 6. [fiction] JS/A, CG (See full booktalk in *Booktalks and Beyond,* 2007, pages 35 to 37.) Eighty-three-year-old Eddie dies and learns in his journey through the after-life that there are no random acts.
2. Rylant, Cynthia. **God Went to Beauty School.** New York: Harper-Collins Publishers, 2003. 64p. $14.99. ISBN 0 06 009433 8. [poetry] MJS, CG (See full booktalk in *Teen Genre Connections,* 2005, pages 84 to 85.) In twenty-three poems, Rylant characterizes God as an almighty being who puts the world in motion and then discovers, when getting involved, the pain and beauty in His creation.
3. Sleator, William. **Hell Phone.** (See full booktalk in "Mystery/Suspense"/"Paranormal," pages 164 to 166.) Seventeen-year-old Nick Gordon finds himself in hell after trusting a voice on a cheap cell phone.

4. Soto, Gary. **The Afterlife.** New York: Harcourt Brace and Company, 2003. 161p. $16.00. ISBN 0 15 204774 3. [fiction] JS, CG with high interest for boys (See full booktalk in *Teen Genre Connections,* 2005, pages 294 to 296.) Stabbed to death in a restroom, eighteen-year-old Jesús, having grown up in a Mexican/Hmong Fresno neighborhood, moves from life to the after-life and briefly touches those left behind.

5. Zevin, Gabrielle. **Elsewhere.** New York: Farrar, Straus and Giroux, 2005. 277p. $19.95. ISBN 0 374 32091 8. [fiction] MJS, G (See full booktalk in *Booktalks and Beyond,* 2007, pages 188 to 190.) Liz dies in a traffic accident shortly before her sixteenth birthday and begins her new life in Elsewhere, a world where she becomes younger each day, learns about her spirit, and prepares to be reborn.

ೞ

Pixley, Marcella. **Freak.**

New York: Farrar, Straus and Giroux/Melanie Kroupa Books, 2007. 131p. $16.00.
ISBN-13: 978 0 374 32453 7. [fiction] MJS, G

Themes/Topics: bullies, middle schools, writing, conduct of life, dysfunctional families

Summary/Description

When senior Artie Rosenberg moves in with her family, twelve-year-old academically precocious Miriam and fourteen-year-old Deborah vie for his attention and affection. Miriam's fantasies about Artie bring teasing and ridicule from the middle school popular girls clique. Deborah, who has decided to throw over academics and be part of the popular high school crowd, begins dating Artie. The harassment and the Deborah/Artie relationship escalate. When a desperate Miriam cuts her hair and eyebrows to try to look like the popular girls, she mutilates them. Her self-absorbed parents see her appearance but allow her to go to school where the extreme reaction results in a cafeteria fight with her most powerful enemy, a girl considered the school slut. Miriam learns that neither she nor her enemy has an adult to turn to. She shaves her head, goes to the popular crowd party, and is the only person there to defend her tormentor from a possible rape. In thanks and apology, the girl gives a leather-bound journal to Miriam.

Read Aloud/Reader Response

The entire book is an excellent read aloud, but the following passages might produce some lively discussions.

1. Chapter 3, pages 18 to 23, beginning "I've never had..." and ending "Even me." This passage describes Miriam, her friend, and the beginning of the harassment.
2. Chapter 4, pages 25 to 27, beginning with the chapter and ending "...put it back on her knee." Miriam describes the pecking order on the bus and the price of popularity for Jenny Clarke, Miriam's major harasser.
3. Chapter 6, pages 35 to 43. This chapter communicates the negative dynamics in Miriam's family.
4. Chapter 22, pages 111 to 113. In this chapter, Miss Garland suggests that Miriam and Jenny may share the same type of problems at home.
5. Chapter 25, pages 121 to 126. In this chapter, Miriam defends Jenny.

Booktalk

Twelve-year-old Miriam receives the best news of her life. The handsome Artie Rosenberg will be spending the year with their family. Besides being a hunk, he is surely her soul mate. The problem is that Miriam's fourteen-year-old sister, Deborah, has some plans for Artie too, and Miriam's sister could care if Miriam were alive. Deborah's whole life centers on the popular crowd. Artie's part of that group. So who do you think has the inside track with Artie? The answer is tough enough to take, but Miriam shouldn't worry so much about whom she would like to be with her as she should about who is against her. In a confused mess, Artie makes her a target for the "watermelon girls," the popular middle school crowd that rules the school. She isn't safe in class, the cafeteria, or on the bus. The year from heaven is turning into the year from hell. But when Miriam decides to fight back, the whole world learns what it means to face the *Freak*.

Get Involved

1. (Research) Using your library resources, find out as much as you can about the causes of bullying and ways to combat it. Act as a resource person during the group discussion.
2. (Discuss) Choose the person in the novel that you believe to be the worst bully. Explain your choice with specifics from the text.
3. (Discuss) Do the bullied make themselves targets?
4. (Create) Write another chapter about the first day that Miriam and Jenny return to school. Share it with the group.
5. (Follow-up) Find out about the anti-bullying policies at your school or recreation centers. Share the information with the group. If there are no policies, form a group to put one into action.

Related Works

1. Anderson, Laurie Halse. **Speak.** New York: Farrar, Straus and Giroux, 1999. 198p. $16.00. ISBN 0 374 37152 0. [fiction] JS, G (See full booktalk in *Booktalks and More,* 2003, pages 75 to 77.) Trying to be part of the popular crowd, Melinda Sordino goes to a party that includes high school seniors and drinking. She is raped, and her recovery centers on two classmates and her art teacher who gradually draw out her story.

2. Clements, Bruce. **What Erika Wants.** New York: Farrar, Straus and Giroux, 2005. 216p. $16.00. ISBN 0 374 32304 6. [fiction] MJS, G (See full booktalk in *Booktalks and Beyond,* 2007, pages 6 to 9.) Fifteen-year-old Erika must decide if she will live with her emotional and indecisive father or her manipulative mother, and whether she will keep an exploitive friend.

3. Cormier, Robert. **Heroes.** New York: Delacorte Press, 1998. 135p. $15.95. ISBN 0 385 32590 8. [fiction] JS, CG (See full booktalk in *Booktalks and More,* 2003, pages 118 to 120.) Francis Joseph Cassavant joins the service and tries to kill himself after he fails to prevent the rape of his friend. Finally he decides to confront the rapist, a former personal hero.

4. Flinn, Alex. **Breaking Point.** New York: HarperTempest, 2002. 240p. $6.99pa. ISBN 0 06 447371 6. [fiction] JS, CG with high interest for boys. (See full booktalk in *Booktalks and Beyond,* 2007, pages 12 to 14.) Now eighteen, Paul Richmond reflects on his experience in an exclusive school where a charismatic and popular student became his "friend" and then pressured him to plant a bomb in a classroom.

5. Korman, Gordon. **Jake, Reinvented.** New York: Hyperion, 2003. 213p. $15.99. ISBN 0 786 81957 X. [fiction] JS, CG Through Rick, the reader learns about Jake, a brainy, social outsider who manufactures a new persona to capture the attention of the cold, popular girl he adores.

Contemporary

Contemporary books also confront teen challenges, but with a bit less intensity and danger. The selections with more interest for girls seem closely related to discovering love as well as passion in life. The selections with more interest for boys tend to address the real meaning of "winning," and often winning involves acknowledging mistakes and feelings. Like the books in other chapters, the stories fit into other categories too. *Small Steps* and *Big Slick* could be Issues or Mystery/Suspense selections. *The Wednesday Wars* could be classified as Issues or History. *Slam* and *Notes from the Midnight Driver* might fit in Issues, but the injection of humor and the competitive spirit in these selections add a little lightness to the challenges of growing up in the modern world.

Learning about Love

ᘓᘔ

Clarke, Judith. **One Whole and Perfect Day.**

Honesdale, PA: Front Street, 2006. 250p. $16.95. ISBN-13: 978 1 932425 95 6. [fiction]
JS, CG with high interest for girls

Themes/Topics: Australia, grandparents, prejudice, brothers and sisters, family dynamics

Summary/Description

Lily, labeled the sensible one in her eccentric family, hopes for one perfect day of togetherness even though that requires healing the conflict between her irascible, prejudiced grandfather and her aimless older brother. Lily's grandmother, who routinely talks to an imaginary friend she created while growing up in an orphanage, plans a celebration for her husband's eightieth birthday that she feels will force everyone to be amiable. Each chapter tells how Lily's family members learn about themselves as they move toward the party and how people in other conflicted, dysfunctional families that touch the lives of Lily's family work out their problems or differences. The party takes place. Lily, a little less sensible, finds a boyfriend. The grandmother reunites with the person who inspired her imaginary friend, and Lily, along with several adult characters, learns that freedom and unbelievable coincidence may be frustrating but more productive than plans and rules.

Read Aloud/Reader Response

1. Chapter 1, pages 7 to 11. In this chapter, Lily introduces her family.
2. Chapter 5, pages 27 to 30, beginning with the chapter and ending with "…across his arms." Lily's grandfather discovers his mother's wedding dress and recalls the regret connected to it.
3. Chapter 13, pages 71 to 74, beginning with the chapter and ending "…really, truly, was." Lily ponders her "freakish" family.
4. Chapter 23, pages 122 to 130. In this chapter, Lily's grandfather returns to his old neighborhood, is infuriated by the changes, and finds himself in a confrontation with Rose, a Chinese woman, who grew up in the same neighborhood.
5. Chapter 29, pages 162 to 164, beginning "Oh, Lily…" and ending with the chapter. Marigold reflects on Lily the bully but finds an overwhelmed Lily at home.

Booktalk

Seventeen-year-old Lily is the sensible one in the family. She does the housework in their ramshackle house while her charming older brother wanders from project to project, and her psychologist mother concentrates on which needy client she will bring home to stay for a while. They trust Lily to keep everything together. But Lily is tired of smelling like cooked vegetables and cleaning supplies. She would like to fall in love. She would like a little excitement. And she is going to get it. Her grandmother, who talks to an imaginary friend, decides to have a family party to smooth feelings and make things perfect. That doesn't seem like a bad plan, but Lily's grandfather recently picked up an ax and chased Lily's brother out of the house. Grandma is inviting both of them. Lily's mother may invite another one of her patients (Lily calls them "lame ducks"), the crazy Mrs. Nightingale. Of course, Lily's father won't be there because he left the family before Lily was born. And did I mention that Lily, with her blocky body and wiry hair, is no beauty? How can anyone who looks like that, thinks like that, or has a family like that ever hope for any happiness, let alone *One Whole and Perfect Day?*

Get Involved

1. (Research) Using your library resources, find as much information as you can about immigration in Australia over the past fifty years. Act as a resource person for your group during discussion.
2. (Research) Using your library resources, find as much information as you can about immigration in North America over the past fifty years. Act as a resource person for your group during discussion.
3. (Create) Using the information from Get Involved 1 and 2, organize a debate about what controls should be placed on immigration.
4. (Discuss) Bullies are an issue in each family. Choose one person who might be considered a bully in the story. Discuss the person's relationships with others. Refer to specifics from the novel.
5. (Discuss) Lily's mother comments that all families are dysfunctional. Do you agree? Be sure to refer to specific details from the novel.
6. (Discuss) What part does prejudice play in the story? Be sure to refer to specific details from the novel.

Related Works

1. Albom, Mitch. **The Five People You Meet in Heaven.** New York: Hyperion, 2003. 196p. $19.95. ISBN 0 7868 6871 6. [fiction] JS/A, CG (See full booktalk in *Booktalks and Beyond,* 2007, pages 35 to 37.) In his journey through the after-life, eighty-three-year-old Eddie learns that there are no random acts, sacrifice brings rewards, letting go of anger allows one to move on, love lasts through memories, and responsibility and integrity bring redemption and salvation.
2. Frost, Helen. **Keesha's House.** New York: Farrar, Straus and Giroux/Frances Foster Books, 2003. 116p. $16.00. ISBN 0 374 34064 1. [fiction] JS, CG with high interest for girls (See full booktalk in *Booktalks and Beyond,* 2007, pages 21 to 24.) In separate sestinas or sonnets, homeless young people, now sheltered in a neighborhood home, tell their stories and express their fears and concerns.
3. Nolan, Han. **A Face in Every Window.** New York: Harcourt Brace and Company, 1999. 264p. $16.00. ISBN 0 15 201915 4. [fiction] JS, CG with high interest for girls. (See full booktalk in *Booktalks and More,* 2003, pages 17 to 19.) When James Patrick O'Brian's mother wins a house, fills it with people experiencing conflict or change, and strikes out on her own, James at first resists his "weird" situation but eventually learns to see individuals rather than stereotypes.

4. Tan, Shaun. **The Arrival.** New York: Scholastic Inc./Arthur A. Levine Books, 2007. 128p. $19.99. ISBN-13: 978 0 439 89529 3. [wordless graphic] MJS, CG with high interest for boys. The story, told completely in dramatic graphics, communicates the joy of arrival to a new country and how that joy is passed to others.

5. Zusak, Markus. **I Am the Messenger.** New York: Alfred A. Knopf, 2002. 357p. $20.50. ISBN 0 375 93099 X. [fiction] S, CG (See full booktalk in *Booktalks and Beyond,* 2007, pages 143 to 146.) A series of seemingly unconnected tasks, directed by a deck of cards, show an average nineteen-year-old underage cabdriver that he can control his own life. Then, ironically, he learns that a writer has created him to convey that message.

ᏣᏤ

Green, John. An Abundance of Katherines.
New York: Dutton Books, 2006. 215p. $16.99. ISBN 0 525 47688 1. [fiction] JS, G

Themes/Topics: friendship, self-perception, conduct of life

Summary/Description

Dumped by the nineteenth Katherine he has dated, Colin Singleton, a self-absorbed, has-been child prodigy, embarks on a road trip with his best friend, the humorous, overweight Hassan. Colin wants time and space to develop his mathematical formula that will predict the length of romantic relationships. He believes that success will prove his worth to the world. The two friends stop in Gutshot, Tennessee, and are hired by the owner of the town's factory to record the stories of the employees and retirees. Lindsey, the daughter of the factory's owner, is a former nerd who has committed herself to popularity. In recording the stories and interacting with each other and the in-crowd, the three discover the importance of doing something positive for the world and then passing on the stories about those deeds to future generations. They decide that the pursuit of fleeting fame and popularity causes an individual to forget the people who really matter and compromise one's principles.

Read Aloud/Reader Response

1. Chapter 7, page 68, beginning "Well, I think..." and ending "...all popular is." Lindsey defines popular.
2. Chapter 9, page 96, beginning "That's why people..." and ending with the chapter. Colin reflects on the sad situation of the Dumpees.

3. Chapter 14, pages 148 to 151, beginning "Let me tell you..." and ending "...private habit." Lindsey tells her story.
4. Chapter 18, pages 195 to 196, beginning "Hollis and Lindsey..." and ending with the chapter. Hassan shares his spiritual revelation.
5. Chapter 19, pages 207 to 208, beginning "And the moral..." and ending "...happens *with* you." Colin reflects on how life shapes stories and stories shape life.
6. Epilogue, pages 210 to 215. In the epilogue, Colin figures out that the future is not knowable or controllable, and all three accept that the joy of life is rooted in journey.

Booktalk

Colin Singleton just graduated from high school. For most of us, graduation means a step up, a new start in life. For Colin it means an end. Colin made a career of being a child prodigy. He has ten thousand dollars to prove it. Suddenly, he is too old to be a child prodigy. Suddenly, he has to be an adult, a genius, and Colin is not too sure that he can make that leap. But he does have an idea. He is working on a special formula. It will tell all the people who are constantly dumped by their heartthrobs if and when the traumatic event will take place. The dumped will no longer be dumbfounded. Colin, who falls in love only with girls named Katherine, has been dumbfounded nineteen times. Katherine the nineteenth, his latest unfortunate choice, may be the one to destroy his confidence, his formula, and his heart. But Colin does have a friend, the laugh-a-minute, irresponsible Hassan. Hassan thinks that he and Colin should take a ride and get away from it all, especially since Colin has the money to finance the trip. The two hit the road to find the formula, but what they discover in a small Tennessee town appropriately named Gutshot is much harder to figure out than even *An Abundance of Katherines*.

Get Involved

1. (Research) Using your library resources, learn more about the meaning of prodigy and genius. Compare what you find with the narrator's explanation in chapter 2, on page 10, beginning "Prodigies can very quickly learn..." and ending with the paragraph.
2. (Research) Using your library resources, learn more about specific child prodigies. Determine why the person was a prodigy and how talent affected his or her life.
3. (Research) Learn more about the life of Archduke Ferdinand. Why do you think Green alludes to him?
4. (React) Read the epilogue several times. List what you feel are the most important realizations. Compare your answers with the answers of someone else who has completed the same exercise.

5. (Discuss) Why is mathematics such an important part of the novel?
6. (React) How do you feel about the role of religion in the story?
7. (Discuss) Read or re-read *The Missing Piece* (Related Work 5). Discuss how it applies to Colin, Lindsey, and Hassan.

Related Works

1. Alexander, Lloyd. **The Golden Dream of Carlo Chuchio.** (See full booktalk in "Adventure/Survival"/"Quest," pages 123 to 126.) In this Arabian Nights-type fantasy, a young man discovers that perhaps the journey rather than the destination is the best part of life.
2. Bagdasarian, Adam. **First French Kiss and Other Traumas.** New York: Farrar, Straus and Giroux/Melanie Kroupa Books, 2002. 134p. $16.00. ISBN 0 374 32338 0. [fiction] JS, CG (See full booktalk in *Teen Genre Connections*, 2005, pages 73 to 74.) In five groups of essays, a fictional character tells his traumatic and sometimes humorous life experiences in becoming a man.
3. Earls, Nick. **48 Shades of Brown.** New York: Houghton Mifflin Company, 2004. 288p. $6.99pa. ISBN 0 618 45295 8. [fiction] S, CG (See full booktalk in *Teen Genre Connections*, 2005, pages 75 to 77.) When the sixteen-year-old sheltered and intellectual narrator decides to stay with his twenty-something aunt during his senior year, he discovers a whole new set of responsibilities and his own sexual awakening.
4. Green, John. **Looking for Alaska.** New York: Dutton Books, 2005. 224p. $15.99. ISBN 0 525 47506 0. [fiction] S, CG (See full booktalk in *Booktalks and Beyond*, 2007, pages 37 to 40.) Sixteen-year-old Miles Halter attends his father's alma mater, Culver Creek, to seek what François Rabelais described in his last words as "a Great Perhaps," and bonds with three students who help him explore the meaning of life and death.
5. Silverstein, Shel. **The Missing Piece.** New York: Harper & Row Publishers, 1976. 98p. $16.99. ISBN 0 06 025671 0. [fiction] J, CG A wandering incomplete circle discovers that hunting for the missing piece is more fun than finding it.

Koja, Kathe. Kissing the Bee.

New York: Farrar, Straus and Giroux/Frances Foster Books, 2007. 121p. $16.00.
ISBN-13: 978 0 374 39938 2. [fiction] JS, G

Themes/Topics: high school, interpersonal relationships, bees, individuality

Summary/Description

Seniors Avra, Dana, and Emil are a trio. The demanding and mercurial Avra, the "queen bee," assumes that Emil is her boyfriend, and that Dana will always support her. In constant conflicts with her mother and older sister, Avra plans on leaving with Emil after the prom and living her own life. Dana and Emil develop feelings for each other. Rather than telling Avra, Dana withdraws from the trio. Avra accuses Dana of feeling superior and turns against her. Emil fully admits his feelings for Dana after he fulfills his promise to take Avra to the prom. When Dana and Emil become a couple, Avra and her mother react with bitterness. Avra gets a new boyfriend, and Dana realizes that her relationship with Avra was not a healthy one. Dana's science project on the life of bees pulls all the story events together as Dana realizes that she has a right to be an independent person who can ignore Avra's often petty and selfish demands.

Read Aloud/Reader Response

1. Chapter 4, pages 24 and 25, beginning *"He likes facts."* and ending with the chapter. Emil raises a significant difference between a bee and a butterfly.
2. Chapter 6, pages 32 and 33, beginning "My mother never..." and ending with the chapter. Dana reflects on her mother's belief that "Anything can happen."
3. Chapter 7, pages 38 and 39, beginning "Sometimes Avra..." and ending with the chapter. Dana reflects on what she and Emil love.
4. Chapter 14, page 96. This brief chapter explores the meaning of wings.
5. Chapter 17, page 116, beginning "'You always know...'" and ending "...never would be." Dana realizes that she is more talented and stronger than Avra.

Booktalk

Dana, Avra, and Emil are seniors and inseparable. Emil is Avra's boyfriend. Dana is Avra's best friend. Dana picks up the slack for any plans Avra has, even Avra's prom date with Emil. Avra is the idea person, and Dana works out the details. That was the way it was even before Emil came into the picture. Now Dana is looking at some details of her own. She has a big science project due, a project about bees. Some of the bee information seems to describe her life. (*Read out loud the italicized description of the bee society on page 4.*) Guess who the worker is and guess who the queen in their three-person hive is. (*Wait for a response.*) Right. But Emil starts talking to Dana about butterflies and love. Bees accept their fate, but butterflies transform themselves. Which will Dana be? Dana has to make some decisions. Those decisions may sting, but bee folklore claims that the pain of the sting is worth the wisdom that it gives. So Dana may have to suffer a little sting to get a grip on her own life and love. The ancients called it *Kissing the Bee.*

Get Involved

1. (Research) Using your library resources, find out as much as you can about bees and butterflies. Act as a resource person during the discussion.
2. (Discuss) Is Dana a bee or a butterfly?
3. (React) How do you feel about Avra as a person? Support your opinion with specifics from the novel.
4. (Discuss) Choose the section of the bee report that was most significant to your life. Explain your choice and compare it to the choices of others in the group.
5. (Create) Design the prom costume that you think Dana should wear.

Related Works

1. Cabot, Meg. **Teen Idol.** New York: HarperCollins Publishers, 2004. 293p. $16.89. ISBN 0 06 009617 9. [fiction] MJS, G Junior Jenny Greenley, who anonymously writes an advice column for the student paper, is in the middle of her own dating dilemmas when she guides a movie star around her high school and prepares for the prom.
2. Hemphill, Stephanie. **Your Own Sylvia: A Verse Portrait of Sylvia Plath.** New York: Alfred A. Knopf, 2007. 261p. $15.99. ISBN-13: 978 0 375 83799 9. [poetry] S/A, G With poems, Hemphill presents and interprets the people, events, and influences of Sylvia Plath.
3. Hosler, Jay. **Clan Apis.** Columbus, OH: Active Synapse, 2000. 158p. $15.00. ISBN 1 4046 1367 6. [graphic] S/A, CG (See full booktalk in *Teen Genre Connections*, 2005, pages 280 to 282.) In five chapters, Hosler describes the life cycle of the honeybee through the life journey of Nyuki, a worker bee.
4. Kidd, Sue Monk. **The Secret Life of Bees.** New York: Penguin Books, 2002. 302p. $14.00. ISBN 0 14 200174 0. [fiction] S/A, G (See full booktalk in *Booktalks and Beyond*, 2007, pages 196 to 199.) Fourteen-year-old Lilly Owens seeks refuge in a bee farm and learns about both bee keeping and life.
5. Plath, Sylvia. "Stings." PoemHunter.com. Available: http://www.poem hunter.com/poem/stings/ (Accessed 29 July, 2008). The speaker in the poem declares her right to be a queen rather than a worker bee. Koja uses a line from the poem to introduce her story.

ℭℨ ℬℨ

Lubar, David. Sleeping Freshmen Never Lie.

New York: Penguin Group/Speak, 2005. 279p. $6.99pa. ISBN-13: 978 0 14 240780 6.

[fiction] MJ, CG with high interest for boys

Themes/Topics: self-confidence, conduct of life, interpersonal relations, writing, brothers, high school, freshman year

Summary/Description

As Scott Hudson and his three buddies grow apart during their freshman year, Scott discovers his writing, organizational, and interpersonal talents. He throws himself into the newspaper, the play, and student council in order to meet one girl whom he sees as glamorous. He finds himself defending and eventually dating an unpopular Goth girl with whom he has more in common. He makes friends with and helps mature a nonacademic senior bully who becomes his protector, and he befriends a social outcast who eventually attempts suicide. At home, Scott writes letters explaining what he learns to his unborn baby brother, supports his older brother's efforts to find himself, and learns to admire his own parents' successful relationship. He discovers that other students envy his stable family and successful life, that the students he thought would be least likely to be his friends are probably his best friends, that he has developed enough physically to defend himself against bullies, and that the little brother he feared might take his place in the family is a welcome addition.

Read Aloud/Reader Response

1. Chapter 16, page 133, letter dated November 19. In this letter to his baby brother, Scott explains why suicide is a bad idea.
2. Chapter 17, page 139, beginning "Tuesday, on the way..." and ending with the chapter. Scott shows his hesitancy to get involved with Lee even though she is sharing with him the literature that he loves.
3. Chapter 19, pages 146 to 147, beginning "I'd been taking..." and ending "...completely flaky." Scott challenges Lee's pseudo-intellectual statements.
4. Chapter 25, pages 195 to 196, beginning "Did you date..." and ending "...what you have to do." Scott and his father talk about dating.
5. Chapter 32, pages 263 to 276. Written in three acts, the chapter brings together all the events of the novel.
6. Chapter 33, pages 277 to 279, Scott talks about his developing writing skills and writes a final letter to his new baby brother.

Booktalk

Scott Hudson is looking forward to starting his freshman year. He and his three buddies plan to be "One for all and all for one." But high school isn't quite what Scott anticipated. He and his friends aren't in the same classes, and the plain Jane he shared his crackers with in kindergarten is now an amazingly good looking girl he is trying to date. Trying to get a date with the gorgeous girl leads him into joining the paper, student council, and the stage crew. Those extra-curricular activities and his academic schedule don't leave him much time for old friends. And if school isn't enough pressure, his home life is getting a little hectic too. Scott's eighteen-year-old brother is moving back home, and their mother just announced that she is pregnant. There goes the quiet house and his status as the youngest member of the family. Suddenly, Scott's life is a whirlwind of disappointments, surprises, and problems that show up faster than he can understand what they mean, even if he has the strength to stay awake. Listen closely to what he finally figures out because *Sleeping Freshmen Never Lie*.

Get Involved

1. (Research) Scott and Scott's English teacher try and use several word games and structures. Using your library resources, find at least two writing structures or suggestions to strengthen writing. Share your findings with the group.
2. (Create) Choose the approach or structure from Get Involved 1 that appeals the most to you. Write a message that uses it.
3. (React) Choose what you feel is the most significant event of Scott's freshman year. Explain your choice. Compare your choice with choices made by others in the group.
4. (React) Choose the character that holds the most appeal for you. Explain your choice with specifics from the text.
5. (Follow-up) Scott mentions several books in the course of the story. Choose one, read it, and share your reactions with the group.

Related Works

1. Connelly, Neil. **St. Michael's Scales.** New York: Arthur A. Levine Books, 2002. 320p. $16.95. ISBN 0 439 19445 8. [fiction] MJS, CG with high interest for boys (See full booktalk in *Teen Genre Connections,* 2005, pages 59 to 61.) Fifteen-year-old Keegan Flannery, the smallest ninth-grader at the almost bankrupt Our Lady of Perpetual Help High School in Allentown, Pennsylvania, plans to commit suicide until he finds his strength in wrestling, but he fails to stop his friend from committing suicide.

2. Garfinkle, D. L. **Storky: How I Lost My Nickname and Won the Girl.** New York: G. P. Putnam's Sons, 2005. 184p. $16.99. ISBN 0 399 24284 8. [fiction] MJ CG (See full booktalk in *Booktalks and Beyond,* 2007, pages 63 to 65.) High school freshman Michael "Storky" Pomerantz seeks popularity in high school and a dating relationship with a gifted student but instead finds one good friend and academic success.

3. Lubar, David. **Hidden Talents.** New York: Tom Doherty Associates, 1999. 213p. $16.95. ISBN 0 312 86646 1. [fiction] MJ CG with high interest for boys (See full booktalk in *Booktalks and More,* 2003, pages 63 to 65.) Thirteen-year-old Martin Anderson enrolls in an alternative school and makes friends with other boys who have unusual talents. They figure out how to harness their powers and protect themselves from the bullies who harass them.

4. McGraw, Jay. **Life Strategies for Teens.** New York: Fireside Press, 2000. 236p. $14.00. ISBN 0 7432 1546 X. [nonfiction] JS, CG (See full booktalk in *Teen Genre Connections,* 2005, pages 52 to 54.) Jay McGraw presents "Ten Laws of Life" dealing with identity, independence, decision-making, and self-respect.

5. Sones, Sonya. **What My Mother Doesn't Know.** New York: Simon Pulse, 2003. 259p. $6.00pa. ISBN 0 689 85553 2. [fiction] JS, G In a series of poems, fourteen-year-old Sophie relates her love journeys in the midst of her cold father's and manipulative mother's marital conflict. She finally discovers that she has more in common with Murphy, the boy in her art class who is labeled a reject.

ఁఁఁ

Myers, Walter Dean. **What They Found: Love on 145th Street.**

New York: Wendy Lamb Books, 2007. 243p. $18.99. ISBN-13: 978 0 375 93709 5.
[related short stories] JS, GC with high interest for boys

Themes/Topics: love, family life, beauty shop,
African-Americans, Harlem, coming of age

Summary/Description

A sequel to *145th Street: Short Stories,* these fifteen interrelated stories explore romantic love, family love, exploitive love, and friendship. The first story focuses on a dying man who plans his funeral around the opening of his wife's beauty shop. That setting and those characters loosely weave together the stories of a young couple trying to remain celibate before marriage, a sister caring for her drug-addicted mother and four-year-old brother, a plain girl deciding to give up the attentions of a handsome philanderer, a shy girl learning to open up to men, tough love leading a girl to turn in her brother to the police, a father deciding that stealing for his little boy's present is not love, a girl challenging a long time boyfriend to grow up, a single mother being perceived as a Madonna, a young man deciding his girlfriend is not worth a jail sentence, a strong-minded young woman finding her own life by managing her husband, and a corporal discovering love in a combat zone.

Read Aloud/Reader Response

1. "the fashion show, grand opening, and bar-b-que memorial service," pages 3 to 6, beginning "A year ago..." and ending "...even from the hospital." As their father is dying, he pushes his family to open the beauty shop.
2. "the life you need to have," pages 55 to 56, beginning "But this morning..." and ending "...then I'll get over it." Gaylee realizes that her potential boyfriend translates all relationships in terms of his life.
3. "burn," page 73, beginning "In the cab uptown..." and ending "'...nothing.'" Noee sees that Burn has a softer side under his tough mask and realizes that she too has a mask.
4. "some men are just funny that way," pages 75 to 85. In this short story, Keisha reveals her character through her narrative about her relationship with sports and her boyfriend.
5. "the man thing," pages 119 to 136. In this short story, Eddie reveals his character through his narrative about his school and love decisions.

Booktalk

Who or what defines love? Is it the father who plans for his family or the father willing to steal for them? Is it the girl looking for handsome and smart or the one just looking into someone's heart? Does love come all in a rush or does it just build slowly day by day? Is it all about hanging on or letting go? The people who live on 145th Street are trying to find out. You met quite a few of them in *145th Street: Short Stories* (*Hold up a copy of the book.*) Now they are looking for love, and these fifteen people are ready to tell you *What They Found.* (*Hold up a copy of the second book.*)

Get Involved

1. (Research) Using your library resources, find as much information as you can on developing healthy relationships. Act as a resource person for the group during the book discussion.

2. (React) Choose your favorite story. Explain your choice.
3. (Create) Share a story about an experience that taught you about love.
4. (React) Choose the female character that you feel learned the most about love. Explain your choice with specifics from the short story.
5. (React) Choose the male character that you feel learned the most about love. Explain your choice with specifics from the short story.

Related Works

1. Flake, Sharon G. **Who Am I without Him?: Short Stories about Girls and the Boys in Their Lives.** New York: Hyperion Books for Children/Jump at the Sun, 2004. 168p. $15.99. ISBN 078680693 1. [fiction, short stories] JS, G (See full booktalk in *Booktalks and Beyond,* 2007, pages 19 to 21.) Ten short stories explore the positives and negatives of the female/male relationship.
2. Johnson, Angela. **The First Part Last.** New York: Simon & Schuster Books for Young Readers, 2003. 131p. $15.95. ISBN 0 689 84922 2. [fiction] JS, CG (See full booktalk in *Booktalks and Beyond,* 2007, pages 24 to 25.) In four parts, Bobby tells about his journey to fatherhood after the baby's mother dies.
3. Myers, Walter Dean. **The Beast.** New York: Scholastic Press, 2003. 176p. $16.95. ISBN 0 439 36841 3. [fiction] JS, CG A senior at an exclusive prep school returns to his Harlem home and discovers that his girlfriend is a drug addict.
4. Myers, Walter Dean. **145th Street: Short Stories.** New York: Delacorte Press, 2000. 151p. $15.95. ISBN 0 385 32137 6. [fiction] JS, CG (See full booktalk in *Booktalks and More,* 2003, pages 91 to 93.) In ten short stories, Myers portrays tragedy, frustration, achievement, and compassion on 145th Street.
5. Myers, Walter Dean. **Sunrise over Fallujah.** New York: Scholastic Press, 2008. 304p. $17.99. ISBN-13: 978 0 439 91624 0. [fiction] JS, CG with high interest for boys. Private Robin Perry participates in the invasion of Iraq, bonds with his comrades, thinks he is in love with one of them, and realizes the horrors and lies of a war he thought would end in just a few days.

ᘓᘔ

Sachar, Louis. Small Steps.

New York: Delacorte Press, 2006. 257p. $16.95. ISBN 0 385 73314 3. [fiction]
MJS, CG with high interest for boys

Themes/Topics: juvenile delinquency, rehabilitation, cerebral palsy, disabilities, singers, friendship, interpersonal relationships, African-Americans

Summary/Description

Seventeen-year-old African-American Armpit (Theodore Johnson), from *Holes*, now works for an irrigation and landscaping firm and acts as a kind of big brother to his neighbor Ginny, a cerebral palsy victim. X-Ray, a friend from Camp Green Lake, proposes a ticket scalping plan that leads Armpit and Ginny to a chance meeting with teen singing sensation Kaira DeLeon who is being exploited by her mother's new husband. Armpit and Kaira are attracted to each other. Kaira's stepfather plans to kill her to cover up his embezzlement and then blame Armpit who has a criminal record. By chance, Armpit saves Kaira's life, becomes a hero, and considers what he was willing to give up for a glamorous date. He returns home a hero and sets his own goals and priorities while Kaira heals from the attack.

Read Aloud/Reader Response

1. Chapter 1, pages 4 to 5, beginning "After leaving Camp Green Lake..." and ending "...the name Armpit." The passage reveals the challenges of an ex-convict.
2. Chapter 5, pages 39 to 42, beginning "The ticket windows..." and ending "...sweating so much." Armpit learns about "fixed costs" versus "variable costs."
3. Chapter 13, pages 90 to 91, beginning "Ginny's mother..." and ending "...no heart and soul." Armpit reacts to Ginny's father deserting her.
4. Chapter 27, pages 204 to 205. In this chapter, Armpit reflects on the donkey story from his economics class.
5. Chapter 36, pages 254 to 257. In this chapter, Armpit hears Kaira's new song but sets his own goals.

Booktalk

Hold up a copy of Holes *and ask how many people read the book.*

  The Camp Green Lake guys are moving on. Two years after Camp Green Lake, seventeen-year-old Armpit is building a new life outside of jail, but he is still digging holes. X-ray, another Camp Green Lake graduate, has a great idea for some fast money. They will buy tickets to the hottest concert in town and then scalp the tickets. Armpit isn't so sure—especially since his money is financing the project. But he doesn't want to dig holes forever, and so he agrees. The plan spins him into a world of rock stars, love, a crash course in economics, and a possible jail sentence. He thinks that it is going to take everything he has to get out of this mess—muscles, brains, and heart. But really, making life right again just depends on whether or not Armpit can make some difficult but *Small Steps*.

Get Involved

1. (Research) Using your library resources, learn more about the challenges of cerebral palsy. Act as a resource person for the group during the book discussion.
2. (Research) Using your library resources, learn more about teen rehabilitation programs. Be sure to consider how the programs incorporate what might be considered small steps. Act as a resource person during the discussion.
3. (Discuss) Compare Armpit's goals at the beginning of the novel (Read Aloud 1) with his goals at the end (Read Aloud 5). Which do you think are better and why?
4. (Discuss) Ask each person in the group to choose a character in the novel and explain, with specifics from the text, what that character reveals about Armpit.
5. (Create) Make up a list of small steps that you think could improve your life. Use them. Keep a journal, and report your success or lack of success to the group.

Related Works

1. Covey, Sean. **The 6 Most Important Decisions You'll Ever Make: A Guide for Teens.** New York: Simon & Schuster/Fireside Books, 2006. 319p. $15.95. ISBN-13: 978 0 7432 6504 1. [nonfiction] JS, CG Using the 7 habits philosophy, Covey addresses the issues of school, friends, parents, dating and sex, addictions, and self-worth. Each chapter concludes with a "Baby Steps" application section for reader application. "Help Desk," at the end of the book, lists applicable Web sites for each chapter. A bibliography lists the references for each chapter.
2. Mikaelsen, Ben. **Petey.** New York: Hyperion, 1998. 280p. $15.95. ISBN 0 7868 0426 2. [fiction] JS, CG (See full booktalk in *Booktalks Plus*, 2001, pages 6 to 8.) Petey is a man born with cerebral palsy, labeled an idiot, and raised in a mental institution.
3. Sachar, Louis. **Holes.** New York: Farrar, Straus and Giroux, 1998. 233p. $16.00. ISBN 0 374 33265 7. [fiction] MJS, CG with high

interest for boys. (See full booktalk in *Booktalks Plus*, 2001, pages 35 to 37.) Stanley Yelnats, wrong fully convicted of theft, is sentenced to a boys' juvenile detention camp, and discovers his own fate and new friendships while uncovering corruption.

4. Shull, Megan. **Amazing Grace.** New York: Hyperion, 2005. 247p. $15.99. ISBN 0 7868 5690 4. [fiction] JS, G Grace, a teenage tennis star, model, cover girl, and spokesperson, finds she is overwhelmed, quits her career, joins her aunt in Alaska, and finds a more grounded life that allows her to return to her tennis career and keep the things that are important to her.

5. Trueman, Terry. **Stuck in Neutral.** New York: HarperCollins Publishers, 2000. 116p. $14.95. ISBN 0 06 028519 2. [fiction] JS, CG Fourteen-year-old Shawn McDaniel, who has cerebral palsy, cannot communicate or control his movements, but believes that his father plans to kill him.

ॐॐ

Schmidt, Gary D. The Wednesday Wars.

New York: Clarion Books, 2007. 264p. $16.00.
ISBN-13: 978 0 618 72483 3. [fiction] MJS, CG

Themes/Topics: Vietnam War, Shakespearian themes, coming of age, friendship, family life, junior high

Summary/Description

At the beginning of the 1967 school year, seventh-grader Holling Hoodhood believes that his English teacher is out to get him. Every Wednesday afternoon the Jewish and Catholic students are released for religious instruction. Holling, a Presbyterian, stays behind. At first his teacher assigns him janitorial duties, but decides that they will read and study Shakespearian plays together. As the year develops, Holling's family is caught up in the turbulent sixties, and Holling applies the plays' themes to his personal and classroom life. His teacher, Mrs. Baker, hopes for her husband's return from Vietnam. Gradually, Holling and Mrs. Baker develop a mutual respect as they support each other through daily crises from escaped classroom rats to cross-country races, and teacher evaluations. Holling finds the courage to stand up to his arrogant and domineering father. Mrs. Baker develops more personal relationships with her students. At the end of the novel, the entire class waits at the airport to witness Mrs. Baker reuniting with her husband, formerly missing in action.

Read Aloud/Reader Response

1. "October," page 48, beginning "We read..." and ending with the chapter. Holling and Mrs. Baker discuss Shylock.
2. "November," pages 70 to 72, beginning "That afternoon..." and ending with the chapter. Holling applies *The Tempest* to tragic events.
3. "January," pages 108 to 110, beginning "The next afternoon..." and ending "...when I left." Holling and Mrs. Baker conflict over *Macbeth*.
4. "February," pages 150 to 155, beginning "For the next Wednesday..." and ending "...bottle of Coke being opened." *Romeo and Juliet* help Holling clarify his feelings for Meryl Lee.
5. "May," pages 234 to 236, beginning "By the end..." and ending with the chapter. Holling applies *Hamlet* to Mrs. Baker's husband being found in the jungle.
6. "June," pages 262 to 263, beginning "Now I smiled." and ending "'...to tell you your future.'" Mrs. Baker tells Holling his future based on their reading of *Much Ado about Nothing*.

Booktalk

Holling Hoodhood is starting seventh grade. That should be no big deal except Holling is convinced that his teacher is out to get him, big time. Nobody else is too worried about Holling's problems. His father is an architect, and for father to be successful, every Hoodhood family member has to be on his or her best behavior. Dad wants Holling just to deal with anything, happily and quietly. Holling's sister is more worried about how she looks than about how Holling feels. The Vietnam War is going on, too, so how concerned is anyone going to be about one seventh-grader's feelings? But Holling is concerned, and he should be. For Holling, nineteen sixty-seven promises to be big. It is filled with cream puffs, rats, yellow tights, a dramatic role as a fairy, bullies, missing soldiers, baseball, track practice, and Shakespeare, Shakespeare, Shakespeare. All because Holling is Presbyterian. It's the sixties. Equal rights is a central issue. Shouldn't someone be protecting the Presbyterians? Holling thinks so, especially when he finds himself, every week, plunged into *The Wednesday Wars*.

Get Involved

1. (Research) Using your library resources, continue to research the Vietnam War. You may wish to start with Related Work 1. Act as a resource person during discussion.
2. (Discuss) By the end of the novel, what is the biggest change in Mrs. Baker? In Holling?

3. (React) Many personal wars occur in the novel. List each war that you perceive. Identify the opposing elements. Explain the resolutions.
4. (Discuss) What role does religion play in the story? Be sure to draw from the specifics of the story.
5. (Discuss) Humor and disaster weave the story together. Cite an instance of each. Explain how each choice you have made might be related to its opposite.
6. (Follow-up) Read a play by Shakespeare cited in the novel. Agree and or disagree with Holling's conclusions.

Related Works

1. Caputo, Philip. **10,000 Days of Thunder: A History of the Vietnam War.** New York: Atheneum Books for Young Readers/A Byron Preiss Visual Publications, Inc., Book, 2005. 128p. $22.95. ISBN-13: 978 0 689 86231 1. [nonfiction] JS, CG with high interest for boys. Pulitzer Prize-winning journalist and Vietnam veteran Philip Caputo explains the historical background, battles, context, politics, cultural influences, and cultural clashes of the Vietnam War.
2. Crist-Evans, Craig. **Amaryllis.** Cambridge, MA: Candlewick Press, 2003. 184p. $15.99. ISBN 0 7636 1863 2. [fiction, mixed format] MJS, CG with high interest for boys. (See full booktalk in *Booktalks and Beyond,* 2007, pages 205 to 207.) With letters from his brother and a narrative describing his own feelings, fifteen-year-old Jimmy tells about his home life, and his brother, Frank, fighting in Vietnam and eventually being reported Missing in Action.
3. Dunton-Downer, Leslie, and Alan Riding. **Essential Shakespeare Handbook.** New York: DK Publishing, Inc., 2004. 480p. $25.00pa. ISBN 0 7894 9333 0. [reference] JS, CG This user-friendly Shakespeare reference includes plot summaries and interpretative material on all thirty-nine plays and an analysis of the poetry. It also has essays on Shakespeare's life and times as well as his impact on world culture.
4. Hobbs, Valerie. **Sonny's War.** New York: Farrar, Straus and Giroux/ Frances Foster Books, 2002. 215p. $16.00. ISBN 0 374 37136 9. [fiction] JS, G (See full booktalk in *Teen Genre Connections,* 2005, pages 230 to 233.) Fourteen-year-old Cory describes her life in a little California town after her father's death and her brother's decision to fight in Vietnam.
5. Morales, Gilbert (ed.). **Critical Perspectives on the Vietnam War.** New York: The Rosen Publishing Group, 2005. 176p. (Critical Anthologies of Nonfiction Writing). $30.00. ISBN 1 4042 0063 0. [nonfiction] JS, CG Articles and official papers from the Vietnam

period show the development of the war, the battlefield difficulties the soldiers faced, and the controversy surrounding it.

ᘓᘔ

Nye, Naomi Shihab. Going Going.

New York: HarperCollins/Greenwillow Books, 2005. 232p. $16.89.
ISBN 0 06 029366 7. [fiction] JS, G

Themes/Topics: political activists, small business, San Antonio (Texas), boyfriends, old vs. new, love

Summary/Description

Sixteen-year-old Florrie loves small, unique businesses and the buildings that hold them. On her sixteenth birthday, she persuades her mother, father, and brother to forgo chain store shopping for sixteen weeks. She also enlists her friends in her campaign, and they stage protest demonstrations. Ramsey is a new boy in the group in whom Florrie is interested, and Zip is Florrie's longtime friend, who is interested in her. As Florrie directs more daring protests and gains publicity, Ramsey pulls back his participation and dates another girl. Zip stays loyal to both Florrie and her causes even though she rejects him. Eventually, Florrie realizes that people can be cast aside as thoughtlessly as old, sturdy buildings and realizes her feelings about Zip. At the end of the novel, Florrie's mother reports that Taco Bell is moving next door to the family's restaurant. Florrie begins planning a promotion that will convince people to stay with small business.

Read Aloud/Reader Response

1. Chapter 3, "Three Weeks Earlier," page 26, beginning "He was always sad..." and ending "...*passage of time.*" Florrie reflects on her father's sad view of birthdays, but the passage also applies to the inevitable change that time brings to communities.
2. Chapter 3, "Three Weeks Earlier," pages 30 to 38, beginning "Her father got an odd grin..." and ending with the chapter. After Florrie announces her birthday wish, she and her brother, True, argue about the merits of small versus chain stores.
3. Chapter 4, "Campaign," pages 39 to 41, beginning "*Once there was a girl...*" and ending "*...To What You Love.*" Florrie recalls her sixth-grade assignment, describing her life in the form of a children's book. It reveals her passion for small business and old things.

4.   Chapter 5, "potato enchiladas," pages 67 to 70, beginning "Florrie's whole family…" and ending with the chapter. The passage explains Florrie's gray apparel policy and her mother's contrasting dress.
5.   Chapter 14, "el viento," pages 159 to 168. This chapter is Florrie's term paper about her beloved grandfather.

Booktalk

Ask how many people shop at chain stores. Ask what the names of their favorite chain stores are. Ask if they think that these stores help or hurt the community.

Florrie hates chain stores. All of them, and they seem to be taking over her hometown of San Antonio, Texas. She decides to put them out of business or at least take a little of it away. On her sixteenth birthday, she makes a wish. Her family has always tried to make each person's birthday wish come true. This time they aren't sure if that is possible. They have to promise that they won't shop in a chain store for sixteen weeks. The sixteen weeks includes the Christmas holidays. And Florrie doesn't stop there. She talks her friends into making the same promise. Not enough? She decides that a few demonstrations might just be the consciousness raisers that this community needs. Watch out Wal Mart, Home Depot, and Gap. Florrie isn't taking it anymore. Nobody is going to corrupt Florrie's world with their smooth sales pitches and flashy merchandise. Well, maybe one person can. A new boy decides to join the cause. He is cuter than anybody she has ever met before, and she just can't wait for his phone calls—all about preserving the best of the past, of course. Or are they? Will Florrie stay dedicated to holding onto her precious past or, like those small businesses she is trying to save, is her dedication *Going Going* gone?

Get Involved

1.   (Research) Using your library resources, research the history of the Alamo. Act as a resource person for the group.
2.   (Discuss) How do Florrie's actions toward Ramsey and Zip agree with or contradict her feelings about old things?
3.   (Discuss) How would you describe Florrie's relationship with her brother?
4.   (Discuss) Is Florrie different by the end of the story?
5.   (Discuss) Choose one protest event that Florrie plans. What does Florrie learn about herself, and what does the reader learn about Florrie in that protest? Be specific.
6.   (Create) Florrie loves old postcards because of the stories that they suggest. Organize a show and tell for old, outdated objects. Invite

each person to guess the item's use and importance. Then ask each person in the group to choose an item brought by a group member and create a short anecdote about it.

Related Works

1. Bloor, Edward. **Tangerine.** New York: Scholastic, 1997. 294p. (An Apple Signature Edition). $4.99pa. ISBN 0 590 43277 X. [fiction] MJ, CG with high interest for boys (See full booktalk in *Booktalks Plus*, 2001, pages 16 to 19.) A new middle school student in Tangerine County, Florida, finds himself in the middle of family and environmental conflict.

2. Granfield, Linda (text), and Arlene Alda (photographs). **97 Orchard Street, New York: Stories of Immigrant Life.** New York: Tundra Books of Northern New York, 2001. 57p. $15.00. ISBN 0 88776 580 7. [nonfiction] MJS/A, CG Based on the research and restoration of the Lower East Side Tenement Museum, this slim volume of pictures, sketches, and text vividly depicts life for the immigrant families of the period and is an excellent example of how the preservation of buildings helps us to remember our history.

3. Hautman, Pete. **Sweetblood.** New York: Simon & Schuster Books for Young Readers, 2003. 180p. $16.95. ISBN 0 689 85048 4. [fiction] JS, G (See full booktalk in *Teen Genre Connections*, 2005, pages 6 to 8.) After a fascination with an Internet chat room puts her in the path of a sexual predator, sixteen-year-old Lucy Szabo realizes that Mark, her best friend, holds true love for her.

4. Hiaasen, Carl. **Hoot.** New York: Alfred A. Knopf, 2002. 292p. $15.95. ISBN 0 375 82181 3. [fiction] MJ, CG with high interest for boys (See full booktalk in *Teen Genre Connections*, 2005, pages 37 to 39.) Roy Eberhardt, a new student in Trace Middle School, is drawn into an environmental fight to save burrowing owls threatened by the construction of a new restaurant.

5. Vaupel, Robin. **My Contract with Henry.** New York: Holiday House, 2003. 244p. $16.95. ISBN 0 8234 1701 8. [fiction] MJ, G Thirteen-year-old Beth Gardner finds herself in conflict with her mother's boyfriend over the use of the local Wayburn Woods for a housing project.

Zevin, Gabrielle. **Memoirs of a Teenage Amnesiac.**
New York: Farrar, Straus and Giroux, 2007. 271p. $17.00.
ISBN-13: 978 0 374 34946 2. [fiction] JS, G

Themes/Topics: amnesia, friendship, high school

Summary/Description

High school junior Naomi Paige Porter hits her head in a fall and forgets her life from puberty on. Naomi, an adopted Russian orphan, discovers and reevaluates her feelings about her popular boyfriend, divorced parents, new step-parents, old friends, academic achievement, and her extra-curricular activities while she dates the brooding, mysterious boy who found her. She becomes more forgiving and accepting of her parents and their partners, sees the flaws in her own choices, and recognizes that her true love is her lifelong friend and yearbook co-editor.

Read Aloud/Reader Response

1. Chapter 1, pages 21 to 22, beginning "I decided to make a more specific..." and ending "...she started to cry." Naomi remembers her mother's sign exhibition.
2. Chapter 1, pages 22 to 24, beginning "About a minute later..." and ending "...I didn't have to hear twenty." Naomi recalls her father's penchant for lists.
3. Chapter 2, pages 41 to 47, beginning "Now that I was..." and ending with the chapter. Naomi tries to learn about herself through her yearbooks and personal possessions.
4. Chapter 4, pages 76 and 77, beginning "'How come...'" and ending "...I said." Will analyzes Naomi's reasons for dropping photography.
5. Chapter 5, page 127, beginning "I had been happy,..." and ending "...opaque to myself." Naomi realizes that Will can see her inner self.
6. Chapter 14, page 259 to 260, beginning "It was noisy..." and ending "We were so much alike really." Naomi's father talks about forgetting.
7. Chapter 14, pages 261, beginning "The week before the wedding,..." and ending "...of hours every morning." Naomi's father decides between "I do" and "I will" for the wedding.

Booktalk

Read the passage that begins, "Above all,..." and ends "...needs to lose." It introduces the novel and precedes the first section, "I was."

When Naomi Porter, high school junior, loses, she loses big. A hit on the head wipes away four years of her life. She doesn't remember that her parents are divorced, that she has a "to die for" boyfriend, or that she co-chairs the yearbook—the book everyone uses to remember their high school years. But losing one thing makes her find something else and that has everything to do with how love changes life. Sometimes, everyone needs a good hit on the head. She can tell you about hers and the future that she started when she lost her past. Her story is in her own private yearbook. It doesn't have one picture, just the *Memoirs of a Teenage Amnesiac.*

Get Involved

1. (Research) Using your library resources, find out more about amnesia. Act as a resource person during the book discussion.
2. (Research) Using your library resources, find out more about photography and the skills that it requires. Act as a resource person during the discussion.
3. (Compare) Read *Rosencrantz and Guildenstern Are Dead* (Related Work 4). Because this is a major reference in the novel, act as a resource person in the group and consider its relationship to the story.
4. (Discuss) In ten minutes, list as many ironic situations or parallels that occur in the novel as you can find. Compare your list with the lists of others in the group. Discuss the similarities and differences.
5. (Discuss) Consider the importance of the word *will* in the novel.
6. (Discuss) Naomi calls her memoirs a love story. Discuss how that classification surprised or failed to surprise you in any way.
7. (React) Did the story need pictures?
8. (React) Identify one part of your life (e.g., your purse, closet, room) and explain what someone examining it might think of you. Consider what you might change before allowing someone else to look at that part of your life.
9. (Create) Compose a photo essay of one aspect of high school life. Display it in the library or media center.

Related Works

1. Anderson, Laurie Halse. **Prom.** New York: Viking Press, 2005. 215p. $16.99. ISBN 0 670 05974 9. [fiction] JS, G (See full booktalk in *Booktalks and Beyond,* 2007, pages 56 to 58.) Eighteen-year-old Ashley Hannigan, the oldest of four in a dysfunctional urban family, focuses on her exploitive juvenile delinquent boyfriend and just tolerates school until she throws herself into saving the prom and discovers her talents and support.
2. Cabot, Meg. **Teen Idol.** New York: HarperCollins Publishers, 2004. 293p. $16.89. ISBN 0 06 009617 9. [fiction] MJS, G (See full booktalk

in *Booktalks and Beyond,* 2007, pages 61 to 63.) When Junior Jenny Greenley guides movie star Luke Striker, researching an upcoming film, around her high school, she sees her experience with new eyes and finds her true friends and real people skills.

3. Nelson, Blake. **The New Rules of High School.** New York: Viking Press, 2003. 227p. $16.99. ISBN 0 670 03644 7. [fiction] JS, CG Seventeen-year-old Max Caldwell decides, in his senior year, that he will build a life based on his own feelings and ambitions rather than his parents' expectations.

4. Stoppard, Tom. **Rosencrantz and Guildenstern Are Dead.** Jackson, TN: Grove Press, 1994. 128p. $10.40. ISBN-13: 978 0802132758. [classic] S/A, CG In this theater of the absurd play, Rosencrantz and Guildenstern try to find out Hamlet's intentions so that they might report to the king, but can't even figure out who or where they are.

5. Zevin, Gabrielle. **Elsewhere.** New York: Farrar, Straus and Giroux, 2005. 277p. $19.95. ISBN 0 374 32091 8. [fiction] MJS, G (See full booktalk in *Booktalks and Beyond,* 2007, pages 188 to 190.) Liz dies in a traffic accident shortly before her sixteenth birthday and begins a new life in Elsewhere, a world where she can evaluate choices, discover her true talents, forgive her hit-and-run killer, and prepare to return to earthly life.

Playing the Game

ᏨᎲᏨᎲ

Carter, Alden. **Love, Football, and Other Contact Sports.**
New York: Holiday House, 2006. 261p. $16.95.
ISBN 0 8234 1975 4. [short stories] JS, CG with high interest for boys

Themes/Topics: high school life, performance, and relationships

Summary/Description

These connected short stories center on the football players and the dynamic that they add to high school life. The topics include dating, vocation, bullying, abuse, pacifism, academic achievement, delinquency, gender roles, extended families, blended families, self-image, and some international points of view. The three introductory pieces are a humorous guide to football players from a girl's point of view, a humorous, almost two-sentence guide to love from a football player's point of view, and an overall view of the team by two of the major characters in the stories. The rest of the stories are organized by sophomore, junior, and senior year. A list of major characters with brief descriptions appears before each story.

Read Aloud/Reader Response

Any of the stories in the collection provide great read aloud/reader response material. The following are just a few specific suggestions.
1. "A Girl's Guide to Football Players," pages 1 to 7. The guide describes the personalities of the offensive, defensive, and special teams. It is a great contrast, in just length, to "A Football Player's Guide to Love," pages 7 to 8.
2. "Trashback," pages 23 to 43. This short story illustrates how joking can be interpreted as perversion and bullying.
3. "Buck's Head," pages 62 to 63, beginning "Okay, let's examine..." and ending "...can't quite do it." The narrator compares the personalities of an unlikely couple.
4. "Satyagraha," pages 79 to 92. On the advice of his pacifist trainer, one football player uses passive resistance to confront another player's bullying.
5. "The Gully," page 133, beginning "I try to remember..." and ending "...he's right." An Amish boy discusses stealing with the younger brother of a star football player.

Booktalk

The football team, the jocks. We all know what they are like. Let me read to you the definition of an offensive lineman that comes from "A Girl's Guide to Football Players." It is written by the female editorial staff of the *Purple Cow Literary Magazine*. (*Read the definition of offensive lineman on page 2. Ask how many people in the group agree with the definition.*) That's how these stories start, with the ladies' definition of football players. But that isn't where these stories end. Football players have lives off the field. They live with the glamorous, the brainy, the outcasts, the bullies, and the artists. The list goes on, but you know all the high school groups. The players, like everyone else, also have families that nobody may know about. This story tells it all, and it may leave you thinking a little differently about the groups that you think you know so well. The groups that survive each day with *Love, Football, and Other Contact Sports*.

Get Involved

1. (Research) Using your library resources, continue to research Gandhi and his relationship to the civil rights movement. Act as a resource person for your group during discussion.
2. (React) Choose the story that you feel was the most enjoyable and believable. Explain your choice.
3. (Discuss) Choose one character who appears more than once throughout the stories. Explain why you think that character is important.
4. (Discuss) The words *love* and *football* in the title obviously relate to the stories. Discuss how the phrase "...and Other Contact Sports" applies.
5. (Create) Carter uses the football team to frame his stories. Choose another group, club, or team in your school or organization. Build a series of related short stories around it.

Related Works

1. Averett, Edward. **The Rhyming Season.** New York: Clarion Books, 2005. 214p. $16.00. ISBN 0 618 46948 6. [fiction] JS, G (See full booktalk in *Booktalks and Beyond,* 2007, pages 65 to 68.) Senior Brenda Jacobsen gains skill and insight as she works with a controversial coach, and deals with the town's conflicts as well as graduation.
2. Bagdasarian, Adam. **First French Kiss and Other Traumas.** New York: Farrar, Straus and Giroux/Melanie Kroupa Books, 2002. 134p. $16.00. ISBN 0 374 32338 0 [fiction] JS, CG (See full booktalk in *Teen Genre Connections,* 2005, pages 73 to 74.) In five groups of essays, a fictional character tells his traumatic and sometimes humorous life experiences in becoming a man.
3. Going, K. L. **Fat Kid Rules the World.** New York: G. P. Putnam's Sons, 2003. 183p. $17.99. ISBN 0 399 23990 1. [fiction] JS, CG with high interest for boys (See full booktalk in *Teen Genre Connections,* 2005, pages 4 to 6.) The unlikely friendship between an outcast and a popular student makes both stronger.
4. Korman, Gordon. **Jake, Reinvented.** New York: Hyperion, 2003. 213p. $15.99. ISBN 0 786 81957 X. [fiction] JS, CG with high interest for boys. Through Rick, the reader learns about Jake, a brainy, social outsider who manufactures a new popular persona.
5. Wilkinson, Philip. **Gandhi: The Young Protester Who Founded a Nation.** Washington, DC: National Geographic, 2005. 64p. $17.95. ISBN 0 7922 3647 5. [nonfiction] MJS, CG With pictures, maps, as well as a simple and clear text, this source is a good introduction to Gandhi's life and principles.

CℜℜC

Fehler, Gene. Beanball.

New York: Clarion Books, 2008. 104p. $16.00. ISBN-13: 978 0 618 84348 0.
[novel in verse] MJS, CG with high interest for boys

Themes/Topics: baseball, high school, sports injuries, interpersonal relations, conduct of life

Summary/Description

Free verse monologues by twenty-eight narrators chronicle the events before, during, and after the baseball game in which Luke "Wizard" Wallace's skull is shattered by a beanball. Losing the vision in his left eye, Luke gains a different perspective on life, his friends, and his family. The monologues record the enthusiasm and confidence of young players who see themselves as invincible, the horror they and the adults experience in the face of the accident, and the true character of each speaker.

Read Aloud/Reader Response

The entire book presents an excellent opportunity for a group dramatic reading. The following are the monologues that may promote special discussions.

1. "Tim Burchard, umpire," pages 20 and 21. The umpire describes the accident.
2. "Sarah Edgerton, Oak Grove student," pages 29 and 30. Sarah Edgerton describes her first encounter with Luke.
3. "Luke 'Wizard' Wallace," pages 58 and 59. Luke reacts to the "good news" that he will be blind in one eye.
4. "Sarah Edgerton, Oak Grove student" and "Luke 'Wizard' Wallace," pages 86 and 87. Sarah anonymously sends Luke articles to support him. He sees the anonymity as a sign that he is too distant.
5. "Luke 'Wizard' Wallace," pages 94 and 95. The pitcher who hit Luke comes to apologize.

Booktalk

Junior Luke "Wizard" Wallace is a star athlete who looks forward to leading his high school baseball team to a state championship. Then he gets in the way of a wild pitch, and the championship is out of sight. In fact, Luke's future is out of sight. The pitch shatters his skull and destroys the vision in his left eye. But like other accidents, this one has more than one victim and more than one hero. Luke is changed forever but so is his team, his family, and his friends. Each one has a lot to say about a few moments in which lives and plans changed, all because of a game and a little white *Beanball*.

Get Involved

1. (Research) Using your library resources, find out as much as possible about athletes with physical handicaps. Act as a resource person during the class discussion.
2. (React) Which speakers surprised you and which speakers did not?
3. (Discuss) How does Fehler frame his story and do you think that the frame is successful?
4. (Discuss) On the basis of the story's details, what happens next?
5. (Create) Using free verse monologues, describe a single event from at least five points of view. Share your poems with the rest of the group.

Related Works

1. Carter, Alden R. **Bull Catcher.** New York: Scholastic Press, 1997. 279p. $15.95. ISBN 0 590 50958 6. [fiction] MJS, CG with high interest for boys (See full booktalk in *Booktalks Plus*, 2001, pages 96 to 98.) Neil Larsen, along with his teammates, decides that baseball cannot be the full focus of life.
2. Deuker, Carl. **Painting the Black.** Boston, MA: Houghton Mifflin Company, 1997. 248p. $14.95. ISBN 0 395 82848 1. [fiction] JS, CG with high interest for boys (See full booktalk in *Booktalks and More*, 2003, pages 121 to 123.) Ryan Ward must decide between personal integrity and his personal loyalty to an unscrupulous star athlete who uses his sports celebrity to break the rules.
3. Jeter, Derek, with Jack Curry. **The Life You Imagine: Life Lessons for Achieving Your Dreams.** New York: Scholastic Inc., 2000. 279p. $4.99pa. ISBN 0 439 35601 6. [nonfiction] JS, CG with high interest for boys (See full booktalk in *Teen Genre Connections*, 2005, pages 61 to 63.) Jeter talks about setting high goals, dealing with setbacks, choosing role models, keeping a balance between focus and fun, being a team leader, thinking before acting, and greeting each day as a new challenge.
4. Johnson, Scott. **Safe at Second.** New York: Philomel Books, 1999. 254p. $17.99. ISBN 0 399 23365 2. [fiction] MJS, CG with high interest for boys (See full booktalk in *Booktalks Plus*, 2001, pages 101 to 103.) When Todd Bannister, the star pitcher of the high school team, loses an eye in a game accident, Paulie, his best friend and a mediocre athlete, faces the fact that his whole life has been in a supporting role to Todd. With this role gone, Paulie discovers his own talents and finds a new direction in his life.

5. Robinson, Sharon. **Jackie's Nine: Jackie Robinson's Values to Live By.** New York: Scholastic Inc., 2001. 192p. $15.95. ISBN 0 439 23764 5. [nonfiction] MJS, CG (See full booktalk in *Booktalks and More*, 2003, pages 123 to 125.) Sharon Robinson's articles illustrate the nine principles she feels guided her father's life—courage, determination, teamwork, persistence, integrity, citizenship, justice, commitment, and excellence.

♋♊

Hornby, Nick. Slam.
New York: G. P. Putnam's Sons, 2007. 309p. $19.99.
ISBN-13: 978 0 399 25048 4. [fiction] JS, CG

Themes/Topics: teenage fathers, teenage parents, Tony Hawk, skateboarding, England, conduct of life

Summary/Description

Sixteen-year-old Sam, a top skateboarder, lives with his thirty-two-year-old single mother and plans to break the family's record of bad decisions by going to college, but discovers that his gorgeous former girlfriend is pregnant with his baby. He tells his problems to a poster of Tony Hawk whose book, *Hawk—Occupation: Skateboarder*, has become Sam's life guide. Sam and his girlfriend work through pregnancy and their parents' conflicts. Recalling Tony Hawk's advice and experiencing time travel glimpses of the future, Sam commits to being a better father than his own absentee dad, does go on to college, helps to care for his mother's new baby, and maintains a friendship with his baby's mother even though he finds someone else to love.

Read Aloud/Reader Response

1. Chapter 1, pages 8 and 9, beginning "Does this sound..." and ending "...let yourself down." Sam justifies confiding in Tony Hawk.
2. Chapter 2, pages 13 and 14, beginning "Here's the other thing..." and ending "...don't even find the stairs." Sam describes his family's history.
3. Chapter 4, pages 64 to 70, beginning with the chapter and ending "...whether I'd ever go back." Sam explains why he falls out of love.
4. Chapter 7, pages 115 to 116, beginning "I knew I was being..." and ending "...to Hastings or wherever." Sam justifies running away.
5. Chapter 13, pages 218 to 219, beginning with the chapter and ending with "...the rest of it." Sam distinguishes between facts and a story.

Booktalk

Read aloud the passages in Chapter 1, beginning with the chapter and ending on page 3 with "...complicated and interesting person, ha ha."

The Sam described in that passage was fifteen years old, but on his sixteenth birthday he gets a present that changes his life. He finds out that he is going to be a father. By the time Sam gets the fatherhood news, the romance with the baby's mother is history. Sam has some big decisions. He knows what it is like to grow up with parents who fell out of love. He knows that his birth ruined his mother's life. He also knows that having a baby may mean that his own life with those dreams of skateboarding and college might be finished forever. So far he has told his problems to the Tony Hawk poster on his bedroom wall, but Sam's life is getting more real all the time. And he needs some real answers. He is learning that taking a risk to learn a new clever trick isn't as hard as it looks. The hard part comes when the trick fails. That's when you take the *Slam*.

Get Involved

1. (Research) Using your library resources, find out more about skateboarding: the tricks and the language. Act as a resource person for the group during discussion.
2. (Research) Using your library resources, find out more about the role of fathers in unwed pregnancies. Act as a resource person for the group during discussion.
3. (Discuss) In Read Aloud/Reader Response 5, Sam distinguishes between the facts and the story. Do you agree with him?
4. (React) What do you think is the most important issue in the story? Support your opinion with details from the text.
5. (Follow-up) Sam relies on Tony Hawk because he claims that Hawk's book talks about life as much as sports. Continue to find sports biographies or how-to books that you feel also deal with life issues. Share the books that you find with the group.
6. (Create) After sharing the advice that you find from Get Involved 5, make up a list of Life Rules that you feel would be most helpful to a teenager.

Related Works

1. Acheson, Alison. **Mud Girl.** Regina, Saskatchewan: Coteau Books, 2006. 319p. $10.95. ISBN-13: 978 1 55050 3548. [fiction] JS, G Abandoned by her mother, sixteen-year-old Aba Zytka Jones lives with her depressed father and fantasizes about irresponsible nineteen-year-old Jude who has a two-year-old son, Dyl. Finally, realizing how

both she and Dyl are neglected, Aba enters foster care and takes Dyl with her.

2. Bechard, Margaret. **Hanging on to Max.** Brookfield, CT: Roaring Brook Press, 2002. 142p. $15.95. ISBN 0 7613 1579 9. [fiction] JS, CG Spending his senior year taking care of his new son, Sam Pettigrew decides his baby needs a stable family.

3. Covey, Sean. **The 6 Most Important Decisions You'll Ever Make: A Guide for Teens.** New York: Simon & Schuster/Fireside Books, 2006. 319p. $15.95. ISBN-13: 978 0 7432 6504 1. [nonfiction] JS, CG Using the 7 habits philosophy, Covey addresses the issues of school, friends, parents, dating and sex, addictions, and self-worth. Each chapter concludes with a "Baby Steps" application section for reader application. "Help Desk," at the end of the book, lists applicable Web sites for each chapter. A bibliography lists the references for each chapter.

4. Johnson, Angela. **The First Part Last.** New York: Simon & Schuster Books for Young Readers, 2003. 131p. $15.95. ISBN 0 689 84922 2. [fiction] JS, CG (See full booktalk in *Booktalks and Beyond,* 2007, pages 24 to 25.) In four parts, Bobby tells about his journey to single fatherhood.

5. Nolan, Han. **Born Blue.** New York: Harcourt, Inc., 2001. 177p. $17.00. ISBN 0 15 201916 2. [fiction] JS, G (See full booktalk in *Teen Genre Connections,* 2005, pages 13 to 15.) Raised in foster care, the rebellious and talented Janie has a baby but decides to leave it with her childhood friend from foster care rather than subject it to the life of a single parent and child.

6. Trapani, Margi. **Reality Check: Teenage Fathers Speak Out.** New York: The Rosen Publishing Group, Inc., 1999. 64p. (The Teen Pregnancy Prevention Library). $29.95. ISBN 0 8239 2995 7. [nonfiction] JS, CG with high interest for boys. Five teenage fathers share their experiences of being a father before they planned to be. The book includes sources for further help and further reading.

ᘓᘔ

Myers, Walter Dean. Game.

New York: HarperTeen, 2008. 218p. $17.99. ISBN-13: 978 0 06 058295 1. [fiction]
MJS, CG with high interest for boys

Themes/Topics: basketball, teamwork, African-Americans, Czech-Americans, self-actualization, family life, Harlem, high school

Summary/Description

Harlem high school senior Drew Larson, a star basketball player who rejects coaching, finds his star spot threatened when a Czech immigrant joins the team. In a series of conflicts with his coaches, he realizes that if he refuses to play as part of a team, he won't play at all. As the team moves up in championship competition, Drew learns about a world different from his own and respects that teamwork brings success. Even though Drew never becomes close friends with the new player, and the team loses their championship bid in a heartbreaking game, Drew receives a bid from DePaul and an opportunity to fulfill his dream of playing in the NBA.

Read Aloud/Reader Response

Because the story does not have chapter numbers, page numbers designate the read aloud/reader response passages.

1. pages 40 to 43, beginning "The whole team..." and ending "...with some people." After being made to sit on the bench, Drew reflects on what makes him uncomfortable about having to change.
2. pages 62 to 63, beginning "I thought..." and ending "...with my B plan." Drew realizes that he may have something in common with the homeless who refuse to play the game of life.
3. pages 120 to 124, beginning "After school..." and ending "...for me, too." Drew eats lunch with Ruffy and Ruffy's brother Tony and realizes how easily a misstep could put Drew in Tony's situation. The placement of this scene in the chapter is a good basis for discussion.
4. pages 148 to 152, beginning "The old fellow..." and ending "...with the Negro Leagues." Mr. Cephus tells about his life and reveals what makes him special.
5. page 215, beginning "I wondered..." and ending "...how deep my game could be." Drew reflects on what he learned in his relationship with Tomas.

Booktalk

Senior Drew Lawson knows he can play basketball. And he knows that he can lead his Harlem team to the playoffs and a championship shot. He is hoping that his starring role gets him a bid to a high-profile school and then to the NBA. But his coach may have another plan, one that involves a new white boy on the team. The plays seem to center on the new kid. He is from the Czech Republic and hungry to be part of the American dream. The coach wants him to be a star, and the media is paying attention. Drew is slowly getting shoved out of the picture. Is Drew going to join the has-beens who hang on Harlem's corners? Or does he have a back-up plan to turn things around? He thinks so, but Drew is about to learn that basketball is about more than taking the ball down the court and putting it in the basket. It has more to do with what is inside the player than what is on the scoreboard. And before Drew can call himself a winner, he has to find the right answer to one question, "How deep is his *Game?*"

Get Involved

1. (Research) Read or view the play *Othello*. Then using your library resources, learn as much about the play as possible. Act as a resource person during the discussion.
2. (Research) Drew mentions the different neighborhoods in Harlem. Using your library resources, find out as much as possible about the neighborhoods in Harlem. Act as a resource person during the discussion.
3. (React) Several games were being played in the story. List as many as you can, and then compare your list with the list of others in the group. Be sure to consider the coaches' game.
4. (Discuss) Were the coaches right in trying to integrate the team? Defend your answer with specifics from the story.
5. (Create) Write a description of a basketball game from the point of view of one of the players. Share your descriptions with the group. Compare your descriptions with Myers's game descriptions.

Related Works

1. de la Peña, Matt. **Ball Don't Lie.** New York: Delacorte Press, 2005. 280p. $16.95. ISBN 0 385 73232 5. [fiction] JS, CG with high interest for boys (See full booktalk in *Booktalks and Beyond*, 2007, pages 68 to 70.) Seventeen-year-old Sticky, a white foster child with obsessive-compulsive behavior, focuses his life in the Lincoln Rec, a basketball court/homeless shelter, where he is challenged, harassed, protected, and eventually accepted by outstanding black street ball players.
2. Myers, Walter Dean. **Bad Boy: A Memoir.** New York: Harper-Tempest, 2001. 206p. $6.95pa. ISBN 0 06 447288 4. [nonfiction] JS, CG with high interest for boys (See full booktalk in *Teen Genre Connections*, 2005, pages 54 to 56.) In this autobiography, Myers tells about his unruly behavior, his passion for reading and writing, descriptions of adults who helped him succeed, the effects of society's unspoken stereotypes, and his own poor and sometimes dangerous teenage choices.

3. Myers, Walter Dean. **Monster.** New York: HarperCollins Publishers, 1999. 281p. $15.95. ISBN 0 06 028077 8. [fiction] JS, CG with high interest for boys (See full booktalk in *Booktalks and More,* 2003, pages 13 to 15.) Sixteen-year-old Steve Harmon creates a play about his murder trial and his experience before the trial. His reflections show the difficulty of making good choices.

4. Myers, Walter Dean. **Slam.** New York: Scholastic Press, 1996. 267p. $15.95. ISBN 0 590 48667 5. MJS, CG with high interest for boys (See full booktalk in *Booktalks Plus,* 2001, pages 110 to 112.) When Greg Harris, AKA Slam, transfers from his neighborhood school to a magnet school, he finally decides that getting through life may mean getting his game and attitude together both on and off the court.

5. Waltman, Kevin. **Learning the Game.** New York: Scholastic Press, 2005. 224p. $16.95. ISBN 0 439 73109 7. [fiction] JS, CG with high interest for boys (See full booktalk in *Booktalks and Beyond,* 2007, pages 33 to 35.) Nate Gilman, whose family is one of the most afflu-ent in town, helps the team rob a college fraternity. His decision to confess teaches him about true loyalty, friendship, and responsibility.

CG

Krech, Bob. **Rebound.**

Tarrytown, NY: Marshall Cavendish, 2006. 271p. $16.99. ISBN-13: 978 0 7614 5319 2.
[fiction] JS, CG with high interest for boys

Themes/Topics: basketball, teamwork, racism, friendship

Summary/Description

In Raymond Wisniewski's town, the Polish boys wrestle, and the African-American boys play basketball. Ray decides that he wants to play basketball, and finally makes the team in his senior year. Ray's de-termination and success force him to deal with his and the town's deep racial prejudices, as well as his criteria for friendship, love, and personal integrity. He discovers that his best friend has become a violent racist, that beautiful girls can be phony, that new friends are willing to cross racial lines to protect him, that plain girls can become beautiful, and that even an enemy might have the courage to do what is right.

Read Aloud/Reader Response

1. "prologue," pages 7 to 15. The prologue reveals Ray's character and the heavily prejudiced situation in which he lives.

2. Chapter 5, pages 64 to 66, beginning "We were in fourth grade…" and ending "…problems with Zulik." Ray recalls how Walter helped him to stand up to bullies.
3. Chapter 15, pages 145 to 150. The chapter reveals the characters of the coach and Ray's father. Discussing the similarities between the two would be interesting.
4. Chapter 25, pages 232 to 234, beginning "In the locker room…" and ending "…onto the announcement board." Coach T reacts to the racist cheers and tension.
5. Chapter 29, page 265, beginning "I glance at…" and ending "…always gonna see it." Ray realizes that Walter can understand only the simplistic categories of black and white.

Booktalk

In Franklin High School, if you are Polish, you wrestle, and if you are African-American, you play basketball. Raymond Wisniewski doesn't want to make a racial statement, but he does want to play basketball. For two years he tries to make the team, no success. Then his luck changes. A new coach is playing a whole new ball game, and Ray is part of it. As a senior, he is a varsity starter. Mission accomplished? Not quite. It is just the beginning. The games off the court are more complicated than basketball. To get on the team, Ray knocks out another player who happens to be African-American. The player isn't going to take that and neither are his friends. Then, because Ray is a team star, the school goddess is taking an interest in him. It is his dream come true. But because she doesn't like African-Americans, she may be his nightmare. Ray's biggest problem is his friends. To them, Ray is the "Great White Hope," and they are willing to back him to the death. Ray doesn't want to fight. He just wants to play ball, but dribbling and shooting alone don't make a winning team. These days his life shots aren't as accurate as his game shots, and if he wants to win on and off the court, he'd better work on his *Rebound.*

Get Involved

1. (Research) In chapter 25, Ray sees a swastika on Walter's arm and indicates that the older Polish members of the community would react negatively to that symbol. Using your library resources, research the relationship between Germany and Poland during World War II.
2. (Discuss) How does Ray earn the respect of the team?
3. (React) List each incident of prejudice in the novel. Describe the event, the person who shows the prejudice, and the result of the prejudice. Compare your list with the lists of others in the group.

4.   (Discuss) Compare the two basketball coaches. How does each coach affect and reflect the team and community?

5.   (Follow-up) What do you think happens the day after the closing confrontation of the story?

6.   (Follow-up) Do the prejudices in your own community affect you?

Related Works

1.   Averett, Edward. **The Rhyming Season.** New York: Clarion Books, 2005. 214p. $16.00. ISBN 0 618 46948 6. [fiction] JS, G In a town geared to boys' basketball, a girls' team, directed by an eccentric coach, drives for a championship. In the experience, senior Brenda Jacobsen finds meaning and direction for her own life.

2.   Conroy, Pat. **My Losing Season.** New York: Doubleday, 2002. 402p. $27.95. ISBN 0 385 48912 9. [nonfiction] S/A, B The author of *The Prince of Tides* explains how his brutal Citadel basketball experience was tied to his abusive home life. The language requires a mature audience. The passage beginning on page 3 with "The lessons I learned while playing basketball..." and ending on page 4 with the words "...sweet, swift game" makes a good strong read aloud indicating the relationship between sports and self-discovery.

3.   de la Peña, Matt. **Ball Don't Lie.** New York: Delacorte Press, 2005. 280p. $16.95. ISBN 0 385 73232 5. [fiction] JS, CG with high interest for boys (See full booktalk in *Booktalks and Beyond,* 2007, pages 68 to 70.) Seventeen-year-old Sticky, a white foster child with obsessive-compulsive behavior, focuses his life in the Lincoln Rec, a basketball court/homeless shelter, where he is challenged, harassed, protected, and eventually accepted by outstanding black street ball players.

4.   McKissack, Fredrick. **Black Hoops: The History of African Americans in Basketball.** New York: Scholastic Press, 1999. 154p. $15.95. ISBN 0 590 48712 4. [nonfiction] MJS, CG (See full booktalk in *Booktalks Plus,* 2001, pages 106 to 107.) *Black Hoops* tells the story of basketball in the larger context of race relations in America and American sports.

5.   Wallace, Rich. **Playing without the Ball.** New York: Alfred A. Knopf, 2000. 213p. $5.99. ISBN 0 679 98672 3. [fiction] S, CG Seventeen-year-old Jay McLeod, deserted by his mother and father, lives in a single room above Shorty's Bar. With Shorty as a kind of guardian, Jay tries to build stability in his life through basketball and girlfriends.

CῸῊ

Luper, Eric. Big Slick.

New York: Farrar, Straus and Giroux, 2007. 234p. $16.00. ISBN-13: 978 0 374 30799 8.
[fiction] JS, CG with high interest for boys

Themes/Topics: poker, gambling, honesty, interpersonal relations, self-perception, restitution

Summary/Description

Sixteen-year-old Andrew Lang, who works in his father's dry cleaning business with a street smart Goth girl named Jasmine, feeds his poker habit by stealing money from his father's cash drawer. Down six-hundred dollars, he tries various ways to make the money, but eventually the father discovers the theft, and Andrew, after an angry confrontation, launches a daring plan with Jasmine and his friend Scott to win it back. Andrew wins the money he needs but decides to make restitution another way when he realizes that his father truly loves him. Father and son make peace. Andrew and Scott become dealers in their own poker club, and Jasmine leaves her drug using and abusive boyfriend to be with Andrew. Subject matter and language could be considered controversial. The names of various playing card combinations designate the chapters.

Read Aloud/Reader Response

1. "Ajax," pages 20 to 21, beginning "Shushie closes his..." and ending "I'll never be like them." Andrew is labeled a gambler for the first time and has a glimpse of his future.
2. "Little Pete," pages 36 and 37, beginning with the chapter and ending with "Crisis averted." Andrew describes a scene at home and misses all the signals that indicate that his parents care about him.
3. "Dead Man's Hand," pages 62 to 65, beginning "It takes a few seconds..." and ending with the chapter. Andrew and Scott conflict over Andrew's stealing and gambling.
4. "Route 66," pages 157 to 158, beginning "It feels like it was..." and ending "'...in your mouth.'" The threesome compares their trip to the casino and Manifest Destiny.
5. "Fido," pages 213 to 217, beginning "For the first time..." and ending with the chapter. Shushie and Andrew discuss Andrew's "tells."

Booktalk

Sixteen-year-old Andrew Lang, math whiz, can handle odds and probabilities. Just show him the figures. So he can't figure out why his poker game is in the sewer. Andrew loses even when he makes the right moves. He is convinced that losing is just bad luck. Bad luck can't last forever, so Andrew bets more, a lot more. His money runs out, but his dad's doesn't. Andrew borrows a little from the cash register in his dad's dry cleaning business. His dad will never miss it. Six-hundred dollars melts away, and all Andrew's ideas on how to pay it back fade fast. Andrew makes the big shift from mathematician to gambler. His once-predictable life is full of lies and uncertainty. He has a couple of friends left who are willing to stick with him, even bet on his new scheme. The three will take on big-time gambling. They are hoping for a change of luck. (They will need it.) And they are looking hard for the *Big Slick*.

Get Involved

1. (Research) Using your library resources, find out as much as possible about poker. Act as the resource person during the book discussion.
2. (Research) Using your library resources, find out as much as possible about compulsive gambling. Act as a resource person during the book discussion.
3. (Compare) After reading *Big Slick*, also read *All-in* (Related Work 2). Compare the two stories and discuss which one seems more realistic.
4. (React) Is Andrew Lang a winner?
5. (Follow-up) Organize a game tournament. Include at least four types of games and give prizes for the winners of the individual games and tournaments.

Related Works

1. Brooks, Martha. **True Confessions of a Heartless Girl.** New York: Farrar, Straus and Giroux/Melanie Kroupa Books, 2003. 181p. $16.00. ISBN 0 374 37806 1. [fiction] JS, G Pregnant seventeen-year-old Noreen Stall steals her boyfriend's truck and money, and drives to the small community of Pembina Lake, where she and the citizens learn the importance of restitution and resurrection in finding personal love and peace.
2. Hautman, Pete. **All-in.** New York: Simon & Schuster, 2007. 181p. $15.99. ISBN-13: 978 1 4169 1325 2. [fiction] JS, CG with high interest for boys. Denn Doyle from *No Limit* finds his gambling shaken up by a young casino dealer hired to destroy him.
3. Mikaelsen, Ben. **Touching Spirit Bear.** New York: HarperCollins Publishers, 2001. 241p. $15.95. ISBN 0 380 97744 3. [fiction] MJ, CG with high interest for boys (See full booktalk in *Booktalks and*

More, 2003, pages 80 to 82.) This story about a radical approach to juvenile rehabilitation includes victim/offender mediation as a means to effect restitution.

4. Murphy, Claire Rudolf. **Free Radical.** New York: Clarion Books, 2002. 198p. $15.00. ISBN 0 618 11134 4. [fiction] MJ, CG with high interest for boys (See full booktalk in *Teen Genre Connections,* 2005, pages 66 to 68.) Luke finally decides to support his mother's efforts to make restitution for an accidental killing during the Vietnam War and learns the lifelong consequences of rash acts.

5. Waltman, Kevin. **Learning the Game.** New York: Scholastic Press, 2005. 224p. $16.95. ISBN 0 439 73109 7. [fiction] JS, CG with high interest for boys (See full booktalk in *Beyond Booktalks,* 2007, pages 33 to 35.) Practicing for his senior season on the local court, Nate Gilman, whose family is one of the most affluent in town, helps the team rob a college fraternity and then wrestles with his pledge of secrecy.

ෆ෨

Lupica, Mike. Heat.

New York: Puffin Books, 2006. 220p. $6.99pa. ISBN-13: 978 0 14 240757 8. [fiction] MJ, CG with high interest for boys

Themes/Topics: Cuban immigrants, family, baseball, teamwork, friendship

Summary/Description

Twelve-year-old Michael Arroyo's unusual height and strong pitching arm cause jealous Little League players and managers to question Michael's age and eligibility. Michael and his seventeen-year-old brother Carlos fear probing questions or publicity since their father's recent death. If the authorities find out that they are orphans, they may be sent to foster care or back to Cuba. With the help of an elderly neighbor whom Michael saves from a mugger, his best friend, the daughter of a famous Cuban pitcher who plays for the Yankees, the Little League coach, and a league commissioner, Michael proves his eligibility, plays in the team's critical game, pitches in Yankee Stadium, and has assurance that he and his brother will have the help and support they need to stay together.

Read Aloud/Reader Response

1. Chapter 1, pages 1 to 5. This opening chapter introduces Victor's ability and character.

2. Chapter 10, pages 64 to 72. This chapter illustrates Justin's character and Michael's reaction to it.
3. Chapter 13, page 90, beginning "I'm too…" and ending "…that's bad." Michael realizes that jealousy may have motivated the attack against him.
4. Chapter 14, pages 91 to 93, beginning with the chapter and ending "…feel worse." Michael realizes how important baseball is in his life.
5. Chapter 19, page 136, beginning "Don't sound so…" and ending "…person to die." Cora reminds him about the dangers of resentment.
6. Chapter 28, pages 213 to 220. In this concluding chapter, Michael realizes the magic and legacy of Yankee Stadium.

Booktalk

Michael Arroyo is twelve years old. He has a pitching arm that most twenty-year-olds would envy. His Little League team may win the World Series this year because of Michael. It's great to be a star, but Michael's star is getting a little tarnished. He and his brother and father came here on a boat from Cuba. Now his father is dead. Michael and his brother Carlos are making it alone, or trying anyway. If the authorities find out, Michael and Carlos may be living in foster care or, even worse—they may be on a boat back to Cuba. Michael leaves his worries behind when he steps on the ball field. Carlos even believes that Michael's talent will eventually save them both. But sometimes a person can be too good, and sometimes people who aren't quite as good get jealous. Suddenly, Michael finds himself in a different game. Some of the players and the coaches are asking if Michael is really twelve, if he is eligible at all. He has to produce a birth certificate, and the authorities are asking why they can't talk to his father about it. He doesn't know how to get that piece of paper from Cuba. He is throwing out answers that are about as good as wild pitches. More than in any other game he has played, Michael is starting to feel the *Heat*.

Get Involved

1. (Research) Using your library resources, continue to investigate the history of Cuban immigration in the United States. Act as a resource person during group discussion.
2. (Research) Using your library resources, discover more about the impact of Cuban players on North American baseball. Share your information as a resource person during group discussion.

3. (Research) Using your library resources, trace the history of the Yankees. Act as a resource person for your group during discussion.
4. (Discuss) The opening chapter illustrates the power of Michael's arm and his integrity. How do those two elements develop the novel?
5. (Discuss) Choose one character in the novel. Explain how that character influences other characters and the plot's final outcome. Compare your answer with the answer of others in the group.
6. (Follow-up) Write two endings for the book. In one ending, the team wins the championship. In the other ending, the team loses. Then discuss with the group how each ending affects the story.

Related Works

1. Jeter, Derek, with Jack Curry. **The Life You Imagine: Life Lessons for Achieving Your Dreams.** New York: Scholastic Inc., 2000. 279p. $4.99pa. ISBN 0 439 35601 6. [nonfiction] JS, B (See full booktalk in *Teen Genre Connections,* 2005, pages 61 to 63.) Derek Jeeter, describing himself as an ordinary guy with extraordinary dreams, talks about setting high goals, dealing with setbacks, choosing role models, keeping a balance between focus and fun, being a team leader, thinking before acting, and greeting each day as a new challenge.
2. Nelson, Kadir. **We Are the Ship: The Story of Negro League Baseball.** (See full booktalk in "History"/"Shaping," pages 252 to 255.) In telling the story of the Negro baseball league, Kadir touches on the leagues in Cuba that welcomed the players instead of discriminating against them.
3. Schmidt, Gary D. **The Wednesday Wars.** (See full booktalk in "Contemporary"/"Learning about Love," pages 56 to 59.) Like Michael, Holling Hoodhood is awed by Yankee magic and surprised by the help he receives from the adults he initially distrusts and the peers who prove to be his loyal friends.
4. Tan, Shaun. **The Arrival.** New York: Scholastic Inc./Arthur A. Levine Books, 2007. 128p. $19.99. ISBN-13: 978 0 439 89529 3. [wordless graphic] MJS, CG The story, told completely in pictures, communicates the joy of arrival and how that joy is passed to others.
5. Woodson, Jacqueline. **Miracle's Boys.** New York: G. P. Putnam's Sons, 2000. 131p. $15.99. ISBN 0 399 23113 7. [fiction] MJS, CG with high interest for boys (See full booktalk in *Teen Genre Connections,* 2005, pages 28 to 30.) Three Puerto Rican brothers learn about each other and their own guilt when they struggle to keep their household together after their mother's death.

CßⅩɁ

Sonnenblick, Jordan. **Notes from the Midnight Driver.**

New York: Scholastic Press, 2006. 272p. $16.99. ISBN 0 439 75779 7. [fiction]
JS, CG with high interest for boys

Themes/Topics: divorce, personal responsibility, guitar, family relationships, inter-generational friendships, forgiveness

Summary/Description

Sixteen-year-old Alexander Gregory gets drunk and takes his mother's car. He plans to storm his father's house, and catch his father with the third-grade teacher. Instead, he drives over the neighbor's lawn gnome, gets arrested, and winds up in the hospital with alcohol poisoning and a head wound. Facing his parents' anger and a no-nonsense judge, he finds himself doing community service in the rest home where his mother works. He is assigned to Solomon Lewis, a shrewd, cantankerous old man who plays "gotcha" with his caretakers and fellow patients. Alex tries to relate to Sol through music and discovers that Sol is a professional musician who teaches him about music, love, and life. The experience comes "Full Circle" when Alex finds pictures of Sol's estranged daughter, the judge who sentenced him, and brings about a reunion and reconciliation before Sol's death.

Read Aloud/Reader Response

1. "Gnome Run," pages 3 to 10. In this chapter, Alex describes his run in with the police, a hilarious incident that could have been tragic.
2. "Laurie Meets Sol," pages 64 to 73. In this chapter, Sol and Laurie bond.
3. "Home Again," pages 137 to 138, beginning "Uh, okay." and ending "…in the world?" The passage reveals the importance of *but* in excuses. *But* plays a central role again on page 196 when Laurie insists on going to the hospital instead of staying at the dance.
4. "A Night for Surprises," pages 151 to 168. In this chapter, the concert reveals a new dimension of Sol and his relationship to Alex.
5. "Darkness," pages 169 to 176. In this chapter, Sol reveals his story, and Alex understands the seriousness of driving drunk.

Booktalk

"It seemed like a good idea at the time." That's how sixteen-year-old Alex Gregory looks back on his decision to get drunk, drive over to his father's house, and confront Dad and Alex's third-grade teacher, the lady who broke up their family. Alex doesn't make it past the neighbor's yard, and he does more damage to the lawn ornament than to his dad's love affair. But he does start a new chapter in his life. After his arrest and hospital stay, Alex faces a hanging judge and her no-nonsense backup, his mother. No leniency for the first offense. Alex is assigned to community service in the nursing home where his mother works. He is supposed to make friends with Solomon Lewis, a man who refuses to talk most of the time and makes people wish that he wouldn't talk when he does. Sol's favorite word is *Gotcha*. That is really bad news for Alex when Alex's love life and guitar get involved. Alex would like to forget about his days at the home. It's bad enough getting through it, but the judge insists on knowing all about his progress. Alex has to write about his nightmare as well as live it, especially when his freedom and future depend on what he has to say about this weird community service, and what he says is called the *Notes from the Midnight Driver.*

Get Involved

1. (Research) Using your library resources, find statistics concerning drinking and driving fatalities. Act as a resource person during the discussion.
2. (Research) Using your library resources, learn more about the concept of Zen. Act as a resource person during the discussion.
3. (Discuss) What is the importance of the word *Gotcha?* Be sure to consider how the word changes in meaning.
4. (Discuss) What is the importance of the word *But?*
5. (Discuss) Why is the novel funny and why isn't it funny? What do your answers tell you about humor?
6. (Follow-up) Plan an activity in a local rest home. Discuss the reactions at the next book discussion group.

Related Works

1. Curtis, Christopher Paul. **Bucking the Sarge.** New York: Random House Children's Books/Wendy Lamb Books, 2004. 272p. $15.95. ISBN 0 385 32307 7. [fiction] MJS, CG with high interest for boys (See full booktalk in *Booktalks and Beyond,* 2007, pages 9 to 12.) Inspired by Chester X, a resident in his mother's group home for mentally disabled men, fourteen-year-old Luther T. Farrell decides to leave his mother's twisted inner-city empire and build a new life of his own.
2. Huser, Glen. **Skinny Bones and the Wrinkle Queen.** Toronto, ON, Canada: Groundwood Books, 2006. 232p. $16.95. ISBN-13: 978

0 88899 732 6. [fiction] MJ, G Tamara, a ninth-grader in foster care, and Miss Barclay, an eighty-nine-year-old nursing home resident, who taught junior high English for forty-one years, join forces to achieve their goals. Tamara agrees to accompany Miss Barclay to a three-night opera performance in Seattle, and, in return, Miss Barclay will pay for Tamara's modeling lessons.

3.   Levin, Betty. **The Unmaking of Duncan Veerick.** (See full book-talk in "Mystery/Suspense"/"Contemporary," pages 135 to 138.) When thirteen-year-old Duncan is sent by his parents to help an elderly woman, he becomes involved in helping her protect her possessions from her greedy nephew.

4.   Muth, Joh. **Zen Shorts.** New York: Scholastic Press, 2005. 36p. $17.99. ISBN-13: 978 0 439 33911 7. [fiction, picture book] CMJS/A, CG In this picture book, Stillwater, the panda, uses three stories that reflect the Zen philosophy to give three siblings a different perspective on the world. The first tells about a poor man who gives a robber gifts. The second warns that luck cannot be judged or predicted. The third deals with keeping burdens. The last two apply most directly to *Notes from the Midnight Driver.* An "Author's Note" answers the question "What is Zen?"

5.   Simmons, Michael. **Pool Boy.** Brookfield, CT: Roaring Brook Press/ A Neal Porter Book, 2003. 164p. $23.90. ISBN 0 7613 2924 2. [fiction] JS, CG with high interest for boys (See full booktalk in *Booktalks and Beyond,* 2007, pages 54 to 56.) After his father is convicted for insider trading, fifteen-year-old Brett discovers a new boss and mentor, an elderly man who formerly cleaned the family pool.

Adventure/Survival

In adventure and survival books, characters tap into their courage, intelligence, and skill to confront danger and disaster. The girls' selections feature girls pushed not only to live, but also to prevail; and prevailing often means preserving their community as well as themselves. The selections tagged as having more interest for boys include more rough-and-tumble confrontations and larger-than-life situations, some even mystical.

Flight

Brooks, Kevin. **Being.**
New York: Scholastic, Inc./Chicken House, 2007. 336p. $16.99.
ISBN 0 439 89973 7. [fiction] JS, CG with high interest for boys

Themes/Topics: identity, friendship, love, trust

Summary/Description

Sixteen-year-old Robert Smith, supposedly an orphan, undergoes a routine endoscopy and is pursued by scientists and thugs when they discover that his body is, not human, but a maze of wires and chemicals. Robert, shocked and afraid, draws on new-found strength and healing power. He escapes from the hospital with his records and seeks out Eddi Ray, a former acquaintance who specializes in researching and creating identities. Newspapers report that Robert murdered the examining doctor, so, at first, Robert coerces Eddi to help him. As Eddi learns Robert's story, they work together and grow to love each other. Hiding in Spain, the two contemplate their futures, but the thugs find them and kill Eddi.

Robert, still not sure of who or what he is, draws on his super-human strength, overcomes his enemies, and escapes again.

Read Aloud/Reader Response

1. Chapter 1, pages 1 to 7. This opening chapter sets the tone of mystery and horror.
2. Chapter 5, page 47, beginning "To take my…" and ending "… 1191212." Robert searches Ryan's jacket.
3. Chapter 8, page 95, beginning "Things and places…" and ending "How do you think?" Robert asks universal questions about how and why he exists.
4. Chapter 9, page 103, beginning "I read something…" and ending "I guess I'll never know." Robert recalls the remarks of one of his social workers.
5. Chapter 17, pages 208 to 214, beginning "I stared at the lights in the darkness." and ending with the chapter. Robert contacts Ryan, and they spar via cell phone.

Booktalk

Sixteen-year-old Robert Smith is scheduled for a routine ulcer exam. The doctors will shove a tube down his throat and into his stomach. What they see isn't routine. Robert is made up of (*Read the passage in Chapter 2, page 22, beginning "Unknown things." and ending "… like blood-dark shimmer.…."*) Soon he is being cut open, helpless on the table. He can feel every cut, and he is sure that he will die. Then he feels a power that he can't explain and that the doctors don't anticipate. He is no longer helpless. He pulls himself off the table, grabs a gun from one of the thugs now in the room, places the gun to the man's head, and whispers, "That's enough." He makes it out of the hospital, runs, and keeps running. Does he have the strength to escape the cold-blooded killers who pursue him? Maybe. More important, can he escape the thoughts that haunt him, the thoughts that tell him that he isn't a human, but someone's wire-and-plastic creation, someone's monster—someone's *Being*.

Get Involved

1. (Research) Using your library resources, find as much information as possible about Kevin Brooks. During the discussion of the book, act as a resource person about Brooks as a writer.
2. (Compare) Read *Frankenstein* (Related Work 4). Compare Robert and the monster as creations.
3. (React) Can Robert's dilemma apply to any teenager?

4. (Create and Follow-up) Trust is a central theme in the story. Create a three- or five-panel graphic that illustrates trust. Explain how it applies to the novel.
5. (React) Were you satisfied with the ending?

Related Works

1. Coville, Bruce (comp. and ed.). **Half-Human.** New York: Scholastic Press, 2001. 224p. $15.95. ISBN 0 590 95944 1. [fiction] JS, CG (See full booktalk in *Booktalks and More*, 2003, pages 101 to 103.) This collection of stories questions what makes a human being. "How to Make a Human," a poem by Lawrence Schimel appearing on pages 94 and 95, presents a negative view of man forgetful of his ties to nature.
2. Farmer, Nancy. **The House of the Scorpion.** New York: Atheneum Books for Young Readers/A Richard Jackson Book, 2002. 380p. $17.95. ISBN 0 689 85222 3. [fiction] JS, CG with high interest for boys (See full booktalk in *Teen Genre Connections*, 2005, pages 208 to 210.) The clone of a notorious drug lord avoids being farmed for body parts, escapes, and returns to take over and reform the country.
3. Patterson, James. **Maximum Ride: The Angel Experiment.** New York: Warner Vision Books, 2005. 440p. $6.99pa. ISBN 0 446 61779 2. [fiction] JS, CG with high interest for boys (See full booktalk in *Booktalks and Beyond*, 2007, pages 181 to 183.) Fourteen-year-old Maximum Ride (Max) leads a six-member "family" made up of children, who have been injected by the government with bird DNA and raised in cages.
4. Shelley, Mary. **Frankenstein.** New York: Pocket Books, 2004. 352p. (Enriched Classics). $4.95pa. ISBN-13: 978 0743487580. [classic] JS/A, CG with high interest for boys. In this Gothic horror story about human life created by man, first published in 1818, Shelley presents the responsibilities each creator has for his or her creation.

ℭℨℭ

Draper, Sharon. **Copper Sun.**
New York: Atheneum Books for Young Readers, 2006. 302p. $16.95.
ISBN-13: 978 0 689 82181 3. [fiction] JS, CG

Themes/Topics: heritage, slavery, Fort Mose (Florida), indentured servants, South Carolina, Colonial period, eighteenth century

Summary/Description

Fifteen-year-old Amari is stolen from her village by slavers. After seeing her entire family killed, she is encouraged to survive by a fellow slave so that she can tell the story. Purchased in the colonies by Percival Derby for his sixteen-year-old son, she bonds with an indentured servant, the plantation cook, and the cook's little boy. Amari, the cook, and the indentured servant help Derby's eighteen-year-old wife hide her newborn biracial baby whose father is the wife's personal slave. Derby discovers the plot, kills the baby and the father, and locks up the three conspirators. He will sell Amari, the indentured servant, and the cook's son. With the help of an old plantation slave and the doctor who attends Derby's wife, the three escape. Anti-slavery people they encounter help them to successfully flee to the Spanish, slavery-free Fort Mose, in Florida. Amari discovers that she is pregnant by Derby's son, and the three, as a free family, start a new life together. The "Afterword" explains the development of Fort Mose and lists Web sites and books for further research about slavery.

Read Aloud/Reader Response

1. Chapter 6, page 37, beginning "So why should…" and ending "…must live." Amari questions why she should live.
2. Chapter 31, page 201, beginning "I am ashamed to be…" and ending "…know how to stop it." The doctor explains why he is helping Amari, Polly, and Tidbit run away.
3. Chapter 33, page 213, beginning "Freedom is…" and ending "…you get it." Polly defines freedom.
4. Chapter 33, page 215, beginning "Why you not…" and ending "…respect for nature?" Amari explains her culture's attitude toward food gathering.
5. Chapter 42, pages 300 to 302, beginning "Amari placed her hands…" and ending with the novel. Amari decides to have her baby and recognizes the unity of human experience in the copper sun.

Booktalk

Fifteen-year-old Amari lives in Africa. She is betrothed to handsome Besa. Her father delights her and the rest of the village with his stories. Life in the village is good, and when strangers come, they are welcome to share it. But these visitors, pale and strange, do not want to share the villagers' lives. They want to destroy them. They kill Amari's entire family in one day. She is shackled, branded, and imprisoned. Soon she is captive on a large boat that sails to another land. She quickly understands that they see her as a possession, an animal. No black faces have authority in this land. Speaking her language is a crime. Should she kill herself and join her family? If she does, these murderers will have taken everything, even her hope. She must survive to tell about the horror of slavery and the triumph of survival. Truth will die in silence and darkness. She is determined to make it live in light of the *Copper Sun.*

Get Involved

1. (Research) In the "Afterword," Draper provides an extensive list of resources. Choose one. Read and/or explore it. Share the information during discussion.
2. (Research and Create) Using your library resources, add sources to Draper's list. Prepare a display of books about slavery for the library or media center.
3. (Research) Using your library resources, make up a bibliography that includes fiction and poetry to hand out during the discussion of the book.
4. (React) What surprised, pleased, or horrified you in the novel?
5. (Discuss) Amari, Polly, and Tidbit all experience physical and personal journeys. Choose one of those characters. Compare their journeys.
6. (Create and Follow-up) Imagine the child that Amari will have and what he will accomplish. Compare your story with others in the group who have done the same.

Related Works

1. Aronson, Marc. **The Real Revolution: The Global Story of American Independence.** New York: Clarion Books, 2005. 238p. $21.00. ISBN 0 618 18179 2. [nonfiction] JS, CG (See full booktalk in *Booktalks and Beyond,* 2007, pages 218 to 221.) Framing the American Revolution in world events, Aronson discusses how slavery contributes to the revolution and the American mindset.
2. Lester, Julius. **Time's Memory.** New York: Farrar, Straus and Giroux, 2006. 230p. $17.00. ISBN 0 374 37178 4. [fiction] JS, CG Amma, the creator god and master of life and death, sends a young man to the New World on a slave ship so that he can quiet the souls of slaves improperly buried. He achieves his task by letting them tell their stories.
3. McMullan, Margaret. **How I Found the Strong.** Boston, MA: Houghton Mifflin Company, 2004. 136p. $15.00. ISBN 0 618 35008 X. [fiction] MJS, CG with high interest for boys (See full booktalk in *Booktalks and Beyond,* 2007, pages 210 to 213.) Ten-year-old Frank

Russell develops a close relationship with the family slave, Buck, when Frank's father and brother leave to fight for the Confederacy. As the Southern position deteriorates, Frank and his father save Buck from local bullies and help him escape to the North.

4. Nelson, Marilyn. Pamela Espeland (notes and annotations). **Fortune's Bones: The Manumission Requiem.** Asheville, NC: Front Street, 2004. 32p. $16.95. ISBN 1 932425 12 8. [nonfiction] JS, CG (See full booktalk in *Booktalks and Beyond,* 2007, pages 247 to 249.) Six poems expressed by multiple narrators tell the story of Fortune's Bones, a skeleton prepared and kept by Dr. Porter, Fortune's owner.

5. Rinaldi, Ann. **The Ever-After Bird.** New York: Harcourt Children's Books, 2007. 240p. $17.00. ISBN-13: 978 0 15 202620 2. [fiction] MJ, G Thirteen-year-old Cecilia learns the horrors of slavery when she journeys through the pre-Civil War South with her abolitionist uncle who directs slaves to freedom as he searches for the rare scarlet ibis.

ᘓᘔ

Haas, Jessie. Chase.

New York: HarperCollins, 2007. 250p. $17.89. ISBN-13: 978 0 06 112851 6. [fiction]
MJS, CG with high interest for boys

Themes/Topics: coal mines and mining, Irish-Americans, Pennsylvania history, nineteenth century, orphans, horses, conduct of life

Summary/Description

Fifteen-year-old Phin, an orphan, witnesses a murder by the "Sleepers," an Irish underground organization, and escapes. Pursued by Fraser, an undercover Pinkerton man riding a tracking horse, and Ned Plume, the underground member who failed to kill him, Phin jumps a train where he is trapped in a car with both Fraser and Plume. Thinking he has hidden from both of them, he gets off the train in wooded farmland, but Fraser follows him. Phin rigs a rope trap that knocks Fraser off the horse. Phin can leave Fraser to die but takes him instead to a nearby farm. The women who run the farm help both Phin and Fraser, even though they know that Phin previously stole from them, and finally side with Phin against Fraser who reveals that the Pinkertons are about to close in on the Sleepers. Phin, knowing that Plume is coming to kill him, leaves the safety of the cabin, faces Plume, assures him that he won't betray him, tells him about the Pinkerton crackdown, advises Plume to go West with the woman he loves, and returns to straighten out his own relationships with Fraser and the farm owners. The "Historical Note" explains the story's context.

Read Aloud/Reader Response

1. Chapter 4, pages 29 and 30, beginning "She wanted him…" and ending "…keep himself awake." The passage illustrates the values that Phin inherited from his parents.
2. Chapter 10, pages 72 to 75, beginning "At Murray's his…" and ending "…make out the words." Fraser and Plume probe each other through conversation in the train car.
3. Chapter 14, pages 109 to 112, beginning "He climbed up…" and ending "…feeling was leaving him." Phin reveals his sources of strength.
4. Chapter 17, pages 140 to 141, beginning "He looked around…" and ending "…attracted to them." Phin sees himself as part of the universe and realizes that he wishes to stay in the mainstream of life.
5. Chapter 21, pages 175 to 186. The chapter brings up the issue of what makes a man.
6. Chapter 25, page 218, beginning "I've lived…" and ending "…wide latitude." Fraser responds to Abby's insisting that he help Phin.

Booktalk

Fifteen-year-old Phin lives in Murray's bar, a tavern in the heart of Pennsylvania coal country. His Irish mother moved them there when her English husband was marched off to fight for the Union and never returned. She worked as a washerwoman. Now she too is dead and Phin makes his living doing chores at Murray's. Phin's mother gave Phin a love of books and thought she could protect him from the dangers of the mines and the bar. So when he takes the early morning to read, Phin believes he is doing a safe and quiet thing that will tie him to the beauty he shared with his parents. But there is no quiet or safety in the coal country of the late nineteenth century. The owners want to drive the men and boys as hard as they can, and the Irish miners aren't about to let them. On that morning, Phin looks up to see the "Sleepers," the Irish underground that dares to fight the owners. They're here to kill a man, a quiet, hard-working man who lets Phin sit in his house and read his books. The murder is quick. It gives neither Phin nor the victim any time to react. Phin sees it, and so he becomes the next man to kill. The gun is in his face. The shooter hesitates. It is enough time for Phin to get away. He does, he thinks. Both his legs and the train carry him. Then another man is after him, too, a man who rides a horse that can track as well as any dog. Why? Phin isn't sure. The man could be a Pinkerton, a Sleeper, or a vigilante. Take your pick. Phin *is* sure that he can't let them catch him. In the few moments it takes for him to glance up from his book, Phin changes from a man of thought to a fugitive forced to action. Now he has only two choices—Will he be the victim or the victor in the *Chase?*

Get Involved

1. (Research) Find out more about the conflict between miners and owners in the Pennsylvania mines of the late nineteenth century. Act as a resource person during the discussion.
2. (Research) Find out more about Ralph Waldo Emerson and Walt Whitman and the works cited in the story. Act as a resource person during the group discussion.
3. (Research) Find more about William Wordsworth and the Romantic Movement. Act as resource person during the discussion.
4. (Discuss) Who are the good guys and the bad guys? Refer to the story to support your opinion.
5. (Follow-up) Based on what you know about the characters, what happens next?

Related Works

1. Bartoletti, Susan Campbell. **A Coal Miner's Bride: The Diary of Anetka Kaminska.** New York: Scholastic Inc., 2000. 217p. (Dear America). $10.95. ISBN 0 439 05386 2. [fiction] MJS, G Set in the 1890s, the diary tells the struggles and hardships of a young Polish immigrant wedded to an American miner. After his death, she is permitted to choose a husband she loves.
2. Bartoletti, Susan Campbell. **Growing up in Coal Country.** Boston, MA: Houghton Mifflin Company, 1996. 127p. $16.95. ISBN 0 395 77847 6. [nonfiction] MJS, CG This source explains the jobs, attitudes, and everyday details of mining life.
3. Poets.org. Available: http://poets.org. (Accessed August 2008). The Web site allows the user to access information about poets, their work, and individual poems. Both Whitman and Wordsworth are in the data base.
4. Poolos, J. **Ralph Waldo Emerson: The Father of the American Renaissance.** New York: The Rosen Publishing Group, Inc., 2006. 112p. (The Library of American Thinkers). $33.25. ISBN 1 4042 0506 3. [nonfiction] MJS, CG Poolos explains Emerson's personal struggles and how they led him to the intellectual crisis that changed American thinking and scholarship. Other books in the series discuss

John Dewey, William James, John Jay, Henry Wadsworth Longfellow, and Henry David Thoreau.

5. Yerxa, Leo. **Ancient Thunder.** Toronto, ON, Canada: House of Anansi Press/Groundwood Books, 2006. 31p. $18.95. ISBN-13: 978 0 88899 746 3. [fiction] C,MJS/A CG. With beautiful art technique that mimics painting on leather, Yerxa celebrates the horse and the role that it played in the lives of Native Americans.

Heneghan, James. Safe House.

Victoria, BC, Canada: Orca Book Publishers, 2006. 151p. $7.95pa.
ISBN-13: 978 1 55143 640 1. [fiction] MJS, CG with high interest for boys

Themes/Topics: Ireland, Catholic/Protestant conflict, grief, circus, peace keeping

Summary/Description

When twelve-year-old Liam Fogarty witnesses his defenseless parents gunned down by Protestant terrorists, he sees the face of the trigger man who has a prominent mole. The terrorists discover Liam, but he escapes out the bedroom window. When the Mole pursues him, the police decide to place Liam in a safe house. The Mole, a policeman, bribes the caretakers, and Liam flees. Throughout the chase, Liam relies on the memories he has of his parents and the circus skills he acquired in a program designed to bring Protestant and Catholic teenagers together. In his final escape, Liam negotiates the parapet of a tall building. The Mole follows and falls. Paralyzed by the accident, he will live the rest of his life in a wheelchair, but his prison sentence is lessened because he gives information about key terrorists. Liam is adopted by his best friend's family. The "Appendix" provides a brief timeline of Protestant/Catholic conflict.

Read Aloud/Reader Response

1. "...lighting a candle..." pages 34 to 35, beginning "Why do you always..." and ending with the chapter. Liam recalls his conversation with his mother about prayer.
2. "...arms of a child..." pages 77 to 78, beginning "Liam is ten..." and ending with the chapter. Liam's father tries to persuade his neighbor that Catholic and Protestants should work together.
3. "...everyone has his price..." pages 104 to 105, beginning "Liam and his da..." and ending "'...you can possibly be.'" Liam's father encourages Liam to always stand by his principles.

4. "...everyone has his price..." pages 105 to 107, beginning "It looked like the Mole..." and ending "Who could be trusted?" Liam is trying to sort out the good and the bad.
5. "...violent protest in Ardoyne..." pages 108 to 115. This chapter reflects on family love, religious conflict, and the futility of violence.

Booktalk

Twelve-year-old Liam is asleep when two men storm into his house, kill both his parents, and then try to kill him. The violence, the noise, and the spray of bullets paralyze him. Then he finds the courage to move, to jump out the bedroom window, and to slide down the drainpipe. He saw the trigger man, and the man knows it. Liam's neighbor tells him that his dead parents are "safe with God," but Liam is far from safe. He is suddenly part of the violent Irish battle between Catholic and Protestant. The killer will try to kill Liam too. Liam knows that, and when the mostly Protestant police force puts him in a "safe house," he can't quite believe that a Catholic boy can be safe. He's right. Money changes hands. The protectors become his enemies, and Liam is on the run again. It's 1999 in Belfast, Ireland. For a Catholic boy who has seen the face of a Protestant killer, no house is a *Safe House*.

Get Involved

1. (Research) Using your library resources, learn more about the Irish Protestant/Catholic conflict. Act as a resource person for the group during discussion.
2. (Research) Using your library resources, find out as much as you can about how a circus works. Act as a resource person for the group during discussion.
3. (Research) Using your library resources, find out more about leaders and movements for peace. Use the information that you find to build a visual presentation or a book display for the library.
4. (React) What surprised you in the novel?
5. (React) Liam reflects on his father's actions and advice. List each one in the novel that you can find. State what you think the advice teaches Liam.
6. (Discuss) How would you describe Liam and his family to someone who never met them? Be sure to re-read the chapter "...a wedding picture..." before doing so.

Related Works

1. Derkins, Susie. **The Irish Republican Army.** New York: The Rosen Publishing Group, Inc., 2003. 64p. (Inside the World's Most

Infamous Terrorist Organizations). $27.95. ISBN 0 8239 3822 0. [nonfiction] MJS, CG Derkins explains how the IRA came into being, the violence it reacted to and created, and the new hopes for peace in Ireland. Reading lists, Web sites, and a bibliography provide additional sources.

2. Heneghan, James. **The Grave.** New York: Farrar, Straus and Giroux/ Frances Foster Books, 2000. 245p. $17.00. ISBN 0 374 32765 3. [fiction] JS, CG (See full booktalk in *Booktalks and More*, 2003, pages 65 to 67.) Tom Mullen falls into a recently uncovered mass grave and time travels from 1974 Liverpool to 1847 Ireland. The journey helps him find the family he thought abandoned him.

3. Mikaelsen, Ben. **Tree Girl.** New York: HarperCollins Children's Books, 2004. 240p. $16.99. ISBN 0 06 009004 9. [fiction] JS, G Fifteen-year-old Gabriela Flores flees her home in Guatemala when U.S.-trained troops begin a systematic Indian massacre that wipes out most of her family. She builds a new family from other refugees and shares her teaching talents with the camp's children.

4. Staples, Suzanne Fisher. **Under the Persimmon Tree.** New York: Farrar, Straus and Giroux/Frances Foster Books, 2005. 275p. $17.00. ISBN 0 374 38025 2. [fiction] MJS, G (See full booktalk in *Booktalks and Beyond,* 2007, pages 236 to 239.) After her father and brother are seized by the Taliban and her mother and newborn brother die in the American bombing, a young Afghan girl journeys in disguise to a refugee camp.

5. Wilkinson, Philip. **Gandhi: The Young Protester Who Founded a Nation.** Washington, DC: National Geographic Children's Books, 2006. 64p. $17.95. ISBN 0 7922 3647 5. [nonfiction] MJS, CG With many pictures and maps as well as a clear text, this is an excellent introduction to Gandhi's life and his work for peace.

☙❧

Van Draanen, Wendelin. **Runaway.**

New York: Alfred A. Knopf, 2006. 250p. $15.95. ISBN 0 375 83522 9. [fiction] MJS, G

Themes/Topics: runaways, homeless persons, orphans, diary

Summary/Description

Twelve-year-old Holly Janquell is an orphan in an abusive foster home. Following her teacher's suggestion, she journals her feelings. She rebels against her foster parents, runs away, and then finds herself in an hour-by-hour struggle to get food and shelter while avoiding the authorities. Her journal begins with a hostile and mocking tone, but gradually, writing helps Holly work through the grief and bitterness that she holds about her mother, a heroin addict who kept Holly in a nomadic life until dying of an overdose. Finally, Holly meets Sammy, who is working off school detentions in a soup kitchen. Sammy saves her from an attack of a homeless man and finds her a permanent home with a mother and daughter who run a pet store. The story was inspired by the author's 1999 mystery, *Sammy Keyes and the Sisters of Mercy*.

Read Aloud/Reader Response

1. "June 12th", page 45. Holly reflects on the last day of school. Her bitterness demonstrates her longing to be part of the day.
2. "Almost Midnight," page 69. Holly's dream reveals her feelings about social services, her abusive classmate, and the teacher who suggested the journal.
3. "Almost Midnight," pages 75 to 76. Holly compares herself to a slave, and hopes for a runaway Underground Railroad.
4. "Some backyard, a couple days later," pages 98 to 100. Holly envies the world of the affluent and reflects on how she should get her own life under control.
5. "A few days later…" pages 178 to 179. Holly takes responsibility for the out-of-control behavior that pushed her into abusive foster homes.

Booktalk

Since her mother died, Holly Janquell has lived in foster homes. Since her new foster father flushed her head in the toilet, she has seriously thought about not living in foster homes at all. She is going to make her break. She ran away before, but the authorities caught her. She had to come back, and things just got worse. This time, like the slaves on the Underground Railroad she reads about in school, she plans for the trip. Holly packs supplies, and she already knows how to pick things up on the road. Her mother taught her all about stealing, and Holly takes only what she needs. She makes the break. But the longer she is on the road, the more tired she gets. Holly begins to think about how hard it will be to steal, run from the authorities, and defend herself from street people for six more years until she is eighteen. Six more years until she can support herself with a good job. And if she can't go to school, she probably won't get a good job. Will she eventually find safety and happiness on her freedom trail? Or will she find only the hunger, fear, and loneliness of a homeless *Runaway*?

Get Involved

1. (Research) Using your library resources, learn more about the lives of runaway, homeless children. Act as a resource person during the group discussion.
2. (Research) Holly is inspired by the Underground Railroad. Find stories about those involved in the movement. You may wish to start by reading Related Work 2. Act as a resource person for the group.
3. (Create and Follow-up) Keep a daily journal. After a month, read your entries. Write an entry explaining what you found out about yourself.
4. (React) Read all the poems that Holly wrote. What did each poem tell you about Holly? Compare your reactions with the reactions of others in the discussion group.
5. (React) Is the story believable?
6. (Follow-up) Ask a speaker who works with the homeless or the poor to speak to your class about the problems children in these situations experience. Compare that information with the information that you found in Get Involved 1.

Related Works

1. Flake, Sharon G. **Money Hungry.** New York: Hyperion Books for Children/Jump at the Sun, 2001. 187p. $15.99. ISBN 0 786 80548 X. [fiction] MJS, G (See full booktalk in *Teen Genre Connections,* 2005, pages 285 to 286.) Thirteen-year-old Raspberry Hill, living in the projects with her mother, constantly tries to make money because she fears living, as she and her mother used to, on the streets.
2. Fradin, Dennis Brindell. **Bound for the North Star: True Stories of Fugitive Slaves.** New York: Clarion Books, 2000. 224p. $21.00. ISBN 0 395 97017 2. [nonfiction] MJS, CG (See full booktalk in *Teen Genre Connections,* 2005, pages 30 to 33.) Fradin uses first-person accounts of Mary Prince, Eliza Harris, Henry "Box" Brown, and Harriet Tubman to illustrate the horrors of slavery and the heroic efforts used to escape it. In addition, he explains how entire families, religions, and towns dedicated themselves to the "Underground Railroad."
3. Leavitt, Martine. **Heck Superhero.** Asheville, NC: Front Street, 2004. 144p. $16.95. ISBN 1 886910 94 4. [fiction] MJ, CG with high interest for boys (See full booktalk in *Booktalks and Beyond,* 2007, pages 28 to 30.) Thirteen-year-old Heck, abandoned by his depression-prone mother, searches for her while surviving on the street and dealing with the pain of a badly infected tooth.

4. Nolan, Han. **Born Blue.** New York: Harcourt, Inc, 2001. 177p. $17.00. ISBN 0 15 201916 2. [fiction] JS, G (See full booktalk in *Teen Genre Connections,* 2005, pages 13 to 15.) Janie tells about her life from four to sixteen, after the near-drowning accident caused by her heroin-addicted mother's neglect places her in foster care.

5. Rapp, Adam (text), and Timothy Basil Ering (illus.). **33 Snowfish.** Cambridge, MA: Candlewick Press, 2003. 179p. $15.99. ISBN 0 7636 1874 8. [fiction] S, CG (See full booktalk in *Booktalks and Beyond,* 2007, pages 30 to 33.) Custis, who is about ten and who is owned by a man who uses him for sex and pornographic films, runs from the law with Curl, a fifteen-year-old prostitute, and Boobie, a seventeen-year-old boy who murdered his parents and plans to sell his baby brother.

Fight

♋♌

Beah, Ishmael. **A Long Way Gone: Memoirs of a Boy Soldier.**

New York: Farrar, Straus and Giroux/Sarah Crichton Books, 2007. 229p. $22.00. ISBN-13: 978 0 374 10523 5. [nonfiction] JS/A, CG with high interest for boys

Themes/Topics: Sierra Leone, civil war, child soldiers

Summary/Description

When Ishmael is twelve, his family's village is wiped out in a rebel raid, and he begins his journey of physical, emotional, and intellectual survival that ends in a United Nations rehabilitation camp and eventually, the United States. After being separated from his older brother, he lives alone in the jungle until he encounters six other boys. Because of the rumors about boy soldiers, the boys are not welcome in the villages, but receive occasional individual acts of kindness. Ishmael discovers the village where his family now lives just before another rebel raid kills them. The boys flee the rebels and are drawn into the army where their lives center on drugs, killing, and violent movies. At fifteen, Ishmael is chosen by UN representatives for placement in a rehabilitation camp. The camp finds an uncle with whom he can stay and selects him for the United Nations First International Children's Parliament in New York, where he bonds with an American story-teller. When he returns to Sierra Leone, he finds that civil war is raging. His uncle dies, and Ishmael decides, with the help of the story-teller, to make his way to New York.

Read Aloud/Reader Response

1. Chapter 1, pages 6 and 7, beginning "The first time..." and ending "...would commence." Ishmael describes the rap music that saves his life several times.
2. Chapter 1, pages 16 and 17, beginning "There was a thick forest..." and ending with the chapter. Ishmael reflects on the moon story from his childhood.
3. Chapter 4, pages 26 to 29. In this chapter, Ishmael and his groups are learning their first lessons in survival.
4. Chapter 8, pages 56 and 57, beginning "We had traveled..." and ending with the chapter. Ishmael, now part of the seven boys, describes their encounter with an old man and the problem of their reputation.
5. Chapter 10, pages 69 to 70, beginning with the chapter and ending with "...my wandering mind." Ishmael reflects on the mental battle of survival.

Booktalk

Let me read to you a short passage. (*Read "New York City, 1998." The opening passage is opposite the map of Ishmael's journey.*) Ishmael Beah is twelve years old when he first learns about war. Before that, his big new interests are rap music and reciting Shakespeare. But when rebels destroy his village, he becomes a wanderer, a survivor. He lives as he can—helping or stealing, or just watching—whether he is in a village or a jungle. At thirteen, he becomes a soldier. For three years, he thinks only about killing, good drugs, and American war movies. At sixteen, he is chosen by the UN for rehabilitation. Rap music, Shakespeare, his childhood memories, his monster deeds, a new family, the United States, and more civil war come crashing together. Amidst it all, Ishmael decides to survive. At twenty-six, he writes about his journey. He decides to tell the world how boys are used today as weapons and how they must survive in a world of war. This is his memoir, the true story of his efforts to again find a "civilized" world after being *A Long Way Gone*.

Get Involved

1. (Research) Using your library resources, find out more about Sierra Leone. Act as a resource person for the group during discussion.
2. (Research) Using your library resources, find out more about the use of boy soldiers in war. Act as a resource person for the group during discussion.

3. (React) Is Beah a hero as well as a survivor?
4. (React) List five passages or details that impacted you the most. Compare your list with others in the group.
5. (Follow-up) Invite a community worker or social worker to speak to your group about violent situations for children in your own community.

Related Works

1. Cain, Timothy (ed.). **The Book of Rule: How the World Is Governed.** New York: DK Publishing, Inc., 2004. 320p. $30.00. ISBN 0 7894 9354 3. [reference] MJS, CG Cain includes the governments of 193 countries. Sierra Leone appears on page 188.
2. Cooney, Caroline B. **Diamonds in the Shadow.** (See full booktalk in "Multiple Cultures"/"Integration," pages 272 to 275.) The Finch family agrees to sponsor the Amabo family, four refugees from a civil war in Africa.
3. Ellis, Deborah. **The Heaven Shop.** Narkham, ON, Canada: Fitzhenry & Whiteside, 2004. 192p. $16.95. ISBN 1 55041 908 0. [fiction] MJ, CG (See full booktalk in *Booktalks and Beyond,* 2007, pages 229 to 231.) A family is shattered when the father dies of AIDS. Greedy relatives take charge of the children and treat them as slaves.
4. Mankell, Henning. Anne Connie Stuksrud (trans.). **Secrets in the Fire.** Toronto, ON, Canada: Annick Press LATD, 2003. 166p. $17.95. ISBN 1 55037 801 5. [fiction] MJS, G Sophia, a young refugee from war-torn Mozambique, builds a new life after losing her sister and her legs in a land mine explosion.
5. Zenatti, Valérie. Adriana Hunter (trans.). **When I Was a Soldier: A Memoir.** New York: Bloomsbury Children's Books, 2005. 235p. $16.95. ISBN 1 58234 978 9. [nonfiction] JS, G (See full booktalk in *Booktalks and Beyond,* 2007, pages 241 to 244.) On her eighteenth birthday, according to Israeli law, Valérie Zenatti becomes a soldier. For two years, she experiences rigorous training that matures her and causes her to question Israel's romantic self-characterizations.

જી જી

Frost, Helen. **The Braid.**

New York: Farrar, Straus and Giroux/Frances Foster Books, 2006. 95p. $16.00.
ISBN 0 374 30962 0. [poetry/novel] JS, G

Themes/Topics: family, sisters, immigration, Mingulay (Scotland), Canada, nineteenth century

Summary/Description

Two teenage sisters, caught up in the Highland Clearances of the 1850s, are separated when Jeannie immigrates with her family to Canada, and Sarah decides to return to their grandmother in Mingulay. The sisters tell their stories in alternating narrative poems. Jeannie, the more protected beauty, supports her mother and baby brother after her father and two sisters die on the voyage. Sarah, the responsible and plain sister, falls in love and becomes pregnant by a young man subsequently forced on an emigration boat to Canada. Jeannie finds shelter, food, and a small income for her family as she battles harsh elements, injury, and discrimination. Sarah keeps her baby and her love by refusing an arranged marriage to cover her disgrace. She plans her own passage to Canada, but her young man meets Sarah's family in Canada and earns his passage back to Mingulay. Jeannie, settling her family in the new world, begins to learn to read and looks forward to a love of her own. Sarah marries and builds a house and family.

The "Introduction" establishes the historical context. "Notes on Form" explains Frost's poetic structure composed of praise and narrative poems, which like Celtic knots are braided horizontally and vertically. "Notes on People, Language, and Places" set the geographical context.

Read Aloud/Reader Response

The entire text is suitable for a dramatic read aloud presentation. Below are some poems appropriate for individual readings and responses.

1. "The Crossing," pages 18 and 19. Jeannie describes the crossing in which she loses her father and two sisters. She realizes the grim consequences and her responsibility within them.
2. "House with Two Doors," pages 66 and 67. "Doors," page 68. Jeannie realizes that John's invitation to his home involves a job instead of courting. "Doors" describes the powerful symbolism of the door.
3. "My Questions Quiet Down," pages 75 and 76. "Answers," page 77. Sarah reviews the risks that she takes and the uncertainty that she faces. "Answers" ponders the elusiveness of answers.
4. "Money," page 80. The poem reflects on the power of money.
5. "Travelers," page 83. The poem suggests how travel allows the world to grow.

Booktalk

Jeannie and Sarah live in Scotland during the 1850s, a period known as the Highland Clearances. People who live in the Western Isles of Scotland are being put off their land. Raising sheep rather than renting to people will bring the landlords more money, so the people must go. Jeannie and Sarah are two of these people. Their father decides to move the family to Canada. Jeannie supports her father's plan. She will leave with her family, but Sarah, the oldest, has other ideas. Sarah decides to stay in Scotland. She will live with her grandmother in Mingulay. She cannot face the family with her decision. In fact, she knows that her parents will not let her make it. So she steals away in the night and hides until they are gone. She leaves only one thing behind, a gift telling her sister that they will be joined forever. And Sarah is right. The sisters' lives twine into one like the hair Sarah leaves behind in *The Braid.*

Get Involved

1. (Research) Read "Notes on People, Language, and Places," pages 93 and 94. Using your library resources, continue to research the Highland Clearances on which this series of poems is based. Act as a resource person for the group.
2. (Research) Read "Notes on Form," pages 91 and 92. Using your library resources, continue to research Celtic knots. Act as a resource person for the group during the discussion.
3. (React) Do you think the title is a good one? Support your opinion with specifics from the text.
4. (Discuss) How does the separation force each sister to grow?
5. (Create) Choose one or more of the praise poems. Create an illustration that reinforces the poem's message and tone.

Related Works

1. Carvell, Marlene. **Sweetgrass Basket.** New York: Dutton Children's Books, 2005. 243p. $16.99. ISBN 0 525 47547 8. [poetry] JS, G (See full booktalk in *Booktalks and Beyond,* 2007, pages 244 to 246.) Sent to an off-reservation school after their mother's death, Mattie and Sarah Tarbell find their Mohawk heritage and their own self-respect challenged by the white world's cruelty, prejudice, and ignorance. They tell about their experiences and relationship in poems.
2. Frost, Helen. **Keesha's House.** New York: Farrar, Straus and Giroux/ Frances Foster Books, 2003. 115p. $16.00. ISBN 0 374 34064 1. [poetry] JS, CG (See full booktalk in *Booktalks and Beyond,* 2007, pages 21 to 24.) A group of young outcasts band together and form a family. Each tells his or her story in poetry.
3. Schmidt, Gary D. **Lizzie Bright and the Buckminster Boy.** New York: Clarion Books, 2004. 219p. $15.00. ISBN 0 618 43929 3. [fiction] MJS, CG (See full booktalk in *Booktalks and Beyond,* 2007,

pages 251 to 254.) In the early 1900s, Turner Buckminster moves to Phippsburg, Maine, when his father becomes the minister of Phippsburg's First Congregational Church, and finds himself in the middle of a plot to grab land from a poor community descended from former slaves.

4. Whelan, Gloria. **Chu Ju's House.** New York: HarperCollins Publishers, 2004. 227p. $16.89. ISBN 0 06 050725 X. [fiction] MJS, G (See full booktalk in *Booktalks and Beyond,* 2007, pages 239 to 241.) Fourteen-year-old Chu Ju knows that her parents will give her baby sister to an orphanage so that they can, as tradition dictates, try to have a boy. She runs away, and in four years, establishes a new and independent life.

5. Wooding, Chris. **Poison.** New York: Orchard Books, 2003. 273p. $16.99. ISBN 0 439 75570 0. [fiction] JS, G (See full booktalk in *Booktalks and Beyond,* 2007, pages 176 to 178.) In this fantasy, sixteen-year-old Poison sets out to recover her baby sister and finds her life purpose.

ভ্য

Grant, Vicki. **Pigboy.**

Victoria, BC, Canada: Orca Book Publishers, 2006. 101p. (Orca Currents). $8.95. ISBN-13: 978 1 55143 643 2. [fiction] MJ, CG with high interest for boys

Themes/Topics: bullies, names, self-esteem, heroism

Summary/Description

Dan Hogg, a fourteen-year-old nerd, joins his class, including the class bullies and a substitute teacher, for a field trip to a "heritage farm." The routine butt of abuse and jokes about his name, Dan knows that the pig setting will escalate his nightmare life. When they arrive, the tour guide proves to be an escaped convict who knocks out the teacher and bus driver, locks up the class in the barn with the farm's injured owner, and attempts to burn it down so there will be no witnesses. Dan, the smallest and smartest, directs the bully to help him, squeezes out of a hole in the roof, and saves everyone. Now a hero, he gains respect from his peers and himself.

Read Aloud/Reader Response

This short book is a great read aloud, but the following passages may warrant special attention.

1. Chapter 1, pages 1 to 4. Dan introduces himself and the situation.

2.   Chapter 2, pages 7 and 8, beginning "Whenever..." and ending with the chapter. Dan's mother explains to him why he is a lucky person.
3.   Chapter 10, pages 58 to 59, beginning "I wanted to find..." and ending "...if I at least tried." Dan realizes why he should take action against the murderer.
4.   Chapter 15, pages 88 to 95. The chapter describes Dan's madcap run and rescue.
5.   Chapter 17, pages 100 to 101, beginning "Shane doesn't..." and ending with the chapter. Dan reveals the attitude changes in both Shane and himself.

Booktalk

Fourteen-year-old Dan Hogg has a big burden in life—his name. On top of that, he is a skinny nerd with glasses and bad teeth. He might as well put a target on his back and tell the bullies to knock him around. They do anyway, and now things are getting worse. The entire class is taking a field trip to a "heritage farm." That means that they'll spend an entire day without electricity, running water, a television, or a pop machine. What they will have is lots of pigs. In that wonderful situation, Dan knows who will be the center of entertainment. He just hopes that he can get out of this nature visit alive. But when the class meets the farm, the trip takes a dangerous turn—for everyone. Who will they find to save the day? Enter *Pigboy*.

Get Involved

1.   (Research) Using your library resources, find out more about names and the effects they might have on a person. Act as a resource person for the group.
2.   (React) List all the words that you would use to describe Dan Hogg. Find specifics from the story that support your word choices. Compare your list with the lists of others.
3.   (Follow-up) Grant centers on a normal situation, a field trip, gone bad. Make a list of normal situations. Then list complications that could make them dangerous.
4.   (Create) Choose one of the situations from Get Involved 3. Describe a character who might neutralize or confront the danger. Be sure to list all the information about that character that Grant included about Dan Hogg.
5.   (Create) Write a short story of your own or one episode of a longer story that uses the situation and character from Get Involved 3 and 4. Share your writing with the group.

Related Works

1. Brooks, Kevin. **Martyn Pig.** New York: Chicken House, 2002. 240p. $10.95. ISBN 0 439 29595 5. [fiction] JS, CG Fifteen-year-old Martyn Pig, fascinated with mystery stories, accidentally kills his abusive father and then decides to cover up the death so that he can live on his own. *Pigboy* and *Martyn Pig* both deal with the name problem, but *Martyn Pig* requires a more mature audience.

2. Covey, Sean. **The 6 Most Important Decisions You'll Ever Make: A Guide for Teens.** New York: Simon & Schuster/Fireside Books, 2006. 319p. $15.95. ISBN-13: 978 0 7432 6504 1. [nonfiction] JS, CG Using the 7 habits philosophy, Covey addresses the issues of school, friends, parents, dating and sex, addictions, and self-worth. Each chapter concludes with a "Baby Steps" application section for reader application. "Help Desk," at the end of the book, lists applicable Web sites for each chapter. A bibliography lists the references for each chapter.

3. Garfinkle, D. L. **Storky: How I Lost My Nickname and Won the Girl.** New York: G. P. Putnam's Sons, 2005. 184p. $16.99. ISBN 0 399 24284 8. [fiction] MJ, CG (See full booktalk in *Booktalks and Beyond,* 2007, pages 63 to 65.) High school freshman Michael "Storky" Pomerantz figures out how to respect the person he is as he seeks approval.

4. Hiaasen, Carl. **Hoot.** New York: Alfred A. Knopf, 2002. 292p. $15.95. ISBN 0 375 82181 3. [fiction] MJ, CG (See full booktalk in *Teen Genre Connections,* 2005, pages 37 to 39.) Roy Eberhardt, a new and bullied student in Trace Middle School, joins forces with a brother and sister to take on a greedy company and save the owls that the company is trying to destroy.

5. Lekuton, Joseph Lemasolai. **Facing the Lion: Growing up Maasai on the African Savanna.** Washington, DC: National Geographic, 2003. 123p. $15.95. ISBN 0 7922 5125 3. [nonfiction] MJS, CG with high interest for boys (See full booktalk in *Booktalks and Beyond,* 2007, pages 234 to 236.) Joseph Lekuton describes his nomadic life as a Maasai. In Chapter 1, he relates an unsuccessful lion encounter that teaches him to confront the other "lions" in his life.

☙❧

McCaughrean, Geraldine. The White Darkness.
New York: HarperTempest, 2005. 373p. $17.89.
ISBN-13: 978 0 06 089036 0. [fiction] JS, CG

Themes/Topics: Antarctica, imaginary friends, coming of age

Summary/Description

Fourteen-year-old Sym, raised by her Uncle Victor to be obsessed with the Antarctic, confides her life wishes and fears to the romantic figure of Captain Oates who died in Captain Robert Falcon Scott's 1911 expedition to the South Pole. Victor takes her on a surprise tourist trip to the Antarctic but steals the high-tech equipment and shifts the expedition to a search for a mythical city inside the earth. As Sym travels into the wilderness with Victor and the two men who conned him into believing that his discovery would become a movie, she discovers that her uncle killed her father, stole her family's money, caused her deafness, drugged the other travelers, and blew up the plane that threatened to take the filmmakers back to the mainland. He poisons and abandons one of the con men and plans for Sym to mate with the other one and populate the mythical city. The second man steals the equipment and abandons them. Sym and Victor continue on foot. Finally, the uncle throws himself into a hole he believes to be the city's entrance. Sym struggles on, still talking to Oates, and eventually discovers that the group left enough clues to effect the rescue of her and the man who deserted her. On the rescue ship, she has the respect and admiration of the rescuers but also information about Oates that she could not have known without his telling her.

Read Aloud/Reader Response

1. Chapter 5, pages 64 to 66, beginning "Now I sat..." and ending with the chapter. Sym reflects with Oates, on fitting in.
2. Chapter 6, pages 68 to 69, beginning "At first the doctors..." and ending "...like big amber tears." Sym recalls her father's illness.
3. Chapter 17, pages 251 to 255, beginning "'Uncle Victor...'" and ending "...monsters in the basement." Victor reveals that Sym's father really loved her and gives her enough information for her to figure out that Victor killed her father.
4. Chapter 19, pages 282 to 283, the quiz "What Could Pick up on Vacation?!!!" This is the quiz Sym writes to her friend Nikki.
5. Chapter 20, page 305, beginning "When the White Darkness..." and ending "Nobody!" Sym explains the meaning of *White Darkness*.

Booktalk

Fourteen-year-old Sym is in love. Let her tell you. (*Read page 1 out loud.*) Titus Oates explored the Antarctic. He died in the Scott expedition of 1911 because Scott, the leader, was too proud to listen to his advice. Sym fell in love with Oates while reading and learning everything she could about Antarctica. Now her Uncle Victor, who gave her all those books, is giving her the chance of a lifetime. They are taking a luxury trip to the bottom of the world. No one else, even Sym's mother, knows about it. He loves Antarctica even more than Sym. But he doesn't tell Sym, or anyone else, about a second planned trip, one that has nothing to do with the travel agency. Inside the earth, he believes there is a city where all the lost explorers remain alive. That is where Uncle Victor plans to take Sym. That is where he plans to leave her. And as Sym finds herself navigating this treacherous, cold desert with a madman, she must draw on all she knows, and on all Titus Oates knows, or she, like those before her, will perish in *The White Darkness.*

Get Involved

1. (Research) Using your library resources, find out as much as you can about the climate of Antarctica. Act as a resource person during the group discussion. You may wish to start with Related Work 2.
2. (Research) Using your library resources, find out as much as you can about exploration in Antarctica. Act as a resource person during the group discussion.
3. (React) Choose what you feel is the most important conversation that Sym has with Oates. Compare your choice with those made by others in the group. Explain your choice with specifics from the novel.
4. (Discuss) Sym explains *White Darkness* on page 305. (See Read Aloud/Reader Response 5.) Sym compares it to perfect ignorance. Do you agree with her comparison?
5. (React and Follow-up) Sym believes her uncle's lies, but has enough truth in her experience to save her. Can you relate an experience in which you sorted out fantasy and reality? Explain how it affected you.
6. (Create) Write an additional scene in which Sym reunites with her mother or with Nikki. You may choose to include Titus Oates as well.

Related Works

1. Atkins, Jeannine. Dusan Petricic (illus.). **How High Can We Climb?** New York: Farrar, Straus and Giroux, 2005. 224p. $17.00. ISBN 0 374 33503 6. [nonfiction] MJ, G The twelve accounts of women explorers include the story of Ann Bancroft, who reached both the North and South Poles and crossed Antarctica on foot with Liv Arnesen.
2. Bledsoe, Lucy Jane. **How to Survive in Antarctica.** New York: Holiday House, 2006. 101p. $16.95. ISBN 0 8234 1890 1. [nonfiction]

MJS, CG Bledsoe reveals the unique ecology and international co-operation of Antarctica as she describes the preparation necessary for a human to survive when encountering snow, extreme temperatures, wildlife, and crevasses.

3. Pullman, Philip. **Once upon a Time in the North.** New York: Alfred A. Knopf, 2008. 96p. $12.99. ISBN-13: 978 0 375 84510 9. [fiction] JS, CG with high interest for boys. Two characters from the world of *His Dark Materials,* Lee Scoresby and Iorek Byrnison, meet and prove that a Texan balloonist and an armored bear can work together to defeat corrupt businessmen and politicians in the frozen Arctic.

4. Sullivan, Paul. **Maata's Journal.** New York: Atheneum Books for Young Readers, 2003. 240p. $16.95. ISBN 0 689 83463 2. [fiction] JS, G Seventeen-year-old Maata, an Inuit, records her survival in an Arctic expedition from April to July of 1924. In addition to the dangers she and her fellow explorers share, Maata uses her journal to reflect on two situations that brought her here—the resettlement of the Inuits by the Canadian government and the expedition itself that intends to measure nature rather than listen.

5. Vanasse, Deb. **Out of the Wilderness.** New York: Clarion Books, 1999. 165p. $15.00. ISBN 0 395 91421 3. [fiction] JS, CG with high interest for boys. This story about two brothers who live in the wilderness is framed by two bear encounters. The first separates the brothers because the younger tries to shoot a charging bear. The second illustrates that the older brother's dedication to nature has grown into a mental illness that will cause his death.

ෆ඼ඬ

McCormick, Patricia. **Sold.**
New York: Hyperion, 2006. 263p. $15.99. ISBN 078685171 6. [fiction] JS, G

Themes/Topics: poverty, prostitution, child-selling, choice, India

Summary/Description

Thirteen-year-old Lakshmi lives with her family in Nepal. After the monsoons wash away the family crops, her step-father sells her into prostitution. Thinking she will be a maid in a wealthy city home and earn money for her family, Lakshmi follows her handlers' instructions and lies to the border guards so that they will not arrest her. She arrives at "Happiness House" in India ruled by the cruel Mumtaz, a fat, old woman who cheats and brutalizes the prostitutes. Lakshmi is beaten and drugged until she becomes one of the regulars and bonds with the other women. One prostitute's son teaches her to read and write and gives her a glimpse of the outside world. Lakshmi watches her friends, diseased or no longer desirable, thrown into the street. She also learns that none of her money goes home, and she will never make enough to buy her freedom. When American "customers" promise her a new life, she fears to believe them, but eventually risks an escape.

Read Aloud/Reader Response

1. "A Tin Roof," pages 1 to 2. This introductory passage introduces Lakshmi's values, the step-father's values, and the family's overwhelming poverty.
2. "Everything I Need to Know," pages 15 and 16. After Lakshmi has her first period, her mother explains the community's expectations for her.
3. "City Rules," pages 50 and 51. Ama advises Lakshmi how to act in the city.
4. "Everything I Need to Know Now," pages 141 to 143. Anita, Pushpa, and Shahanna explain the rules she will need to survive in Happiness House.
5. "Revelation," pages 238 to 239. Lakshmi learns her real situation from Shilpa.

Booktalk

Thirteen-year-old Lakshmi lives in Nepal. (*Show Nepal on a map.*) Her family's biggest dream is to have a tin roof on their shack. The Himalayan monsoons destroy their crops and that dream. Lakshmi's step-father, a gambler, says that they no longer have enough money to feed her. He will send her to the city with a beautiful stranger and arrange for her to work as a maid. Her money will buy her food and support the family. If she works hard, someday they will have a tin roof. Someday she will successfully return to her village to marry. So Lakshmi travels to India (*Show India and possibly Calcutta on the map.*) with this mysterious stranger. But too late she discovers that she has not been hired, but *Sold.* She is not a maid but a prostitute. If she disobeys her mistress or tries to escape her new home, Happiness House, she can be beaten, deformed, or murdered. Isolated and trapped, she knows nothing about what is outside this Happiness House. Then a strange customer arrives, an American. He makes promises about a new life. But she believed new life stories before. New is not always better, and the girls in the house tell her that Americans will make her walk naked in the streets. They may kill her. Does she dare take the risk? She must decide. Is torture, even death, better than being *Sold?*

Get Involved

1. (Research) Using your library resources, learn more about the world slave trade. Act as a resource person during discussion.
2. (Research) Using your library, learn more about child labor in the world. Act as a resource person during discussion.
3. (React) Each character in the novel has a picture of reality. Choose one character's picture. Discuss how accurate it is and how it affects the person's life.
4. (Discuss) Television, movie, and sports stars play a special role in the novel. Note each time one is mentioned. How do these references affect the story?
5. (Discuss) Choose three objects mentioned in the text. How do you think each one characterizes the person with whom it is associated?
6. (Follow-up) Investigate how you can become involved in helping teenagers who are victims of adult exploitation through crime or child labor.

Related Works

1. Cameron, Ann. **Colibrí.** New York: Farrar, Straus and Giroux/ Frances Foster Books, 2003. 240p. $17.00. ISBN 0 374 31519 1. [fiction] MJS, G (See full booktalk in *Teen Genre Connections*, 2005, pages 269 to 271.) Twelve-year-old Colibrí travels with the man who kidnapped her when she was four until a Day-Keeper counsels her to leave the obviously abusive relationship.
2. Ellis, Deborah. **The Heaven Shop.** Narkham, ON, Canada: Fitzhenry & Whiteside, 2004. 192p. $16.95. ISBN 1 55041 908 0. [fiction] MJ, CG (See full booktalk in *Booktalks and Beyond,* 2007, pages 229 to 231.) Thirteen-year-old Binti Phiri sees her family fall apart after her father dies of AIDS and greedy relatives force them to live in slave conditions.
3. Ellis, Deborah. **I Am a Taxi.** (See full booktalk in "Multiple Cultures"/"Conflict," pages 285 to 289.) Twelve-year-old Diego lives in San Sebastián Women's Prison in Cochabamba, Bolivia, until he loses his privileges to earn money and enslaves himself to drug dealers to support his incarcerated family.
4. Lunde, Paul. **Organized Crime: An Inside Guide to the World's Most Successful Industry.** New York: DK Press, 2004. 192p. $30.00. ISBN 0 7894 9648 8. [reference] JS, CG with high interest for boys. Lunde describes world-wide crime organizations, including the exploitation of children and teenagers for prostitution.
5. Whelan, Gloria. **Homeless Bird.** New York: HarperCollins Publishers, 2000. 216p. $15.95. ISBN 0 06 028454 4. [fiction] MJS, G

(See full booktalk in *Booktalks and More,* 2003, pages 215 to 217.) Thirteen-year-old Koly marries a dying boy to free her family of the burden of supporting her. Suffering the abuse and abandonment of her mother-in-law after her husband dies, she rebuilds her life through her embroidery talent.

ᘓᘔ

Pow, Tom. Captives.

New Milford, CT: Roaring Brook Press/A Neal Porter Book, 2007. 185p. $17.95. ISBN-13: 978 1 59643 201 7. [fiction] JS, CG

Themes/Topics: kidnapping, Caribbean, truth, terrorism

Summary/Description

While on a Caribbean vacation, two families are kidnapped by rebels. The father of one family writes a best-selling, carefully sanitized and edited, book about their captivity. His son reads the book and then writes the version he knew as the truth. The father's narrative portrays rebels full of bitterness and hate. The son's version expands on the reasons behind the rebellion against a dictator backed by American greed and includes the stories of the rebels: the poet leader whose uncle is the dictator; the union leader and thief abused in jail; the young boy whose university parents have been liquidated by the government; and the leader's companion lover and fellow leader who lives to see the group's efforts bear fruit. The second couple's teenage daughter draws the attention of both the teen author and the teen rebel. She becomes the rebel's lover and dies trying to protect him when the government troops "rescue" the tourists and, in their mission, massacre most of the rebels (terrorists).

Read Aloud/Reader Response

1. Part I, Captives 2, pages 47 to 48, beginning "I don't hate..." and ending "...*this* is a choice." In the father's version, Maria responds to the question about choices.
2. Part I, Captives 2, page 49, beginning "Do you know..." and ending "We know." In the father's version, Maria responds to one of the captive's questions about consequences.
3. Part I, Captives 3, "Day Twenty," pages 68 to 72. Rafael reveals that he is a poet.
4. Part II, Chapter 1, pages 109 to 113, beginning "Louise was still..." and ending with the chapter. Louise's memory of July 4th suggests the vulnerability of the soldier.

5.   Part II, Chapter 6, pages 138 to 142. The chapter demonstrates how Mason, the company representative, persuades Gabriel to betray his friends.
6.   Part II, Chapter 10, page 171, beginning *"The woman is born..."* and ending *"...death is a lie."* Eduardo shares the creation song.

Booktalk

Martin and his family are on vacation in the Caribbean. Louise and her family are too. Suddenly, their guide's car is stopped. The six are blindfolded, shoved into a truck, and driven to the island's interior. Surrounded by guns and machetes, they don't ask too many questions. The truck is gone, and the group continues on foot. Exhausted by the sun and rugged terrain, they don't have the power to escape. Even threatened and afraid, the six U.S. citizens begin to understand the danger and greed they represent from their government and why the rebels hold them hostage. But as they move deeper into the forest, every group member, rebel and prisoner, depends more and more on the other for survival. The rebels are humans after all. The prisoners too have lives, families, and loves. They could almost understand each other. They could almost be friends. But in a life-and-death situation, each person must consider the inevitable bottom line. And that bottom line is that one group is captors, with the power to grant life or death. And the other group is *Captives.*

Get Involved

1.   (Research) Using your library resources, find out more information about U.S. involvement in just one country south of its borders. Act as a resource person for the group during discussion.
2.   (Discuss) The title *Captives* has many applications in this story. List each character in the story. List how each might be considered a captive. Compare your list and reasons with those made by others in the group.
3.   (Discuss) Martin comments that truth often lives in fiction more than nonfiction. Agree and/or disagree. Use specifics from the text to support your opinion.
4.   (Create and Follow-up) Ask two people to observe the same event and then tell their observations. Compare the two versions.
5.   (Create and Follow-up) Using a newspaper report as a base, create a fiction story of your own in which you treat one of the subjects more sympathetically than the other.

Related Works

1.   Allende, Isabel. Margaret Sayers Peden (trans.). **City of the Beasts.** New York: HarperCollins Publishers, 2002. 406p. $21.89. ISBN 0

06 050917 1. [fiction] MJ, CG with high interest for boys (See full booktalk in *Teen Genre Connections,* 2005, pages 87 to 90.) Fifteen-year-old Alex Cold accompanies his eccentric grandmother on a writing assignment and saves a Brazilian tribe from extinction.

2. Cameron, Sara, in conjunction with UNICEF. **Out of War: True Stories from the Front Lines of the Children's Movement for Peace in Colombia.** New York: Scholastic Press, 2001. 224p. $15.95. ISBN 0 439 29721 4. [nonfiction] JS CG (See full booktalk in *Booktalks and More,* 2003, pages 58 to 61.) Nine teenagers, members of the UNICEF-related Children's Movement for Peace in Colombia, tell about their attempts to seek peace in the Colombian civil conflict. Each believes that any hope for peace lies in the hearts of Colombian children who must learn to overcome the violence, hate, and poverty in their own homes.

3. Ellis, Deborah. **I Am a Taxi.** (See full booktalk in "Multiple Cultures"/"Conflict," pages 285 to 289.) A young man living in a Bolivian prison with his parents who are falsely accused of drug trafficking becomes involved in American-backed drug production to make money for his family's survival.

4. Freedman, Russell. **Who Was First? Discovering the Americas.** New York: Clarion Books, 2007. 88p. $19.00. ISBN-13: 978 0 618 66391 0. [nonfiction] MJS CG Freedman explores the many groups who may have been the first to discover the Americas. Pages 11 to 13 tell the story of the Tainos, the Native Americans referred to in the naming of the rebel character El Taino.

5. Mikaelsen, Ben. **Tree Girl.** New York: HarperCollins Children's Books, 2004. 240p. $16.99. ISBN 0 06 009004 9. [fiction] JS, G (See full booktalk in *Teen Genre Connections,* 2005, pages 94 to 96.) Fifteen-year-old Gabriela Flores finds herself struggling to survive when U.S.-trained government troops begin a systematic Indian massacre in Guatemala.

Quest

✿✿

Bell, Hilari. **The Last Knight: A Knight and Rogue Novel.**
New York: HarperCollins/EOS, 2007. 357p. $17.99. ISBN-13: 978 0 06 082504 1.
[fiction] JS, CG with high interest for boys

Themes/Topics: conduct of life, friends, father/son relationships, mystery, fantasy, adventure

Summary/Description

Idealistic eighteen-year-old Sir Michael decides to commit to the outmoded career of knight errant, and redeems street-wise seventeen-year-old Fisk for his squire. They rescue a "damsel-in-distress" accused of murdering her husband and are arrested, but Michael's father, a baron, redeems them and then specifies the terms of their redemption to him. Michael must return the lady to justice, offer an apology to the kinsmen of the murdered man, and return to his father's manor where he will act as estate steward to the Baron of Seven Oaks for as long as the Baron wills it. In their quest to capture the accused, Michael and Fisk are pursued and thwarted by the lady's supporters. They arrive at her home where she experiments with infusing magic into simple-minded people abandoned by their families. Her men capture Michael, but Fisk flees. She decides to extend her experiments to Michael, an intelligent person. Fisk returns to rescue Michael who figures out that the lady's husband killed himself while using his wife's potions to achieve fertility. Michael releases her, but stops her experimenting on unsuspecting subjects by telling her that her potions had no effect on him. Michael's prison experience influences Michael to release Fisk, but Fisk stays with Michael. Together, they will quest as outcasts of society. Michael and Fisk tell the story in alternating chapters.

Read Aloud/Reader Response

1. Chapter 5, page 85, beginning "She summoned a boy..." and ending "...that includes the simple ones." Fisk comments on "simple" people.
2. Chapter 7, pages 128 and 129, beginning "As a child I knew..." and ending "...redeem the destruction of magica." Fisk explains the Savant.
3. Chapter 11, pages 222 to 224, beginning "But she settled..." and ending "...for the first time in days." Fisk tells Mistress Kara their story and reveals his growing admiration and affection for Michael.
4. Chapter 14, page 277, beginning "My captors weren't..." and ending "...get out of an ordinary cell." Michael is beginning to see the difference between romance and reality.
5. Chapter 18, pages 353 to 357, beginning "I met her eyes..." and ending with the chapter. Michael decides to free the lady, lie, free Fisk, and continue the life he loves as an outlaw instead of living under his father's judgments.

Booktalk

Eighteen-year-old Michael is a self-appointed knight errant. Since that job ended hundreds of years ago, he is the only knight errant in the world. Luckily, he finds a squire. Seventeen-year-old Fisk is not a willing squire. Michael redeems Fisk just before he is sentenced for conning the villagers. According to the law, Fisk is obligated to his redeemer until the redeemer frees him. But since Fisk is a clever criminal and more street-wise than Michael can ever hope to be, Fisk starts looking for the loophole the day he starts the job. Their first task is rescuing a "damsel-in-distress." Unfortunately, the damsel is accused of murdering her husband, and when Fisk meets her, he is sure that it wouldn't bother her to murder them too. Michael and Fisk are arrested for helping a fugitive escape. Michael's wealthy and very angry father arrives to redeem Michael, and suddenly, the two have a real live quest. Michael, a redeemed man, and Fisk, Michael's redeemed man, are sent to right their wrong. They have to bring the fair damsel back to face justice or be condemned. By now they know that the damsel is dangerous and that the justice she faces may not be just, but in a world where quests are hard to find, this team can't be picky. So they are off to save the day and their necks. And the not-so-loyal squire discovers that it is all just a too-typical day in the life of his dreaming redeemer, *The Last Knight*.

Get Involved

1. (Research) Using your library resources, research the story of Don Quixote. Act as a resource person during the discussion.
2. (Discuss) How are Fisk and Michael different? Be sure to use specifics from the text.
3. (Discuss) How are Fisk and Michael alike? Be sure to use specifics from the text.
4. (React) Do you agree with Michael's conclusions at the end of the story? Be sure to use specifics from the text to defend your answer.
5. (Create and Follow-up) Describe the quests that a modern knight errant might undertake and the difficulties he or she might encounter.
6. (React) Define heroism. Is it, as Fisk often observes, "highly overrated"?

Related Works

1. Anderson, John David. **Standard Hero Behavior.** New York: Clarion Books, 2007. 273p. $16.00. ISBN-13: 978 0 618 75920 0. [fiction] JS, CG with high interest for boys. Thinking that he can never be a hero, fifteen-year-old Mason applies for a job as a bard

and discovers that the real heroism is far different from the kind he reads about in books as he organizes a battle to save his town from orcs, goblins, and trolls.

2.   Cadnum, Michael. **Forbidden Forest: The Story of Little John and Robin Hood.** New York: Orchard Books, 2002. 218p. $17.95. ISBN 0 439 31774 6. [fiction] JS, CG with high interest for boys. In four parts, Cadnum tells the story of Little John becoming an outlaw, joining Robin Hood's band, and falling in love.

3.   Kerven, Rosalind. **King Arthur.** New York: DK Publishing, 1998. 63p. (Eyewitness Classics). $14.95. ISBN 0 7894 2887 3 [nonfiction]. MJS, CG with high interest for boys (See full booktalk in *Booktalks Plus,* 2001, pages 131 to 133.) In her description of King Arthur's legend, Kerven explains how the need for Arthur came about and why his legend included codes of knightly conduct as well a strong leadership.

4.   Reuter, Bjarne. Tiina Nunnally (trans.). **The Ring of the Slave Prince.** New York: Dutton Children's Books, 2003. 373p. $22.99. ISBN 0 525 47146 4. [fiction] MJ, CG with high interest for boys (See full booktalk in *Beyond Booktalks,* 2007, pages 97 to 100.) Hoping to save his mother and half-sister from drudgery and abuse, fourteen-year-old Tom O'Connor pursues a slave whom he thinks he can return for riches.

5.   Voigt, Cynthia. **Jackaroo: A Novel of the Kingdom.** New York: Simon Pulse, 2003. 358p. $5.99. ISBN 0 689 86435 3. [fiction] JS, CG As sixteen-year-old Gwyn sees the suffering of the common people and hopes that Jackaroo, a legendary Robin Hood-type character, will return, she takes on the persona to save others and discovers that other "common" people do the same.

ɔʃɛ

Colfer, Eoin. Airman.

New York: Hyperion Books for Children, 2008. 412p. $17.99. ISBN-13: 978 142310750 7.
[fiction] MJS, CG with high interest for boys

Themes/Topics: flight, good vs. evil, coming of age, friendship, family, conduct of life

Summary/Description

Born in a hot air balloon at the Paris World's Fair, Conor and his family live in the 1890s world of the sovereign Saltee Islands, off the Irish coast where his father is a guard and confidant to the progressive king. Conor lives an idyllic life as the playmate to the princess. The royal tutor teaches him the science of flight. At fourteen, Conor intervenes in a plot to kill the king. Conor is declared dead but secretly sent to the prison island of Little Saltee where he is forced to live underground and mine for diamonds. With the brief help of his cellmate, Conor overcomes the prison's inhumane conditions and brutality. He focuses on building a flying machine and effects a successful escape. He reunites with his cellmate, and together they defeat the man who killed the king, imprisoned Conor, and now plans to kill Conor's parents and the queen, his former playmate.

Read Aloud/Reader Response

1. Chapter 2, pages 46 to 49, beginning "Someone else came…" and ending "…rest of the night." Marshall Bonvilain comes to see Conor after Conor's rescue of the princess.
2. Chapter 2, pages 53 to 54, beginning "Victor Vigny…" and ending "…*you might be needing it.*" Vigny tells Conor why he needs the skill to defend himself.
3. Chapter 5, pages 111 to 118. Conor is admitted to the prison.
4. Chapter 8, pages 164 to 167, beginning "The cell itself…" and ending "'I have a dream.'" Wynter and Conor discuss the keys to survival in prison, and Conor finds his focus.
5. Chapter 18, pages 397 to 407, beginning "Conor hurtled…" and ending with the chapter. Conor arrives in Bonvilain's tower and saves the day.

Booktalk

Conor Broekhart is born in a hot air balloon at the 1878 Paris World's Fair. The balloon is being shot down by rebels. As a child, Conor takes to the skies again when he propels himself and his princess away from an exploding tower. Conor's cool head and brave act make him the darling of both the princess and her father, the king of the sovereign Saltee Islands off the Irish coast. He becomes Sir Conor Broekhart, and, as his father guards the king, Conor enjoys the same indulgent life as the princess. Plus he has a tutor who shares his love of flying. But when Conor is fourteen, his life changes. He discovers a plot to kill the king. Naturally, our hero tries to defend the king. This time he doesn't succeed. Conor is labeled a traitor. His good name is lost. His new name is Conor Finn. He is sent to the dark side of the Saltees, the prison island where most prisoners die mining diamonds to support the kingdom. The guards plan to break him, even if that means beating him to death, and what little life he has, he lives buried underground. The pampered hero must become a survivor. But to survive these prison years he needs a dream. And for Conor that dream means freedom by way of the sky, the only possible escape. Now he pursues an old dream in a new way. Once again he will become a legend. Once again his name will change, and this time his name will be *Airman.*

Get Involved

1. (Research) Using your library resources, learn more about the history of flight. Act as a resource person during the discussion.
2. (React) Is Princess Isabella a damsel-in-distress? Use specifics from the text to support your answer.
3. (React) List the traits that you think make Conor successful. Compare your list with the lists of others in the group.
4. (Research) Using your library resources, research the concept of hero. Act as a resource person during the discussion.
5. (React) List the traits that you think make Conor a hero. Compare your list with the lists of others in the group.
6. (Create) Using graphic style, portray the characters and settings as you picture them.

Related Works

1. Eden, Maxewell. **The Magnificent Book of Kites: Explorations in Design, Construction, Enjoyment & Flight.** New York: Sterling Publishing Co., Inc., 2002. 464p. $14.95pa. ISBN 1 57912 025 3. [nonfiction] JS/A, CG with high interest for boys. This comprehensive reference teaches the reader how to design, build, and fly thirty different kites as well as understand the aerodynamics involved.
2. Lawrence, Iain. **The Convicts.** New York: Delacorte Press, 2005. 198p. $17.99. ISBN 0 385 90109 7. [fiction] MJ, CG with high interest for boys (See full booktalk in *Booktalks and Beyond,* 2007, pages 128 to 131.) When his father is taken to debtor's prison, a pampered Tom Tim leaves home, is thrust into a new street identity, joins child thieves, goes to prison, and eventually reunites with his father.
3. Oppel, Kenneth. **Airborn.** New York: HarperCollins/EOS, 2004. 355p. $17.89. ISBN 0 06 053181 9. [fiction] MJS, CG with high interest for boys (See full booktalk in *Booktalks and Beyond,* 2007, pages 107 to 110.) Fifteen-year-old Matt Cruse, a cabin boy on the *Aurora,* an airship on which his deceased father served, rescues a dying man who tells exotic stories. One year later Matt explores the man's journey with the man's granddaughter and enters a world of adventure and danger.

4. Oppel, Kenneth. **Skybreaker.** New York: HarperCollins Publishers, 2006. 369p. $17.89. ISBN-13: 978 0 06 053228 4. [fiction] MJS, CG with high interest for boys. In this *Airborn* sequel, Matt and Kate join the owner of the *Skybreaker* and a mysterious gypsy girl. The four battle pirates and fantastical creatures to salvage the valuables from a legendary ghost ship.

5. Updale, Eleanor. **Montmorency: Thief, Liar, Gentleman?** New York: Orchard Books, 2003. 233p. $16.95. ISBN 0 439 58035 8. [fiction] MJS, CG with high interest for boys (See full booktalk in *Booktalks and Beyond,* 2007, pages 131 to 133.) Montmorency, a petty thief, learns the ways of a gentleman during his prison term and uses them to become a more prosperous thief when he is released. Eventually, he becomes a government spy.

Klass, David. **The Caretaker Trilogy.**
Concluding volume forthcoming.
New York: Farrar Straus and Giroux/Frances Foster Books. [fiction]
JS, CG with high interest for boys.

Firestorm: Book I.
2006. 287p. $17.00. ISBN 0 374 32307 0. [fiction] JS, CG with high interest for boys

Themes/Topics: identity, environmental concerns, conduct of life, good vs. evil

Summary/Description

Jack Danielson, a brilliant, athletic, and good-looking high school senior, discovers that his entire life has been a protective cover, and that his real mission, as a visitor from the future, is to save the earth at a critical ecological "Turning Point." When Jack tells his "parents" that he saw a man no one else saw, the father sacrifices his life so that Jack can escape. In his subsequent journey, he meets Gisco, a telepathic dog, and Eko, a shape-shifting female battle instructor. The two slowly reveal Jack's identity, family heritage, and mission to find Firestorm as they help him discover his powers and survive in the battle with Dargon, Jack's evil cousin whose mission is to kill Jack and destroy Firestorm. Jack connects with Firestorm and kills Dargon, but both Gisco and Eko disappear at the end of the battle, and Jack finds himself successful but alone.

Read Aloud/Reader Response

1. Chapter 26, pages 115 to 117. This chapter is Jack's first deep sea trip. It introduces the beauty and danger of the sea that he will face later. Chapter 27 shows the danger of the bull shark that he faces in his battle with Dargon.
2. Chapter 28, pages 124 to 127, beginning "I glance at her face..." and ending with the chapter. Eko reveals her complicated nature. She also recites a passage from Ecclesiastes that addresses the re-generation of the earth.
3. Chapter 32, pages 136 to 137, beginning with the chapter and ending "...she says." Eko explains the battle between the Caretakers and the Dark Army, the natural and unnatural.
4. Chapter 49, pages 191 to 194. This chapter describes the catch and the bycatch.
5. Chapter 51, pages 197 to 201. In this chapter, the cook brags on his family history in the destructive fishing industry.
6. Chapter 71, page 269, beginning "I still don't know..." and ending "...waiting for me." Jack is beginning to comprehend Firestorm.

Booktalk

Read Chapter 1, pages 3 to 5, beginning with the chapter and ending "'...mind-bending drugs.'"

That's Jack. He just experienced one of the best days of a very good life. That man with the rolling eyeballs, however, changes everything. He pulls Jack away from success and safety to a battle for survival. Everything Jack thought he knew changes to a lie—even time and space. In this new world, a telepathic, snobby, monster of a dog and a shape-shifting ninja girl tell him that his job is to save the earth from ecological disaster. And they aren't kidding. To do that, he must find a source of power he knows nothing about. He must find the power of the earth. He must find *Firestorm*.

Whirlwind: Book II.

2008. 295p. $17.00. ISBN-13: 978 0 374 32308 0.

Themes/Topics: environmental concerns, good vs. evil, love, destiny, Amazon rain forest

Summary/Description

Jack returns home to see P. J. and discovers that he is going to be arrested for her recent disappearance and his parents' death. Gisco reappears and helps him escape the police and the Dark Army. Then they flee to the Amazon rain forest to rescue P. J. from the Dark Lord, the father of Dargon. Jack and Gisco are captured by the Dark Lord who holds P. J. also. The Dark Lord releases Jack, P. J., and many other prisoners so that Jack can lead him to the only person who can defeat the Dark Lord. The possible savior is a powerful time-traveling shaman now lost in the present. In an ambush staged by the Dark Lord, Jack loses contact with the group. Eko returns to save his life, guide him to the shaman, revive him, and rediscover their love. The shaman raises a rain forest army that destroys the prison, and continues to pursue the now-fleeing Dark Lord. Jack rescues P. J. and decides that he and P. J. deserve a normal life despite the insistence that he fulfill his destiny of saving the future.

Read Aloud/Reader Response

1. Chapter 23, pages 73 to 76. In this chapter, Gisco attempts to explain the time-space relationship that makes Jack's mission possible.
2. Chapter 33, pages 104 to 106, beginning with the chapter and ending "…*back on his feet.*" The discussion about the rescued boy and Kidah highlights the importance of each individual's life.
3. Chapter 40, pages 128 to 130, beginning with the chapter and ending "…under heavy guard." Ernesto explains the groups of prisoners and reveals that P. J. is in the prison.
4. Chapter 49, pages 160 to 164. In this chapter the colonel confronts Jack and reveals his ultimate threat of torture.
5. Chapter 73, pages 233 to 234, beginning "I get to know…" and ending "…few wrong turns?" Jack rethinks his definition of savage.

Booktalk

Jack Danielson from *Firestorm* (*Hold up the book.*) plans to recapture part of his old life. He wants to see his girlfriend P. J. again, and so he returns to his hometown where he used to be the normal teenage football star. WRONG MOVE! P. J. is missing. The town blames Jack for her disappearance and his parents' gory deaths. The police arrest him, and the Dark Army is on its way to destroy him. Things look grim, and then a rhino-sized dog appears. You guessed it. Gisco is back. Together they go on the run to the Amazon. The Dark Lord, the father of Dargon who Jack destroyed in *Firestorm*, is waiting there, and he wants revenge. He is holding P. J. to lure Jack into his trap, and it works. But someone else is trapped in the Amazon, a shaman, the only person who can destroy the Dark Lord and save the future. Once again, Jack gets the good jobs: rescue P. J., find the shaman, save the rain forest and the future. It seems a little bit much for somebody who hasn't even graduated from high school, but Jack takes it on and finds himself swept up in the *Whirlwind*.

Get Involved

1. (Research) Using your library's resources, learn more about the role of the coral reefs in ecology. Act as a resource person for the discussion of *Firestorm*.
2. (Research) Jack often refers to the Romantic poets. Using your library resources, learn more about the Romantic poets. Act as a resource person during the discussion.
3. (Research) Jack also uses references to Greek and Roman mythology. Using your library resources, learn about these allusions. Act as a resource person during the discussion.
4. (Research) In Chapter 9 of *Firestorm* Gisco tells Jack to read *Oedipus*. Using your library resources, research that reference and discuss how it applies to both *Firestorm* and *Whirlwind*.
5. (Discuss) Describe the good guys and the bad guys.
6. (Create and Follow-up) Rewrite one of the chapters as a graphic novel. Share it with the group.

Related Works

1. Allende, Isabel. Margaret Sayers Peden (trans.). **City of the Beasts.** New York: HarperCollins Publishers, 2002. 406p. $21.89. ISBN 0 06 050917 1. [fiction] MJ, CG with high interest for boys (See full booktalk in *Teen Genre Connections,* 2005, pages 87 to 90.) Fifteen-year-old Alex Cold and twelve-year-old Nadia Santos save the day when they become embroiled in a plot to destroy the rain forest and a native tribe that inhabits it.
2. Collard, Sneed B. **Flash Point.** Atlanta, GA: Peachtree, 2006. 240p. $15.95. ISBN-13: 978 1 56145 385 6. [fiction] MJ, CG with high interest for boys. Luther Wright, high school sophomore, chooses to preserve his integrity and the environment as he resists pressure from his family and the high school football team to fit in and chooses, instead, to challenge misinformation that keeps the forest fires and anger burning in his town of Heartwood, Montana.
3. Evans, Kate. **Weird Weather: Everything You Didn't Want to Know about Climate Change but Probably Should Find Out.** Toronto, ON, Canada: Groundwood Books, 2007. 96p. $15.95. ISBN-13: 978 0 88899 838 5. [graphic, nonfiction] JS, CG Evans makes the case that we must act now against global warming. She includes "Take Action" Web sites, Web sites with climate change news, "Interactive Online Games," and "Recommended Further Reading."
4. Haddix, Margaret Peterson. **Found: Book I.** New York: Simon & Schuster Books for Young Readers, 2008. 314p. (The Missing).

$15.99. ISBN-13: 978 1 4169 5417 0. [fiction] MJ, CG with high interest for boys. Two adopted thirteen-year-old boys discover that they came to earth, along with a plane load of other babies, through time travel. At the end of the novel, they are heading to the fifteenth century with the sister of one of the boys. The series considers how changing one event of one life can change the history of the world.

5. Hobbs, Will. **Leaving Protection.** New York: HarperCollins Publishers, 2004. 178p. $16.89. ISBN 0 06 051632 1. [fiction] MJ, CG with high interest for boys. Sixteen-year-old Robbie Daniels signs on for a summer fishing job to catch salmon off southeastern Alaska and discovers that his captain is secretly hunting for buried Russian plaques that claim ownership of Alaska and the Northwest.

6. Pfeffer, Susan Beth. **The Dead & the Gone.** New York: Harcourt, Inc., 2008. 321p. $17.00. ISBN-13: 978 0 15 206311 5. [fiction] JS, CG with high interest for boys. After a meteor hits the moon, seventeen-year-old Alex Morales fights to keep his sisters and himself alive as the city and world deteriorate.

ဟူ သူ

Alexander, Lloyd. **The Golden Dream of Carlo Chuchio.**

New York: Henry Holt and Company, 2007. 320p. $16.95. ISBN-13: 978 0 8050 8333 0.
[fiction] JS, CG with high interest for boys

Themes/Topics: coming of age, conduct of life, love, loyalty, friendship

Summary/Description

In this Arabian Nights-type tale, orphaned and romantic Carlo Chuchio seeks a treasure after he loses his job and home by reversing figures and almost ruining his employer and guardian. In Carlo's first stop, a thief robs him but only wants a job for himself and his assistant, a slave girl fleeing a cruel master who killed her parents. The three continue and are joined by a wise man. Guided by mysterious and disappearing characters (the bookseller who sells Carlo the map, a story-teller who tells a tale of love and common sense, a dream seller who points each character to personal fulfillment, and a clairvoyant who clarifies their experiences), the group comes closer to the gold, their personal treasures, and the slave dealer who killed the girl's parents. With the help of his three companions, Carlo defeats the villain and discovers that his treasure lies in the journey he will continue with the slave girl whom he loves. The story combines action, humor, and serious life choices.

Read Aloud/Reader Response

1. Chapter 2, pages 12 to 15, beginning with the chapter and ending "... put my plans in motion." Carlo argues with his conscience.
2. Chapter 6, pages 54 to 56, beginning "My good deed..." and ending "... nothing after that." Shira and Carlo first discuss "The Road of Golden Dreams."
3. Chapter 10, pages 89 to 94, beginning "Once, there was..." and ending with the chapter. This is the story of "The Well-Digger and the Princess," which becomes the basis of the novel.
4. Chapter 12, pages 103 to 110. This chapter introduces Salamon to the story.
5. Chapter 15, pages 128 and 129, beginning "I still heard it..." and ending with the chapter. Carlo realizes his responsibility in executing the thieves.
6. Chapter 21, pages 166 to 169, beginning "As the legend goes..." and ending "... for themselves elsewhere." The tale of Tarik Beg and the Dark Fortress illustrates why a person should keep his or her word and how a love of gold corrupts.

Booktalk

Carlo Chuchio is a dreamer. His uncle tries to teach him how to keep good records and accounts, but Carlo would rather waste his time reading and thinking about genies and flying carpets. Then a disaster and a blessing change Carlo's life. The disaster is that he reverses the uncle's accounts and almost destroys the business. The mistake loses Carlo his home and his job. The blessing comes in a purchase, a new book. Tucked inside is a treasure map. When Carlo returns to the bookseller the next day to give him back the map, the man has disappeared. Not only has he disappeared, but no one can remember ever seeing him. It seems to be a lucky and mysterious beginning. So Carlo decides to find the treasure, but luck changes again. Carlo is robbed of everything he owns. The robber, however, isn't really a robber. He returns with new supplies and clothes. He wants to join Carlo, not trick him. The robber's assistant, a beautiful slave girl, wishes to come too. Who else will he meet? A wise man, a story-teller, a dream seller, a clairvoyant, an entire nomadic tribe, and the worst villain ever imagined. Does he ever find the treasure? That depends on how you look at things. Carlo learns that each man sees treasure a little differently. And, for Carlo—failure, hero, and prince—treasures in life seem to fade and return in this new mysterious and magical world of *The Golden Dream of Carlo Chuchio.*

Get Involved

1. (Research) Using your library resources, research the elements needed to create an Arabian Nights adventure. Act as a resource person during the discussion.
2. (Discuss) After reading *The Golden Dream of Carlo Chuchio,* define a *chooch.* Compare your definition with others who have read the book.
3. (Create) Complete your own ending of "The Well-Digger and the Princess" (See Read Aloud/Reader Response 3).
4. (React) List the events that you think teach Carlo about himself. Compare your list with those of others in the group. Discuss your choices.
5. (Discuss) List each of the characters in the novel. Are they stereotypes? Explain your answer.
6. (Compare) Read *The Legend of the Wandering King* (Related Works 3). How is it similar and different from *The Golden Dream of Carlo Chuchio?*

Related Works

1. Bruchac, Joseph. **Wabi: A Hero's Tale.** (See full booktalk in "Fantasy/Science Fiction/Paranormal"/"Retelling an Old Story," pages 189 to 191.) In this Native American myth, Wabi tells about his life in which he chose to be human and eventually won the heart of a human girl.
2. Coelho, Paulo. Alan R. Clarke (trans.). **The Alchemist.** San Francisco, CA: HarperSanFrancisco, 1998. 174p. $13.00pa. ISBN 0 06 250218 2. [fiction] JS/A, CG In this fairy tale-like novel, Santiago, a young shepherd, seeks his personal calling, learns about the world and himself, finds love, and discovers his riches and treasure at home.
3. García, Laura Gallego. **The Legend of the Wandering King.** New York: Arthur A. Levine Books, 2005. 213p. $16.95. ISBN 0 439 58556 2. [fiction] JS, CG A proud prince learns to be a great poet and a responsible adult by making up for an injustice driven by his jealousy of another poet.
4. McCaughrean, Geraldine. **The Stones Are Hatching.** New York: HarperCollins Publishers, 1999. 230p. $15.95. ISBN 0 06 028765 9. [fiction] MJ, CG with high interest for boys. Living with an older abusive sister after World War I, eleven-year-old Phelim discovers the house is filled with creatures from the Old Magic who guide him on his hero's journey, which eventually connects him with his father.

5. Napoli, Donna Jo. **Beast.** New York: Atheneum Books for Young
    Readers, 2000. 260p. $17.00. ISBN 0 689 83589 2. [fiction] JS, CG
    (See full booktalk in *Teen Genre Connections,* 2005, pages 171 to 173.)
    After the spirits exile him and change him into a lion as punishment
    for an imperfect sacrifice, Orasmyn, a young Persian prince, begins a
    journey to learn about humanity and love.

Mystery/Suspense

Mystery and suspense combine why and how questions with edge-of-the-seat excitement. The girls' selections have girls front and center as victims or detectives—sometimes both. The boys' selections focus on more danger, violence, and drama in the discovery process.

Contemporary

✿✿

Brooks, Kevin. Candy.

New York: Scholastic, Inc./Chicken House, 2005. 364p. $16.95.
ISBN 0 439 68327 0. [fiction] JS, CG

Themes/Topics: drug addiction, prostitution, falling in love, brothers and sisters, music, recovery, rescue

Summary/Description

Joe Beck, a teenager from an affluent but broken home, falls in love with Candy, a teenage prostitute and drug addict. To see Candy, he is willing to lie to his father, defy Candy's pimp, abandon his band, and eventually endanger his sister Gina. When Candy comes to hear Joe's band, Iggy, her pimp, arrives, takes her back, and beats her. Joe finds the house of prostitution where she lives, makes love to her, defends himself from Iggy, and ties up him up. Joe and Candy flee to the Beck cottage where Joe helps Candy withdraw from drugs, but Iggy finds them and demands that Candy return to him or he will kill Gina, whom he kidnapped. Pretending to agree to Iggy's demands, Candy stabs Iggy in the throat and frightens his accomplices by telling them that police are coming. Her plan saves Gina, but Candy is placed in a juvenile home.

At a reunion between Candy and Joe, Joe realizes that Candy is still emotionally unstable and addicted, but holds on to his dream of a future, positive relationship. The content could be considered controversial and requires a mature audience.

Read Aloud/Reader Response

1. Chapter 1, page 2, beginning "When the girls…" and ending "… even *more* embarrassed…." In a casual encounter with some laughing girls on the train, Joe reveals his inexperience and naiveté.
2. Chapter 3, page 48, beginning "He grinned…" and ending with the paragraph. Joe realizes that the differences between Mike and Iggy are in their characters.
3. Chapter 4, page 59, beginning "Yeah, when they were getting…" and ending with "…what's the point?" Gina explains their mother's reason for wanting a divorce. Joe resents the explanation that she didn't want any more to do with her children.
4. Chapter 11, page 165, beginning "What's the matter…" and ending "…moving back." When searching for Iggy, Joe encounters a street kid who questions why Joe is there.
5. Chapter 12, pages 182 to 183, beginning "Imagine…" and ending "…was swollen and bandaged." Joe's description of opening the door to Candy's room suggests that he is entering a new life.
6. Chapter 20, pages 306 to 307, beginning with the chapter and ending *"Why does it have to hurt so much?"* Joe questions the person he has become in relation to Candy.
7. "Epilogue," pages 363 to 364, beginning "It's been almost six months…" and ending with the chapter. Joe reflects on staying faithful to Candy.

Booktalk

Joe Beck lives in a big house. He has a devoted older sister, and all the money he wants. One day he takes a trip to London, just a doctor's appointment. By chance he meets a girl, Candy. She is prettier than he can believe and smart enough to save him from some street guys he also happens to meet. Candy knows those guys and her way around. Joe walks out of that world and back into his safe, predictable one, but Candy's memory haunts him. He wants to see her again, talk to her, and discover who she is. Who she is ties into the violence of drugs, sex, and death. Underneath it all can Joe discover the sweet and loving girl in whom he wants to believe? Or is this girl just a bad dream—a nightmare filled with bittersweet, sickening *Candy?*

Get Involved

1. (Research) Using your library resources, research heroin, addiction, and the possibility of recovery. Act as a resource person during the discussion.
2. (React) Do the roles of Mike and Gina strengthen or weaken the novel for you?
3. (React) Is Iggy believable?
4. (React) At the end of the novel, do you agree with Joe's conclusion that he is changed?
5. (Discuss) Do you think that the relationship between Candy and Joe has a chance for success?
6. (Create) Write a letter to Joe about his experience with Candy. Share your letter with others in the group.

Related Works

1. Brooks, Kevin. **Martyn Pig.** New York: Chicken House, 2002. 240p. $10.95. ISBN 0 439 29595 5. [fiction] JS, CG with high interest for boys (See full booktalk in *Booktalks and Beyond,* 2007, pages 114 to 116.) Naïve fifteen-year-old Martyn Pig becomes involved with a manipulative and street-wise older girl who helps him hide his dead father's body and collect the inheritance.
2. Hautman, Pete. **Sweetblood.** New York: Simon & Schuster Books for Young Readers, 2003. 180p. $16.95. ISBN 0 689 85048 4. [fiction] JS, G (See full booktalk in *Teen Genre Connections,* 2005, pages 6 to 8.) Sixteen-year-old Lucy Szabo rebels against her father whom she believes caused her diabetes. She abandons her schoolwork, goes Goth, becomes involved with a middle-aged man through a chat room, and, through a near-death experience, realizes that her friend and parents are her major supporters.
3. Myers, Walter Dean. **Monster.** New York: HarperCollins Publishers, 1999. 281p. $15.95. ISBN 0 06 028077 8. [fiction] JS, CG with high interest for boys (See full booktalk in *Booktalks and More,* 2003, pages 13 to15.) Naïve sixteen-year-old Steve Harmon, on trial for murder, creates a play about his trial and his experiences before the trial. By the end of the novel, both Steve and the reader question his innocence.
4. Koja, Kathe. **The Blue Mirror.** New York: Farrar, Straus and Giroux/Frances Foster Books, 2004. 119p. $16.00. ISBN 0 374 30849 7. [fiction] JS, G Seventeen-year-old Maggy lives with her cat, Paz, and her alcoholic mother. She rarely attends school and hangs out downtown at a café, The Blue Mirror. Drawn into a world

of stealing and homelessness by street kids, she eventually finds a
more stable life through her art.

5. Nolan, Han. **Born Blue.** New York: Harcourt, Inc., 2001. 177p.
    $17.00. ISBN 0 15 201916 2. [fiction] JS, G (See full booktalk in
    Teen Genre Connections, 2005, pages 13 to 15.) As the daughter of a
    heroine-addicted mother, Janie tells about her life from the time she
    is four years old when she is rescued from drowning to when she is
    sixteen and decides to leave her illegitimate daughter with a loving
    and caring family. She realizes that she is not stable enough to take
    on another life or relationship.

෬෯

Gratz, Alan. Something Rotten.

New York: Penguin Group/Dial Books, 2007. 207p. (A Horatio Wilkes Mystery).
$16.99. ISBN-13: 978 0 8037 3216 2. [fiction] JS, CG with high interest for boys

Themes/Topics: family conflict, murder, water pollution,
Tennessee, *Hamlet*

Summary/Description

In this modern *Hamlet* mystery, Horatio Wilkes visits his school friend
Hamilton Prince in Denmark, Tennessee, to investigate the recent
death of Rex Prince, Hamilton's father. Rex told Hamilton, on a videotape, that he was being murdered. Hamilton is convinced that Uncle
Claude is the murderer, but because Hamilton is moody, overdramatic,
and possibly alcoholic, Horatio sorts through other suspects. Olivia, the
daughter of Claude's solicitor and a spurned girlfriend of Hamilton, is an
environmentalist who is furious about the local river being polluted by
the Princes' Elsinore Paper Plant. Candy, a prissy and obsequious servant,
has an alliance with Ford Branff who wishes to buy the company. Roscoe
Grant and Gilbert Stern, dumb and dumber acquaintances of Hamilton's
from middle school, are mysteriously invited to the house. As he investi-
gates, Horatio deduces that Claude slowly poisoned Rex with the dioxin
from the river and now plans to kill Hamilton. Horatio rescues Hamilton
who exposes Claude's crime. Roscoe and Gilbert die in a fiery crash engi-
neered by Claude. Hamilton and Olivia rekindle their relationship.

Read Aloud/Reader Response

1. Chapter 5, pages 38 to 44. In this chapter Hamilton and Horatio talk
    about the family conflicts, and Hamilton demonstrates his drinking
    problem.

2. Chapter 6, page 46, beginning "I've visited friends…" and ending "…rest of their days." Horatio ponders Candy's motive.
3. Chapter 7, pages 53 to 58, beginning with the chapter and ending "…and I nodded." Olivia shows Horatio the landscape and explains how the Princes have polluted the Copenhagen River and harmed the people around it.
4. Chapter 21, pages 171 to 173, beginning "What was it in the water…" and ending "…same as anyone else's." The doctor explains the danger of dioxin.
5. Chapter 22, pages 178 to 180, beginning "Back at the ranch…" and ending with the chapter. Horatio consults his sister Rosalind and her husband, both doctors, and solves the mystery.

Booktalk

"Something is rotten in Denmark." Denmark, Tennessee, that is. Hamilton Prince invites his school friend, Horatio Wilkes, to his mansion for the summer to find out just how rotten things really are. Hamilton came home from school and learned that his mother married his Uncle Claude, the uncle he can't stand, just two months after Hamilton's father died. Soon Uncle Claude will have control of the business, the Elsinore Paper Company that is turning the Copenhagen River from blue to brown. And even though everyone says that Dad died of cancer, he left a videotape just for his son's eyes. A videotape in which he appears as white as a ghost and tells Hamilton that if he dies, Hamilton will know that it is murder. Hamilton is too sad, too love sick, and too drunk to figure out what is going on and what to do about it. That is what friends are for. So Horatio Wilkes accepts the invitation to sniff out the bad guys and soon discovers that even a mansion can't hide the smell of *Something Rotten.*

Get Involved

1. (Research) The novel is a modern version of Shakespeare's *Hamlet* with a twist. Using your library resources, read the play, view the play, or read about it. Act as a resource person during the discussion.
2. (Research) *Rosencranz and Guildenstern Are Dead* (Related Work 4) is also used in the novel. Using your library resources, read the play, view the play, or read about it. Act as a resource person during the discussion.
3. (Research) Horatio's sisters also have names that appear in Shakespeare. Using your library resources, find out about those characters and how the sisters in the novel reflect them.

4. (React) Do you think that using the play as a base for the novel was a good idea?
5. (Discuss) What universal issues do you think that the novel shares with the play?
6. (Create) Sketch a modern plot for another Shakespearean play.

Related Works

1. Cooney, Caroline. **Enter Three Witches: A Story of Macbeth.** (See full booktalk in "Fantasy/Science Fiction/Paranormal"/"Retelling an Old Story," pages 191 to 193.) Lady Mary, the daughter of the Thane of Cawdor and the Ward of the Macbeths, works through her fears, allies herself with Fleance, and helps Malcolm defeat Macbeth.
2. Dunton Downer, Leslie, and Alan Riding. **Essential Shakespeare Handbook.** New York: DK Publishing, Inc., 2004. 480p. $25.00. ISBN 0 7894 9333 0. [reference] MJS, CG This user-friendly reference includes plot summaries and interpretative material on all thirty-nine plays and an analysis of the poetry. It also includes essays on Shakespeare's life, times, and impact on world culture. Pages 324 to 335 discuss *Hamlet.*
3. Shakespeare, William. Jeff Dolven (ed.). **Hamlet.** New York: Barnes and Noble Shakespeare, 2007. 434p. $6.95. ISBN-13: 978 1 4114 0034 4. [classic] S/A, CG Young Prince Hamlet comes home from Wittenburg to discover that his father is dead and that his mother is married to his uncle. Horatio, his school friend, is the only person he can trust as he sets out to test the ghost of his father who wants revenge. The play is often hailed as Shakespeare's greatest tragedy and is based on another story, an Old Norse legend in which the hero feigns madness so that he can accomplish his revenge.
4. Stoppard, Tom. **Rosencrantz and Guildenstern Are Dead.** Jackson, TN: Grove Press, 1994. 128p. $10.40. ISBN-13: 978 08021 32758. [classic] S/A, CG In this theater of the absurd play, Rosencrantz and Guildenstern try to find out Hamlet's intentions so that they might report to the king, but can't even figure out who or where they are.
5. Sweeney, Joyce. **The Spirit Window.** New York: Delacorte Press, 1998. 243p. $15.95. ISBN 0 385 32510 X. [fiction] MJ, G (See full booktalk in *Booktalks Plus*, 2001, pages 19 to 21.) In this novel based on Shakespeare's *The Tempest,* a young girl must heal her family in order to hold on to them and the land they value.

ᘓᘔ

Hartnett, Sonya. Surrender.

Cambridge, MA: Candlewick Press, 2005. 248p. $16.99.
ISBN-13: 978 0 7636 2768 3. [fiction] JS, CG

Themes/Topics: guilt, insanity, parent/child relationships, alter ego, brothers, dogs, city/town life, isolation

Summary/Description

Mentally ill twenty-year-old Anwell (Gabriel) recalls his life. He lies restrained in bed and wills himself to die. When he was seven years old, he accidentally killed his physically and mentally handicapped older brother. His small town and distant, self-centered parents will not allow him to forget it. Isolated, he creates a friend, Finnigan, who renames Anwell, Gabriel, the angel. Finnigan wills Gabriel to perform all his bad acts, demands Gabriel's exclusive loyalty, and launches a series of arsons against anyone who hurts Gabriel. The fires end when Gabriel's father purchases Surrender, a dog with whom Gabriel and Finnigan bond. When Surrender kills a local farmer's sheep, the father orders Gabriel to borrow a gun and kill the dog. Because Gabriel rebels before the shooting, the father decides to beat his son, now sixteen, with a belt. Gabriel goes to fetch the belt, but spies an ax and kills both parents. Now deciding to die so that Finnigan will die also, Gabriel is revisited by Finnigan who reveals himself as the brother Gabriel killed.

Read Aloud/Reader Response

The entire book would be an interesting dramatic read aloud for two performers: one reading the Gabriel chapters and the other reading the Finnigan ones. Below are some passages for special consideration.

1. "Gabriel," pages 1 to 5. In this chapter, Gabriel describes his situation.
2. "Finnigan," pages 24 to 26. In this chapter, Finnigan describes himself in relation to the town.
3. "Finnigan," pages 72 to 74. In this chapter, Finnigan describes himself again as the person in control of the town.
4. "Gabriel," pages 86 to 87, beginning "I smiled..." and ending "...had to be pure." Gabriel vows to enhance his own goodness by making Finnigan completely wicked.
5. "Finnigan," page 110, beginning with the chapter and ending with "...only Surrender." Finnigan describes his natural ownership of Surrender.

6. "Finnigan," pages 216 to 220. In this chapter, Finnigan again tries to get Gabriel to rationalize evil, and Gabriel rejects him.

Booktalk

Gabriel is twenty years old, and he is dying. All the members of his immediate family are gone. He takes comfort in knowing that his devoted aunt cares for him and will miss him. He also knows that the small world outside of his room whispers about him and the bones it took them so long to find. In his entire life before he got sick, Gabriel has only one friend, Finnigan. Finnigan does the things that Gabriel does not dare do. No matter how others tease him or pick on him, Gabriel knows that Finnigan will defend him—quietly and secretly so that no one will guess that they are friends. It is exciting to know someone so brave, so smart. Then the fires start. And after the fires, come other things, worse things. Gabriel discovers that friendships like theirs come with a price. Finnigan wants to be paid, and Gabriel knows that Finnigan will come for that payment soon, a payment Gabriel fears more than death. Gabriel must prepare. He just isn't sure how, but he is sure that he must fight Finnigan with all of his will or *Surrender.*

Get Involved

1. (Research) Using your library resources, find out as much as possible about good parenting. Act as a resource for the group during discussion.
2. (Discuss) In "Gabriel," pages 1 to 5 (Read Aloud/Reader Response 1) Gabriel describes his situation. In "Finnegan," pages 24 to 26 (Read Aloud/Reader Response 2) Finnegan describes himself in relation to the town. After reading the entire novel, discuss the reliability of the speakers in both passages.
3. (Research) Using your library resources, find out as much as possible about the Angel Gabriel. Act as a resource person for the group during discussion.
4. (React) Rate the title on a scale of 1 to 10. Explain your rating to the group.
5. (React and Create) Find passages that physically describe each character. Explain what you feel these descriptions add to the novel. Try to draw portraits of these characters.
6. (Follow-up and Compare) Read *Thursday's Child* (Related Work 2) and *What the Birds See* (Related Work 1), also by Hartnett. How does she use the usual and unusual to build suspense and horror?

Related Works

1. Hartnett, Sonya. **What the Birds See.** Cambridge, MA: Candlewick Press, 2002. 196p. $15.99. ISBN 0 7636 2092 0. [fiction] JS, CG In 1977, nine-year-old Adrian, whose mother is mentally unstable and whose father left him with a distant and abusive maternal grandmother, is bullied at school and turns to his neighbor Nicole, a social isolate, who leads them both to their deaths when she persuades him that they can become heroes.

2. Hartnett, Sonya. **Thursday's Child.** Cambridge, MA: Candlewick Press, 2000. 261p. $15.99. ISBN 0 7636 1620 6. [fiction] JS, CG (See full booktalk in *Teen Genre Connections,* 2005, pages 276 to 278.) Harper Flute recalls her dysfunctional family life that produces her brother who lives in tunnels that he digs under the house and eventually emerges as a wild, almost mythological figure to kill a man who attacks her.

3. Hautman, Pete. **Invisible.** (See full booktalk in "Issues"/"Facing Our Own Choices," pages 29 to 32.) Seventeen-year-old Doug Hanson, a brilliant loner beset by bullies, sets a fire that deforms him. He lives in what he describes as the Madham Hospital Burn Unit where he continues to see and talk to Andy, his popular, now deceased, friend.

4. Leavitt, Martine. **Heck Superhero.** Asheville, NC: Front Street, 2004. 144p. $16.95. ISBN 1 886910 94 4. [fiction] MJ, CG with high interest for boys (See full booktalk in *Booktalks and Beyond,* 2007, pages 28 to 30.) Thirteen-year-old Heck, abandoned by his depression-prone mother, deals with surviving on the street by moving back and forth between real and comic book worlds and finally realizes that the coping method is unhealthy and unwise.

5. Poe, Edgar Allan. Michael McCurdy (illus.). **Tales of Terror.** New York: Alfred A. Knopf, 2005. 89p. $15.95. ISBN 0 375 83305 6. [fiction] S/A, CG This Poe collection, accompanied by a CD and illustrated with stark black-and-white pictures, includes "The Masque of the Red Death," "The Black Cat," "The Pit and the Pendulum," "The Tell-Tale Heart," "The Cask of Amontillado," and "The Fall of the House of Usher."

ℭℑℜ

Levin, Betty. The Unmaking of Duncan Veerick.

Asheville, NC: Front Street, 2007. 212p. $16.95. ISBN-13: 978 1 932425 96 3. [fiction] MJ, CG with high interest for boys

Themes/Topics: old-age, friendship, swindlers and swindling, conduct of life

Summary/Description

When an elderly neighbor has a stroke, thirteen-year-old Duncan is sent by his parents to her home to check the house and help her. Her nephew arrives and hires Duncan and a neighbor girl, Tracy, to take inventory of all the items left over from the salvage business owned by the woman's deceased husband. The elderly neighbor suspects that her nephew is stealing several of the items that are rare and now illegal to trade. She instructs Duncan to take some and hide some. He stores part of the inventory in the shed, which burns down. The woman suffers another stroke. Duncan is a prime suspect for arson and theft. Tracy supports him in revisiting the area and the details. He figures out that the nephew sold the objects and then reported them to the insurance company as burned. In the final chapter, Duncan stands on the front porch of the woman's now empty house and trumpets the song she requested as her send-off, "When the Saints Go Marching In."

Read Aloud/Reader Reaction

The chapters are designated only by page numbers.
1. Pages 55 to 56, beginning "When Duncan walked up the road..." and ending with the chapter. Duncan meets Eddie for the first time.
2. Page 80, beginning "'Duncan,' she said..." and ending with the chapter. Astrid asks Duncan to play "When the Saints Go Marching In" at her funeral.
3. Pages 107 to 112. In this chapter, Duncan tries to follow his good instincts about the situation but is overruled by adults.
4. Pages 117 to 120. In this chapter, Tracy and Duncan wrestle the mummy.
5. Pages 198 to 199. In this chapter, Duncan reflects on how the situation has changed his life.

Booktalk

Thirteen-year-old Duncan has a life. He goes to school, has friends, and is learning how to play the trumpet. His parents think he doesn't have a life. They volunteer him to help an elderly neighbor, Astrid Valentine, after she has a stroke. It isn't enough that he takes care of the dog and looks after the house while she is in the hospital. Now he is supposed to do odd jobs for her—on command. Things aren't too bad until the nephew shows up. He wants Duncan to inventory all the old stuff that Astrid saved from her husband's salvage business. And the stuff includes more than old doorknobs and hinges. Some of it, like the bones, is downright creepy. Some of it, like the body from Peru, is illegal. Then items start to disappear. Maybe Duncan forgets and leaves a doorknob or a bone in his pocket once in a while, but Astrid is worried about more than those trifles. She pleads with Duncan to hide her things, the most valuable and the most dangerous, before her nephew makes them disappear. He agrees, and that unfortunate decision turns out to be *The Unmaking of Duncan Veerick*.

Get Involved

1. (Research) Using your library resources, find out as much as possible about mummies. Act as a resource person for your group.
2. (Research) As a mystery writer, Levin uses "red herrings." Find the definition of red herrings. Act as a resource person during the class discussion.
3. (React) Both Duncan and his mother feel that Duncan is greatly changed by the end of the novel. Do you like Duncan better at the beginning or at the conclusion of the story? Be sure to support your answer with specifics from the text.
4. (React) Who do you think is the most important character, besides Duncan, in the story? Support your answer with specifics from the text.
5. (Create) Arrange a display of books from your library that deal with salvage and salvage expeditions.

Related Works

1. Abrahams, Peter. **Down the Rabbit Hole: An Echo Falls Mystery.** New York: HarperCollins Publishers/Laura Geringer Books, 2005. 375p. $16.89. ISBN 0 06 073702 6. [fiction] MJ, G (See full booktalk in *Booktalks and Beyond,* 2007, pages 111 to 114.) Eighth-grader Ingrid Levin-Hill solves a local murder by using the methods of Sherlock Holmes.
2. Harrison, Michael. **Facing the Dark.** New York: Holiday House, 2000. 128p. $15.95. ISBN 0 8234 1491 4. [fiction] MJS, CG with high interest for boys (See full booktalk in *Teen Genre Connections,* 2005, pages 135 to 137.) An accused murderer's son and the victim's daughter join forces to solve the crime according to the methods of Hercule Poirot.
3. Hiaasen, Carl. **Flush.** New York: Alfred A. Knopf, 2005. 263p. $16.95. ISBN 0 375 82182 1. [fiction] MJ, CG with high interest for boys (See full booktalk in *Booktalks and Beyond,* 2007, pages 121 to 123.) A brother and sister team proves that a gambling boat pours raw sewage into the Florida waters.

4. konigsburg, e. l. **Silent to the Bone.** New York: Atheneum Books, 2000. 261p. $16.00. ISBN 0 689 83601 5. [fiction] MJS, CG with high interest for boys (See full booktalk in *Booktalks and More,* 2003, pages 151 to 152.) A teenage sleuth constructs a language so that he and his friend can work together and save the friend from child abuse charges.

5. Malam, John. Dr. Joann Fletcher (consultant). **Mummies and the Secrets of Ancient Egypt.** New York: DK Publishing, Inc., 2001. 96p. $14.95. ISBN 0 7894 7975 3. [nonfiction] MJS, CG with high interest for boys. Explaining the deities and beliefs that produced the mummy, Malam includes graphic descriptions of mummy preparation and meaning.

ᛯᛰ

Schmidt, Gary D. First Boy.

New York: Henry Holt and Company, 2005. 197p. $16.95. ISBN 0 8050 7859 2.
[fiction] MJS, CG with high interest for boys

Themes/Topics: presidents, elections, politics, family, identity, courage, New Hampshire

Summary/Description

After his grandfather dies, fifteen-year-old Cooper Jewett learns that his grandparents adopted him after he was abandoned by his real parents, a politically ambitious couple who are now the President and First Gentleman, and that the family farm is heavily mortgaged to a neighbor. A senator, running for president, wants to capitalize on the political scandal, and, with the help of hired thugs and the local sheriff, pressures Cooper to travel with him and tell his story of abandonment and relative poverty. Cooper refuses. His house is burgled, and one of his barns is burned. The president's aide arrives and takes Cooper to meet the first couple who tell him that he will be hidden in a secluded cabin. Cooper escapes, and with the help of two elderly friends, returns home. The senator kidnaps him and tells Cooper that if he refuses to tell the story at a press conference, he will lose his farm and be turned over to social services. The senator misjudges the New Hampshire press. At the conference, the medical witnesses fail to corroborate the senator's claims. Cooper leaves under his friends' protection, and the senator promises to ruin him. Cooper stands guard that night and confronts the sheriff who attempts to burn the remaining barn. A reporter records the incident with pictures, and the publicity ruins the senator's presidential bid. Cooper returns to farm life. The community raises a new barn in the spring, well-wishers send enough money to pay off the farm and the barn, and the president's aide, admiring Cooper's guts, promises to take Cooper on a trip to Peru to see the bigger world.

Read Aloud/Reader Response

1. Chapter 3, pages 36 to 53. This chapter reveals the personalities of several characters, and Cooper's general environment.
2. Chapter 4, pages 60 to 72, beginning "The embers were still glowing..." and ending with the chapter. The passage illustrates Cooper's courage and maturity in the face of Mr. Searle, Senator Wickham's hired thugs, and Mrs. Pearley's illness and shock.
3. Chapter 6, page 110, beginning "You are..." and ending "...Cooper Jewett." Mrs. Hurd helps Cooper define himself, and Cooper repeats a modified form of that statement in Chapter 9, pages 177 and 178.
4. Chapter 7, pages 126 to 132, beginning with "Cooper had imagined..." and ending with the chapter. Cooper meets the president.
5. Chapter 8, pages 133 to 135, beginning with the chapter and ending "...that he's lying." Cooper realizes the difference between real love and ambitious alliance as he confronts the First Gentleman.

Booktalk

Fifteen-year-old Cooper Jewett lives on a farm in New Hampshire with his grandfather. His grandparents raised him after his own parents died in a car accident. That is the world that Cooper Jewett knows. Then his grandfather, who seems to have just a little cold, dies. Everything that Cooper thought he knew changes. His grandfather isn't really his grandfather, the family farm doesn't belong to him or the family, and his parents aren't dead. Cooper thinks that the best thing to do is to just keep milking the cows, take care of the farm, and stay awake long enough to go to school. Others disagree. Some want him to give up the farm. A senator wants him to campaign with him for president. The President and First Gentlemen want to talk to him. Some very big men in big, black, official-looking cars keep appearing in town. His barn burns down, his house is burgled, and he almost has his arm twisted out of its socket. It seems that Cooper, a teenager who doesn't even have a dog, might determine the direction of the nation. The stakes are high, and some very important people are willing to kidnap him, beat him up, or take what little he has left to win a presidential race. Cooper learned a lot about life on that quiet New Hampshire farm. Now he has to use what he learned to survive in another world that includes lying, cheating, and terrorism. Because now he is more than Cooper Jewett. Now he is also the *First Boy.*

Get Involved

1. (Research) Using your library resources, learn more about the presidential primary process. Prepare a graphic organizer depicting the process. Act as a resource person for the group during the discussion.
2. (Research) Using your library resources, investigate the importance of New Hampshire in presidential primaries. Act as a resource person for the group during discussion.
3. (React) Which supporting character had the most appeal for you?
4. (Follow-up) After reading the novel, what characteristics might you consider in voting for an elected official?
5. (Discuss) After reading the novel, try to list the qualities that you think might be important to the people of New Hampshire when they are selecting a candidate.

Related Works

1. Blackwood, Gary. **Second Sight.** New York: Dutton's Children's Books, 2005. 279p. $16.99. ISBN 0 525 47481 1. [fiction] MJS, CG Joseph Ehrlich, who shares a mind-reading act with his father, meets a young clairvoyant, who draws him into the political intrigue of Lincoln's assassination. In this version, Lincoln lives, and Joe learns more about himself, his father, and personal integrity.
2. Schmidt, Gary D. **Lizzie Bright and the Buckminster Boy.** New York: Clarion Books, 2004. 219p. $15.00. ISBN 0 618 43929 3. [fiction] MJS, CG (See full booktalk in *Booktalks and Beyond*, 2007, pages 251 to 254.) In the early 1900s, Turner Buckminster moves to Phippsburg, Maine, where he and his family confront the rigid expectations and prejudices of the community.
3. Schmidt, Gary D. **The Wednesday Wars.** (See full booktalk in "Contemporary"/"Learning about Love," pages 56 to 59.) A young man learns to make tough decisions as he bonds with his teacher, stands up to his father, and chooses his friends.
4. St. George, Judith. **In the Line of Fire: Presidents' Lives at Stake.** New York: Holiday House, 1999. 144p. $18.95. ISBN 0 8234 1428 0. [nonfiction] JS, CG St. George describes the assassinations of Presidents Abraham Lincoln, James Abram Garfield, William McKinley, and John Fitzgerald Kennedy. Each story is introduced by a brief narrative passage about an event a few hours before the assassination. In four parts, the text explains each president's

background, character, and politics, as well as the circumstances of his death; the assassin or assassins; the president's goals and policies; and the impact and implications of the assassination for the nation and the president's legacy. A fifth chapter includes the assassination attempts against Presidents Theodore Roosevelt, Franklin Delano Roosevelt, Harry S. Truman, Gerald Ford, and Ronald Reagan. The "Author's Note" briefly outlines the history of presidential protection.

5. Weaver, Will. **Full Service.** New York: Farrar, Straus and Giroux, 2005. 232p. $17.00. ISBN 0 374 32485 9. [fiction] JS, CG with high interest for boys (See full booktalk in *Booktalks and Beyond*, 2007, pages 257 to 259.) Fifteen-year-old Paul Sutton takes a job outside his religious community and finds challenges to his religious and family beliefs as well as his personal integrity.

Historical

Avi. **The Traitors' Gate.**

New York: Atheneum Books for Young Readers/A Richard Jackson Book, 2007. 351p. $17.99. ISBN-13: 978 0 689 85335 7. [fiction] MJ, CG with high interest for boys.

Themes/Topics: spies, family life, Great Britain, nineteenth century, conduct of life

Summary/Description

When his father is sent to debtor's prison, fourteen-year-old John Huffam takes on the responsibilities of contacting a distant, hostile relative for help, securing his sister's marriage, and finding out the reasons for his father's lies and the spies who hound the family. His father, who has gambled away his money, works in the Naval Ordinance Office where he copies ordinances specifications for cannon manufacturing. His photographic memory allows him to sell rifle plans to international spies, but the government finds out about his activities and pressures him to lure the possible purchasers into a trap. The housekeeper's brother (Ireland), the sister's suitor (France), and John's militaristic teacher (Russia) vie for the plans. A ragged street girl helps John but then steals the plans herself when she realizes that the sale will bring enough money to bring her father home from Australia. John retrieves them as she escapes, and secures his father's freedom with the reward for his actions. John's money sets the family back on track, and John enters a better school. In the "Author's Note," Avi explains the connections between the story and the life of Charles John Huffman Dickens.

Read Aloud/Reader Response

1. Chapter 1, pages 10 to 18, beginning "The nature of this school..." and ending with the chapter. John describes his school and his difficulties with "Old Moldy," his teacher.
2. Chapter 13, page 93, the passage "...*The more a sailor...weather the gales*..." The clerk at the Naval Ordinance Office suggests that John needs to know more about his father.
3. Chapter 17, pages 110 to 118. The chapter reveals the father's duplicity and fears.
4. Chapter 35, pages 251 to 256, beginning "I walked down the nave..." and ending "'...to keep my distance.'" John meets Mr. Snugsbe.
5. Chapter 40, page 288, beginning "I'll tell you..." and ending "'...of a scoundrel.'" Mr. Tuckum listens to John's description of Old Moldy and agrees that he makes a likely suspect.

Booktalk

Fourteen-year-old John Huffam comes home from school one day in November 1849 and sees his family's possessions out on the street. His father is going to debtor's prison. Their belongings will be sold, and the family will join the father in prison. Suddenly, John is the man of the family. His mother, sister, father, and even the jolly bailiff taking them to jail expect him to solve the family's problems. His plain Jane sister wants John to ensure that she still has a suitor. His father wants John to petition Lady Euphemia Huffam, their distant and hostile aunt, to lend them the money for his debt. And the bailiff? Well, he seems to expect John to do something more than pay the debt, but John can't figure out what that is. He also can't figure out why the Irish Mr. O'Doul wants John's father in prison in the first place, why his sister's French suitor is so interested in the job of John's father, or why a strange Mr. Copperfield appears with dire warnings. As John tries to meet everyone's expectations, he gradually discovers that his father has another life. It deals in gambling and secrets for sale. Secrets that can take lives and control countries. Now they are becoming John's secrets too. Many strangers would like to share his burden, his secrets. A street-wise, ragged girl named Sary the Sneak knows all the strangers. Can he trust her? Or is everyone he meets leading him carefully and skillfully into treason and death through *The Traitors' Gate*?

Get Involved

1. (Research) Using your library resources, research Charles Dickens and his writing. Act as a resource person during the discussion.
2. (Research) Using your library resources, research the debtor's prison of nineteenth-century England. Act as a resource person during the discussion.
3. (React) Choose your favorite character. Explain your choice, and compare your choice with those of others in the group.
4. (Discuss) Mr. Snugsbe describes his life and John's job in terms of a coat. How does the coat idea apply to the rest of the novel?
5. (Create) Choose another piece of apparel such as a wallet, a ring, or a shoe. Use it to describe a person's life as Mr. Snugsbe uses his coat.

Related Works

1. Altman, Steven-Elliot, and Michael Reaves. Bong Dazo (illus.). **The Irregulars...in the Service of Sherlock Holmes.** Milwaukee, OR: Dark Horse Books, 2005. 126p. $12.95. ISBN 1 59307 303 8. [graphic] MJS, CG with high interest for boys. A band of street children penetrate an underground other world as they help clear the name of falsely accused Mr. Watson.
2. Dickens, Charles. George Stade (ed.). **David Copperfield.** New York: Barnes and Noble Classics, 2003. 742p. $7.95pa. ISBN-13: 978 1 59308 063 1. [classic] JS/A, CG Written in 1849 to 1850, this novel was a favorite of Dickens because it reflected his own rags to riches life. The hero of *Traitors' Gate* faces similar challenges.
3. Hausman, Gerald, and Loretta Hausman. **Escape from Botany Bay: The True Story of Mary Bryant.** New York: Orchard Books, 2003. 224p. $16.95. ISBN 0 439 40327 8. [fiction] JS, G Nineteen-year-old Mary Bryant, in 1786, is sentenced to hang for stealing a bonnet but is sent instead to pioneer in an Australian prison colony. Her arrest, journey, landing, colonization, escape, apprehension, return to England, and liberation all illustrate her integrity and bravery in the face of a cruel injustice system.
4. Lawrence, Iain. **The Convicts.** New York: Delacorte Press, 2005. 198p. $17.99. ISBN 0 385 90109 7. [fiction] MJ, CG with high interest for boys (See full booktalk in *Booktalks and Beyond*, 2007, pages 128 to 131.) Tom leaves his near-insane mother when his father is marched off to debtor's prison and begins a journey through the criminal system that eventually reunites him with his father on a ship to Australia.

5.   Updale, Eleanor. **Montmorency: Thief, Liar, Gentleman?** New York: Orchard Books, 2003. 233p. $16.95. ISBN 0 439 58035 8. [fiction] MJS, CG with high interest for boys (See full booktalk in *Booktalks and Beyond*, 2007, pages 131 to 133.) In 1875, Montmorency, a petty thief, gravely injured in an escape, is physically rebuilt by an ambitious surgeon. He reinvents himself as a dual personality, gentleman and criminal. This book is the first in the Montmorency series.

Kasischke, Laura. Feathered.

New York: HarperTeen, 2008. 261p. $17.89. ISBN-13: 978 0 06 081318 5. [fiction] S, G

Themes/Topics: spring break, friendship, missing persons, coming of age, Cancún (Mexico), rape, Maya mythology

Summary/Description

Three high school seniors travel to Cancún, Mexico, for spring break. The more experienced girl stays in the hotel area and bar to party. The two best friends, Anne and Michelle, withdraw from the party atmosphere and accept an offer from Ander, a middle-aged man, to tour Mayan ruins. Michelle sees Ander as the father she never knew and embraces the experience. Anne grows suspicious of Ander and arranges an escape, a ride for both Michelle and her with a group of "normal" looking boys. The boys take the girls to an isolated jungle road. Michelle knows that she has been drugged and warns Anne not to drink the water offered by the boys. Anne fights off her attacker, but is left on the road, and cannot rescue Michelle who is later raped and left naked in the jungle. Ander rescues Anne and begins the search for Michelle. Ten months later with the direction of Ander and Michelle's mother, Michelle is found living with a native tribe. She has amnesia and cannot speak. Finally, Anne reaches her by showing her a feather that Michelle gave to her on the day that they toured the Mayan ruins. The story is told in chapters that alternate between Anne and Michelle. The Mayan mythology suggests a parallel between the rights of passage in drunken parties and the ancient virgin sacrifices to Quetzalcoatl.

Read Aloud/Reader Response

Each passage cited is a complete chapter.
1.   Part 1, Chapter 7, pages 32 to 34. An incident of a dead baby bird is tied to the girls' arrival in Cancún, Mexico.

2. Part 2, Chapter 3, pages 104 to 108. Ander's story about Quetzalcoatl makes Anne fear him.
3. Part 2, Chapter 10, pages 137 to 140. Michelle identifies with the maidens willing to sacrifice themselves to Quetzalcoatl.
4. Part 3, Chapter 3, pages 174 to 175. Ander demonstrates his sensitivity.
5. Part 4, Chapter 8, page 228. Two sentences explain Michelle's situation.

Booktalk

Seniors Michelle and Anne are best friends. They are about ready to graduate and can't think of anything more exciting than a trip to Cancún, Mexico, on their spring break. Sun, fun, and boys. What's not to like? But when their flight arrives, the party life is just a little faster than they anticipated. They step back to watch the scene for a while, and they meet a middle-aged man with a strange accent. He sees they are alone and makes them an offer. He will take them on a tour of ancient Mayan ruins. At first they say no. After all, from the time they were small, their mothers told them not to talk to strangers. Then they say yes. And the next day they start a whole new vacation—one that will change them from little girls to women, one that will mean that they will never be innocent again. They try their wings. Their lives entwine with the dark mysteries of ancient Mayan rituals, and their senior trip becomes a horrific confrontation with evil. Suddenly, what was solid and familiar is gone. Now they have to survive in a world where they don't know the people or the language, and where the directions for right and wrong, life and death, are both fragmented and *Feathered.*

Get Involved

1. (Research) Using your library resources, continue to learn more about Mayan mythology. Act as a resource person during the discussion.
2. (React) Is the historical parallel appropriate?
3. (Discuss) Judge the characters' judgments.
4. (React) Is this novel just a scare tactic or an exploitation of headlines?
5. (React) How did you feel about Ander's question to Anne and Michelle in Part 1, Chapter 14: "Where are your fathers?"
6. (Create) Anne fantasizes about how this terrible experience will end. What do you think happens after the story? Compare your answer with others in the group.

Related Works

1. Anderson, Laurie Halse. **Speak.** New York: Farrar, Straus and Giroux, 1999. 198p. $16.00. ISBN 0 374 37152 0. [fiction] JS, G (See full booktalk in *Booktalks and More*, 2003, pages 75 to 77.) After Melinda Sordino is raped, she withdraws until a teacher and two students draw her out by advice and example. When she finally tells, her life changes positively.

2. Dogar, Sharon. **Waves.** New York: Scholastic, Inc./Chicken House, 2007. 344p. $16.99. ISBN-13: 978 0 439 87180 8. [fiction] S, CG The Ditton family decides to go to their summer vacation home even though sixteen-year-old Charley, the oldest daughter, lies in an irreversible coma, from a vacation injury from the year before. Her brother, fifteen-year-old Hal, receives telepathic messages from Charley who wants to tell about the love and violence that caused her accident.

3. Green, John. **Looking for Alaska.** New York: Dutton Books, 2005. 224p. $15.99. ISBN 0 525 47506 0. [fiction] S, CG (See full booktalk in *Booktalks and Beyond*, 2007, pages 37 to 40.) Sixteen-year-old Miles Halter, bored and isolated in his local high school, attends his father's alma mater, Culver Creek, and finds a more complicated society filled with choices about drugs, alcohol, and sex. Three students support and befriend him and sort through their sometimes destructive alternatives.

4. Vance, Susanna. **Deep.** New York: Delacorte Press, 2003. 272p. $15.95. ISBN 0 385 73057 8. [fiction] MJS, G (See full booktalk in *Teen Genre Connections*, 2005, pages 123 to 125.) An indulged thirteen-year-old girl and a street-wise seventeen-year-old girl cooperate to escape a serial killer and then secure his arrest.

5. West, David. Mike Taylor (illus.). **Mesoamerican Myths.** New York: The Rosen Publishing Group, Inc./Rosen Central, 2006. 48p. (Graphic Mythology). $29.25. ISBN 1 4042 0802 X. [graphic] MJS, CG with high interest for boys. This presentation of Mesoamerican myths includes three myths that explain the creation of the world; the creation of the sun, moon, and people; and the Hero Twins. The first two are labeled Aztec, and the third is Mayan.

ᏨᏫ

konigsburg, e. l. The Mysterious Edge of the Heroic World.

New York: Atheneum Books for Young Readers/Ginee Seo Books, 2007. 244p. $16.99. ISBN-13: 978 1 4169 4972 5. [fiction] M, CG

Themes/Topics: friendship, art world, Nazi Germany,
heroism, family secrets

Summary/Description

Amedeo Kaplan and William Wilcox both attend Lancaster Middle
School in St. Malo, Florida. Amedeo and his mother just moved
into town. William and his mother run an estate sale business. Amedeo
begins to work with them because he is fascinated by Mrs. Zender, the
owner of a deteriorating house. His dream is to discover something valuable or significant. Mrs. Wilcox and William have contracted to help
Mrs. Zender downsize to a retirement home. Each of Mrs. Zender's possessions has a story that she tells, but she also listens to the boys' conver-
sations and knows Amedeo's wish to discover something. She allows him
to find a sketch, a wedding gift from her Austrian husband, which proves
to be a piece of "decadent" art seized by the Nazis in exchange for safe
passage for the recently deceased father of Amedeo's godfather who is
now a museum director. The father's memoirs tell about his brother, an
art dealer and homosexual, who gave his own life so that his orphaned
younger brother could leave Germany during the Holocaust.

Read Aloud/Reader Response

1. Chapter 5, pages 52 to 59, beginning "'When Mrs. Zender…'" and
    ending "…took the dishes." Amedeo and William discuss the prob-
    lems of the rich and their own financial situations.
2. Chapter 7, pages 70 to 71, beginning "When Mrs. Wilcox…" and
    ending "…subconscious anger." The passage explains how the sale
    of the screen changed Mrs. Wilcox's situation with Bert and Ray.
3. Chapter 9, pages 102 and 103, beginning "Ninety percent…" to the
    end of the chapter. Mrs. Zender explains that we can see only ten
    percent of who a person is.
4. Chapter 18, pages 186 to 187, beginning "There was a lot…" and
    ending "…quiet dignity." Mrs. Zender is described as a bond be-
    tween the two boys.
5. Chapter 19, pages 218 to 219, beginning "*It was the Nazis…*" and
    ending "…*good brother.*" The narrative about the brother's heroism
    reflects on the inaccurate labels used by the Nazis.

Booktalk

A new town, an old house, a possible friend. These are the three things
that push twelve-year-old Amedeo to introduce himself to William, the
quiet, aloof classmate who can walk, without knocking, into the most interesting house in town. Amedeo seems to think that the house and the

lady who lives there will give him the opportunity he dreams of, the opportunity to discover something lost, valuable, and important. And he is right. Mrs. Zender is downsizing because even the wealthy can't hire good people anymore. William and his mother have contracted to help her. When Amedeo joins them, the three find themselves sorting wall-to-wall possessions. And the job becomes even more complicated because Mrs. Zender has a story for each item. And when Amedeo makes his big discovery, he opens the book not only of a valuable piece of lost art but also of a tragic story that takes them all to *The Mysterious Edge of the Heroic World.*

Get Involved

1. (Research) Using your library resources, continue to learn as much as possible about Decadent Art in Hitler's Germany. Act as a resource person during the discussion. Be sure to have pictures of the art with you.
2. (Research) Using your library resources, continue to research the undesirable labels used in Hitler's Germany and the use of those same labels outside of Hitler's Germany. Act as a resource person during the group discussion.
3. (Discuss) What was the most interesting part of the memoir written by Peter's father?
4. (Discuss) Point out some of the flaws of the various characters. Why do you think that konigsburg uses so many flawed characters in her story?
5. (Follow-up) *The Mysterious Edge of the Heroic World* is a sequel to *The Outcasts of 19 Schuyler Place* (Related Work 2) and *Silent to the Bone* (Related Work 3), but many readers would not realize that they are connected. After reading all three books, discuss the connections among the three books.

Related Works

1. Giblin, James Cross. **The Life and Death of Adolf Hitler.** New York: Clarion Books, 2002. 246p. $21.00. ISBN 0 395 90371 8. [nonfiction] MJS, CG (See full booktalk in *Teen Genre Connections,* 2005, pages 250 to 252.) Giblin portrays a disturbed and dedicated individual who, with an exceptional gift for politics and speech making, appealed to the prejudices and fears of the German people after World War I.
2. konigsburg, e. l. **The Outcasts of 19 Schuyler Place.** New York: Atheneum Books for Young Readers, 2004. 296p. $16.95. ISBN 0 689 86636 4 [fiction] MJS, G (See full booktalk in *Booktalks and*

Beyond, 2007, pages 199 to 202.) A woman recalls the summer of 1983 when she was twelve and helped her uncles save three giant towers they built for forty-five years.

3. konigsburg, e. l. **Silent to the Bone.** New York: Atheneum Books, 2000. 261p. $16.00. ISBN 0 689 83601 5. [fiction] MJS, CG with high interest for boys (See full booktalk in *Booktalks and More,* 2003, pages 151 to 152.) An extremely intelligent teenager accused of hurting his baby sister loses his power of speech.

4. Nir, Ycluda. **The Lost Childhood: A World War II Memoir.** New York: Scholastic Press, 2002. 288p. $16.95. ISBN 0 439 16389 7. [nonfiction] JS, CG This memoir of a Polish Jew explains the massacre of the Jews by the Nazis and Ukrainians, his own disguise as a Catholic, and life in German work camps.

5. Spinelli, Jerry. **Milkweed.** New York: Alfred A. Knopf, 2003. 208p. $15.95. ISBN 0 375 81374 8. [fiction] JS, CG (See full booktalk in *Teen Genre Connections,* 2005, pages 240 to 243.) The approximately eight-year-old gypsy narrator lives on the streets, steals to survive, and survives the Holocaust, although he tries to follow his Jewish friend to the ovens. In his adult life, he feels compelled to tell his story repeatedly.

Lisle, Janet Taylor. **Black Duck.**

New York: Philomel/Sleuth, 2006. 252p. $15.99. ISBN 0 399 23963 4. [fiction]
MJS, CG with high interest for boys

Themes/Topics: Prohibition, friendship, adventure, gangsters, Newport, twentieth century

Summary/Description

When fourteen-year-old Ruben Hart and Jeddy McKenzie find a man's body on the beach, the boys become embroiled in a conflict between rival Prohibition bootleggers. Ruben inadvertently picks up a fifty-dollar bill torn in half, a "ticket" that will pick up the payload. After the beach incident, Ruben is interested in possibly cashing it in, and realizes that Jeddy, firmly on the side of the police, is pulling away from him. Jeddy's sister, Marina, loves Billy Brady, the captain of the *Black Duck,* a legendary, elusive bootlegging transport. A traitor joins the *Black Duck* crew on the night that Ruben finally sails with them. The spy informs Jeddy who calls the Coast Guard. All the crew, with the exception of Ruben and one other man, are killed. Ruben carries the news of Billy's death to Jeddy's sister, Marina, whom he secretly loves. Ruben eventually marries Marina but never tells her of Jeddy's betrayal.

Read Aloud/Reader Response

1. "Tom Morrison," pages 73 to 75, beginning "Well, you know, what…" and ending with the chapter. Jeddy's story about Marina and Charlie reveals that her father blames her in any problem that she might have with a boy or man.
2. "The Killers Return," page 84, beginning "Life wasn't being…" and ending with the chapter. Ruben reflects on Tom Morrison's life.
3. "The Breakup," pages 111 and 112, beginning "Jeddy didn't look…" and ending "…as we'd sworn to do." Ruben reflects on the moment between Jeddy and him that could have prevented a tragedy.
4. "The Squeeze," pages 116 to 117, beginning "I couldn't help…" and ending "…have used his help." Ruben encounters his father being dishonest for the first time.
5. "The Last Interview," page 245, beginning *What happened then?*" and ending "…*do what was right.*" Ruben assesses the reasons that Jeddy reported the *Black Duck.*

Booktalk

Ask how many in the group have ever heard of Prohibition and the Depression. Invite them to share what they know with the group.

A dead man in an evening suit. That's what fourteen-year-old Ruben Hart and Jeddy McKenzie find one night while they are walking the beach and looking for lobster pots. The two are best friends The year is 1929, and they know that the dead man is probably a bootlegger. Smuggling liquor from Canada is a fast and dangerous way to make money. And the dark hole in the man's neck, probably a bullet hole, says that chances are that he didn't just fall overboard. They inform the police, and take something off the body, just a souvenir. Then the body disappears, and people, dangerous people, start to show up looking for a "ticket" that the man had when he died. The ticket could give the holder a fortune in stolen goods. Jeddy's father is the police chief. That should give them protection, but maybe not. Maybe lots of quiet citizens are making some money too. If enough people have a lot to lose, protection could be impossible. And one of the smugglers is a local hero, a teenager. If he helps them use the ticket, he could give both Ruben and Jeddy more money and more excitement than they ever could hope for. Life is offering a wild and dangerous ride. The name of the boat is the *Black Duck,* no destination or satisfaction guaranteed.

Get Involved

1. (Research) Find out more about Prohibition. Act as a resource person during the discussion.
2. (Research) Find out more about the Great Depression. Act as a resource person during the discussion.
3. (Discuss) Both Chief McKenzie and Tom Morrison face grief and trouble in their lives. Compare how those situations affect each man.
4. (React) With which of Ruben's decisions do you agree? Disagree?
5. (React) With which of Jeddy's decisions do you agree? Disagree?
6. (Discuss) How central is Marina to the story?
7. (React) Did you think that the interview format strengthened or weakened the story?

Related Works

1. Beyer, Mark. **Temperance and Prohibition: The Movement to Pass Anti-liquor Laws in America.** New York: The Rosen Publishing Group, Inc./Primary Source/Rosen Central, 2006. 32p. (The Progressive Movement 1900–1920: Efforts to Reform America's New Industrial Society). $23.95. ISBN 1 4042 0195 5. [reference] MJ, CG Beyer briefly explains why Prohibition came about and why it ended.
2. Gallo, Donald R. (ed.). **Time Capsule: Short Stories about Teenagers throughout the Twentieth Century.** New York: Delacorte Press, 1999. 221p. $16.95. ISBN 0 385 32675 0. [short stories] JS, CG Ten stories focus on the ten decades of the twentieth century. "Bootleg Summer" by Will Weaver on pages 39 to 59 tells how the sheriff uses a young man as a pigeon in a bootleg run in which two men are killed.
3. Kupperberg, Paul (ed.). **Critical Perspectives on the Great Depression.** New York: The Rosen Publishing Group, 2005. 176p. $30.60. ISBN 1 4042 0061 4. [reference] JS, CG This collection of articles depicts the people, government, institutions, culture, and end of the Great Depression. It explains how the New Deal, by ending Prohibition, increased government revenue and decreased crime.
4. Newton, Robert. **Runner.** (See full booktalk in "History"/"Growing," pages 230 to 233.) In 1919, fifteen-year-old Charlie Feehan makes liquor runs for a crime boss so that he can support his newly widowed mother and baby brother.
5. Weaver, Will. **Full Service.** New York: Farrar, Straus and Giroux, 2005. 232p. $17.00. ISBN 0 374 32485 9. [fiction] JS, CG (See full booktalk in *Booktalks and Beyond*, 2007, pages 257 to 259.) When Paul begins working in a service station, he meets a mixture of local

sports heroes, gangsters, law breakers, and hippies who challenge the standards of his fundamentalist community.

ᕙᕗ

Selznick, Brian. **The Invention of Hugo Cabret.**
New York: Scholastic Press, 2007. 544p. $22.99.
ISBN-13: 978 0 439 81378 5. [fiction] M, CG

Themes/Topics: orphans, theft, automaton, magic, movies, Georges Méliès, Paris, 1930s

Summary/Description

Twelve-year-old orphan Hugo Cabret maintains the train station clocks. His alcoholic uncle, the paid employee, is gone. Hugo's father, who also built and repaired clocks, died in a fire while rejuvenating an automaton he found in the museum where he worked. After the fire, Hugo finds the automaton in the ashes. Using his father's diagrams, he decides to fix it. He steals supplies from an old toymaker at the station. The toymaker catches Hugo, takes the notebook containing the diagrams, and says he will destroy it. The toymaker's adopted daughter befriends Hugo, returns the notebook, and inadvertently supplies the automaton's start-up key. In their efforts and their love of movies, Hugo and the girl discover that the toymaker is Georges Méliès, a pioneer French movie maker who is thought to be dead. Their efforts renew his interest in the magic of film, and he, in turn, brings Hugo into his family. In this unique combination of text and illustration, part of the story is told completely in illustrations, which have the movement and depth of a silent movie.

Read Aloud/Reader Response

1. "The Thief," pages 1 to 61. The first chapter establishes the old man, the girl, Hugo, and the automaton.
2. "Secrets," pages 162 to 163, beginning "So I was right..." and ending with the chapter. The old man sets the conditions under which Hugo might win back his notebook, and Hugo surprises him by saying he has a job.
3. "The Invention of Dreams," pages 354 and 355, beginning "*The filmmaker...*" and ending "...face of movies." Hugo discovers the history of Georges Méliès.
4. "Purpose," pages 370 to 371, beginning "Isabelle read the stories..." and ending "There had to be something else." Hugo is delighted to learn that Prometheus, like him, is a thief, but feels there must be something more than punishment for daring.

5. "The Visit," pages 386 to 390, beginning "Madame Méliès…" and ending "…I can repay him." Monsieur Tabard explains how Méliès impacted his life.

Booktalk

Magic, movies, mystery, and a machine that writes all by itself. This book has it all and one more thing: pictures, hundreds of them. (*Flip the pages in front of the group as you speak.*) They don't just sit there and help us understand the words. They actually move the story along. These pictures make movies that don't move and graphic novels that don't talk. You have never been in a book like this before so you may need some help. Let Professor H. Alcofrisbas, magician extraordinaire, tell you what to do. (*Read "A Brief Introduction," page before Part One begins.*) Yes, Hugo Cabret has secrets. Some he doesn't even know he has. The ones he doesn't know are popping out to reveal some of the secrets he does know but would like to keep quiet. Any one of them could connect him to his dead father, get him a beating from his abusive uncle, lead him to new friends, get him arrested, or pull him into a world of endless dreams. What will happen? Pay close attention to both the words and the not-so-silent pictures in *The Invention of Hugo Cabret.*

Get Involved

1. (Research) Using your library resources and/or the Web site provided by Brian Selznick, find out more information about Georges Méliès and his contribution to film. Act as a resource person during the discussion.
2. (Research) Using your library resources, locate one or more of the films or information about the films listed on pages 530 to 531. Act as a resource person during the discussion.
3. (React) How would the application of the title change if you replaced *Invention* with another word?
4. (Discuss) How does Selznick use machines, magic tricks, and movies to tell the story?
5. (React) What happens to time in the story?
6. (Create) Choose a section of pictures and write text for them.
7. (Create) Choose a section of text and try to express it entirely in pictures.
8. (Follow-up) Plan a silent film festival.

Related Works

1. McCaughrean, Geraldine. **The Kite Rider.** New York: Harper-Collins Publishers, 2001. 272p. $15.95. ISBN 0 06 623874 9. [fiction]

MJS, CG with high interest for boys (See full booktalk in *Booktalks and Beyond,* 2007, pages 105 to 107.) Twelve-year-old Haoyou sees his father die when a ship's first mate ties the father to a kite to test the wind and predict the success of a voyage. He joins a circus, attaches himself to a kite as an act, rids himself of an exploitive uncle, saves his mother and sister from servitude, and eventually makes his living as a kitemaker.

2. Muth, Joh. **Zen Shorts.** New York: Scholastic Press, 2005. 36p. $17.99. ISBN-13: 978 0 439 33911 7. [fiction, picture book] CMJS/A, CG In this picture book, Stillwater, the panda, uses three stories that reflect the Zen philosophy to give three siblings a different perspective on the world. The first tells about a poor man who gives a robber gifts. The second warns that luck cannot be judged or predicted. The third deals with keeping burdens. An "Author's Note" answers the question "What is Zen?"

3. Park, Linda Sue. **A Single Shard.** New York: Clarion Books, 2001. 152p. $15.00. ISBN 0 395 97827 0. [fiction] MJS, CG (See full booktalk in *Teen Genre Connections,* 2005, pages 282 to 285.) Tree-ear, a homeless boy living in twelfth-century Korea, works for a famous, but bitter, potter to make up for breaking a piece of his pottery. Eventually he is allowed to learn the craft and accepted into the man's family.

4. Pullman, Philip (text), and Leonid Gore (illus.). **Clockwork: Or All Wound Up.** New York: Arthur A. Levine Books, 1998. 112p. $14.95. ISBN 0 590 12999 6. [fiction] MJS, CG (See full booktalk in *Booktalks and More,* 2003, pages 153 to 155.) Man and machine blend in this tale of a greedy apprentice and redeeming love.

5. Tan, Shaun. **The Arrival.** New York: Scholastic, Inc./Arthur A. Levine Books, 2007. 128p. $19.99. ISBN-13: 978 0 439 89529 3. [wordless graphic] MJS, CG with high interest for boys. The story, told completely in pictures, communicates the joy of arrival to a new country and how that joy is passed to others.

Paranormal

❧❧

Becker, Tom. **Darkside.**

New York: Orchard Park, 2007. 294p. $16.99. ISBN-13: 978 0 545 03739 6. [fiction] MJ, CG with high interest for boys

Themes/Topics: family roots, evil, weremen, vampires

Summary/Description

Twelve-year-old Ricky Thomas and fourteen-year-old Jonathan Starling are both stalked by bounty hunters from Darkside because each has one parent from Darkside and one from Lightside. Lightside holds "normal" people, and "Darkside" holds the evil and paranormal beings that Lightside people ignore. Jonathan's father is obsessed with returning to Darkside. He has spent most of Jonathan's life in mental institutions. During his father's latest hospital stay, Jonathan's house is attacked. The attack gives Jonathan access to his father's private library where Jonathan learns about Darkside. He travels there with his father's instructions to find Carnegie, a wereman (a werewolf who walks on two legs). Two Darkside citizens want Jonathan. One already has Ricky and wants the two boys to be torn apart by wild jackals in a Darkside-type circus act. The other, a vampire, regularly feeds on the blood of the patients in the hospital where Jonathan's father stays and in Lightside heads the investigation of the boys' disappearance from the Lightside community. Jonathan, Ricky, and Carnegie destroy the circus plan, and with the help of the vampire's maid, and a bumbling policeman, foil the vampire's plot to drain the blood from Jonathan's father and Jonathan.

Read Aloud/Reader Response

1. Chapter 3, pages 30 to 31, beginning with the chapter and ending "...was her name." Jonathan ponders the mystery of Mrs. Elwood and his mother.
2. Chapter 4, pages 47 to 49, beginning "But now he was here..." and ending "...began to cry." Jonathan enters the father's study and finds a picture of his parents.
3. Chapter 5, pages 60 to 63, beginning "According to the introduction..." and ending "...onto a piece of paper." Jonathan reads excerpts from *The Darkest Descent*.
4. Chapter 9, pages 108 to 111, beginning "Jonathan began to cough..." and ending "...tried to wriggle free." The passage describes Jonathan's initial search for Carnegie in Darkside.
5. Chapter 11, pages 131 to 135, beginning with the chapter and ending "'Come on.'" Carnegie gives Jonathan a tour and explanation of Darkside.

Booktalk

Fourteen-year-old Jonathan Starling has a pretty difficult life. He doesn't know his mother, and his father has been in and out of mental hospitals for as long as Jonathan can remember. So when his dad has another episode, Jonathan sees it as just more of the same. But this time things are different. This time Jonathan's house is attacked. This time Jonathan confronts the darkening that his father mumbles about. This time Jonathan is pursued by a woman with fluorescent pink hair and a perfume that puts him to sleep. This time he finds himself crossing over to a hidden part of London that is filled with vampires, werewolves, evil, and death. This time he is running into danger and running for his life in London's dirtiest secret, *Darkside*.

Get Involved

1. (Research) Using your library resources, learn more about werewolf and vampire lore. Act as a resource person during the discussion.
2. (Create) Draw some of the characters and setting described. Compare your images with the images of others in the group who have also drawn the characters.
3. (Discuss) Who is Mrs. Elwood, really?
4. (React) Does this fantasy contain any reality?
5. (React) Do you agree with the ending?

Related Works

1. Becker, Tom. **Darkside Book 2: Lifeblood.** New York: Orchard Books, 2008. 288p. $16.99. ISBN 978 0 545 03742 6. [fiction] MJ, CG with high interest for boys. Jonathan must solve a series of murders and find his mother before the descendants of Jack the Ripper find him.
2. Bunting, Eve. **The Presence: A Ghost Story.** New York: Clarion Books, 2003. 195p. $15.00. ISBN 0 618 26919 3. [nonfiction] JS, G (See full booktalk in *Teen Genre Connections*, 2005, pages 156 to 158.) Noah Vanderhost died 120 years ago at the age of seventeen. He calls himself a Presence rather than a ghost and haunts the church where he murders young girls who have recently experienced trauma.
3. Funke, Cornelia. **Inkheart.** New York: Chicken House, 2003. 544p. $19.95. ISBN 0 439 53164 0. [fiction] MJS, G (See full booktalk in *Booktalks and Beyond*, 2007, pages 162 to 163.) When Dustfinger, a mysterious and sinister stranger, arrives, twelve-year-old Meggie and her father Mo, whom Dustfinger calls Silvertongue, enter Mo's secret world of fictional characters where Meggie's mother disappeared.
4. Horowitz, Anthony. **Raven's Gate.** New York: Scholastic Press, 2005. 256p. (The Gatekeepers). $17.95. ISBN 0 439 67995 8. [fiction] MJ, CG (See full booktalk in *Booktalks and Beyond*, 2007, pages 138 to 141.) Orphaned fourteen-year-old Matt Freeman is sentenced to a

foster home in a town of witches and discovers his own supernatural powers.

5. Nix, Garth. **Mister Monday: Book One.** New York: Scholastic Press, 2003. 361p. (The Keys to the Kingdom). $5.99pa. ISBN 0 439 55123 4. [fiction] MJ, CG. In this first book of the series, twelve-year-old Arthur Panhaligon receives a magical key that pulls him into a parallel universe of monsters, mythical figures, and bizarre environments where he is expected to take on a hero's role and obtain all Seven Keys to the Kingdom.

6. Yancey, Rick. **The Extraordinary Adventures of Alfred Kropp.** New York: Bloomsbury, 2005. 339p. $16.95. ISBN 1 58234 693 3. [fiction] MJ, CG with high interest for boys. Fifteen-year-old oversized, no-confidence, orphaned Alfred Kropp steals a sword. He discovers that the sword is Excalibur, that he is the descendant of Lancelot, and that he has unusual powers and strength.

Brooks, Kevin. The Road of the Dead.

New York: Scholastic, Inc./Chicken House, 2006. 352p. $16.99. ISBN 0 439 78623 1.

[fiction] JS, CG with high interest for boys

Themes/Topics: family, gypsies, criminal conspiracy, bullies, fighting, death

Summary/Description

When fourteen-year-old Ruben Ford and his sixteen-year-old brother Cole travel to an isolated village to retrieve the body of his sister who was beaten, raped, and murdered, they discover her death to be the accidental result of a land-grabbing scheme and fight the perpetrators who want to drive them away or kill them. Ruben, who receives telepathic messages from his sister, insists on accompanying Cole, a bare-knuckle fighter like their gypsy father who is now in prison for manslaughter. The police will not release the body until the crime is solved. The brothers travel to the crime scene and encounter a gang of thugs pressuring the townspeople to sell their property for resort development. With the help of a gypsy colony called to the town in a vision, the two discover the reasons for their sister's death, defeat the gang, and find the murderer's body to take back to the police. By the end of the novel, the brothers have bonded. Ruben is tougher, and also receives telepathic messages from his now more sensitive brother Cole. Full of suspense, but also violence, the story requires a mature audience.

Read Aloud/Reader Response

1. Chapter 3, pages 23 to 24, beginning "He told me once…" and ending "…in their blood." Ruben recalls his father's stories and his gypsy roots.
2. Chapter 5, pages 82 to 83, beginning "Outside the hotel…" and ending "…stars on my own." The passage describes the village setting and the difference between the brothers.
3. Chapter 9, pages 152 to 163. The chapter illustrates the sadistic bullying that the brothers and gypsies face.
4. Chapter 10, page 175, beginning "Cole was quiet…" and ending "…what it's doing." The passage contrasts how the two brothers process information.
5. Chapter 11, pages 193 to 194, beginning "He sighed…" and ending "'…came out.'" Cole tells his "barrel of bees" dream.

Booktalk

Fourteen-year-old Rubin Ford hears his sister's voice. She is dead—brutally killed on a lonely trail. His sixteen-year-old brother Cole hears their mother's request to bring the body home so that the family can bury her. The police won't release the body until the murderer is found. Cole knows that may be never. After all, the Ford children are "breeds," half gypsy, and "breeds" just don't seem to count as much as "regular" people. So Cole decides to go to the scene and solve the crime himself. Rubin knows that he had better go with Cole. Otherwise, his tough and angry brother could wind up like their father, in prison for manslaughter. But the brothers discover that they may be looking for more than one murderer. They may be facing an entire gang, a gang with large amounts of money at stake. Gypsies are natural fighters, aren't they? Don't they have to be? So with brains, bare knuckles, grief, guns, knives, guts, and a little help from the unexplained, they start their strange and perilous journey that could leave them forever on *The Road of the Dead.*

Get Involved

1. (Research) Using your library resources, learn more about gypsies in relation to European history. Act as a resource person for the group during the discussion.
2. (Discuss) What causes the brothers to bond? Be sure to support your statements with specifics from the text.
3. (Discuss) How do you think Brooks establishes the brothers' enemies as evil?

4. (React) The relationship between Abigail and Vince is central to the story. Describe the relationship and then explain how you reacted to it.

5. (React) Does the story need gypsies? Defend your answer by using details from the text.

6. (React) In Chapter 12, Rubin observes, "My brother knew how to turn off his heart." Do you agree?

Related Works

1. Blackman, Malorie. **Naughts & Crosses.** New York: Simon & Schuster Books for Young Readers, 2005. 387p. $15.95. ISBN 1 4169 0016 0. [fiction] JS, CG (See full booktalk in *Booktalks and Beyond,* 2007, pages 16 to 19.) Sephy Hadley, a dark-skinned cross, and Callum McGregor, a light-skinned naught, become friendly and then romantically involved in a drastically segregated and prejudiced society.

2. Brooks, Kevin. **Lucas: A Story of Love and Hate.** New York: Chicken House, 2002. 432p. $16.95. ISBN 0 439 45698 3. [fiction] JS, CG with high interest for boys (See full booktalk in *Booktalks and Beyond,* 2007, pages 4 to 6.) Sixteen-year-old Caitlin McCann decides to help Lucas, a stranger with no friends, family, or last name.

3. Brooks, Kevin. **Martyn Pig.** New York: Chicken House, 2002. 240p. $10.95. ISBN 0 439 29595 5. [fiction] JS, CG with high interest for boys (See full booktalk in *Booktalks and Beyond,* 2007, pages 114 to 116.) Fifteen-year-old Martyn Pig decides to cover up his father's death and finds himself tied into exploitation and murder by an older female accomplice.

4. Dogar, Sharon. **Waves.** New York: Scholastic, Inc./Chicken House, 2007. 344p. $16.99. ISBN-13: 978 0 439 87180 8. [fiction] S, CG The Ditton family decides to go to their summer vacation home even though sixteen-year-old Charley, the oldest daughter, lies in an irreversible coma, from a vacation injury from the year before. Her fifteen-year-old brother, Hal, receives telepathic messages from Charley who wants to tell about the love and violence that caused her accident.

5. Zusak, Markus. **Fighting Ruben Wolfe.** New York: Arthur A. Levine Books, 2000. 224p. $15.95. ISBN 0 439 24188 X. [fiction] S, CG with high interest for boys (See full booktalk in *Teen Genre Connections,* 2005, pages 70 to 72.) The working-class Ruben brothers decide to fight for money and discover that their brotherhood is more important than the crowd's cheers.

ℭ℈℈℩

Knox, Elizabeth. Dreamhunter Duet.

New York: Farrar, Straus and Giroux/Frances Foster Books. [fiction] MJS, CG

Themes/Topics: family life, coming of age, creation,
conduct of life, parallel worlds

Dreamhunter: Book I.

2005. 365p. $19.00. ISBN 0 374 31853 0.

Summary/Description

Fifteen-year-old Laura and her cousin, Rose, will each attempt a "Try"
to become dreamhunters when they are sixteen. Laura's father and
Rose's mother, both part of prestigious, early twentieth-century families, are already dreamhunters. Laura's obviously troubled father is contracted by his government to dream punishing nightmares to disruptive
prisoners. He leaves before Laura's successful "Try," gives her a cryptic
message before he goes, tries to kill himself, mysteriously disappears,
and is declared dead. Laura, with the help of Nown, a servant her father
created from sand, refuses to accept the death, suspects a government
plot, and follows instructions her father left for her. She learns the "old
ways," reincarnates her father's servant, now her creation, and decides
to expose an elite dream audience to the horrible nightmare, the sensation of being buried alive, that drove her father mad. By the end of the
first book, Laura is in hiding, protected by the servant she has freed. Her
father returns and reunites with his brother-in-law, a famous filmmaker.

Read Aloud/Reader Response

1. "Prologue," pages 3 to 5. Laura's father dreams his healing dream
    for the audience of the Rainbow Opera but shelters them from the
    dream's dark turn that haunts him.
2. "A Talented Family," Chapter 3, pages 21 to 24, beginning with the
    chapter and ending "...embarrassed by it." The passage introduces
    the Hame history and the possible link between the old songs and
    creation or bringing forth.
3. "A Talented Family," Chapter 9, pages 67 to 69, beginning "His
    voice had acquired..." and ending "Remember that." Laura's father
    gives her the clues that she will need from the ancient times.
4. "The Try," Chapter 1, page 128, beginning "Now a curtain..." and
    ending with the chapter. Laura realizes that since she succeeded
    and Rose failed, their different talents have separated them.

5. "The Sandman," Chapter 4, pages 209 to 216, beginning "Laura
    slept for a..." and ending with the chapter. Laura establishes her
    relationship with the sand servant.

Booktalk

Laura Hame lives at the beginning of the twentieth century. Her family
is wealthy and famous, and soon she will have the opportunity to share
their wealth and fame. At sixteen, Laura will be eligible for her "Try."
She will attempt to enter the Place, a mysterious world her father accidentally fell into years before. Only the Place decides who will enter. It
doesn't judge by wealth, or family, or intelligence. Seemingly barren, it
is a mystical world full of dreams that just a chosen few can experience
and share with the world. If the Place accepts Laura, she will live like
both her father and her aunt, a celebrity on the edge of a world that looks
very much like ours. The public will pay her, pamper her, but never really understand her. And so the event is an opportunity that brings her
both joy and fear. Her famous father won't be there for that day. He is
now thin and distracted. His hands and mouth are bleeding. He talks
nonsense about the old ways. Government officials insist that he leave
with them immediately. His fame and wealth have become tangled with
dread and suffering. Should Laura reject her opportunity, a life that is
separating them, or should she pursue it even more? She might learn
about what haunts her father. But learning about what haunts him might
pull her into his overwhelming nightmare, the unpredictable, dangerous
world of *The Dreamhunter.*

Dreamquake: Book II.
2007. 449p. $19.00. ISBN-13: 978 0 374 31854 3.

Summary/Description

After terrorizing an audience with the buried alive nightmare, Laura
is hidden from the authorities by The Grand Patriarch and Father
Roy, who reunites her with her father. Rose, sent away to boarding
school, becomes friends with Cas Doran's daughter and spies on the
Dorans. Slowly, evidence emerges that Cas Doran plans to control
the government by slipping propaganda into dreams and subduing the
population with the Contentment Dream generated by imprisoned
dreamhunters. Laura, in trying to foil Doran, learns that the Place is
a Nown, a man-made creation. Opening the grave she finds there, she
discovers her son, an escaped prisoner from the future, who created
the Nown and destroys the Place. The dreams from the Place were
visions of her fate and the memories of his life. With the Place gone,

Doran's plan is defeated, and the evidence that the family gathered sends him to jail. Because of her extraordinary deeds, Laura changes her future and fate. She lives in a parallel world where she raises her son with her husband and extended family, including her son from the other future.

Read Aloud/Reader Response

1. Section I, "The Isle of the Temple," Chapter 5, pages 52 to 53, beginning "Faith doesn't mean..." and ending "...*sold* the truth." The Grand Patriarch explains faith.
2. Section I, "The Isle of the Temple," Chapter 7, page 62, beginning "Lots of people..." and ending "...have in common." Rose tells Laura that she must examine their likenesses instead of their differences.
3. Section II, "Foreigner's North," Chapter 5, page 111, beginning "She started to..." and ending "...sleepy with happiness." Laura reflects on her feeling for Nown.
4. Section III, "Summer and Christmas," Chapter 3, pages 156 to 157, beginning "When she and Laura were children..." and ending "'...*ever* catch up with her?'" Rose reflects on her responsibility to develop her own character.
5. Section VI, "Epidemic Contentment," Chapter 7, beginning "Rose scooted next..." and ending "...very old and lonely." Rose realizes that Laura must meet her own destiny.

Booktalk

Dreamhunter ended in a nightmare. Laura exposed the government's terrible secret. The government uses nightmares to control a prisoner's behavior—nightmares so horrible that the men see themselves clawing their way out of the ground. Now the whole world knows it, but they don't want to thank Laura for the revelation. They want to punish and terrorize her just as she terrorized them. She has to run and hide to save her life. But the government has even more sinister secrets. If they can control the minds of prisoners, they can do the same to their "law-abiding" citizens as well. They can even control the minds of dreamhunters like Laura, her father, and her aunt. Laura must choose. Will she stay in hiding and protect herself? After all, she has warned the world. Or will she go back to the two worlds she knows so well—her loving family and her powerful dreams? Both have defined her, and yet now they can never be quite the same. Should she turn to Nown, her new protector and guide, or should she search for a new dream, a dream that can change the worlds forever, even destroy them? She will not hide, not Laura. She will uncover those secrets. She will open up undiscovered ground. She will understand these dreams that she hunts, and she will create a *Dreamquake.*

Get Involved

1.   (Research) Using your library resources, learn more about the meaning of dreams. Act as a resource person for the group during the discussion.
2.   (Research) Using your library resources, learn more about the technology at the beginning of the twentieth century. Act as a resource person for the group during the discussion.
3.   (Discuss) After learning about the beginning of the twentieth century, consider why Knox selected this time period for her setting.
4.   (Discuss) What are the conflicts between the religious and secular worlds?
5.   (Discuss) How does the relationship between Laura and Rose change and develop throughout the two novels?
6.   (Discuss) How do the two families change and stay the same?
7.   (React) Are the men stronger than the women?

Related Works

1.   Pullman, Philip. **His Dark Materials Trilogy.** New York: Alfred A. Knopf. [fiction] MJS, CG with high interest for boys (See full booktalk in *Booktalks and More,* 2003 pages 161 to 166.)
     The Golden Compass. 1995. 399p. $20.00. ISBN 0 679 87924 2. Lyra, an orphan, discovers the identity of her parents, and as the lone reader of *The Golden Compass,* finds herself in a struggle between good and evil.
     The Subtle Knife. 1997. 362p. $20.00. ISBN 0 679 87925 0. Will, seeking his father, enters an alternative reality and meets Lyra. Together they find Will's father and Will's role in the universe as the keeper of *The Subtle Knife.*
     The Amber Spyglass. 2000. 518p. $19.95. ISBN 0 679 87926 9. As the new Adam and Eve, Lyra and Will use their powers to keep their two worlds separate.
2.   Shelley, Mary. **Frankenstein.** New York: Pocket Books, 2004. 352p. (Enriched Classics). $4.95pa. ISBN-13: 978 07434 8758 0. [classic] JS, CG with high interest for boys. Dr. Frankenstein creates a monster and realizes that he is responsible for and to his creation.
3.   Sleator, William. **The Last Universe.** New York: Amulet Books, 2005. 215p. $16.95. ISBN 0 8109 5858 9. [fiction] MJ, CG (See full booktalk in *Booktalks and Beyond,* 2007, pages 186 to 188.) Fourteen-year-old Susan and her dying sixteen-year-old brother, Gary, explore

a mysterious maze created by her scientist uncle. They discover, according to a theory of quantum physics, alternative worlds.

ɕʒɕ

Sleator, William. **Hell Phone.**

New York: Amulet Books, 2006. 237p. $16.95. ISBN 0 8109 5479 6. [fiction]
MJ, CG with high interest for boys

Themes/Topics: horror, Hell, cell phones

Summary/Description

Poverty stricken seventeen-year-old Nick Gordon buys a cheap used cell phone so that he can talk to his girlfriend. He begins receiving calls from Fleck, a man in Hell who forces him to bring him to earth, and Lola, a woman on earth who pleads with Nick to protect her from Fleck. Per Fleck's instructions, Nick contacts Trang, the phone's former owner who has tried to escape Fleck and Lola. As the phone gains more power over Nick, Fleck and Lola involve him in a plot to secure inheritance money for them and eventually set him up to kill the legal heir, a man who has begun dating Nick's girlfriend. Nick is found guilty of murder, dies by lethal injection, and goes to Hell where he reunites with Fleck, Trang, and the murder victim. Using the cell phone, the four attempt to escape Hell. Nick leaves successfully, hopes the innocent Trang broke away also, sells his story to the tabloid press, and continues his life with his understanding girlfriend.

Read Aloud/Reader Response

1. Chapter 5, pages 45 to 53, beginning with the chapter and ending with "...it was doing to me?" The phone gradually changes Nick.
2. Chapter 7, pages 66 to 81, beginning with the chapter and ending with "'...takes a lot out of you.'" Fleck arrives from Hell.
3. Chapter 10, pages 126 to 127, beginning "'You said you...'" and ending "'...beneath us somehow.'" Jen distinguishes between the words *fine* and *interesting*.
4. Chapter 14, pages 182 to 183, beginning "My lawyer made..." and ending "...out of the courtroom." Nick explains his sentence.
5. Chapter 15, pages 194 to 198, beginning with the chapter and ending "'Jealousy, perhaps?'" Nick meets Fleck and Trang in Hell.

Booktalk

Seventeen-year-old Nick Gordon doesn't have much money, but he would like to have a cell phone to get a little more personal talk time with his girlfriend. He buys a cheap used one and some minutes. Before he can get serious about making calls, he starts getting them. A threatening voice makes some very strange demands. A pleading, desperate voice begs Nick to save her. When Nick calls the phone's former owner to find out what is going on, the man tells him to throw the phone away immediately. Nick's girlfriend and her parents agree. But Nick wants to keep it. The phone is a puzzle, a mystery that Nick wants to solve. He soon discovers the price for that solution. Is Nick willing to pay the one painful automatic deduction for the unique long distance package offered by the *Hell Phone*?

Get Involved

1. (Research) Using your library resources, find as many images as possible of Hell to compare with Sleator's. Act as a resource person during the discussion.
2. (Create) Select a character or scene from the novel. Represent the character or scene in graphic format.
3. (Discuss) What does the novel say about justice and fairness?
4. (Discuss) Why is Trang an important part of the story?
5. (React) Do you agree that doing a wrong thing because you are trying to help another person is not really wrong?

Related Works

1. Rylant, Cynthia. **The Heavenly Village.** New York: The Blue Sky Press, 1999. 95p. $15.95. ISBN 0 439 04096 5. [fiction] MJS, CG (See full booktalk in *Booktalks Plus*, 2001, pages 53 to 54.) In this village between heaven and earth, souls who still have business on earth complete their tasks before moving on.
2. Sleator, William. **The Boxes.** New York: Dutton, 1998. 196p. $15.99. ISBN 0 525 46012 8. [fiction] MJ, CG (See full booktalk in *Booktalks Plus*, 2001, pages 189 to 192.) Anne Levi opens boxes left in her care and discovers a supernatural world and a new maturity and confidence.
3. Sleator, William. **The Last Universe.** New York: Amulet Books, 2005. 215p. $16.95. ISBN 0 8109 5858 9. [fiction] MJ, CG (See full booktalk in *Booktalks and Beyond*, 2007, pages 186 to 188.) Fourteen-year-old Susan and her dying sixteen-year-old brother, Gary, explore a mysterious maze created by her scientist uncle and discover alternative worlds that could mean health for Gary and death for Susan.
4. Soto, Gary. **The Afterlife.** New York: Harcourt, Inc., 2003. 161p. $16.00. ISBN 0 15 204774 3. [fiction] JS, CG (See full booktalk in *Teen Genre Connections*, 2005, pages 294 to 296.) Stabbed to death

in a restroom when he comments on a man's yellow shoes, eighteen-year-old Jesús, having grown up in a Mexican/Hmong Fresno neighborhood, moves from life to the after-life, sees how much his family loves him and wanted to protect him, realizes how much he meant to his friends, saves a life, and falls in love with seventeen-year-old Crystal, who committed suicide.

5. Zevin, Gabrielle. **Elsewhere.** New York: Farrar, Straus and Giroux, 2005. 277p. $19.95. ISBN 0 374 32091 8. [fiction] MJS, G (See full booktalk in *Booktalks and Beyond,* 2007, pages 188 to 190.) Liz, who dies in a traffic accident shortly before her sixteenth birthday, begins her new life in Elsewhere, a world where she becomes younger each day, learns about her spirit, and has the option of returning to earth.

Fantasy/Science Fiction/ Paranormal

Fantasy, science fiction, and paranormal stories make the unbelievable believable by combining magic, futuristic visions, and the unexplained with survival, adventure, mystery. The books tagged as girls' selections here, like selections in other genres, focus on love, mutual support, and talents. The boys' selections center on themes of mission, adventure, and sometimes, monsters. Both groups of books communicate that coming of age, whether in magical or high-tech worlds, is a mystical and unexplainable phenomenon.

Discovering Our Place

Carey, Janet Lee. **The Beast of Noor.**
New York: Atheneum Books for Young Readers, 2006. 497p. $16.95.
ISBN-13: 978 0 689 87644 8. [fiction] MJ, CG with high interest for boys

Themes/Topics: love, loyalty, restitution, redemption, conduct of life, coming of age

Summary/Description

Fifteen-year-old Miles Ferrell and his thirteen-year-old sister Hanna discover their own magic and strengths as they struggle to destroy the Shriker, a huge and raging beast of the dark woods. The Shriker was a brave and loyal dog until his master, an ancestor of Miles and Ferrell, betrayed him three hundred years ago. Defying his teacher of magic, Miles steals a spell that connects him to a parallel magical world. He becomes a shape-shifter and pursues the Shriker. Miles also becomes a powerful and violent Shriker. Hanna follows him and coaxes him away from the power he holds. Attacked by the Shriker, Miles's kindness instead of violence returns the Shriker to his loyal dog form, and the dog helps them return to the real world. Carey's "Author's Note" explains the story's inspiration and roots. A "Glossary" at the end of the novel defines unfamiliar words used in the text.

Read Aloud/Reader Response

1. "The Wild Hunt," pages 18 to 25, beginning "In the dimly lit cave…" and ending with the chapter. The grandfather tells the Shriker's story.
2. "Brother Adolpho's Garden," pages 92 to 100. Brother Adolpho discusses other worlds and the conflict of good and evil.
3. "Visitors from Afar," pages 301 to 303, beginning "Hanna led the guests…" and ending "blinked them back." Hanna learns that her mismatched eyes signal her special gifts.
4. "Essha, Hannalyn," pages 327 to 337. In this chapter, Hanna learns about Enoch.
5. "The Dog," pages 445 to 448. In this chapter, Miles finds the dog within the Shriker.

Booktalk

Fifteen-year-old Miles Ferrell and his thirteen-year-old sister Hanna are outcasts in the village of Noor. Miles studies magic and hopes, someday, to become a *meer*, a wielder of magic. His sister Hanna has one brown eye and one blue eye. She is already rumored to be a witch. At her birth, the mother's midwife was killed by the Shriker, a monster of the black forest. Three-hundred years ago this monster was a loyal dog. What changed him? His owner's betrayal. That owner was an ancestor of Miles and Hanna, so the villagers blame them and their family for the monster and the magic that keeps him alive. Now the beast has claimed a new victim, a beautiful young girl. Miles decides to end the dying and his family's shame. He steals a spell from his teacher and follows the monster into his magical retreat. But the magic proves as dangerous as the monster, and Hanna resolves to find and save Miles. To survive, both must confront their fears, faults, and family secrets, battles more dangerous than *The Beast of Noor*.

Get Involved

1. (Research) Using your library resources, learn more about the "phantom hound" legend that Carey cites in the "Author's Note." Act as a resource person during the discussion.
2. (React) List the truths from this fantasy that you feel can be carried into the real world. Use specifics from the text to illustrate your choices.

3. (Create) Illustrate the characters or settings in graphic format.
4. (Discuss) Should a personal journey or coming of age story be tied to a battle against a monster?
5. (Create) Write another chapter from the monster's point of view.

Related Works

1. Coville, Bruce, comp. and ed. **Half-human.** New York: Scholastic Press, 2001. 224p. $15.95. ISBN 0 590 95944 1. [short stories] MJS, CG (See full booktalk in *Booktalks and More*, 2003, pages 101 to 103.) Each story in this fantasy collection describes a person "like us, but not quite" who must decide how that difference will affect his or her relationship to the human world. Coville points out that each unusual character shares with the reader the universal journey of identity. Lawrence Schimel's poem, "How to Make a Human," defines humanity.
2. Funke, Cornelia. **Dragon Rider.** New York: Scholastic, Inc., 2004. 528p. $12.95. ISBN 0 439 45695 9. [fiction] MJ, CG with high interest for boys. An orphan and a silver dragon join with a host of fantasy characters and supportive humans to defeat the evil golden dragon and in the process find their homes.
3. Gardner, John. **Grendel.** New York: Vintage Books, reissue edition, 1989. 192p. $10.95pa. ISBN 0 679 72311 0. [fiction] S/A, CG The monster from *Beowulf*, whose life has been characterized by the "Shaper," tells his own story.
4. Napoli, Donna Jo. **Beast.** New York: Atheneum Books for Young Readers, 2000. 260p. $17.00. ISBN 0 689 83589 2. [fiction] JS, CG (See full booktalk in *Teen Genre Connections*, 2005, pages 171 to 173.) When Orasmyn, a young Persian prince, selects an imperfect camel for sacrifice, an animal who has suffered, the spirits punish him by changing Orasmyn into a lion, an animal banished from the kingdom. They wish him to learn, like the camel, about suffering. Only a woman's love can break the curse.
5. Wooding, Chris. **Poison.** New York: Orchard Books, 2003. 273p. $16.99. ISBN 0 439 75570 0. [fiction] JS, G (See full booktalk in *Booktalks and Beyond*, 2007, pages 176 to 178.) When the pharies steal her baby sister, sixteen-year-old Poison sets out to bring her back. In the journey, Poison discovers that she has the power to write the stories.

Hautman, Pete. Rash.
New York: Simon & Schuster Books for Young Readers, 2006. 249p. $15.95.
ISBN-13: 978 0 689 86801 6. [fiction] JS, CG with high interest for boys

Themes/Topics: self-control, individuality, football, artificial intelligence

Summary/Description

Bo Marsten, who, like other members of his family, has issues with self-control, lives in an antiseptic non-violent future society. When he is falsely accused of causing a skin rash in his school, his angry reaction results in his being sentenced to work in a Canadian tundra pizza factory surrounded by polar bears. Bo becomes part of an illegal football team formed by the factory's abusive manager. While Bo adjusts to his new life, Bork, an artificial intelligence that Bo created for his science project, becomes an independent entity and works to get Bo out of jail. His efforts cause the manager to release Bo to the tundra where he is almost killed by a polar bear. Rescued and sent back to his family, he realizes that he cannot exist in his structured, safe life and decides, with money provided to him by Bork, to leave home and play football in South America, a society that still allows risk.

Read Aloud/Reader Response

1. Chapter 1, pages 3 and 4, beginning with the chapter and ending with "...when he'd been drinking." Bo and his grandfather discuss the society's penal system.
2. Chapter 13, pages 57 to 60. In this chapter, Bo and his grandfather reflect on how longevity has affected the society.
3. Chapter 19, pages 85 to 92. In this chapter, Bo gets his first look at prison.
4. Chapter 27, pages 129 to 130, beginning with the chapter and ending "'Self-control'." Rhino illustrates to Bo how Bo can develop self-control.
5. Chapter 42, pages 213 to 214, beginning "That is not always..." and ending "...'are likely to'?" Bork explains his reason for not taking death seriously.
6. Chapter 49, pages 246 to 249. In this final chapter, Bo bonds with his grandfather and decides to leave home.

Booktalk

For Bo Marsten, our society is ancient history. He lives in a super-refined future. Gourmet pizza is $89.95. Plastic permanently replaced paper money long ago. McDonald's controls the prison system. Everything that could possibly hurt or upset someone else is outlawed, and people live well over a hundred—well, live may be an overstatement. Maybe we should say that people exist until they are well over a hundred. But Bo, like several members of his family, doesn't seem to appreciate a nice, quiet, risk-free life. Bo causes conflict. He gets angry, loses his temper, and hurts people. He goes completely out of control when his classmate falsely accuses him of causing a skin rash that is rapidly spreading throughout the population. He throws a punch and is on his way to the Canadian tundra where he will be making those expensive gourmet pizzas and defending himself from other violent prisoners and polar bears. Is there any hope for *his* future? Just his science project, an independent artificial intelligence named Bork who follows him to Canada. Bork is sure that he can get Bo released. Bo doesn't know if that is the good or bad news. Bork now looks much scarier than Bo remembers him to be, and Bork seems to be making some very questionable decisions. Considering the guards, the inmates, and the bears, Bo thinks peace, quiet, and risk-free looks better all the time. Sure, Bo would like to get out, but when and how are big questions. He just doesn't want to do something *Rash*.

Get Involved

1. (Research) Using your library resources, find one law intended to protect us in society. During the discussion, share the law and its purpose with the group.
2. (Discuss) How does each law mentioned in Get Involved 1 bring us closer to Bo's society or distinguishes us from it?
3. (Create) Try to recreate one scene from the novel in graphic form.
4. (Compare) Read at least one of the works listed in Related Works 1 through 4. How are they similar and different from the world described in *Rash*? Be sure to be specific.
5. (React) Which world would you have chosen either in *Rash* or in the worlds described in Related Works 1 through 4? Be sure to explain your choice.

Related Works

1. Adlington, L. J. **The Diary of Pelly D.** New York: HarperCollins/ Greenwillow Books, 2005. 282p. $16.99. ISBN 0 06 076616 6. [fiction] JS, CG (See full booktalk in *Booktalks and Beyond*, 2007, pages 178 to 181.) Fourteen-year-old Toni V is the runt of a work gang clearing land after a war and discovers the private diary of an upper-class girl who is marginalized and finally eliminated.
2. Anderson, M. T. **Feed.** Cambridge, MA: Candlewick Press, 2003. 235p. $16.99. ISBN 0 7636 1726 1. [fiction] JS, CG with high interest for boys (See full booktalk in *Teen Genre Connections*, 2005, pages 201 to 203.) In this world of the future, corporations

communicate news, advertising, and emotional reactions through the feed, a chip implanted in the brain.

3. Farmer, Nancy. **The House of the Scorpion.** New York: Atheneum Books for Young Readers/A Richard Jackson Book, 2002. 380p. $17.95. ISBN 0 689 85222 3. [fiction] JS, CG with high interest for boys (See full booktalk in *Teen Genre Connections,* pages 208 to 210.) Matteo Alacrán discovers that he is the seventh clone of a drug lord who will use Matteo's body parts to extend his 140-year-old life, but Matteo, with the help of his caretakers, escapes, finds new friends, and vows to return to save his country.

4. Philbrick, Rodman. **The Last Book in the Universe.** New York: The Blue Sky Press, 2000. 224p. $16.95. ISBN 0 439 08758 9. [fiction] JS, CG with high interest for boys (See full booktalk in *Booktalks and More,* pages 146 to 148.) In this novel, the world, void of thought, is ruled by gangs.

5. Sachar, Louis. **Holes.** New York: Farrar, Straus and Giroux, 1998. 233p. $16.00. ISBN 0 374 33265 7. [fiction] MJS, CG with high interest for boys. Stanley Yelnats is unjustly sentenced to the isolated and dangerous Camp Green Lake, where he discovers friends, riches, his family history, and his own identity.

෴

Klause, Annette Curtis. **Freaks: Alive, on the Inside!**
New York: Margaret K. McElderry Books, 2006. 336p. $16.95.
ISBN-13: 978 0 689 87037 8. [fiction] JS, CG with high interest for boys

Themes/Topics: freak shows, abnormalities, supernatural, reincarnation, adventure

Summary/Description

Abel Dandy, a normal child of a father with no legs and a mother with no arms, lives in Faeryland where people with physical abnormalities live and perform. He decides that his difference isolates him from this community, and he makes his way in the outside world. Miss Dibble, the Pixie Queen of Faeryland, gives him a gold ring with a turquoise that connects him to a mummy who was her lover in an earlier life and whom Abel has the ability to resurrect. Her spirit guides him to the freak show of Dr. Mink who secures his acts by manipulating adults and stealing and imprisoning children with abnormalities. Abel joins the show, and bonds with the adults. With their help, he rescues the children and brings the mummy back to life. In a final confrontation with the evil Mink, the positive people whom Abel met on his journey arrive. Mink is defeated. Abel and the "freaks" from Mink's show decide to live in Faeryland. The "freaks" bring the promise of new life to the show, and Abel hopes that one day he will learn to manage the business that supports these misunderstood humans he cares about. Some of the content may be considered controversial.

Read Aloud/Reader Response

1. Chapter 1, pages 4 and 5, beginning "Faeryland had formerly..." and ending "'...physiognomy.'" Abel describes Faeryland, his childhood home.
2. Chapter 4, pages 36 to 38, beginning "I went to my chamber..." and ending "...bread and cheese." Abel departs Faeryland after an encounter with the Pixie Queen.
3. Chapter 13, pages 121 to 129, beginning with the chapter and ending with "...have a career after all." Abel sees Dr. Mink's show and decides that he might have an opportunity to join them as a knife thrower.
4. Chapter 19, pages 202 to 203, beginning "A sigh bubbled up..." and ending with the chapter. Abel meets the mummy.
5. Chapter 30, pages 325 to 328, beginning "I was going home—..." and ending with the chapter. Abel reflects on how he has changed even though he is returning to where he started.

Booktalk

Ask what the term freaks *means to the members of the group.*

Abel Dandy is normal. He grew up in Faeryland, a town populated by "human oddities." His father has no legs. His uncle, his father's twin brother, has those legs growing out of his chest. Abel's mother has no arms. The girl who wants to date Abel has a body covered with fur. The rest of his family and friends includes dwarves, fat ladies, and Siamese twins. In 1899, "normal" people call Faeryland people freaks. One of the few ways that freaks can make a living is to show off their differences and build an act around them. They call it show business. In this world, Abel is dull, a failure. He leaves home to prove that a normal person can succeed too. On the road, "human oddities" and abnormal take on new meanings. The very human comforts of Abel's home are gone. He faces lies, violence, prejudice, and death. Physical differences may make a person look twisted, even shocking, but never as repulsive as the *Freaks: Alive, on the Inside!*

Get Involved

1. (Research) Continue to research sideshows and freaks in the early twentieth century. Act as a resource person during the group discussion.
2. (Research and Discuss) What makes a freak? You may wish to use library resources to research the word's history and etymology before discussing the question.
3. (Research and Discuss) Using your library resources, research the meaning of resurrection and reincarnation. How does each term apply to the novel?
4. (React) What is the relationship between appearance and performance in the novel? How does that relationship relate to your own life?
5. (Create) Abel emphasizes that each member of Faeryland has an act as well as a difference. Develop or explain your own personal "act" that makes you competitive.

Related Works

1. Gordon, Susan. **Meet the Mummy.** New York: The Rosen Publishing Group, Inc., 2005. 48p. (Famous Movie Monsters). $26.50. ISBN 1 4042 0273 0. [nonfiction] MJ, CG with high interest for boys. Gordon summarizes the movie and explains its place in the context of history and motion pictures. Other books in the series deal with *The Blob, The Creature from the Black Lagoon, Dracula, Frankenstein, Godzilla, King Kong, Wolf Man.*
2. Gruen, Sara. **Water for Elephants.** Chapel Hill, NC: Algonquin Books of Chapel Hill, 2006. 335p. $23.95. ISBN-13: 978 4 56512 499 8. [fiction] S/A, CG Ninety-three-year-old Jacob Jankowski recalls his life with the circus, which began, when, as an orphaned and penniless young man, he inadvertently jumped a circus train and entered a world of love, fantasy, and terror. The content and situations could be controversial for younger audiences.
3. Hearn, Julie. **Sign of the Raven.** New York: Atheneum Books for Young Readers/Ginee Seo Books, 2005. 336p. $16.95. ISBN 0 689 85734 9. [fiction] JS, CG (See full booktalk in *Booktalks and Beyond,* 2007, pages to 152 to 154.) Twelve-year-old Tom moves through a time gap and joins the world of eighteenth-century circus "freaks" or monsters.
4. Lawrence, Iain. **Ghost Boy.** New York: Delacorte Press, 2000. 326p. $15.95. ISBN 0 385 32739 0. [fiction] MJS, CG with high interest for boys (See full booktalk in *Teen Genre Connections,* 2005, pages 11 to 13.) Fourteen-year-old Harold Kline, an albino, runs away to join a circus managed by The Cannibal King who is also an albino.

5. Lerangis, Peter. **Smiler's Bones.** New York: Scholastic Press, 2005. 160p. $16.95. ISBN 0 439 34485 9. [fiction] JS, CG Minik, taken from his home by Robert Peary in 1897, becomes the only living Polar Eskimo in New York, for twelve years, and discovers that his hosts have kept his father's bones to display in a museum. Lerangis makes clear that the public considers the Eskimo visitors as oddities.

6. Weaver, Will. **Defect.** New York: Farrar, Straus and Giroux, 2007. 199p. $16.00. ISBN-13: 978 0 374 31725 6. [fiction] JS, CG Sixteen-year-old David Anderson has physical differences that others find repulsive, and he must decide to change them medically or embrace the person that he is.

Landon, Dena. **Shapeshifter's Quest.**
New York: Dutton Children's Books, 2005. 182p. $16.99.
ISBN 0 525 47310 6. [fiction] JS, G

Themes/Topics: fairy tales, identity, adventure and adventurer, voyages and travels, mothers and daughters, magic, shape-shifters, atonement, prejudice, balance

Summary/Description

Eighteen-year-old Syanthe, a shape-shifter, leaves her forest home to find the cure for the disease destroying her people. Syanthe is chosen because, as a twin, she was hidden at birth, and she avoided being tattooed by the priests. The tattoos turn to poison if the shape-shifters try to leave the forest. Syanthe agrees to the mission because her mother is mortally ill, and also because she feels an obligation to atone for her great-great-grandfather's betrayal that led to the shape-shifters' defeat and imprisonment. In her journey, she meets twenty-year-old Jerel, a tribal chieftain with his own magical powers. His men travel in a caravan to the capital where they hope to assassinate the king. The corrupt king drains the life from his subjects to extend his life unnaturally. Combining their powers, Syanthe and Jerel secure the medicine, assassinate the king, and rescue a young priest's apprentice. Jerel and Syanthe return to their respective kingdoms. Syanthe's return is in time to save her mother. Both Syanthe and Jerel are destined to be leaders in a new kingdom where powerful factions will vie for power, but they hope that their affection will reunite them someday.

Read Aloud/Reader Response

1. Chapter 3, pages 21 to 22, beginning "Master Ralyna, why can't we…" and ending "…let him heal on his own." As Ralyna teaches a class in healing, she points out the magic is not limitless and must be used carefully. Her explanation suggests that, in the real world, the same principles apply. One should help another to heal rather than expend all one's energies to heal completely for them.
2. Chapter 3, pages 25 to 28, beginning "When the king conquered us…" and ending "…strength of a promise." Ralyna explains the debt that Syanthe owes to the shape-shifters and shows her their original home that was lost by the betrayal.
3. Chapter 7, pages 68 and 69, beginning "I don't understand…" and ending "…just trying to survive." Dell explains the evil that priests must embrace to survive.
4. Chapter 8, pages 83, beginning "Syanthe, the reason the King…" and ending "…in order to survive." Jerel explains how the king uses metal to control the kingdom and how that control is related to the shape-shifters.
5. Chapter 11, page 115, beginning, "Why doesn't her ride…" and ending "…deny its existence." Jerel explains how Syanthe's magic is different from that of others.

Booktalk

Ask the group what they know about shape-shifters.

Eighteen-year-old Syanthe is a shape-shifter. All her life she has lived in the Carlbine Forest. Now the shape-shifter tribe is asking her to leave. Why? The forest, the tribe, the world, is afflicted with a wasting disease. The other shape-shifters want Syanthe to travel to the capital and bring back the cure. Why Syanthe? All the other shape-shifters wear tattoos. The tattoos become poisonous when the shape-shifters try to leave the forest. Syanthe was hidden from the priests at birth. She wears no tattoo. Only she can leave without the fear of instant death. Plus she owes her people a huge debt. Her ancestors betrayed the shape-shifters. The king used that betrayal to imprison them all. Syanthe has the freedom, and she has a debt to pay, but how? She has never left the forest. How can she possibly fool the priests and the king's spies? Perhaps, alone, she can't, but there is another traveler to the capital. Twenty-year-old Jerel, a stranger, also has magic and a mission. They meet and join forces. Soon both are moving to the capital. Both against the king. But the king has prolonged his life for hundreds of years. He has great power, too, and knows how to suck life from his subjects to lengthen his own. As they move toward the capital, do they move toward death? Can anyone, even the anointed Syanthe, have any hope of successfully completing the *Shapeshifter's Quest?*

Get Involved

1. (Research) Using your library resources, learn more about the legends tied to shape-shifters. Act as a resource person for the group during the discussion.
2. (React) List the talents of Syanthe. Then list the talents of Jerel. How do you think these talents complement each other?
3. (Discuss) How important is Matthe to the story?
4. (React) Are the family values in the story too strong? Support your opinion with details from the story.
5. (React) Do you agree with the priorities of Jerel and Syanthe? Support your opinion with details from the text.

Related Works

1. Bell, Hilari. **The Goblin Wood.** New York: HarperCollins Publishers, 2003. 294p. $17.99. ISBN 0 06 051372 1. [fiction] MJS, G (See full booktalk in *Booktalks and Beyond,* 2007, pages 150 to 152.) Makenna and Tobin, at first enemies, join forces and look forward to a life together while leading the goblin camp to a safe Otherworld.
2. Constable, Kate. **The Singer of All Songs.** New York: Arthur A. Levine Books, 2004. 304p. $16.95. ISBN 0 439 55478 0. [fiction] MJS, G Sixteen-year-old Calwin, who shares the responsibility of protecting her kingdom, joins forces with a young man who breaks into the kingdom. Together they defeat the powerful and corrupt Samos who wishes to be *The Singer of All Songs* and control the world's magic.
3. Farland, David. **The Runelords: The Sum of All Men.** New York: TOR Books, 1998. 479p. $25.95. ISBN 0 312 86653 4. [fiction] S/A, CG with high interest for boys. *The Runelords* drain the wits, stamina, and even beauty of their subjects to become the best in their kingdoms, but one man wishes to become the most brilliant, powerful, and beautiful so that he can command the entire world.
4. Farmer, Nancy. **The House of the Scorpion.** New York: Atheneum Books for Young Readers/A Richard Jackson Book, 2002. 380p. $17.95. ISBN 0 689 85222 3. [fiction] JS, CG with high interest for boys (See full booktalk in *Teen Genre Connections,* 2005, pages 208 to 210.) Matteo Alacrán, the seventh clone of a Mexican drug lord, avoids destruction and takes on the job of reforming his country's government.

5. Jennings, Patrick. **The Wolving Time.** New York: Scholastic Press, 2003. 208p. $15.95. ISBN 0 439 39555 0. [fiction] MJS, CG with high interest for boys. A young man and his parents, who are were-wolves, save the woman who is tortured to testify against them, and the four form a new family.

ʊʃʋ

Leavitt, Martine. **Keturah and Lord Death.**
Asheville, NC: Front Street, 2006. 216p. $16.95.
ISBN-13: 978 1 932425 29 1. [fiction] JS, G

Themes/Topics: death, self-sacrifice, terminal disease, unconditional love

Summary/Description

Sixteen-year-old Keturah Reeve becomes lost in the forest after following a legendary hart, realizes that death is near, and learns that Lord Death is a young, stern, but compassionate young man who allows her a reprieve if she finds her true love within a day. She does not complete her task, gains more reprieves, helps her two friends realize their true loves, convinces Lord Death to save specific lives in the town, including the life of her grandmother, and revives the spirit of her community, Tide-by-Rood. Eventually, Lord Death agrees to protect the entire town from the plague. For her efforts, she wins the admiration of the Lord's son who wishes to marry her and make her royalty. Instead, she chooses to marry Lord Death, the suitor she loved all along because she realizes how much beauty he brought into her life and how he loves her unconditionally. In her acknowledgments, Leavitt explains that writing this romantic/fantasy was a way for her to empathize with the journey of her sister who died at the age of eleven from cystic fibrosis.

Read Aloud/Reader Response

1. Chapter 1, pages 11 to 25. Both Keturah and Lord Death reveal their characters.
2. Chapter 3, pages 45 to 46, beginning "Grandmother..." and ending "...soul-and-heart love." The grandmother explains the relationship between love and death.
3. Chapter 3, page 52, beginning "We all know..." and ending "...we breathe with magic." Soor Lily explains how Lord Death gives her power.
4. Chapter 4, page 162, beginning "If untimely death..." and ending "...means of death." Death explains why death is random and illogical.

5. Chapter 12, page 173, beginning "I have observed..." and ending "...Tailor yourself." Keturah suggests to Gretta that love relies on appreciation rather than criticism.
6. Chapter 14, pages 208 to 209, beginning "I love her,..." and ending "...with their beauty." Lord Death and Keturah explain themselves to John.

Booktalk

(*Read the Prologue, page 9, aloud.*) Yes, sixteen-year-old Keturah tells a story. It is the story that she promises her audience, but there is a strange twist, a surprise that won't be equaled at the village fire for some time. Even the story-teller is not in control when the subject is death, and this story is about both the story-teller and death. That makes it more complicated. But it is not even as simple as that. It is a story that each of us, in some way, shares, in our past, present, and future. It starts out as an innocent journey into the forest and ends with some bitter and not-so-bitter truths and confusing conclusions—all because of the common, but magical, meeting of *Keturah and Lord Death.*

Get Involved

1. (Research) Using your library resources, find other personas that have been given to Death. Act as a resource person during your group discussion.
2. (Research) In the "Acknowledgments" on pages 215 to 216, Leavitt explains that she was inspired to pursue this book by the death from cystic fibrosis of her eleven-year-old sister. Learn more about cystic fibrosis or another disease that involves a long-term struggle. Share your information with the group during the group discussion. Discuss how this story reflects or mirrors the life of a person struggling with the long-term terminal disease.
3. (Discuss) Keturah cares deeply that all the people around her stay healthy and alive. Is this desire consistent with her own decision to be the bride of Death?
4. (React) Do you agree with Keturah's decision? Can you distinguish her decision from the suicide decision of John Temsland?
5. (React) List what you feel Keturah learns about living in her journey to Death.

Related Works

1. Albom, Mitch. **The Five People You Meet in Heaven.** New York: Hyperion, 2003. 196p. $19.95. ISBN 0 7868 6871 6. [fiction] JS/A, CG (See full booktalk in *Booktalks and Beyond,* 2007, pages 35 to 37.) Eighty-three-year-old Eddie dies saving a little girl's life during

an amusement park accident and his journey to the after-life includes visits to five people central to his after-life.

2. Almond, David. **Skellig.** New York: Delacorte Press, 1999. 182p. $15.95. ISBN 0 385 32653 X. [fiction] MJS, CG (See full booktalk in *Booktalks and More*, 2003, pages 99 to 101.) Skellig appears and helps out a young boy and his family, who have moved into a new home and are struggling with the possible death of the new baby.

3. Cabot, Meg. **Haunted: A Tale of the Mediator.** New York: HarperCollins Publishers, 2003. 246p. $15.99. ISBN 0 06 029471 X. [fiction] JS, G In her junior year, Susannah Simon finds herself in a supernatural struggle with seventeen-year-old Paul Slater whom she believes tried to kill her and eliminate Jesse, the 150-year-old ghost she loves and who lives in her bedroom.

4. Rice, Ben. **Pobby and Dingam.** New York: Alfred A. Knopf, 2000. 94p. $16.00. ISBN 0 375 41127 5. [fiction] JS, CG Ashmol Williamson tells how his little sister's imaginary friends, Pobby and Dingam, reshape the perception of his family and their Australian mining town in a commingling of imagination, life, and death.

5. Zevin, Gabrielle. **Elsewhere.** New York: Farrar, Straus and Giroux, 2005. 277p. $19.95. ISBN 0 374 32091 8. [fiction] MJS, G (See full booktalk in *Booktalks and Beyond*, 2007, pages 188 to 190.) Fifteen-year-old Liz dies and discovers a new world and her true spirit in *Elsewhere*.

❧❧

McNamee, Eoin. The Navigator: Chosen to Save the World.

New York: Random House/Wendy Lamb Books, 2006. 342p. $15.99.
ISBN-13: 978 0 375 83910 8. [fiction] MJS, CG with high interest for boys

Themes/Topics: time, identity, good vs. evil, mission

Summary/Description

Owen, whose father supposedly committed suicide, now lives a lonely and isolated life with his depressed mother. In a time shift, his world disappears, and, after an encounter with the Watcher for the Resisters, he finds himself to be a key player in a battle between the Resisters and the Harsh. The two ancient communities repeatedly emerge from extended sleeps and battle for the survival of the world. The negative Harsh, whose weapon is freezing cold, aims to reverse time, wipe out history, and destroy the world. The Resisters try to stop them but need the Navigator to find the lost Mortmain that will secure their survival for another battle. The "Watcher" takes Owen with him to join the awakening and the eventual battle that leads both Owen and a small group of Resisters to a confrontation with the Harsh in the center of the earth. Because of the journey and successful battle, Owen overcomes his personal fears and learns that he, like his father, is a Navigator. Owen restores the Mortmain, saves time, returns to his old world, and finds proof that his experience was real.

Read Aloud/Reader Response

1. Chapter 1, pages 4 to 12, beginning "Owen crossed…" and ending with the chapter. The passage describes Owen's Den and his first encounter with the Watcher.
2. Chapter 7, pages 102 to 106, beginning "It took them…" and ending with the chapter. Johnston comes to make a final offer before the battle begins. Owen learns about each person in the room.
3. Chapter 10, pages 141 to 144, beginning "Owen remembered…" and ending "…the old chest." Owen learns about his life, his father, and their relationship to the Resisters.
4. Chapter 14, pages 200 to 201, beginning "And so Boat…" and ending with the chapter. The Boat leaves to confront the Harsh and save the world.
5. Chapter 22, page 293, beginning "The Navigator…" and ending "…believe it now." The Long Woman defines the Navigator.

Booktalk

Owen is a loner. His father committed suicide. His mother is depressed most of the time. People his age stay away from him. Owen knows he is different and is happy to stay away from anyone who reminds him that he is different. But one day the whole world, as well as Owen, is different. Time is moving backward. The old and familiar world is shifting and disappearing bit by bit. Two new groups of people, the Resisters and the Harsh, appear. They will fight a war to determine the world's fate, its very existence. He has never met a Resister, but the Resisters recognize him. Words and pictures that he can't explain jump into his head. The Harsh try to destroy him, so Owen is definitely part of the battle he doesn't understand. And more frightening—even though he doesn't understand where this jumble is going—Owen may be *The Navigator.*

Get Involved

1. (Research) Using your library resources, research the many ways that man has expressed time. Act as the resource person during the discussion.

2. (Discuss) The relationship between parents and children is a central theme of the story. List all the parent/child relationships. Describe each one. Discuss how each relationship might be related to Owen.
3. (Discuss) How could a method of time measurement change the way that culture or period of history perceives the world?
4. (React) Who are the good guys and the bad guys? Explain your choices. Compare your choices with the choices of others in the group.
5. (Create) Draw a picture of one of the characters or settings in the novel. Point to the details from the story that you used to craft your picture.

Related Works

1. Del Vecchio, Gene. **The Pearl of Anton.** Gretna, LA: Pelican Publishing Co., Inc., 2004. 256p. $16.95. ISBN 1 58980 172 5. [fiction] JS, CG with high interest for boys. This story tells about the battle among the Chosen One, Pure Evil, and Evil Less than Pure.
2. Horowitz, Anthony. **Raven's Gate.** New York: Scholastic Press, 2005. 256p. (Gatekeepers). $17.95. ISBN 0 439 67995 8. [fiction] MJ, CG with high interest for boys. (See full booktalk in *Booktalks and Beyond,* 2007, pages 138 to 141.) Orphaned fourteen-year-old Matt Freeman, held in a foster home situation after a robbery, discovers that he has supernatural powers from his previous life that will allow the Old Ones to come into the world through *Raven's Gate* and renew the battle between good and evil.
3. McCaughrean, Geraldine. **The Stones Are Hatching.** New York: HarperCollins Publishers, 1999. 230p. $15.95. ISBN 0 06 028765 9. [fiction] MJ, CG Based on Irish mythology, this story tells how an ordinary boy receives the task of saving the world.
4. Oppel, Kenneth. **Airborn.** New York: HarperCollins/EOS, 2004. 355p. $17.89. ISBN 0 06 053181 9. [fiction] MJS, CG with high interest for boys (See full booktalk in *Booktalks and Beyond,* 2007, pages 107 to 110.) Fifteen-year-old Matt Cruise, a cabin boy on the ship his father serves, enters a world of danger and adventure when he rescues a dying man and follows the man's granddaughter who wishes to recreate his journey.
5. Wooding, Chris. **The Haunting of Alaizabel Cray.** New York: Orchard Books, 2004. 304p. $16.95. ISBN 0 439 54656 7. [fiction] MJS, CG with high interest for boys (See full booktalk in *Booktalks and Beyond,* 2007, pages 141 to 143.) Seventeen-year-old Thaniel Fox, an orphaned wych hunter, discovers Alaizabel Cray who exhibits the personality of Thatch, an evil spirit who can open the gates for other evil spirits to control the world.

ʊʑʊ

Paolini, Christopher. **The Inheritance Cycle.**
Concluding volume forthcoming.
New York: Alfred A. Knopf. [fiction] MJS, CG with high interest for boys

Themes/Topics: dragons, coming of age, identity, family, love, loyalty, fate, choice

Description Note: A map introduces each book. Explanations of names, a pronunciation guide, and definitions follow the text of each novel.

Eragon, Book One.
2003. 509p. $18.95. ISBN 0 375 82668 8.

Summary/Description

In his fifteenth and sixteenth years, Eragon becomes the first in a new generation of Dragon Riders when he discovers a mysterious stone, a dragon egg. As the dragon grows, Eragon and the dragon develop empathy. The Rá zac, superhuman creatures sent by the evil king, come for them. They destroy Eragon's home and kill his grandfather. Brom, a legendary former Dragon Rider posing as a story-teller, helps Eragon escape and becomes his mentor in battle and magic before dying. Eragon then meets Murtagh, the son of a traitorous Dragon Rider whom Brom killed in a duel. Murtagh helps Eragon rescue a beautiful elf from the evil powers who wish to control her and the Dragon Riders. Against Murtagh's wishes, the party arrives in Tronjheim, an elf kingdom. Eragon's powers are directed to a battle between good and evil. The elves triumph, but Eragon is beginning to distrust the affable but enigmatic Murtagh.

Read Aloud/Reader Response

1. "Prologue: Shade of Fear," pages 1 to 5. The Prologue sets the stage for Eragon finding the dragon egg, saving the beautiful lady elf, and battling the evil Shade.
2. "Dragon Tales," pages 31 to 34, beginning "The sands of time..." and ending "...he has ruled us." Brom tells about the beginning of Galbatorix's rule.
3. "Tea for Two," pages 49 to 54, beginning "Dragons have no beginning..." and ending "...watched it waft away." Brom explains dragons and their relationship to man.
4. "Strangers in Carvahall," page 64, beginning "I have words for..." and ending "That is all I have to say." Garrow gives his parting words of advice to Roran and Eragon.

5. "Vision of Perfection," page 236 to 239, beginning "The rhythmic thump…" and ending with the chapter. Brom concludes that teaching Eragon discretion is as important as teaching him "how to."
6. "Bless the Child, Argetlam," pages 428 to 429, beginning "Before she could take off…" and ending "…*gave her a future.*" When asked to bless a child, Eragon finds the reaction confusing and out of proportion to his power.

Booktalk

Read "Prologue: Shade of Fear" out loud.

Elves, Shades, and monster warriors. All are magic. All are focused on a sapphire stone. None of these powerful figures leaves the forest with the stone that night. Its magic waits for a simple farm boy who finds it by accident, hopes to sell it, and feed his family for the winter. But the stone has other ideas. It pulls the farmer into a powerful, magical journey. It chooses him, and, with the help of an old story-teller, joins his life with the world of legends. The stone will unfold its secrets and anoint another hero for the ages—a hero called *Eragon.*

Eldest, Book Two.

2005. 680p. $21.00. ISBN 0 375 82670 X.

Summary/Description

After triumphing in the battle against the evil King Galbatorix, Eragon and Saphira travel to Ellesméra, land of the elves, for further Rider training. Their mentors, an ancient Dragon Rider and his battle-scarred dragon, train them physically, mentally, and emotionally for a rematch with King Galbatorix. Eragon combats his pain, prejudice, and love for the beautiful elf princess Arya as he expands his mind and develops elf powers.

In a parallel story, Eragon's cousin Roran leads the village of Carvahall against Galbatorix forces who try to capture him. When Rá zac capture Katrina, Roran's betrothed, Roran and the villagers evacuate and eventually discover a Varden agent and Eragon supporter who helps them steal a ship. They sail to the battle between Eragon's forces and Galbatorix. In the battle, Eragon eventually faces the Dragon Rider Murtagh, Eragon's older brother controlled by Galbatorix. Roran destroys the Twins who betrayed Eragon in the concluding battle of *Eragon,* and Eragon and Roran reunite and resolve to find and rescue Katrina. Pages xiii to xii present a "Synopsis of *Eragon,* Book One of Inheritance."

Read Aloud/Reader Response

1. "Hrothgar's Gift," pages 80 to 82, beginning "Approaching were Nasuada..." and ending with the chapter. Eragon learns that following his instinct to honor multiple allegiances is good, and he begins another formidable journey.
2. "Celbedeil," pages 111 to 123. The chapter reveals the dwarf culture.
3. "Drifting," pages 154 to 155, beginning "Eragon woke," and ending "...that manner before." Eragon realizes his connection with Arya.
4. "On the Crags of Tel'naeír." The chapter describes Eragon's new school and teacher.
5. "Why Do You Fight?" pages 340 to 352. The chapter presents Eragon's physical, emotional, and mental training. His teacher forces him to think through the "why" of his battle.
6. "The Obliterator," pages 400 to 402, beginning "The next morning..." and ending with the chapter. Oromis explains the reason for the pain of his journey.

Booktalk

With the help of Saphira and Arya, Eragon kills Durza, but is left with a huge and painful scar. The scar is similar to the one on Murtagh, his trusted fellow warrior. But the faithful Murtagh, is gone, dead or captured. Now Eragon hears another voice, a voice that identifies itself as Togira Ikonoka—The Cripple Who Is Whole. The voice promises Eragon the answers he seeks. But the answers require further training in battle, magic, and wisdom. To get these, Eragon must travel to Ellesméra, the land of the elves. Here he falls in love. Here he meets the creature behind the voice, The Cripple Who Is Whole.

As Eragon struggles with his personal battles, his cousin Roran faces his own challenges back in Carvahall. The Rá zac still hunt for Eragon. They are sure that Roran knows where he is. They are willing to hurt anyone close to Roran who can give them information about Eragon or help them lure him into their trap. The Rá zac call for Roran's surrender. Roran refuses to give himself up. He endangers all of Carvahall as the Rá zac promise them death if they resist or slavery if they cooperate. Roran understands that if he is the community's path to destruction, then he must also be its path to salvation. So as Eragon searches, Roran directs the town's flight. The cousins' danger-filled lives slowly edge closer to each other and promise to destroy them both. Together, they face that destruction. Their common enemy is a common relative, a man who believes that he has the power of evil as well as the rights and power of the *Eldest*.

Brisingr, Book Three.

2008. 784p. $27.50. ISBN-13: 978 0375826 726.

Summary/Description

Eragon helps Roran rescue Katrina, discovers the traitor Sloan, and kills the last Rá zac. Roran, Katrina, and Saphira travel to join the Varden army. Eragon stays behind to sentence Sloan. With Ayra's help, Eragon returns later, re-establishes himself in the community, successfully battles Murtagh, and marries Roran and Katrina. Then he travels to the dwarves to ensure a leadership favorable to the Vardens. He also visits the land of the elves where he reunites with Oromis, his teacher; learns that Brom is his real father; discovers that Galbatorix draws power from dragon hearts; and finds his true sword, Brisingr. Meanwhile, Roran fights bravely in the Varden army, awaits the birth of their first child, and, after a confrontation with a superior, becomes a commander. Eragon rejoins the army at the siege of Feinster where he and Ayra kill a shade conjured to confuse and destroy the forces. Fighting in Feinster, Eragon and Saphira experience the battle between Murtagh and Oromis via the dragon heart Oromis and his dragon gave to Eragon. Oromis is killed, and Glaedr, his dragon, is alone. Eragon realizes the strength of his friends and supporters as he and Saphira resolve to battle and destroy Galbatorix. A summary of *Eragon* and *Eldest*, the first two books in the series, appears on pages xiii to xix.

Read Aloud/Reader Response

1. "Around the Campfire," pages 12 to 13, beginning "*Murtagh.*" and ending "...would forevermore." Eragon contemplates Murtagh's evil.
2. "To Walk the Land Alone," pages 93 and 94, beginning "The butcher..." and ending with the chapter. Eragon reveals that he has given Sloan the possibility of redemption and that he is ever loyal to Brom.
3. "Shadows of the Past," pages 191 to 200, beginning "Eragon leaned back..." and ending "...withdrew his hand." Eragon ponders killing in battle, and Arya reveals her sorrows.
4. "To Answer a King," pages 238 to 239, beginning "Orrin and Nasuada..." and ending "...did not divulge them." Orrin explains why he agrees with Eragon's decision not to kill Sloan.
5. "Over Hill and Mountain," pages 389 to 393, beginning "...Long ago,..." and ending "...hold most dear." Garzhvog tells an Urgal story about fate.

6. "Inheritance," pages 621 to 625, beginning "Eragon did as she directed…" and ending "…*as my parents.*" Brom speaks to Eragon through a memory left with Saphira.

Booktalk

The battle of *The Eldest* is over. Roran and Eragon are together again. Together, each is stronger. Galbatorix still threatens to release evil throughout the land. Should they pursue him? Not yet. Eragon has promises to keep. He must help Roran rescue Katrina. He must help the Vardin, the dwarves, and the elves. All face the danger of Galbatorix, and all hold alliances with Eragon even though their connections with each other are questionable. So, Eragon's position is questionable, some would say dangerous. And now he is without a weapon. Murtagh has taken Zar'roc. But in the battle, Eragon has lost more than a sword. The fire of grief and battle is spent. He buried loved ones and held off his enemies. Eragon is battle tired. He wants peace even though he knows he must fight. Most important, he questions his or any man's right to kill or decide the fate of others. Without determination, without resolve, Eragon will find no weapon strong enough to defeat Galbatorix, and yet in mind, body, and spirit, he is the only man strong enough to do it. For a time, Roran will be the soldier, and Eragon will renew his alliances. He will return to the dwarves and to the elves. Here he may rediscover his resolve. Here, he may prepare the thunder and lightning of war. Here, as expressed in the Ancient Language, he may find *Brisingr.*

Get Involved

1. (Create) Draw pictures of each of the characters described in the novels. Compare your interpretations with an artist or moviemaker who has undertaken the same project.
2. (Research) Using your library resources, find out as much as you can about the role of dragons in literature and story-telling. Act as a resource person during the discussion.
3. (Discuss) In the stories, Garrow, Brom, and Oromis die violently. Discuss whether or not you agree with the author's use of death and violence.
4. (Discuss) After reading the book, how would you describe the problems and strengths of making alliances? How do alliances help shape Eragon?
5. (Discuss) Magic comes with many forms and motivations in the novels. How does it affect the story?
6. (React) In the stories, names are extremely important. Why? What do you think your own true name might be?

7. (React) Using characters in the story, define a good leader. Use positive and negative examples to support your opinion.
8. (Create) Define family as Eragon might define it. Then compare it with your own idea of family.
9. (Create) If you had a sword, what would you name it and why?

Related Works

1. Bass, L. G. **Sign of the Qin: Book One.** New York: Hyperion Books for Children, 2004. 383p. (Outlaws of the Moonshadow Marsh). $17.99. ISBN 0 78681918 9. [fiction] MJS, CG with high interest for boys. When the Emperor's wife gives birth to a son marked with the outlaw sign of the Qin, the Emperor recognizes him as the new Starlord who will return justice to the land. He plans to assassinate him, but a tattooed monk blocks the assassination. Thus the Starlord begins a life of battling both earthly and mythological opponents to realize his fate.
2. Dickinson, Peter. **The Ropemaker.** New York: Delacorte Press, 2001. 375p. $15.95. ISBN 0 385 72921 9. [fiction] MJS, G In this coming-of-age fantasy adventure, Tilja, who does not possess her family's natural magic, journeys to her grandmother's home to discover why the forest's magic is failing. The book's divisions tell magic's origins, present function, and future.
3. Funke, Cornelia. **Dragon Rider.** New York: Scholastic Inc., 2004. 528p. $12.95. ISBN 0 439 45695 9. [fiction] MJ, CG with high interest for boys. An orphan and a silver dragon join with a host of fantasy characters and supportive humans to defeat the evil golden dragon and in the process find their homes.
4. Hill, Stuart. **The Cry of the Icemark.** New York: Chicken House, 2005. 496p. $19.95. ISBN 0 439 68626 1. [fiction] JS, CG When King Redrought dies defending his kingdom from the Polypontian Imperial Forces, his daughter, fourteen-year-old Thirrin, inherits the kingdom and battle. Oskan, son of a good witch and now a powerful warlock, becomes her friend and ally. With his supernatural powers, and her tutor's wisdom, she hopes to defeat the evil Scipio Bellorum.
5. Krensky, Stephen. **Dragons.** Minneapolis, MN: Lerner Publications Company, 2007. 48p. (Monster Chronicles). $26.60. ISBN 0 8225 6543 9. [nonfiction] MJ, CG with high interest for boys. Although this book is clearly directed to the younger reader, the historical and literary information that includes drawings and photographs is extensive. A "Selected Bibliography," a list provided in "Further Reading and Websites," and a list of movies provide any reader with

many additional options. An index gives easy access to information within the text.

Retelling an Old Story

 భ్మ

Bruchac, Joseph. **Wabi: A Hero's Tale.**

New York: Dial Books, 2006. 198p. $16.99. ISBN 0 8037 3098 5. [fiction] MJS, CG

Themes/Topics: Abenaki Indians, love, great horned owl, wolves, human/animal relationships

Summary/Description

Wabi tells the story of his life, his hatching to his performing heroic human deeds that give him his love. Pushed out of the nest by his bullying brother, Wabi encounters his great-grandmother who teaches him that he has the ability to think and talk to many different creatures, including humans. Guarding the local village from predators, Wabi falls in love with the chief's headstrong daughter. She refuses all suitors, and so her father stages a hunting contest to find her husband. Wabi decides he will compete as a human, discovers he has human ancestors, wins the contest, and is berated by his would-be bride. He leaves the village in shame and decides to find the home of his pet wolf that he found abandoned in a cave. In spite of super-human challenges, Wabi completes his task and acquires another wolf also. With his companions, he returns to the Indian village and discovers that Bad Bear was poised to attack the village and that the girl Wabi loves left to confront him. Wabi wounds himself saving her, and she realizes that he is the village guardian that she wanted to marry.

Read Aloud/Reader Response

1. Chapter 6, pages 20 to 23, beginning "Why is there..." and ending "...anyone else but me?" The grandmother tells Wabi the story of the Great Darkness.
2. Chapter 9, pages 40 to 41, beginning "Urp." and ending "How sad!" Wabi explains eating and giving thanks.
3. Chapter 11, pages 52 to 58. In this chapter, Wabi adopts the wolf cub.
4. Chapter 15, pages 76 to 79. In this chapter, Wabi becomes a human.

5. Chapter 36, pages 188 to 190. Wabi describes his brave deed and the suffering in the mad bear that attacks him.

Booktalk

Wabi is born a bird, a great horned owl his brother pushed out of the nest. Does Wabi die? No, but he doesn't stay a bird. He changes—to a human being. Not right away. Right away he meets his great-grandmother who promises him that he is much different than the average owl. He can think. He can feel like a human feels, and he can communicate with other animals as well as humans. He starts to watch and guard the nearby village, and he begins to fall in love. Unfortunately, he falls in love with a girl who doesn't want to fall in love. How will he get her attention? Certainly not as a bird. Her father declares a contest to win her hand. Many suitors want the prestige of marrying the chief's daughter. Wabi just wants her love. Wabi will enter the contest. He has to be human to do it. Can he do it? Is she worth it? You be the judge after you listen to his story, *Wabi: A Hero's Tale.*

Get Involved

1. (Research) The Dial publishers note that Bruchac combines fantasy, legend, and romance. Using your library resources, find definitions for each of the three terms and then identify at least one example of each in the text. Act as a resource person for the group during the discussion.
2. (Research) Using your library resources, research another Native American legend or myth. Act as a resource person during the group discussion. Be sure to consider what the myth or legend reveals about the culture.
3. (React) Who are the good guys and the bad guys? Support your answers with specifics from the text.
4. (Discuss) In Chapter 16, on page 86, the great-grandmother assures Wabi that his essence will never change even as a human. How does that statement apply to each of us?
5. (Create) Choose one of the chapters. Transform it into a graphic novel.

Related Works

1. Coville, Bruce (comp. and ed.). **Half-Human.** New York: Scholastic Press, 2001. 224p. $15.95. ISBN 0 590 95944 1. [fiction] JS, CG (See full booktalk in *Booktalks and More,* 2003, pages 101 to 103.) This collection of stories questions what makes a human being. "How to Make a Human," a poem by Lawrence Schimel appearing on

pages 94 and 95, presents a negative view of man forgetful of his ties to nature.

2. Napoli, Donna Jo. **Beast.** New York: Atheneum Books for Young Readers, 2000. 260p. $17.00. ISBN 0 689 83589 2. [fiction] JS, CG (See full booktalk in *Teen Genre Connections*, 2005, pages 171 to 173.) Orasmyn, a young Persian prince, offends the gods, is turned into a lion, and then learns, through love, what it means to be human.

3. Philip, Neil. **The Great Mystery: Myths of Native America.** New York: Clarion Books, 2001. 145p. $25.00 ISBN 0 395 98405 X. [nonfiction] JS, CG with high interest for boys (See full booktalk in *Booktalks and More*, 2003, pages 103 to 105.) In the first chapter, "Trail of Beauty," Philip defines myth, explains its evolution, describes the purpose of related rituals, and identifies the common themes and motifs of Native American belief. Subsequent chapters focus on the specific myths for each region of North America from the Southwest to the Arctic.

4. Spinner, Stephanie. **Quiver.** New York: Alfred A. Knopf, 2002. 176p. $15.95. ISBN 0 375 81489 2. [fiction] JS, G (See full booktalk in *Teen Genre Connections*, 2005, pages 177 to 179.) Combining the boar hunt, the race with the golden apples, and the transformation of Atlanta and her husband Hippomanes into lions, Spinner explains the why behind Atlanta's cruel marriage competition and how one man changed her feelings.

5. Wilkinson, Philip. Neil Philip (consultant). **Illustrated Dictionary of Mythology: Heroes, Heroines, Gods, and Goddesses from around the World.** New York: DK Publishing, 1998. 127p. $25.00. ISBN 0 7894 3413 X. [reference] MJS, CG with high interest for boys. In this extensive, illustrated reference of world mythology, the discussion of "The Americas" appears on pages 94 to 111. Eastern North America, the Great Plains, West Coast, and Southwest appear on pages 98 to 105. A general discussion of the role of heroes and tricksters appears on pages 12 and 13.

ᘓᘔ

Cooney, Caroline B. Enter Three Witches: A Story of Macbeth.

New York: Scholastic Press, 2007. 288p. $16.99.
ISBN-13: 978 0 439 71156 2. [fiction] JS, G

Themes/Topics: ambition, family, friendship, love, *Macbeth*, witches, loyalty, Scotland, castle life

Summary/Description

Lady Mary is the ward of Lord and Lady Macbeth when her father, Thane of Cawdor, betrays Duncan and is killed as a traitor. As the Macbeths attain and hold the throne through murder, deceit, and war, Mary lives through the fears of her own execution and the realization that the kingdom is run by criminals. She gradually becomes closer to the shy and awkward Fleance, and together they help Malcolm defeat Macbeth at Dunsinane, save Mary from a marriage to the Satanic Seyton (the third murderer), and receive thanks, rewards, and an announcement of their betrothal from Malcolm, the new king. The novel uses the play *Macbeth* and many of the questions about it to build the plot and the characters' motivation.

Read Aloud/Reader Response

1. Chapter 1, page 7, beginning "The only person..." and ending "...dreaming...*wanting*." Ildred characterizes Lady Macbeth.
2. Chapter 2, pages 27 to 28, beginning "Three of them..." and ending "Runnnnn!" Mary meets the witches for the first time.
3. Chapter 2, pages 29 to 31, beginning "Lord Banquo looked down..." and ending "...valuable as honor." Banquo, Fleance, and Seyton ponder the body of Asleif, Mary's betrothed. The reflections reveal the characters.
4. Chapter 12, pages 231 to 232, beginning "Mary could see..." and ending "...inside a great stone?" Mary contemplates what Dunsinane means for the Macbeths.
5. Chapter 14, pages 258 to 259, beginning "Everyone rushed around,..." and ending "The Queen of Scotland laughed." Mary rebels against Macbeth's tomorrow speech.

Booktalk

Show a copy of Macbeth *and* Enter Three Witches.

Here are two very powerful stories. One is by Shakespeare and one is by Caroline Cooney. Shakespeare tells a story about ambition and greed. Cooney imagines what happened to some of the people who happened to be in the way.

Fourteen-year-old Mary is a ward, kind of a foster child, of one of the most powerful couples in Scotland, the Lord and Lady Macbeth. Her mother is dead, and her father, the Thane of Cawdor, is at war, fighting for his king—or so she thinks. Her betrothed is with her father. Then word of the battle reaches the castle. Duncan's forces are victorious, but her father is not. Her father was on the other side. He will die for his choice. Will Mary? Mary didn't know about her father's ambition or his plans. Will anyone believe that? Lord and Lady Macbeth are hosting the king, the very man her father tried to kill. Will he demand that she be executed too? Will she lose her lands as well as her future husband? Will she become like the workhorses, abused servants who spend their lives serving nobles? She can't answer any of these questions, and she can't ask anyone else for answers. It's all a mystery, a hurly burly, and then *Enter Three Witches.*

Get Involved

1. (Research) Cooney employs a sustained allusion. After using your library resources to check on the definition of the term, discuss why Cooney might have chosen *Macbeth* as the basis of her story. You may wish to act as a resource person during the discussion.
2. (Research) Using your library resources, learn more about the plots of additional Shakespeare plays. Choose another play that you think would be an appropriate base for a story. Explain your choice and the way you might develop it.
3. (Compare) Read Shakespeare's *Macbeth*. List the elements from the play upon which Cooney capitalizes. Act as a resource person during the discussion.
4. (Compare) Choose one of the scenes upon which Cooney focuses. Explain how she uses it to accomplish her purpose.
5. (Discuss) What do you think that the witches represent?
6. (Discuss) How does each character in the story relate to the witches? How does each reaction affect the character's life?

Related Works

1. Banks, Lynne Reid. **The Dungeon.** New York: HarperCollins Publishers, 2002. 279p. $17.89. ISBN 0 06 623783 1. [fiction] MJS, G Bruce MacLennan, a fourteenth-century Scottish laird, focuses on revenge after his wife is captured and his children are killed by a neighboring laird in retaliation for the murder of a nephew and uses his power to abuse and eventually kill a small slave girl instead of opening himself to her love.
2. Dunton, Downer, Leslie Riding, and Alan Riding. **Essential Shakespeare Handbook.** New York: DK Publishing, Inc., 2004. 480p. $25.00pa. ISBN 0 7894 9333 0. [reference] JS, CG. This user-friendly Shakespeare reference includes plot summaries and interpretative material on all thirty-nine plays and an analysis of the poetry. It also has essays on Shakespeare's life and times as well as his impact on world culture. Pages 358 to 367 deal with *Macbeth* and some productions of the play.

3. Gaiman, Neil (text), and Andy Kubert (illus.). **Marvel 1602: # 1–8.**
    New York: Marvel Comics, 2005. 348p. $19.99pa. ISBN 0 7851
    1073 9. [graphic, fiction] JS/A, CG with high interest for boys (See
    full booktalk in *Booktalks and Beyond,* 2007, pages 171 to 173.) A
    collection of Marvel characters (Dr. Strange, Nick Fury, Spiderman,
    the Fantastic Four, Irish-American Matt Murdock, Thor, Hulk, Mag-
    neto, Professor Charles Xavier, the X-Men, Captain America, Doctor
    Victor von Doom, and Uatu the Watcher) interacts with historical
    characters (Queen Elizabeth I, James I of Scotland, Virginia Dare
    and the Roanoke colony) to produce a fantastical conflict of good
    versus evil.
4. Shakespeare, William, and John Crowther (ed.). **Macbeth.** New
    York: SparkNotes, 2003. 230p. (No Fear Shakespeare). $5.95pa.
    ISBN-13: 978 15866 38467. [drama] JS, CG with high interest for
    boys. Probably first performed in the court of James I in 1605, the
    play deals with the unbridled ambition of a man of action and his wife
    who are willing to fulfill the witches' prophecy by killing their king.
5. Yolen, Jane, and Robert J. Harris. **Girl in a Cage.** New York:
    Philomel Books, 2002. 234p. $18.99. ISBN 0 399 236279. [fiction]
    MJ, G Eleven-year-old Marjorie Bruce, imprisoned in a public cage
    by Edward Longshanks when her father, Robert Bruce, rebels, finds
    her role as a princess and turns public opinion against Longshanks.

✿✿

Hale, Shannon. **Book of a Thousand Days.**
New York: Bloomsbury, 2007. 306p. $17.95.
ISBN-13: 978 1 59990 051 3. [fiction] JS, G

Themes/Topics: love, fairy tale, conduct of life

Summary/Description

Fifteen-year-old Dashti, a lady's maid, and sixteen-year-old Lady
Saren, her mistress, are walled into a tower for seven years because
Lady Saren prefers a suitor of her own choice over the suitor chosen by
her father. The two suitors visit the tower. The first, the evil, sadistic, and
powerful Lord Khasar, whom her father chose, threatens the girls, and
on a second visit, tries to burn them out. The second, Khan Tegus, is the
man Lady Saren promised to marry. In both cases, Lady Saren orders
Dashti to speak for her. Dashti and Tegus fall in love, but Tegus believes
she is Lady Saren. After Khasar's second visit, the guards stop bringing
the girls fresh supplies. Dashti finds a way to escape. They learn that

Khasar destroyed the father's city, travel on to Tegus's city, work in his household, and find that Tegus is now betrothed. Dashti's healing talents and skills in reading bring her attention and promotion. She becomes close to Tegus. Khasar threatens to destroy the city unless they give up Lady Saren, Dashti poses as the lady again, tricks him into showing his werewolf side, saves the city, and with the help of Lady Saren, who now admits her identity, marries Tegus. A map of the Eight Realms introduces the story.

Read Aloud/Reader Response

1. Part 1, Day 11, pages 8 to 12. This diary entry tells how Dashti came to work for Lady Saren.
2. Part 1, Day 160, pages 64 to 66. In this diary entry, Dashti talks to her unsympathetic guard.
3. Part 1, Day 281, pages 78 to 81. Dashti sees Lady Saren as a person rather than gentry.
4. Part 2, Day 64, pages 142 to 143, beginning "One was like..." and ending "...into a corpse." Dashti relates the story of the skinwalker, which anticipates Lord Khasar's shape-shifting.
5. Part 2, Day 113, pages 178 to 187. Dashti and Khan Tegus reveal themselves to each other.
6. Part 2, Day 178, pages 304 to 306. Dashti and Khan Tegus wed.

Booktalk

Fifteen-year-old Dashti has a new job with all the food she can eat for seven years. It seems a dream come true for the poor orphaned girl marked for bad luck at birth, but there is one catch. She will be bricked up in the tower with the lady she serves. The Lady Saren, her new mistress, refused to marry the suitor her father chose for her. She promised herself to another. Her father is so angry that he imprisons her. Of course, Lady Saren, as gentry, needs someone to take care of her, and that will be Dashti. Dashti knows how to fight the rats that will come, how to measure the food so that it will last, and how to survive in the extreme heat and cold. She cannot understand why her mistress is so upset. After all, they are guaranteed a safe home for seven years. Then Lady Saren's suitors come to the tower. One threatens to kill them. Another makes them laugh and look forward to tomorrow. Which one will figure out how to enter the tower? What will happen when he does? Lady Saren can only accept what happens. She is helpless gentry. Dashti must find the answers. And as Dashti searches her thoughts, plans, and fears, she finds not only answers but also herself, in what becomes her *Book of a Thousand Days*.

Get Involved

1. (Research) The novel is based on a fairy tale, "Maid Maleen," recorded by the Brothers Grimm. Using your library resources, find the original tale, read it, and share the differences that you find with the group during the discussion.
2. (Discuss) Dashti and Lady Saren both change in the course of the novel. How do their personal changes affect their relationship?
3. (React) How did the novel affect your own definition of beauty?
4. (React) Identify what you feel is Dashti's most important quality. Explain your choice with specifics from the novel. Compare your opinion with that of others in the group.
5. (Create) Using your library resources, find another Grimm tale. Use it as a basis for a short story of your own. You may wish to start with Related Work 1.

Related Works

1. Hettinga, Donald R. **The Brothers Grimm: Two Lives, One Legacy.** New York: Clarion Books, 2001. 180p. $22.00. ISBN 0 618 05599 1. [nonfiction] JS, CG Within this story of two close and scholarly brothers, Hettinga lists all the brothers' publications and the tales they gathered.
2. Napoli, Donna Jo. **Beast.** New York: Atheneum Books for Young Readers, 2000. 260p. $17.00. ISBN 0 689 83589 2. [fiction] JS, G (See full booktalk in *Teen Genre Connections*, 2005, pages 171 to 173.) In this interpretation of Beauty and the Beast, Orasmyn, a young Persian prince, must live as a lion to learn about suffering, and only the true love of a woman, who does not realize his identity, can break his curse.
3. Napoli, Donna Jo. **Breath.** New York: Atheneum Books for Young Readers, 2003. 260p. $16.95. ISBN 0 689 86174 5. [fiction] JS, CG (See full booktalk *Teen Genre Connections*, 2005, pages 173 to 175.) In this interpretation of the Pied Piper of Hamelin, twelve-year-old Salz, a victim of cystic fibrosis, participates in a coven to cure his disease, but eventually leaves his community that distrusts him and cheats the Pied Piper who tried to save the town from a mysterious disease.
4. Schmidt, Gary D. **Straw into Gold.** New York: Clarion Books, 2001. 172p. $15.00. ISBN 0 618 05601 7. [fiction] MJS, CG (See full booktalk in *Teen Genre Connections*, 2005, pages 175 to 177.) In this revised "Rumpelstiltskin," Rumpelstiltskin's foster son saves a lost prince from death and discovers that relationships are more important than gold.

5.   Voigt, Cynthia. **Elske.** New York: Atheneum Books for Young
     Readers/Anne Schwartz, 1999. 245p. $18.00. ISBN 0 689 82472
     6. [fiction] JS, G (See full booktalk in *Booktalks and More,* 2003,
     pages 111 to 113.) In this Anglo-Saxon-type fantasy, Elske, the
     granddaughter of a Wolfer captive, runs away from her community
     to escape an early death and eventually uses her wits and knowledge
     of languages to help the rebellious princess Beriel take back her
     kingdom.

Sandell, Lisa Ann. Song of the Sparrow.

New York: Scholastic Press, 2007. 416p. $16.99.
ISBN-13: 978 0 439 91848 0. [fiction, poetry] JS, G

Themes/Topics: Lady of Shalott, King Arthur, Lancelot,
Gwynivere, love, loyalty, friendship, coming of age,
battle, bravery

Summary/Description

Seventeen-year-old Elaine lives in Arthur's war camp with her father and brothers. She sews for the men and studies healing from
Morgan, Arthur's older sister. Although the warrior Tristan has feelings
for her, Elaine loves Lancelot, who has given her special attention since
she has been small. Her jealousy rages when Lancelot brings the seemingly cold and haughty Gwynivere to Arthur for marriage but clearly
loves her himself. When Arthur, a newly elected leader, decides to attack
the invading Saxons, Elaine secretly follows the army to provide healing. Instead, she is captured along with Gwynivere. In the Saxon camp,
the women overhear a spy revealing Arthur's location. Elaine creates a
diversion so that Gwynivere can warn Arthur. Elaine escapes, although
seriously wounded, builds a friendship with Gwynivere, earns the admiration of Arthur and his men, discovers that her true love is the attentive
Tristan, and earns, with Tristan, a place at the Round Table where all
pledge to build Camelot. In the "Author's Note," Sandell explains how
she built on the Arthurian legends and literature that she researched.
References listed in "Suggestions for Further Reading" provide more
information.

Read Aloud/Reader Response

1.   II, pages 6 and 7, beginning "Arthur's stance..." and ending "...so
     terribly unalike." Arthur reveals his view of war.

2. VII, pages 54 to 55, beginning *"Why ever would British clansmen..."* and ending *"...beautiful girl."* Lancelot and Elaine talk about politics and Lancelot notices her growing beauty.
3. XIII, pages 108 to 113, beginning "The Merlin steps..." and ending with the chapter. Merlin conducts the ceremony that proclaims Arthur *"...dux bellorum, defender of the land, protector of all of Britain!"*
4. XXXIV, pages 295 to 302. In this chapter, Gwynivere reveals her jealousy and feelings of inferiority.
5. XLIII, pages 360 to 373. In this chapter, Elaine and Tristan explain their true love.

Booktalk

Seventeen-year-old, fiery-tempered Elaine lives in a military camp with her father and brothers. Before her mother died, she taught Elaine to sew. All these years, sewing has given Elaine an important place in the Britons' war camp. Arthur, leader of her camp, is not yet the great King Arthur of Camelot. He is just struggling to obey his commander, stay alive, and defend his country. Then, the high commander of the Britons is poisoned. Young Arthur is tapped to take his place, but he is a controversial choice. As his support disintegrates, Elaine feels that she must do more to help him than sew. From Morgan, Arthur's older sister, Elaine has also learned the healing arts. If she follows the army to the battle, her skill will save many, especially the handsome Lancelot. And there is another reason to follow the battle. A woman named Gwynivere has come to marry Arthur. Her eyes, however, wander to Lancelot. He returns her attention. If Elaine saves Lancelot in battle, perhaps his love will be hers. These many feelings—jealousy, love, commitment, loyalty, fear, and anger—like the wings of a sparrow, flutter inside her. Which should be her focus? Or should she ignore the small bird's flutters completely and listen instead to the bravery and determination that ring in the *Song of the Sparrow?*

Get Involved

1. (Research) Using your library resources or Sandell's "Suggestions for Further Reading," find out as much information as possible about the Arthurian legends. Act as a resource person for the group during the discussion.
2. (Research) Using your library resources, continue to learn more about the role of women during the period. Act as a resource person for the group during the discussion.
3. (Research) The story of Tristan and Isolde is also a major allusion in the story. Learn as much as possible about the story and share it with the group.

4. (Create) Write a short story or a series of verses that might present Gwynivere's point of view. Should she also be considered a heroine?
5. (React) Write down what you feel the story communicates about love. Refer to specifics from the text to support your opinion. Compare your feelings with the feelings of others in the group.
6. (Discuss) Does this story apply to today?

Related Works

1. Bray, Libba. **A Great and Terrible Beauty.** New York: Delacorte Press, 2003. 405p. $18.99. ISBN 0 385 90161 5. [fiction] S, G (See full booktalk in *Booktalks and Beyond,* 2007, pages 157 to 159.) Living in 1895 Bombay, India, sixteen-year-old Gemma, during a vision, sees her mother's suicide and the murder of two mysterious caped men. After her mother's real death, she attends a girl's boarding school where she explores the occult and becomes vulnerable to her mother's connections to the evil supernatural forces.
2. Kerven, Rosalind. **King Arthur.** New York: DK Publishing, 1998. 63p. (Eyewitness Classics). $14.95. ISBN 0 7894 2887 3. [nonfiction] MJS, CG (See full booktalk in *Booktalks Plus,* 2001, pages 131 to 133.) Kerven explains the Arthurian legend and the themes of good and evil surrounding it.
3. Mathews, John. **King Arthur: Dark Age Warrior and Mythic Hero.** New York: Rosen Publishing, 2008. 127p. (Prime Time History). $39.95. ISBN-13: 978 1 4042 1364 7. [reference] JS, CG. Mathews presents a scholarly history of the Arthurian legends as well as its influence on modern culture. The volume includes beautiful artwork and extensive sources for further information. Chapter 5, "Ladies of the Lake," explains the stories of the women surrounding the legend. Elaine is included in those explanations.
4. Springer, Nancy. **I Am Mordred: Tales from Camelot.** New York: Philomel Books, 1998. 184p. $14.95. ISBN 0 399 23143 9. [fiction] MJ, CG Mordred, whose life hovers between the natural and supernatural worlds, loves his father in spite of his fate to battle and kill him.
5. Tennyson, Lord Alfred. "The Lady of Shalott." Poets.org. Available: http://poets.org/viewmedia.php/prmMID/16080. (Accessed January 2009). The site provides the full text of "The Lady of Shalott."

☙❧

Vande Velde, Vivian. **The Book of Mordred.**
Boston, MA: Houghton Mifflin Company, 2005. 342p. $18.00.
ISBN 0 618 50754 X. [fiction] JS, CG

Themes/Topics: King Arthur, mothers and daughters, knighthood, wizards

Summary/Description

Three connected stories portray Mordred as a questioning rebel in the disintegrating and rigid Arthurian court. In Part I, Mordred champions Lady Alayna whose five-year-old daughter, Kiera, is kidnapped by an evil wizard, Halbert, and his nephew, Bayard. Because Merlin is absent from Camelot, the kidnappers want Kiera's wizard powers to help them control the kingdom. Mordred wins the love of both mother and daughter. In Part II, Nimue, who is believed to hold Merlin imprisoned, transforms herself into a boy when knights attack a village and accompanies the young men captured to a dungeon where Halbert takes the boys' lives to regenerate his own. Nimue changes her disguises and cooperates with Mordred and a village girl to defeat Halbert and Bayard again. But Bayard manages to avoid condemnation when Lancelot protects him with the code of chivalry. In Part III, Kiera, now fourteen, is trapped in the Arthurian court torn by the love affair of Lancelot and Guinevere. Although Mordred and Arthur try to negotiate their differences, the treacherous Bayard and Morgan le Fay undermine them. After the fated battle, Arthur joins the Lady of the Lake, but Mordred rejects power and chooses the life with the love of Alayna instead. Kiera walks away.

Read Aloud/Reader Response

1. Part I, Chapter 2, page 13, beginning "But it was..." and ending "...burned them all." Alayna is against magic to protect her daughter.
2. Part I, Chapter 4, pages 23 and 24, beginning with the chapter and ending "...festival atmosphere." Alayna recalls Camelot through colors.
3. Part II, Chapter 1, pages 101 to 102, beginning "Sitting around..." and ending "...apprentice magician." The passage introduces the practical and magical Nimue.
4. Part III, Chapter 1, pages 185 to 188, beginning with the chapter and ending, "So she didn't ask." Magic creates conflict between Kiera and Alayna.
5. Part III, Chapter 20, pages 338 to 242. The characters make their final choices.

Booktalk

Ask how many in the group have heard of King Arthur and Camelot. Discuss what they know.

Most of us have heard of King Arthur and his ideal city, built on chivalry and knighthood. Most of us know about the magical Merlin, beautiful Guinevere, and dashing Lancelot. Many of us even know about Mordred, Arthur's evil son who destroyed the kingdom. But could one man really destroy a paradise? Were there cracks growing in Camelot's foundation before Mordred came along? And what about Mordred? Is he evil at all? Maybe his press agent just wasn't as good as Arthur's. Let me read you this excerpt from a letter written about Sir Malory, the man who praised Arthur. (*Read the passage before the opening of Part I.*) You have all heard Arthur's story. Sir Malory was the man who wrote it. But today we have another story about that ideal kingdom, from another point of view. Today we have *The Book of Mordred.*

Get Involved

1. (Research) Using your library resources, find out as much as possible about chivalry. Act as a resource person for the group during the discussion.
2. (React) Find as many references to chivalry in the novel as you can. Then explain the statements with which you agree and disagree.
3. (Discuss) Did the three-part format help strengthen the story?
4. (Discuss) What strengths do Alayna, Nimue, and Kiera demonstrate?
5. (React) In the novel, what events remind you of modern times? Identify them and explain your choices with specifics from the story and reports from modern times.

Related Works

1. Farmer, Nancy. **The House of the Scorpion.** New York: Atheneum Books for Young Readers/A Richard Jackson Book, 2002. 380p. $17.95. ISBN 0 689 85222 3. [fiction] JS, CG with high interest for boys. Matt, a clone that will be used for body parts, breaks away from his drug lord owner and destroys the drug kingdom.
2. Jones, Diana Wynne. **The Merlin Conspiracy.** New York: Harper-Collins/Greenwillow Books, 2003. 468p. $17.89. ISBN 0 06 052319 0. [fiction] MJS, CG. Divided between the perceptions of Roddy and Nick, this fantasy unfolds in the islands of Blest that keep the balance of magic for half of the multiverse. After the Merlin of Blest dies, Roddy, her good friend Grundo, and Nick, who blunders into Blest from another world, discover their own magical powers, forge relationships, discover powerful family members, and defeat the evil powers. Grundo and Nick reconnect with their fathers, and Roddy begins training as the female counterpart to the male Merlin.

3. Kerven, Rosalind. **King Arthur.** New York: DK Publishing, 1998. 63p. (Eyewitness Classics). $14.95. ISBN 0 7894 2887 3. [nonfiction] MJS, CG (See full booktalk in *Booktalks Plus,* 2001, pages 131 to 133.) The format that includes large full-page pictures and sidebars creates an appealing and motivating presentation of King Arthur. It clearly distinguishes between the magic of Merlin and Morgan le Fay.

4. Mathews, John. **King Arthur: Dark Age Warrior and Mythic Hero.** New York: Rosen Publishing, 2008. 127p. (Prime Time History). $39.95. ISBN-13: 978 1 4042 1364 7. [reference] JS, CG. Mathews presents a scholarly history of the Arthurian legends as well as its influence on modern culture. The volume includes beautiful artwork and the following sources for further information: "Major Sources of the Arthurian Legend"; a list of the court members; a dictionary of the characters mentioned within the volume; a glossary; a list "For Further Reading"; a "For More Information" section that includes journals, addresses, Web sites, and newsletters; and an extensive bibliography. An index provides easy access to information within the text.

5. Springer, Nancy. **I Am Mordred: Tales from Camelot.** New York: Philomel Books, 1998. 184p. $14.15. ISBN 0 399 23143 9. [fiction] MJ, CG Mordred, whose life hovers between the natural and supernatural worlds, loves his father in spite of his fate to battle and kill him.

6. Thomson, Sarah L. **The Dragon's Son.** New York: Orchard Books, 2001. 192p. $17.95. ISBN 0 531 30333 0. [fiction] JS, CG This historical novel is a combination of four stories told by four different characters: Nimue, Morgan, Luned, and Medraud. Set in A.D. 500 Britain, the story explores the country's need for a strong king who must rule with both compassion and strength.

Choosing and Achieving

ɔʃɔ

Farmer, Nancy. **The Land of the Silver Apples.**
New York: Atheneum Books for Young Readers/A Richard Jackson Book, 2007. 491p. $18.99. ISBN-13: 978 1 4169 0735 0. [fiction] MJ, CG with high interest for boys

Themes/Topics: bards, druids, Saxons, goblins, elves, myths, Christianity

Summary/Description

Jack's willful sister, Lucy, violates the rules of the Need-Fire Ceremony and begins a disruption in the family that leads to the revelation that hobgoblins stole Jack's real sister and substituted Lucy. Defending Lucy from a corrupt exorcism, Jack causes an earthquake that releases the elf-queen imprisoned by Christians. The queen takes Lucy and all the water. Under threat of his father's death, Jack begins his journey to Elf-land to retrieve the water and Lucy. He reunites with Thorgil, finds his real sister living happily with the hobgoblins, and learns that Lucy is a selfish elf whom he need not rescue. In this multi-faceted journey that climaxes with a confrontation between the truth (the Life Force) and illusion, Jack restores the Life Force to the land and realizes that both beauty and fear are in the eye of the beholder. Farmer provides an appendix that explains places, people, and symbols referred to in the story as well as a list of her sources.

Read Aloud/Reader Response

1. Chapter 12, pages 101 to 106, beginning with the chapter and ending with "...magic it contained." Jack learns the great conflict between magic and Christianity in the monastery.
2. Chapter 21, pages 216 to 217, beginning "Jack and Pega..." and ending with the chapter. Thorgil describes the knocker hole.
3. Chapter 37, pages 348 to 357. This chapter shows Lucy's true character and the power of the authentic, the truth, or the Life Force.
4. Chapter 40, pages 382 to 384, beginning "They all shaded their eyes..." and ending "...Father Severus said." Thorgil and Severus compare the concepts of fate and "Heaven's purpose."
5. Chapter 42, pages 403 to 404, beginning "THE BEST..." and ending "...nail in the ark." Father Severus tells the story of the best and worst nail in the ark.

Booktalk

Hold up The Sea of Trolls *(Related Work 3) by Nancy Farmer. Ask how many people remember it. Ask a few to fill in the story without spoiling the ending.*

Those who have read *The Sea of Trolls* know Jack, the rejected son who is learning to be a Bard. Well, Jack is back with another magical journey. Favored sister Lucy is convinced she is a princess, and when the Lady of the Lake steals her, it is once again Jack's job to come to the rescue. What does Jack have to face? Rogue monks, knocker holes, elves, and hobgoblins. Who will help him? An ugly slave girl he freed in a weak moment, a questionable descendent of Lancelot, and his old buddy, the Berserker Thorgil. And while he is accomplishing his mission, he also has to sort out the beliefs of the old gods and Christianity. If you already know Jack, you will enjoy this spine-tingling journey as much as the last one. If this is your first meeting, don't hesitate, you will be able to follow every twist and turn of fate in Jack's magical journey to *The Land of the Silver Apples.*

Get Involved

1. (Research) Farmer shows many overlaps between the beliefs in the old gods and Christianity. Using your library resources, learn more about those overlaps, and act as a resource person for your group during the discussion.
2. (React) The difference between the real and the imagined seems to be a major theme in the story. Choose the scene, person, or place that you think most vividly illustrates that idea. Compare your choice with the choices of others in the group.
3. (React) Who for you is the most appealing character? Explain your choice with specifics from the text. Compare your choice with the choices of others in the group.
4. (React) Who for you is the most repulsive character? Explain your choice with specifics from the text. Compare your choice with the choices of others in the group.
5. (Create) Describe or illustrate your understanding of the Life Force.

Related Works

1. Bell, Hilari. **The Goblin Wood.** New York: HarperCollins Publishers, 2003. 294p. $17.99. ISBN 0 06 051372 1. [fiction] MJS, CG
   Eleven-year-old Makenna lives in the Realm of the Bright Gods but leaves and floods the village when she sees her mother, a hedge-witch, killed by a village mob. She comes to lead a goblin army and love a would-be knight sent to kill her.
2. Cadnum, Michael. **Raven of the Waves.** New York: Orchard Books, 2001. 208p. $17.95. ISBN 0 531 30334 9. [fiction] MJS, CG
   with high interest for boys. When seventeen-year-old Lidsmod rides the sea in the Norse ship *Raven* to make his first raid on the peaceful monasteries and villages that line the English rivers, he learns about the courage, cruelty, madness, and kindness that make up his fellow warriors and that forgiveness can be as strong as or stronger than the sword.
3. Farmer, Nancy. **The Sea of Trolls.** New York: Atheneum Books for Young Readers/A Richard Jackson Book, 2004. 459p. $17.95. ISBN

0 689 86744 1. [fiction] MJ, CG with high interest for boys (See full booktalk in *Booktalks and Beyond,* 2007, pages 160 to 162.) Eleven-year-old Jack, overworked and underappreciated by his father, apprentices to the local Bard, also known as Dragon Tongue. He and his spoiled sister Lucy are captured when Beserkers raid the Saxon village. In the subsequent journey, Jack learns that understanding good means acknowledging evil.

4. Funke, Cornelia. **Dragon Rider.** New York: Scholastic, Inc., 2004. 528p. $12.95. ISBN 0 439 45695 9. [fiction] MJ, CG with high interest for boys. An orphan and a silver dragon join with a host of fantasy characters and supportive humans to defeat the evil golden dragon and in the process find their homes.

5. Voigt, Cynthia. **Elske.** New York: Atheneum Books for Young Readers/Anne Schwartz Books, 1999. 245p. $18.00. ISBN 0 689 82472 6. [fiction] JS, G In this fantasy set in an Anglo-Saxon-like time period, Elske, the granddaughter of a Wolfer captive, escapes certain death and becomes the valued warrior for a rebellious princess.

Petersen, David. **Mouse Guard: Fall 1152.**

Fort Lee, NJ: ASP Comics LLC, 2007. 192p. $24.95. ISBN-13: 978 1 932386 57 8.

[graphic] MJS, CG with high interest for boys

Themes/Topics: community, survival, spies, tradition

Summary/Description

Within the mouse community, the Mouse Guard guides fellow mice from community to community without confrontation with enemies and so improves each community's quality of life. In this collection of six episodes, Mouse Guards Lieam, Kenzie, and Saxon search for a missing mouse who peddles grain. They discover that he was killed by a snake, but was a traitor carrying plans of Lockhaven to an enemy. Sadie, another guard, has been sent to make contact with Conrad, a missing guard member who tells about the grain peddler giving information to a mouse who remains in the shadows. Lieam decides to infiltrate a militia known as "the Axe," the center of the plot. While creating a diversion for Lieam, Kenzie and Saxon are attacked, left for dead, and dragged to a hermit's house. The hermit interrogates them and eventually reveals himself as the Dark Axe, an ancient mouse hero. He helps them so that he might retrieve his legendary axe now in the possession of the militia leader. Lieam is discovered as a spy. The militia leader plans to execute him just before he attacks Lockhaven. Sadie warns Lockhaven about the treachery and attack just in time. The good forces win, acknowledge the complaints of the militia members, and banish the leader, who was exploiting the unrest among the country mice and planned to establish a dictatorship. The story is supplemented by an appendix of "Maps, Guides, and Assorted Extras" and "A Gallery of Pinups by Esteemed Authors & Friends." The Pinups appeared in the original Mouse Guard series.

Read Aloud/Reader Response

Because there are no page numbers, the passages are indicated by chapter placement.

1. Each segment has an introductory quotation. The quotations introducing Chapters 3, 4, and 5 apply to real life as well as mouse life. The Chapter 3 quotation applies to discerning friends and enemies. The Chapter 4 quotation applies to the long-term implications of killing an enemy. The Chapter 5 quotation applies to the "storms of life."
2. Chapter 5 includes the book's central legend and therefore presents the values of the mouse community.
3. Chapter 6. The last three pages give Gwendolyn's reaction to the leader of the rebellion and her commitment to the community.

Booktalk

Ask how many members of the group have heard about Tom and Jerry. Ask how many have watched the Disney movie Cinderella.

Mouse Guard: Fall 1152 is another story about mice. But these mice aren't funny or cute. These mice are guards, leaders, mentors, spies, and warriors. As one of the lowest links of the food chain, their lives are full of danger. If they don't work together, if they don't get tough, they will die. Let me read you what the author, David Petersen, says about his mouse stories. (*Read the first three paragraphs of the preface by David Petersen.*) So Petersen created a world with both his words and pictures. He took this world seriously. And the first glimpse is *Mouse Guard: Fall 1152*.

Get Involved

1. (Research) Using your library resources, find out as much as possible about the life of the mouse. Act as a resource person during the discussion.
2. (Discuss) List the values of Petersen's mouse world. Be sure to support what you say with specifics from the text. Compare your list with the lists of other members of the group.

3. (Discuss) Consider the time period that Petersen chose for his story. Consider how the story would have changed if it were set in modern day.
4. (Research) Choose another animal or insect. Research its living situation.
5. (Create) Using the specifics from Get Involved 4, create a world for that animal or insect.
6. (Follow-up) Petersen introduces each chapter with a key quotation. Choose or create a series of quotations that keynote the values of the world you created in Get Involved 5.

Related Works

1. Clement-Davies, David. **Fire Bringer.** New York: Firebird, 1999. 498p. $6.99pa. ISBN 0 14 230060 8. [fiction] JS, CG with high interest for boys. In this animal fantasy based on the real facts of deer life, Rannoch becomes the leader of the deer and decides to direct them away from a life of violence.
2. Hosler, Jay. **Clan Apis.** Columbus, OH: Active Synapse, 2000. 158p. $15.00. ISBN 1 4046 1367 6. [graphic] JS/A, CG (See full booktalk in *Teen Genre Connections,* 2005, pages 280 to 282.) In five chapters, Hosler describes the life cycle of the honeybee through the life journey of Nyuki, a worker bee.
3. Jarvis, Robin. **The Dark Portal: Book One of the Deptford Mice Trilogy.** New York: Sea Star Books, 2000. 239p. $17.95. ISBN 1 58717 021 3. [fiction] MJ, CG In a mice versus rats tale of good and evil, the mice (good guys) live in a deserted Deptford home, and the rats (bad guys) live in the sewers. Victorian grillwork in the house's cellar divides the two worlds, and mysteriously draws mice into the sewers.
4. Johnson, Spencer, M.D. **Who Moved My Cheese?** New York: G. P. Putnam's Sons, 1998. 94p. $19.95. ISBN 0 399 14446 3. [fiction] JS/A, CG. This allegory about mice teaches people how to deal with change in their lives.
5. Zindel, Paul. **Rats.** New York: Hyperion Books for Children, 1999. 203p. $13.99 ISBN 0 7868 2820 X. [fiction] MJ, CG with high interest for boys. Fifteen-year-old Sarah Macafee and her ten-year-old brother Michael live next to a toxic landfill breeding mutant rats able to destroy the entire community unless Sarah and Michael destroy them first.

ᛊᛊ

Pierce, Tamora. **The Will of the Empress.**
New York: Scholastic Press, 2005. 320p. $17.99. ISBN 0 439 44171 4. [fiction] MJS, G

Themes/Topics: friendship, maturation, responsibility, conduct of life, women's rights, magic

Summary/Description

Sixteen-year-old Sandry finds her reunion with her foster sisters and brother strained. After two years, they no longer share their thoughts and cannot return to their old life at Discipline Cottage. The foursome travels to the Namorn Empire, Sandry's royal home. Wanting to keep Sandry's wealth in the kingdom, the Empress tries to marry Sandry off and bribe her friends to stay. Two frustrated suitors resort to a Namorn kidnapping custom that forces a woman's marriage. The four magically defeat their efforts as well as the Empress's plots. Sandry decides to relinquish her lands to her cousin, her overseer, so that her subjects will have caring, hands-on leadership. The cousin will abolish the forced marriage custom. Sandry, Daja, Tris, and Briar, bonded through their struggles, confess that they did not share their thoughts because they each feared rejection. The story is based on the *Circle of Magic* and the *Circle Opens* quartets.

Read Aloud/Reader Response

1. Chapter 9, pages 227 to 228, beginning "Uncaring…" and ending "…face with her hands." Sandry realizes that ownership and leadership carry responsibilities.
2. Chapter 10, page 264, beginning "If you weren't fighting…" and ending "…wanting my family back!" Sandry expresses her frustration over their changed relationship.
3. Chapter 16, page 432, beginning "Ealaga sighed." and ending "…actions of a few?" Ambros's wife points out why women might judge all men by the irresponsible ones.
4. Chapter 20, pages 529 and 530, beginning "It occurs to me…" and ending "…drawled Tris." Daja and Tris reflect on the meaning of determined.
5. Chapter 20, page 538, beginning "Not being able…" and ending "…we are on ourselves." The four understand why they held their thoughts back.

Booktalk

Sandry, Briar, Tris, and Daja are back together but they aren't too happy about it. They all have had their own adventures, and they aren't about to share them. So they are closing their minds—even to each other. Everyone waits for the other one to talk first. Silence. Things get tense. But the magic four better get over their communication problems, and fast. Sandry, the stay at home, needs help with a capital "H." Sandry is royalty, but she hasn't been back to her lands in Namorn for years—especially her older years. If she is going to take this ruling thing seriously, for sixteen-year-old Sandry, it is time. The Empress realizes how wealthy Sandry is. She wants Sandry to marry, stay, and keep her money in Namorn. So on this visit, Sandry needs an escort, people who understand what *she* wants. When Sandry and the tense, confused, but supportive threesome shows up, the Empress sees both money and talent pouring into Namorn. She decides that all should stay. Maybe Sandry's escort needs an escort—maybe even an army. And even an army may be no match for *The Will of the Empress*.

Get Involved

1. (Research) Using your library resources, research the marriage laws of a non-Western country. Act as a resource person for the group during the discussion.
2. (React) Determination and responsibility are two central themes. List incidents from the story that you feel illustrate those themes. Share your choices with the group.
3. (Discuss) Why do you think that Pierce included Gudruny and Zhegorz?
4. (Create) Draw one of the characters or scenes from *The Will of the Empress*.
5. (React) This story focuses on true love as well as true friendship. On the basis of specifics from the story, state where you feel these two feelings separate and overlap. Compare your opinions with those of other members of the group.

Related Works

1. Pierce, Tamora. **The Circle Opens Quartet.** New York: Scholastic Press. [fiction] MJ
   Magic Steps. 2000. 272p. $16.95. ISBN 0 590 39588 2. G Fourteen-year-old Sandry realizes her responsibilities for using magic in the real world when she leaves her school to live with her uncle, trains a dancer to realize his magical powers, and finds herself in confrontation with two assassins and a decadent mage.
   Street Magic. 2001. 304p. $16.95. ISBN 0 590 39628 5. CG Fourteen-year-old Brian Moss uses his plant power to mentor a stubborn young street girl and defeat the evil woman who wishes to control her magic.
   Cold Fire. 2002. 368p. $16.95. ISBN 0 590 39655 2. G Supposedly on vacation, Daja and Frostpine find themselves teaching meditation to magically gifted twins and uncovering a pyromaniac.

Shatterglass. 2003. 368p. $16.95. ISBN 0 590 39683 8. G Trisana
Chandler uses her powers as a glass mage to help a glassmaker gifted
with lightning magic to focus his powers and clear himself of accusa-
tions of murder. Like the other three lead characters in *The Circle
Opens Quartet,* she also mentors a young orphan who does not realize her own magic.

2. Pierce, Tamora. **Melting Stones.** New York: Scholastic Press, 2008.
320p. $17.99. ISBN-13: 978 0 545 05264 1. JS, G First written as an
audiobook released by Full Cast Audio in October 2007, the story
returns to the *Circle of Magic* and the *Circle Opens* quartets. Evvy,
a young stone mage in training, tries to save an island nation from
disaster.

ᘓᘔᘓᘔ

Rowling, J. K., and Mary Grandpré (illus.). **Harry Potter and the Deathly Hallows.**

New York: Scholastic, Inc./Arthur A. Levine Books, 2007. 759p. $34.99.
ISBN-13: 978 0 545 01022 1. [fiction] MJS, CG with high interest for boys

Themes/Topics: courage, love, family, friends, good vs. evil,
conduct of life

Summary/Description

Harry, Hermoine, and Ron set out to destroy Voldemort by destroying the Horcruxes that give him immortality. Without Dumbledore,
the three experience frustration, anger, division, and confusion as they
hide out, hatch plans, and figure out the importance of the objects
Dumbledore bequeaths to them in his will. Their inheritance leads
them to the secrets of the three Deathly Hallows: the invisibility cloak,
the Resurrection Stone, and the Elder Wand. Together, these objects
give the possessor power over death. In the final battle with Voldemort,
Harry travels to the land of death where he sees all the loved ones he
has lost. He reunites with Dumbledore who explains how, in his youth,
he pursued the Deathly Hallows, which would give him power over
death. Harry can choose to stay with him or return to life. Harry chooses
life, and with the help of all his supporters, destroys Voldemort through
Voldemort's ignorance of the Hallows. Although Harry eventually pos-
sesses all three Hallows, he keeps only the invisibility cloak to ensure that
no one person will be tempted by the power again. The epilogue shows
the married couples of Harry and Ginny as well as Ron and Hermoine
sending their children to Hogwarts.

Read Aloud/Reader Response

1. Chapter 11, pages 211 to 216, beginning "Harry hesitated..." and ending "...his old friend?" Harry refuses Lupin's offer for help and calls him a coward because of his willingness to leave his mixed-blood family.
2. Chapter 16, page 325, "Where your...be also." This sentence is on the grave of Kendra and Ariana Dumbledore.
3. Chapter 16, page 328, "The last...is death." This sentence is on the grave of Harry's parents.
4. Chapter 19, pages 370 to 379, beginning "Harry had no strength..." and ending "...surprisingly short time." Ron and Harry are re-united.
5. Chapter 35, pages 705 to 723. In this chapter, Harry crosses over, reunites with Dumbledore, and must decide if he will return to the living world.

Booktalk

Harry Potter and the Deathly Hallows, the end at last. In this final volume, every detail, plot, and character created by Rowling come together. Is it a happy ending? For some. Is it a just ending? For some. But Harry Potter is about much more than happiness and justice. It is about everyday life, even if that life is described in larger-than-life terms. It is about courage in the face of unhappiness and injustice. It is about the power of love and friendship in the best and worst of times. And, on top of everything else, Rowling can tell a good story. This final book is an action-packed, non-stop tale about the deciding face-off between good and evil. Can three teenagers stop a villain who wants to control this world and the next? You'll know when you read the final chapter in the Harry Potter epic, *Harry Potter and the Deathly Hallows.*

Get Involved

1. (Research) Using your library resources, define and find historical examples of fascism. Act as a resource person for the group during the discussion.
2. (Research) Using your library resources, find author interviews and comments that explain Rowling's reactions to and relationship with the Harry Potter series.
3. (Discuss) Is Voldemort's government fascist?
4. (React) Rowling includes an epilogue. Would you have included an epilogue?
5. (Create) Create a library display for the Harry Potter series. Include quotations from Get Involved 2 in your display.

6. (Discuss) How are the major conflicts in this story similar to and different from the conflicts in the other volumes?
7. (React) Identify the characters or places in the series that you feel will become significant references in the future. Explain your choices.

Related Works

1. Rowling, J. K. **Harry Potter and the Chamber of Secrets.** New York: Arthur A. Levine Books, 1998. 341p. $17.95. ISBN 0 439 06486 4. [fiction] MJS, CG with high interest for boys (See full booktalk in *Booktalks Plus,* 2001, page 182.) In this second volume, Harry, the Weasleys, and Hermione return to Hogwarts and discover that Ginny Weasley is under Voldemort's power.
2. Rowling, J. K. **Harry Potter and the Goblet of Fire.** New York: Arthur A. Levine Books, 2000. 734p. $25.95. ISBN 0 439 13959 7. [fiction] MJS, CG with high interest for boys (See full booktalk in *Booktalks Plus,* 2001, pages 184 to 187.) In this fourth volume, Harry finds it more difficult to distinguish between friend and foe as he fights his own pride and jealousy.
3. Rowling, J. K. **Harry Potter and the Half-Blood Prince.** New York: Arthur A. Levine Books, 2005. 652p. $29.99. ISBN 0 439 78454 9. [fiction] MJS, CG with high interest for boys (See full booktalk in *Booktalks and Beyond,* 2007, pages 155 to 157.) In this sixth volume, Harry discovers that double-agent Snapes is the Half-Blood Prince. Dumbledore dies at Snape's hand.
4. Rowling, J. K. **Harry Potter and the Order of the Phoenix.** New York: Arthur A. Levine Books, 2003. 870p. $29.99. ISBN 0 439 35806 X. [fiction] MJS, CG with high interest for boys (See full booktalk in *Teen Genre Connections,* 2005, pages 190 to 192.) In this fifth volume, Harry joins with the Order of the Phoenix to fight Voldemort who lures Harry and his friends into danger through false visions.
5. Rowling, J. K. **Harry Potter and the Prisoner of Askaban.** New York: Arthur A. Levine Books, 1999. 431p. $19.95. ISBN 0 439 13635 0. [fiction] MJS, CG with high interest for boys (See full booktalk in *Booktalks Plus,* 2001, page 183.) In this third volume, Harry discovers the importance of Sirius Black in his family's life.
6. Rowling, J. K. **Harry Potter and the Sorcerer's Stone.** New York: Arthur A. Levine Books, 1997. 509p. $17.95. ISBN 0 590 35340 3. [fiction] MJS, CG with high interest for boys (See full booktalk in *Booktalks Plus,* 2001, pages 181 to 182.) In this first volume, Harry Potter discovers that he is wizard, and, with the help of Ron and Hermoine, confronts Voldemort.

ɾʒ ʕɔ

Wooding, Chris. Storm Thief.

New York: Scholastic Press, 2006. 320p. $16.99. ISBN 0 439 86513 1. [fiction]
JS, CG with high interest for boys

Themes/Topics: orphans, creation, change, haves vs. have-nots, friendship

Summary/Description

In five parts, the story describes the journey of two child ghetto thieves who steal a magical artifact, manage to elude their pursuers, and escape the island. Rail and Moa, the thieves, live on Orokos, a city in the middle of the ocean, which is subject to probability storms that change the island and people constantly. The Protectorate and the Revenants, ghost-like entities that create living dead, engage in an ongoing battle for control. When Rail and Moa discover the artifact, they decide to keep it instead of taking it to their boss. In flight from the boss's trusted soldier and the authorities, they encounter Vago, a golem, created by the Protectorate to battle the Revenants. Although Vago is captured and reprogrammed by the Protectorate, his love for Moa overcomes his jealousy of Rail. With his help and the power of the artifact, Moa and Rail escape the island. Vago cannot save himself, and lives a limbo existence in the sea.

Read Aloud/Reader Response

1. Chapter 1.5, pages 31 to 34, beginning "Vago lived..." and ending with the chapter. Vago finds the seabird. The reader learns about Vago's appearance, his disposition, and his relationship to Cretch and Ephemera.
2. Chapter 1.6, pages 35 to 38, beginning with the chapter and ending with "...lair of the thief-mistress." The reader learns about Rail and Moa and their situation in the city.
3. Chapter 1.8, pages 55 to 60, beginning "Whenever Vago returned..." and ending with the chapter. Cretch and Vago talk about Vago's creation. Cretch demonstrates his abuse, and Vago reacts violently.
4. Chapter 2.1, pages 89 to 94. In this chapter, Lysander Bane, Chief of the Protectorate Secret Police, reveals himself and his society's structure. The chapter also introduces Bane's relationship to the golem.
5. Chapter 5.4, pages 265 to 266, beginning "I tried,..." and ending "...went on in silence." Moa wants to act to save others, but Rail sees saving others as impossible.

6.   Chapter 5.6, pages 276 to 285. In this chapter, Moa and Rail meet Benejes Frine, who explains the history of Orokos and the function of the Chaos Engine.

Booktalk

Rail and Moa live in the ghetto of Orokos. Orokos is an island city plagued by probability storms that can happen anytime. These violent, mysterious, and almost supernatural events can change the color of someone's fingernails or turn the entire population into mice. With no parents and no money, Rail and Moa are among the least likely to survive the chaos that the storms bring. To try to keep alive, the two are part of a theft ring, and Rail is one of the best. When Rail is sent to rob one of the most dangerous parts of the city, he discovers an ancient artifact. He knows that it contains great power. He knows that he should give it to his boss. But he also knows that he doesn't want to share it. The artifact pushes Moa and him to danger and adventure. The duo join a half-monster, half-machine called a golem. Together, they take on the secret police, and change a world. Rail knew he was a master thief. But he never knew that by stealing something small enough to carry, he could become the most powerful person in the world. He never knew that he could become a *Storm Thief.*

Get Involved

1.   (Research) Using your library resources, prepare a bibliography of anti-utopian literature. Share it with your discussion group.
2.   Choose one of the books from the bibliography you prepared in Get Involved 1. Read it and compare the issues that it discusses with those in *Storm Thief.* Ask others in the group to choose one of the books in your bibliography also. Share the similarities and differences that you find.
3.   (Create) Using a graphic format, draw a picture of each character.
4.   (Create) Using a graphic format, depict a scene from the story.
5.   (Compare) Vago is a man-made creature living in a technologically manufactured community. After reading *Storm Thief* and *Frankenstein* (Related Work 4), compare the two monsters. Discuss the responsibility of each creator.
6.   (React) Trace the journey of Moa and Rail. What do you think each part of that journey represents? Consider the characters and experiences that appear within each part.

Related Works

1.   Adlington, L. J. **The Diary of Pelly D.** New York: HarperCollins/ Greenwillow Books, 2005. 282p. $16.99. ISBN 0 06 076616 6. [fiction]

JS, CG (See full booktalk in *Booktalks and Beyond,* 2007, pages 178 to 181.) Fourteen-year-old Toni V, the runt on a work gang clearing land after a war in a future society on a non-earth planet, finds the diary of Pelly D and discovers his own identity as he reads her story of marginalization and persecution.

2. Anderson, M. T. **Feed.** Cambridge, MA: Canlewich Press, 2003. 235p. $16.99. ISBN 0 7636 1726 1. [fiction] JS, CG with high interest for boys (See full booktalk in *Teen Genre Connections,* 2005, pages 201 to 203.) This science fiction novel projects what our world would be like if it centers on consumerism instead of spiritual growth.

3. Blackman, Malorie. **Naughts & Crosses.** New York: Simon & Schuster Books for Young Readers, 2005. 387p. $15.95. ISBN 1 4169 0016 0. [fiction] JS, CG (See full booktalk in *Booktalks and Beyond,* 2007, pages 16 to 19.) In a futuristic society defined by skin color, Sephy Hadley, a dark-skinned cross, and Callum McGregor, a light-skinned naught, become friends and eventually forbidden lovers. Sephy and Callum tell the story in alternating chapters.

4. Shelley, Mary. **Frankenstein.** New York: Pocket Books, 2004. 352p. (Enriched Classics). $4.95pa. ISBN-13: 978 07434 8758 0. [classic] JS/A, CG with high interest for boys. In this Gothic horror story about human life created by man, first published in 1818, Shelley presents the responsibilities each creator has for his or her creation.

5. Sleator, William. **The Last Universe.** New York: Amulet Books, 2005. 215p. $16.95. ISBN 0 8109 5858 9. [fiction] MJ, CG (See full booktalk in *Booktalks and Beyond,* 2007, pages 186 to 188.) Fourteen-year-old Susan and her dying sixteen-year-old brother Gary explore a mysterious maze created by her scientist uncle and discover, according to a theory of quantum physics, alternative worlds that change their lives.

History

History and historical fiction give us a bigger picture and illustrate how the individual might personally struggle in, grow from, and create world-changing circumstances. The girls' selections address coping, realizing personal growth, and clarifying loyalties during critical world events. The boys' selections share those issues but include more action and confrontation.

Struggling

Anderson, M. T. The Astonishing Life of Octavian Nothing: Traitor to the Nation; Volume I: The Pox Party.

Cambridge, MA: Candlewick Press, 2006. 351p. (The Astonishing Life of Octavian Nothing: Traitor to the Nation). $17.99. ISBN 0 7636 2402 0. [fiction] JS, CG

Themes/Topics: slavery, American Revolution, philosophers

Summary/Description

During the period of the American Revolution, Octavian and his mother Cassiopeia live in a Boston house, the Novanglian College of Lucidity, with rational philosophers who address each other by numbers. Pampered and classically schooled, Octavian learns he is a slave being assessed in the research of African intelligence. When his mother refuses to be the mistress to the school's benefactor, the benefactor beats them, lowers their status, and insists that the school focus on practical application. Octavian realizes that his education has been redesigned to make him fail and prove him inferior. Then, fearing a smallpox epidemic, the scholars stage a "Pox Party," in which the guests are inoculated and supervised through a milder disease. Cassiopeia dies. Octavian sees her being dissected, reacts violently, and runs away. He joins the revolutionaries and fights heroically, but slavers track him down. Returned to the school, he is imprisoned, shackled, and eventually interrogated about any connection he has to a slave rebellion. As the interrogation takes place, one of the philosophers poisons the other two interrogators and flees with Octavian from the crime scene.

Read Aloud/Reader Response

1. Part I: "The Transit of Venus," pages 8 and 11, beginning "I was taught..." and ending with the chapter. Octavian recalls his education and observation instruction in the college.
2. Part II: "The Pox Party," pages 134 to 136, beginning "I remember..." and ending with the chapter. Bono teaches Octavian the role of the slave and how to survive.
3. Part II: "The Pox Party," pages 147 to 156, beginning with one chapter and ending with the second. The two chapters involving music reveal both Mr. Sharpe's and Octavian's characters.
4. Part II: "The Pox Party," "Observations upon the Progression of the Smallpox in Homo Afri," pages 225 to 230, the entire report. The scholars report on the death and subsequent dissection of Octavian's mother as well as his reaction to it.
5. Part IV: "The Great Chain of Being," pages 323 to 326, beginning "The Africans amongst..." and ending with the chapter. Octavian ponders the abuses of slavery amid the revolution for freedom.

Booktalk

As the American colonies struggle for freedom, Octavian lives like a prince. He wears white wigs and embroidered satins. He does not work in fields to feed himself. His mother, too, lives like royalty. In fact, she is a real princess in exile. But he is discovering that his kingdom is a frail and dangerous one. His Boston home houses philosophers. They do not use names but numbers. They decide what and when he eats and learns. They supervise his every move. They warn him to stay within the house's walls for his own safety, but Octavian begins to wonder if those walls form his protection or his prison. Does one of these men have the power of a father, or do they all somehow have a claim on him? He knows there is a mystery in this house. The key is behind the forbidden door. When he opens that door, he learns an ugly truth, but Octavian cannot really understand his place, in this different world or in this coming revolution for freedom, until he attends the most frightening event of his life, *The Pox Party*.

Get Involved

1. (Research) Using your library resources, learn more about slavery in New England. Act as a resource person during the discussion.
2. (Research) Using your library resources, learn more about the slave restraints used in the colonies. Share pictures and descriptions of that equipment with the group.
3. (Research) Using your library resources, research the disease of small-pox. Act as a resource person for your group. Discuss why the entire volume is titled *The Pox Party*.
4. (Discuss) What are the ironies and hypocrisies involved in the Novanglian College of Lucidity?
5. (Discuss) Dr. Trefusis is one of the most eccentric supporting characters. Note each time he appears. On the basis of those passages, consider his role in the book.

Related Works

1. Anderson, M. T. **The Astonishing Life of Octavian Nothing: Traitor to the Nation; Volume II: The Kingdom on the Waves.** Cambridge, MA: Candlewick Press, 2008. 592p. (The Astonishing Life of Octavian Nothing: Traitor to the Nation). $22.99. ISBN-13: 978 0 76 3629502. [fiction] JS, CG. When Octavian escapes to Boston, he discovers an offer of freedom from counter-revolutionary forces.
2. Aronson, Marc. **The Real Revolution: The Global Story of American Independence.** New York: Clarion Books, 2005. 238p. $21.00. ISBN 0 618 18179 2. [nonfiction] JS, CG (See full book-talk in *Booktalks and Beyond,* 2007, pages 218 to 221.) Framing the American Revolution in world events, Aronson considers the dynamics of slavery, communication, Indian relations, American Western expansion, financial movement, economic booms and busts, and the developing American character.
3. Cox, Clinton. **Come All You Brave Soldiers.** New York: Scholastic Press, 1999. 189p. $15.95. ISBN 0 590 47576 2. [nonfiction] JS, CG (See full booktalk in *Booktalks Plus,* 2001, pages 155 to 157.) Cox explains how slaves and indentured servants tried to choose the side that would give them liberty and then, after the war, had freedom denied.
4. Lerangis, Peter. **Smiler's Bones.** New York: Scholastic Press, 2005. 160p. $16.95. ISBN 0 439 34485 9. [fiction] JS, CG Minik, taken from his home by Robert Peary in 1897, becomes the only living Polar Eskimo in New York, for twelve years, and discovers that his hosts have kept his father's bones to display in a museum.

5. Nelson, Marilyn. Pamela Espeland (notes and annotations). **Fortune's Bones: The Manumission Requiem.** Asheville, NC: Front Street, 2004. 32p. $16.95. ISBN 1 932425 12 8. [nonfiction] JS, CG (See full booktalk in *Booktalks and Beyond,* 2007, pages 247 to 249.) With notes and pictures accompanying six poems, the author tells the story of Fortune, one of the last slaves in Connecticut. When he died about 1798 at the age of sixty, his master, a doctor, boiled the bones and used the skeleton for study.

ᘒᘓ

Connolly, John. The Book of Lost Things.
New York: Atria Books, 2006. 339p. $23.00.
ISBN-13: 978 0 7432 9885 8. [fiction] S/A, CG

Themes/Topics: World War II England, grief, blended families, coming of age, conduct of life

Summary/Description

In 1939, twelve-year-old David loses his mother after a prolonged illness and then faces adjusting, five months later, to a blended family. His father marries the administrator of the hospice where his mother died, and they have a baby boy. After struggling with grief and resentment that pushes him to mental illness, David is knocked unconscious during a German air raid. In his coma, he visits a world made up of the old stories his mother told him and the worlds he has read about in his stepmother's home. Various good and evil characters from these fantasies help him and deceive him on his coming-of-age quest to consult the king and *The Book of Lost Things.* David discovers that the king, his stepmother's lost relative, was drawn into the kingdom and throne by the same jealous feelings for a new sibling. He returns to the real world and lives a positive life. When he dies, he returns to the fantasy world, his heaven, where he reunites with his family.

Read Aloud/Reader Response

1. Chapter 1, page 3, beginning "Before she became ill,..." and ending "...give them life." David's mother explains how stories come alive.
2. Chapter 1, pages 8 to 9, beginning "In the weeks..." and ending "...they were irritating him." The distinction that David's mother makes between stories and newspaper articles suggests a conflict between the father and mother.

3. Chapter 10, page 94, beginning "Eventually the Woodsman," and ending "'...govern your life.'" The Woodsman distinguishes between compulsive and productive routines.

4. Chapter 13, page 230, beginning "Then you must decide..." and ending "...than he reveals." Roland cautions David about striking a bargain, especially with the Crooked Man.

5. Chapter 32, page 328, beginning "And what would..." and ending "...becoming a man." The Woodsman explains how David, like each person coming of age, must find his own strength.

Booktalk

The year is 1939. The place is England. The English are fighting the Germans, but twelve-year-old David is engaged in another war. It is with himself. Five months after the death of David's mother, his father announces that he will remarry, and that they all will welcome a new baby. David doesn't like this world he is in, a world that seems cold, forgetful, and out of control. He retreats into the ancient stories his mother told him and then into the strange books that he finds in his stepmother's house. But this is World War II. Retreat from pain and horror is almost impossible. One night, both pain and horror fly into his life on German wings. On that night, David finds another world, the world that his mother assured him he could make come alive. This world, like the other, is filled with beauty, joy, deceit, and treachery. But this world's king has a special book. David hopes that the answers to his life are in this book. He will find the king and ask, but what he finds may be much more important and surprising than any information, or spell, or person that may dwell in *The Book of Lost Things*.

Get Involved

1. (Research) Using your library resources, find out more about the home front struggle in England during World War II. Act as a resource person during the discussion.

2. (Discuss) Re-read, perhaps out loud, all the stories told by the fantasy characters. Discuss the purpose of each in relation to David's journey.

3. (Discuss) As a group, sort out the good and evil characters in the novel. Feel free to create a gray category.

4. (Discuss) Trace David's journey. How does each incident change him?

5. (Research) Using your library resources, find original fairy tales. Discuss how they differ from modern animated versions. You may wish to start by reading *The Brothers Grimm* (Related Work 4).

6. (Create and Follow-up) Write a new story or rewrite a traditional fairy tale so that it speaks to teenage life.

7. (Create and Follow-up) Using graphic illustrations, rewrite one of the stories from Get Involved 2 or Get Involved 6 in graphic novel format.

Related Works

1. Farmer, Nancy. **The Sea of Trolls.** New York: Atheneum Books for Young Readers/A Richard Jackson Book, 2004. 459p. $17.95. ISBN 0 689 86744 1. [fiction] MJ, CG with high interest for boys (See full booktalk in *Booktalks and Beyond,* 2007, pages 160 to 162.) When Jack, captured by the Beserkers, journeys to the land of the Trolls to save the life of his spoiled seven-year-old sister, he discovers that understanding good means acknowledging evil.

2. Funke, Cornelia. **Inkheart.** New York: Scholastic Press/Chicken House, 2003. 544p. $19.95. ISBN 0 439 53164 0. [fiction] MJS, CG (See full booktalk in *Booktalks and Beyond,* 2007, pages 162 to 163.) Twelve-year-old Meggie enters the fictional world in order to keep released evil characters from destroying the real one. By the end of the novel, she decides to become a writer and create the magic of her own world.

3. Hearn, Julie. **Sign of the Raven.** New York: Atheneum Books for Young Readers/Ginee Seo Books, 2005. 336p. $16.95. ISBN 0 689 85734 9. [fiction] JS, G (See full booktalk in *Booktalks and Beyond,* 2007, pages 152 to 154.) When twelve-year-old Tom accompanies his mother, suffering from breast cancer, on a visit to his estranged grandmother, he rediscovers a gap in the basement that catapults him to an eighteenth-century London world of freaks. Helping the freaks, he works through mother/grandmother conflicts, the repulsion he feels for his mother's mastectomy, and his fear of her death.

4. Hettinga, Donald R. **The Brothers Grimm: Two Lives, One Legacy.** New York: Clarion Books, 2001. 180p. $22.00. ISBN 0 618 05599 1. [nonfiction] JS, CG Included in this story are lists of all the brothers' publications and gathered tales.

5. Wooding, Chris. **Poison.** New York: Orchard Books, 2003. 273p. $16.99. ISBN 0 439 75570 0. [fiction] JS, G (See full booktalk in *Booktalks and Beyond,* 2007, pages 176 to 178.) When the phaeries steal her baby sister Azalia, sixteen-year-old Poison sets out to bring her back and ultimately becomes the master writer who controls human lives.

Cʒʔɔ

Ferris, Jean. Underground.
New York: Farrar, Straus and Giroux, 2007. 168p. $16.00.
ISBN-13: 978 0 374 37243 9. [fiction] MJ, G

Themes/Topics: Mammoth Cave (Kentucky), slavery,
Underground Railroad, life choices

Summary/Description

In May 1839, sixteen-year-old Charlotte, a new maid and slave at Mammoth Cave Hotel, meets Stephen, an eighteen-year-old slave who is the cave's expert guide. They fall in love. Stephen feels secure in his position and loves his life in the cave. Charlotte, no matter how comfortable, desires freedom over slavery and tries to convince Stephen that they should run away together. Stephen helps with Underground Railroad efforts and understands that he could be sold at any time but commits to staying in Mammoth Cave, Kentucky. Charlotte chooses Stephen over her freedom. The "Author's Note" distinguishes between the fact and fiction in the story.

Read Aloud/Reader Response

1. Chapter 3, pages 16 to 17, beginning "I'd never been inside..." and ending with the chapter. Charlotte explains why she won't go in a cave and compares the "one way out" of the cave to the "one way out" of slavery.
2. Chapter 8, pages 40 to 47. The chapter reflects on the good and bad of slavery.
3. Chapter 17, pages 103 to 105, beginning "Finally I had to ask..." and ending "Course I didn't have any answer for that." Stephen and Charlotte discuss the price of a human being and the price of freedom.
4. Chapter 19, pages 113 to 117, beginning with the chapter and ending "...where he felt the most free." Stephen relates an incident in which his authority of a tour guide and his role of a slave come into conflict.
5. Chapter 23, pages 135 to 138, beginning with the chapter and ending "...the same as Stephen did." Charlotte and Stephen discuss running to freedom or staying in slavery.

Booktalk

Sixteen-year-old Charlotte has a new job and a new master at the Mammoth Cave Hotel. Her sale wasn't the first or the most painful. Charlotte remembers seeing her entire family sold at her first sale, and she knows that the next one might be just as painful. She is ready to grab her freedom and take control of her life as soon as she can figure out how. That is why she can't understand another slave at Mammoth Cave. Eighteen-year-old Stephen is content with his slavery. As the cave's head guide, he roams and explores the cave as much as he likes.

He has his master's respect, and he has never been sold—yet. For him slavery is a good and comfortable life. And because slavery gave Stephen to Charlotte, she also begins to wonder about how much better freedom could be. Then she discovers that runaways are coming to the cave. If she doesn't help them, they may be caught or killed. If she does help them, she might be caught or killed. The safest escape is the cave. The best guide is Stephen. Can she ask him to help and risk his life too? Worse, yet, if he doesn't want to help, will he turn her in? Charlotte doesn't know the answers, but she does know that her greatest safety and her greatest threat both are *Underground.*

Get Involved

1. (Research) Using your library resources, find out as much as possible about the Underground Railroad. Act as a resource person during the book discussion. You may wish to start by reading Related Work 1.
2. (Research) Using your library resources, find pictures and additional information about the Mammoth Cave. Act as a resource person during the discussion.
3. (Research) Using your library resources, learn more about the origins of slavery. Act as a resource person for the group during the discussion.
4. (Discuss) Should Charlotte have stayed with Stephen or sought her freedom?
5. (Create and Follow-up) In the "Author's Note," Ferris explains the basis of her story. Using a newspaper or magazine article, write a short story based on the article's facts.

Related Works

1. Fradin, Dennis Brindell. **Bound for the North Star: True Stories of Fugitive Slaves.** New York: Clarion Books, 2000. 205p. $20.00. ISBN 0 395 97017 2. [nonfiction] MJS, CG with high interest for boys (See full booktalk in *Teen Genre Connections*, 2005, pages 30 to 33.) Outlining the horrors of slavery and the efforts to escape it, Fradin uses first-person accounts of Mary Prince, Eliza Harris, Henry "Box" Brown, and Harriet Tubman.
2. Litwin, Laura Baskes. **Benjamin Banneker: Astronomer and Mathematician.** Berkeley Heights, NJ: Enslow Publishers, Inc., 1999. 112p. (African-American Biographies). $20.95. ISBN 0 7660 1208 5. [nonfiction] MJS, CG Another African-American genius of the post-Civil War era, Banneker lived in relative isolation because of racial prejudice.

3. Nelson, Marilyn. **Carver: A Life in Poems.** Asheville, NC: Front Street, 2001. 103p. $16.95. ISBN 1 886910 53 7. [biography in poems] MJS, CG (See full booktalk in *Teen Genre Connections,* 2005, pages 42 to 44.) Beginning with baby Carver, his mother, and his brother being bushwhacked, this series of poems concludes with the dying religious Professor Carver ruminating on the shame of war pilots training on his beloved Tuskegee Campus.

4. Nelson, Marilyn. Pamela Espeland (notes and annotations). **Fortune's Bones: The Manumission Requiem.** Asheville, NC: Front Street, 2004. 32p. $16.95. ISBN 1 932425 12 8. [nonfiction] JS, CG (See full booktalk in *Booktalks and Beyond,* 2007, pages 247 to 249.) The story of Fortune illustrates that even death did not always end the indignities and abuse of slavery.

5. Taylor, Mildred D. **The Land: Prequel to Roll of Thunder, Hear My Cry.** New York: Phyllis Fogelman Books, 2001. 275p. $17.99. ISBN 0 8037 1950 7. [fiction] JS, CG (See full booktalk in *Teen Genre Connections,* 2005, pages 267 to 269.) As the son of a slave and a plantation owner, Paul Logan struggles to find his own identity as a free man.

෴

Hostetter, Joyce Moyer. **Blue.**

Honesdale, PA: Calkins Creek Books, 2006. 193p. $16.95.
ISBN-13: 978 1 59078 389 4. [fiction] MJS, G

Themes/Topics: polio, race discrimination, friendship, North Carolina, World War II, family

Summary/Description

Thirteen-year-old Ann Fay Honeycutt becomes the man of the house when her father leaves to serve in World War II. She shoulders the responsibility of taking care of the vegetable garden and her siblings until polio strikes, first killing Ann's little brother and then paralyzing her. Like her brother, she is sent to "The Miracle of Hickory," an emergency hospital constructed for the epidemic. Here she meets Imogene Wilfong, a colored girl with whom she bonds. Ann Fay recognizes the prejudice against her friend. Although they are separated after the contagious stage of their disease, they fight to keep in touch. When Ann Fay finally reunites with her family, she resolves to help bridge the gap between the colored and white worlds. An "Author's Note" explains the fiction and nonfiction in the story. A bibliography including books and videos explores polio, Franklin D. Roosevelt, and World War II.

Read Aloud/Reader Response

1.   Chapter 1, pages 17 and 18, beginning "Wisteria is the only thing..." and ending with the chapter. Ann Fay explains her bond with her father in relation to the wisteria.
2.   Chapter 8, page 63, beginning "I thought how..." and ending with the chapter. Ann Fay realizes Junior is a true friend.
3.   Chapter 19, pages 132 to 136. In this chapter, Imogene explains why Ann Fay should not feel guilty and how God stores tears in his bottle collection.
4.   Chapter 22, page 150, the letter to Ann Fay from her daddy. The father expresses his distress in killing his fellow man, but believes that Ann Fay should not associate with Imogene.
5.   "Epilogue," page 187. Ann Fay reflects on what she learned about 1945.

Booktalk

In 1944, the newspapers are full of stories about World War II and polio. Thirteen-year-old Ann Fay Honeycutt doesn't pay much attention. She lives a good life with her family and friends on a beautiful piece of land in Hickory, North Carolina. Even though they don't have much, they know how to get by and stick together. But when her dad joins the fight against Hitler, things have to change. Ann Fay is supposed to take her father's place. She wears the blue overalls now. She tends the garden and rides herd on her sisters and brother. It is hard work, but Ann Fay handles it. Then the family finds itself in another war—a war against polio. Nobody has a magic bullet for that either, and like Hitler, it engineers death and takes prisoners. Honeycutts join the fighting and face the devastation. Will Ann Fay let the disease defeat them? No. Ann Fay is her father's daughter. She has her own overall uniform, and the strength to fight back. Now her overalls don't stand just for work but for character too. Ann Fay is not about to cut and run in a crisis, because, like her uniform tells the world, she is true *Blue*.

Get Involved

1.   (Research) Hostetter suggests many additional sources. Choose one and review it for the group during the book discussion.
2.   (Research) Using your library resources, learn more about the history of polio. Share your information with the group. You may wish to start with Related Work 2.
3.   (Research) Using your library resources, learn more about the presidential terms of Franklin Roosevelt. Act as a resource person during the book discussion.

4. (Compare) Continue to read about discrimination during World War II. You may wish to start with Related Works 1, 3, and 5.
5. (Discuss) Consider how the issues of World War II, polio, and discrimination are related.

Related Works

1. Bruchac, Joseph. **Code Talker: A Novel about the Navajo Marines of World War Two.** New York: Dial Books, 2005. 231p. $16.99. ISBN 0 8037 2921 9. [fiction] MJS, CG with high interest for boys. A former World War II soldier recalls the prejudice against him as a Native American and how his skills overcame that prejudice.
2. Draper, Allison Stark. **Polio.** New York: Rosen Publishing Group, 2001. 64p. (Epidemics: Deadly Diseases throughout History). $19.95. ISBN 0 8239 3348 2. [nonfiction] MJS, CG Tracing the history of the disease and treatment, Draper points out polio's potential for biological terrorism.
3. Freedman, Russell. **The Voice That Challenged a Nation: Marian Anderson and the Struggle for Equal Rights.** New York: Clarion Books, 2004. 114p. $18.00. ISBN 0 618 15976 2. [nonfiction] MJS, CG with high interest for girls (See full booktalk in *Teen Genre Connections,* 2005, pages 248 to 250.) Anderson's life illustrates the great prejudice that African-Americans struggled against during the 1930s and 1940s.
4. Giff, Patricia Reilly. **All the Way Home.** New York: Dell Yearling, 2001. 169p. $5.99pa. ISBN 0 440 41182 3. [fiction] MJ, G Eleven-year-old Muriel, a polio victim, runs away from her adopted home to find the mother she remembers from the polio hospital and discovers that the woman who adopted her was the one who cared for her through her illness and the one she truly remembers.
5. Patneaude, David. **Thin Wood Walls.** Boston, MA: Houghton Mifflin Company, 2004. 240p. $16.00. ISBN 0 618 34290 7. [fiction] MJS, CG (See full booktalk in *Teen Genre Connections,* 2005, pages 238 to 240.) In three parts, Joe Hanada describes how World War II and the Japanese Internment impact his family and the growing desire of young men to prove their loyalty to the United States.

&

Lemelman, Gusta, and Martin Lemelman (illus.).
Mendel's Daughter: A Memoir.

New York: Free Press, 2006. 218p. $19.95. ISBN-13: 978 0 7432 9162 0.

[nonfiction, graphic] MJS, CG

Themes/Topics: World War II, Poland/Ukraine, Nazi invasion, anti-Semitism, Jewish persecution

Summary/Description

Martin Lemelman illustrates his mother's story of her childhood in Poland during the 1930s, which included her escape from Nazi persecution. Part One, 1919 to 1939, opens in Germakivka, an area that is now Ukraine. Martin's mother, Gusta, is part of a large and prosperous Jewish family, and although the family is generally respected and accepted, she experiences some prejudice. Part Two, 1940 to 1945, sees the takeover of the Russian Communists and the subsequent German occupation. Gusta's brothers hide in the forest. Gusta eventually joins them, and her sister follows. They miss the German "Action" that massacres Jews, and in 1944, they are liberated. The "Epilogue" explains how the four make their way out of Poland and to America.

Read Aloud/Reader Response

1. Part I, page 25, beginning "When I am thinking…" and ending "…go to America." The mother reveals her prejudices, and Gusta reveals her desire to move to America.
2. Part I, pages 34 and 35, beginning "My Mother…" and ending "…they kill her." These pages briefly describe her parents' marriage and her mother's death.
3. Part II, pages 59 to 62, beginning "The Russians march…" and ending "…I see it." Gusta describes life under the Russian Communists.
4. Part II, pages 69 to 73, beginning "June 22, 1941" and ending "They will be rich!" Gusta explains how the Germans garnered Ukrainian support.
5. Part II, pages 147 to 171, beginning "We lived in the woods…" and ending "Water, oh, water." Gusta describes their survival in the woods.

Booktalk

In 1989, Martin Lemelman asked his mother to record her life story on tape. He did not look at that tape again until after she died in 1996. And the night that she died she told him that he must share those memories. Gusta Lemelman grew up in Poland during the 1930s. Even though there was some anti-Semitism in her country, Gusta's family was accepted and well respected. Then the Russian Communists came, and finally, the Germans. When the Communists came, her family was targeted because they had more than others. When the Germans came, her family was targeted simply because they were Jews. Gusta and some other members of her family survived the massacres. Others did not. She wanted her son to tell this generation the why and how. She wanted them to know how prejudice and greed can produce blind cruelty. He recorded her words, and, instead of making a tape or a movie, he drew pictures, haunting pictures (*Select pictures that you feel have the most impact for the group and show them as you are speaking.*) so that we could take the experience of *Mendel's Daughter* and make it ours.

Get Involved

1. (Research and Discuss) Lemelman closes his book with the statement from "The Passover Hagaddah": "In every generation, one must look upon himself, as if he personally came out of Egypt." Using your library resources, research the story of Exodus. Share your information with the group, and, together, discuss why Lemelman chose this quotation for his conclusion.
2. (Research) Using your library resources, research the part that Poland played in World War II. Be sure to consider Hitler's plans for that country. Act as a resource person for the group during the discussion.
3. (Research and Create) Using your library resources, research the place of Poland in European history. Construct a timeline of events for the members of the group to use during the discussion.
4. (Research) Using your library resources, research the symbols and ceremonies of the Jews. Act as a resource person for the class discussion. Use as many visual aids as possible.
5. (Discuss) Consider why Lemelman opens his book with the Yiddish saying, "Man plans and God laughs."
6. (React) Write down the most important part of the Gusta's story for you. Explain your choice and compare it with the choices of others in the group.

Related Works

1. Lobel, Anita. **No Pretty Pictures: A Child of War.** New York: Greenwillow Books, 1998. 193p. $16.00. ISBN 0 688 15935 4. [nonfiction] JS, G (See full booktalk in *Booktalks Plus*, 2001, pages 39 to 41.) Anita Lobel tells about leaving her parents to hide unsuccessfully in a country convent when she is five and her brother is three and then trying to reunite all four members of the family after the war when she is ten and her brother is eight.
2. Millman, Isaac. **Hidden Child.** New York: Farrar, Straus and Giroux/Frances Foster Books, 2005. 73p. $18.00. ISBN 0 374 33071 9. [nonfiction] MJS, CG Using narrative, and colored illustrations

to accompany the narrative, Millman describes how, as a child, he survived the Holocaust in hiding. His parents, who both died in concentration camps, were immigrants from Poland where his father was persecuted for being a Communist.

3.   Nir, Yehuda. **The Lost Childhood: A World War II Memoir.** New York: Scholastic Press, 2002. 288p. $16.95. ISBN 0 439 16389 7. [nonfiction] JS, CG Nir tells how his family successfully disguised themselves as Catholics in World War II. He explains the complicated position of the Polish Jews in relation to the Poles, Russians, and Germans.

4.   Opdyke, Irene Gut, with Jennifer Armstrong. **In My Hands: Memories of a Holocaust Rescuer.** New York: Alfred A. Knopf, 1999. 276p. $18.00. ISBN 0 679 89181 1. [nonfiction] JS, CG with high interest for girls (See full booktalk in *Booktalks and More*, 2003, pages 255 to 257.) Opdyke describes how her family life and personal beliefs led her to help and hide Jews persecuted during the German occupation of Poland.

5.   Zenatti, Valérie. Adriana Hunter (trans.). **When I Was a Soldier: A Memoir.** New York: Bloomsbury Children's Books, 2005. 235p. $16.95. ISBN 1 58234 978 9. [nonfiction] JS, CG with high interest for girls (See full booktalk in *Booktalks and Beyond*, 2007, pages 241 to 244.) Zenatti remembers her two years of compulsory military service and the Holocaust stories that kept her dedicated to protecting Israel.

Growing

☙❧

Newton, Robert. **Runner.**

New York: Alfred A. Knopf, 2007. 201p. $18.99. ISBN-13: 978 0 375 93744 6. [fiction] MJ, CG with high interest for boys

Themes/Topics: running, poverty, mothers and sons, organized crime, Australia, conduct of life

Summary/Description

In 1919, fifteen-year-old Charlie Feehan works for a crime boss so that he can support his newly widowed mother and baby brother. Running a race fixed by his new employer, Charlie makes a friend, Norman Heath (a.k.a. Nostrils), and bitter enemies, the infamous Jimmy Barlow and family. Charlie also finds a girlfriend when he generously buys her father out of debt to the mob. He persuades Nostrils to help him make liquor deliveries. On their second run, they are confronted by Jimmy Barlow and his gang. Charlie escapes but Nostrils is almost beaten to death. Guilt-ridden, Charlie quits organized crime, trains for and wins a prestigious running race, and uses his money primarily to buy a wood yard for himself and Nostrils.

Read Aloud/Reader Response

1. Chapter 1, pages 2 to 4, beginning "Let me tell you..." and ending "..., I gladly surrendered." Charlie explains his complicated relationship with running.
2. Chapter 2, page 19, beginning "Alone..." and ending with the chapter. Charlie explains why he doesn't admit how the race he won was fixed.
3. Chapter 9, pages 64 to 65, beginning "The streets of Richmond..." and ending "...horse manure, empty tins, and rats." Charlie describes the neighborhood.
4. Chapter 16, pages 135 to 138, beginning "After only a short..." and ending "'No...'" Charlie watches Barlow beat Nostrils.
5. Chapter 20, pages 170 to 171, beginning "While the others..." and ending "Even just a slice." Charlie realizes that he is driven by the hope for something better.
6. Chapter 23, pages 198 to 201. The concluding chapter shows the successful Charlie presenting the wood yard to his new and stunned business partner, Nostrils.

Booktalk

Fifteen-year-old Charlie Feehan lives in Richmond, Australia. The year is 1919. His father just died, and Charlie is the sole support of his mother and baby brother. Charlie isn't going to feed them or keep them warm if he stays in school. But if he hits the streets, their lives may get better. Charlie has some talent. He can run. The rich and powerful crime boss, Squizzy Taylor, needs a good runner. Charlie can collect bad debts, deliver illegal liquor, and get messages to anyone in town fast. It's easy money, lots of it, and armed protection to boot. Charlie takes the job but doesn't anticipate the problems that come with the perks. Can a man be more than his job? In fact, can Charlie ever become a real man while he is a *Runner*?

Get Involved

1. (Research) Using your library resources and the information given in the "Author's Note," learn more about organized crime in a

particular country during the early twentieth century. Act as a resource person during your group discussion.

2. (Research) Using your library resources, research the flu epidemic
of the early twentieth century. Act as a resource person during your
group discussion.

3. (React) Charlie is a talented runner. List his other talents and how
those talents allow him to be successful.

4. (React) Which supporting character is the most appealing? How
does that character complement Charlie?

5. (Discuss) How does Newton use shoes in the story?

6. (React) After discussing Get Involved 3 and 4, list the qualities that
lead a person to success. Support your list with specific examples.

Related Works

1. Brown, Don. **The Notorious Izzy Fink.** New Milford, CT: Roaring
Brook Press/A Deborah Brodie Book, 2006. 150p. $16.95. ISBN
1 59643 139 3. [fiction] MJ, CG with high interest for boys. Irish/
Jewish Sam Glodsky stands up to the Russian Izzy Fink, the head
of a New York Lower East Side gang, when both thirteen-year-olds
hire on to work for a local gangster.

2. Dueker, Carl. **Runner.** New York: Houghton Mifflin Company,
2005. 216p. $16.00. ISBN 0 618 54298 1. [fiction] JS, CG with high
interest for boys (See full booktalk in *Booktalks and Beyond,* 2007,
pages 70 to 73.) When a gangster offers high school senior Chance
Taylor an opportunity to make easy money, he finds himself involved
in smuggling and terrorism.

3. Karr, Kathleen. **The Boxer.** New York: Farrar, Straus and Giroux,
2000. 169p. $16.00. ISBN 0 374 30921 3. [fiction] MJ, CG with high
interest for boys (See full booktalk in *Booktalks and More,* 2003,
pages 128 to 130.) Fifteen-year-old John Aloysius Xavier Woods
works in a sweatshop in New York's Lower East Side during the late
nineteenth century to help support his mother and five brothers and
sisters. When he takes a saloon's offer of a five-dollar purse for a box-
ing match, he finds himself in trouble with the law.

4. Karr, Kathleen. **The Great Turkey Walk.** New York: Sunburst,
2000. 197p. $4.95pa. ISBN 0 374 42798 4. [fiction] MJ, CG with
high interest for boys (See full booktalk in *Booktalks and More,* 2003,
pages 77 to 80.) Fifteen-year-old Simon Green, failing school and rejected by his adopted family, decides to make his fortune by driving
turkeys to Denver. In the process, he gains friends and self-respect.

5. Myers, Walter Dean. **Harlem Summer.** (See full booktalk in
"Multiple Cultures"/"Identity," pages 267 to 269.) During a 1920s

Harlem summer, sixteen-year-old Mark Purvis learns about the sunny and shady sides of his community.

ᘓᘔ

Pressler, Mirjam, and Eric J. Macki (trans.). Let Sleeping Dogs Lie.

Asheville, NC: Front Street, 2007. 207p. $16.95.
ISBN-13: 978 1 932425 84 0. [fiction] S, G

Themes/Topics: Holocaust, family heritage,
Nazi Party, conduct of life

Summary/Description

Eighteen-year-old Johanna believes that her grandfather built his successful clothing business from the ground up, but on a class trip to Israel discovers that the business originally belonged to a Jewish family who lost it during the Holocaust. After her grandfather's suicide, Johanna probes the family history, and learns that the grandfather who championed her was a proud bully who took advantage of the political situation to buy the store, was unfaithful to his wife who also committed suicide, used his money to control his son's family, and declined to share his wealth with his other relatives. Conflicting with her own father as she seeks information and justice, Johanna realizes that restitution in 1995 is not an easy task, but decides to give some of the money inherited from her grandfather to the woman she met in Israel whose family originally owned the store. The sexual content requires a mature reader and could be considered controversial.

Read Aloud/Reader Response

1. "White Roses," pages 13 and 14, beginning "Standing behind…" and ending "…*in their own best interest.*" Johanna reflects on the mourners at her grandfather's funeral.
2. "Moon Thoughts," pages 34 to 43. In this chapter, Johanna reflects on her grandfather's life and death and the family's relationship to Israel.
3. "Antiquities," pages 70 to 77, beginning "Mom has always opened…" and ending "… not for the time being." The family sorts out grandfather's belongings and Johanna reflects on her inheritance.
4. "Profiteers," pages 164 to 176. In this chapter, Mrs. Fachinger explains the Nazi period to Johanna.
5. "Thin Ice," pages 177 to 188. In this chapter, Johanna and her father confront each other over the injustice and resulting money.

Booktalk

Johanna is eighteen years old and very rich. Her family owns a clothing store, one of the most successful businesses in their German town. Then her grandfather, the man who built the business, commits suicide. The money he leaves Johanna will make her rich the rest of her life. Does his death have anything to do with Johanna's trip to Israel last summer? Johanna met a woman there, a woman who called Johanna's loving grandfather a Nazi. She claimed that he stole her family's store. Is this woman right? Did Johanna's grandfather help these Jews as he claimed, or steal from them? Does the answer make Johanna's family righteous and hard-working or profiteers who have built an empire on blood money? Johanna wants to know. No one really wants to tell her. Life is good now. Life is prosperous. Why can't Johanna just be content to *Let Sleeping Dogs Lie?*

Get Involved

1. (Research) Using your library resources, research efforts of the German government or German families to make restitution to Jewish survivors. Act as a resource person during the discussion.
2. (Discuss) Mrs. Levin states that "Treasures of wickedness profit nothing." Based on the specifics of the story, do you agree or disagree?
3. (Discuss) Doran is a central part of the story even though he appears only briefly. Why do you think that Pressler included him?
4. (Create) Write the scene that might occur between Johanna and Mrs. Levin when Johanna returns to Israel. Share the scene with others.
5. (Research and Follow-up) Using your library resources, research your own family tree through three generations. Share what you learned that surprised you.

Related Works

1. Baer, Edith. **Walk the Dark Streets.** New York: Farrar, Straus and Giroux/Frances Foster Books, 1998. 280p. $18.00. ISBN 0 374 38229 8. [fiction] JS, CG (See full booktalk in *Booktalks Plus,* 2001, pages 153 to 155.) Telling Germany's story and Eva Bentheim's story during the Nazi rise to power, the novel opens in 1933 and ends in 1940, when Eva leaves Germany for America.
2. Chotjewitz, David. Doris Orgel (trans.). **Daniel Half Human.** New York: Simon Pulse, 2004. 325p. $5.99pa. ISBN 9 780689 857485. [fiction] JS, CG with high interest for boys (See full booktalk in

Booktalks and Beyond, 2007, pages 191 to 194.) As an interpreter for the U.S. Army in 1945, Daniel returns to now bombed-out Hamburg, Germany, where he grew up and lost his best friend. The friend joined the Hitler Youth, and Daniel was revealed to be a Jew.

3. konigsburg, e. l. **The Mysterious Edge of the Heroic World.** (See full booktalk in "Mystery/Suspense"/"Historical," pages 146 to 149.) Amedeo Kaplan discovers a valuable piece of art as well as a story of a heroic World War II sacrifice when helping to organize a wealthy woman's downsizing household.

4. Müller, Melissa. Rita Limber and Robert Kimber (trans.). **Anne Frank: The Biography.** New York: Henry Holt and Company, 1998. 330p. $14.00pa. ISBN 0 8050 5997 0. [nonfiction] JSA/CG This work places Anne Frank in a family, social, and political context.

5. Zenatti, Valérie. Adriana Hunter (trans.). **When I Was a Soldier: A Memoir.** New York: Bloomsbury Children's Books, 2005. 235p. $16.95. ISBN 1 58234 978 9. [nonfiction] JS, G (See full booktalk in *Booktalks and Beyond,* 2007, pages 241 to 244.) On her eighteenth birthday, according to Israeli law, Valérie Zenatti becomes a soldier. Her experiences lead her to question the romanticism of the Jewish state in relation to their historic persecution.

ᘓᘔ

Sturtevant, Katherine. A True and Faithful Narrative.

New York: Farrar, Straus and Giroux, 2006. 250p. $17.00.
ISBN 0 374 37809 6. [fiction] MJ, G

Themes/Topics: Great Britain, courtship, Muslim culture, piracy, seventeenth century, types of writing

Summary/Description

In this sequel to *At the Sign of the Star,* sixteen-year-old Meg Moore working in her father's bookstore, The Sign of the Star, finds herself receiving the attentions of Will Barlow, her father's apprentice and Edward Gosse, her best friend's brother. Because she knows that marriage duties could destroy her writing ambitions, she considers staying single. Edward indicates his wishes to court her before he sails for Livorno, but she deflects his advances with jokes about his being captured by pirates. When he is captured and requires a ransom, a guilt-ridden Meg uses her writing to plea for funds. Will Barlow helps her. They become close and begin to court. Edward returns and asks her to write his story. They meet secretly, and Edward describes an exciting Arab world filled with both cruelty and wisdom to which he wishes to return. Will discovers the meetings, and tells Meg's father. The conflict that results causes Meg to choose Edward, who supports her writing ambitions, over Will and persuades her father to publish the narrative even though he will not allow Meg to put her name on it. The "Author's Note: On Piracy" gives a short history of piracy and slavery in the Mediterranean.

Read Aloud/Reader Response

1. Chapter 1, section 1, pages 3 and 4, beginning with the chapter and ending "...not what to say." Meg recalls Edward Goss on the day that he first began to show interest in her.
2. Chapter 2, section 2, pages 33 to 34, beginning "Will it be..." and ending "...give me the manuscript at last." Meg first senses her superiority over Will in writing.
3. Chapter 2, section 3, pages 38 to 44. In this section, the issues of marriage, love, and slavery intertwine.
4. Chapter 6, section 1, pages 124 to 130, beginning "Indeed, the door opened..." and ending with the section. Edward Gosse returns on Valentine's Day and Meg mistakes his Valentine gift.
5. Chapter 10, section 2, pages 224 to 228, beginning "You have spared me." and ending *"The light shines."* Together, Meg and Edward explore the truth of Meg's writing.

Booktalk

Sixteen-year-old Meg Moore works in her father's bookstore, The Sign of the Star. She would like to fill its shelves with her own writing. But because she lives in seventeenth-century England, that dream is next to impossible. Women writers concentrate on romances. They are women of questionable character, and Meg's father wants anything but a woman of questionable character. He wants a respectable daughter and son-in-law. And he has a way to get both. He can marry his daughter to his apprentice, the annoying Will Barlow. But Will Barlow has some competition. Meg's best friend Anne Gosse has a brother Edward. He will be going away soon, but before he goes he would like something from Meg, a sign that she will have some interest in him. Meg tells him that her only interest is telling his story if he is captured by pirates. It is just a jest, another attempt to push away another pesky suitor. Then the jest comes true. Edward is captured. Guilt-ridden, Meg feels compelled to rescue him. Her writing can do it. She can persuade people to contribute to his ransom. The annoying Will Barlow is less annoying now, and he agrees to help her raise the money. Together they work hard. Together they begin to see their two lives becoming one. Together, they achieve their goal. Edward returns. Does everyone live happily ever after?—not quite. An entirely new and unexpected story begins to unfold at *The Sign of the Star,* a story only Meg can tell in *A True and Faithful Narrative.*

Get Involved

1. (Research) Using your library resources, learn more about piracy in the seventeenth century. Act as a resource person for the group during the discussion.
2. (Research) Using your library resources, find information about one woman writer of the seventeenth or eighteenth centuries. Act as a resource person for the group during the discussion.
3. (React) Should Meg choose Edward over Will? Explain your answer with references to the story.
4. (React) Point out when you agree and disagree with Meg's father.
5. (Create and Follow-up) Choose a friend or relative who will share with you a family story. Write it so that it becomes both entertaining and instructive. Share it with the group.

Related Works

1. Johansen, Jonathan (ed.). **Critical Perspectives on Islam and the Western World.** New York: The Rosen Publishing Group, 2006. 182p. (Critical Anthologies of Nonfiction Writing). $30.60. ISBN 1 4042 0538 1. [nonfiction] JS, CG This series of selected documents, essays, and articles explains the background of East/West relations and the rise of Islamist or Islamic fundamentalist movements.
2. McCaughrean, Geraldine. **The Pirate's Son.** New York: Scholastic Press, 1998. American ed. 294p. $16.95. ISBN 0 590 20344 4. [fiction] MJ, CG with high interest for boys (See full booktalk in *Booktalks Plus,* 2001, pages 74 to 77.) Three eighteenth-century teenagers leave traditional English roles and embrace the pirate world.
3. Rees, Celia. **Pirates!** New York: Bloomsbury Children's Books, 2003. 380p. $16.95. ISBN 1 58234 816 2. [fiction] MJS, G (See full booktalk in *Booktalks and Beyond,* 2007, pages 95 to 97.) In this eighteenth-century adventure, fifteen-year-old Nancy inherits her English family's Jamaican plantation, discovers her father's second family, and, with them, flees the danger of the island and joins the pirates.
4. Reuter, Bjarne. Tiina Nunnally (trans.). **The Ring of the Slave Prince.** New York: Dutton Children's Books, 2003. 373p. $22.99.

ISBN 0 525 47146 4. [fiction] MJ, CG with high interest for boys (See full booktalk in *Booktalks and Beyond,* 2007, pages 97 to 100.) In this adventure set in the seventeenth century, Tom O'Connor hopes to save his mother and sister from poverty by returning a slave to his royal family. His arduous journey throws him into piracy and makes him realize the true meaning of riches.

5.   Sturtevant, Katherine. **At the Sign of the Star.** New York: Farrar, Straus and Giroux, 2000. 140p. $16.00. ISBN 0 374 30449 1. [fiction] M, G Twelve-year-old Margaret Moore, a daughter of a successful, seventeenth-century London book merchant, looks forward to a good marriage in the comfort of the books and city that surround her until her father remarries. In her turmoil, she decides to rely on her love of reading and writing, and emulate women emerging as teachers, nurses, and playwrights. Eventually, she accepts her new stepmother and baby brother.

ᏨᎧ

Whelan, Gloria. Summer of the War.
New York: HarperCollins Children's Books, 2006. 176p. $15.99.
ISBN-13: 978 0 06 008072 3. [fiction] MJ, G

Themes/Topics: family life, change, World War II

Summary/Description

Fourteen-year-old Mirabelle treasures her predictable summers on an island in the upper Great Lakes with her grandparents, parents, and three siblings. In 1942, however, her father decides to work for the Air Force, and her mother decides to renew her medical practice. The grandparents will supervise the children and welcome Caroline, Mirabelle's cousin, who has grown up with her father in Europe. Transferred to England, the father, an unpopular and romantic son-in-law, sends Caroline to the island for her safety. Sophisticated and spoiled Caroline divides the family, rebels against the routine, and almost steals Mirabelle's boyfriend. When word comes of her father's death, however, the family reaches out to her in very human ways. They all discover that with love and respect, difference does not threaten cohesion, and routine and safety do not mean restriction.

Read Aloud/Reader Response

1.   Chapter 4, pages 55 to 56, beginning with the chapter and ending "...like he looked at Carrie." Mirabelle reflects on how Carrie's perception changes the group.

2. Chapter 4, pages 63 to 64, Carrie's letter from her father. The father reveals his distaste for the island life.
3. Chapter 9, pages 110 to 111, beginning "She's changed all of us..." and ending "...from the whole human race." Mirabelle's grandmother forces Mirabelle to take responsibility for her own decisions.
4. Chapter 11, pages 133 to 136, beginning "Carrie was actually talking..." and ending with the chapter. When Mirabelle asks Ned to take Carrie sailing, he reveals his opinions of Mirabelle, Carrie, and the family.
5. Chapter 12, page 146, beginning "Will you..." and ending with the chapter. Mirabelle responds to Carrie's request for help in planting an island garden.

Booktalk

Fourteen-year-old Mirabelle is looking forward to another great summer. Her grandparents have their own island in the Great Lakes. Her family spends every summer there. It's quiet. It's predictable, and Mirabelle loves it. But this summer of 1942 will be a little different. Because the United States has entered World War II, Mirabelle's mother is returning to her medical practice, and Mirabelle's father is helping the government build airplanes. Mirabelle's grandparents take care of the island anyway, so Mirabelle and her brothers and sisters can still look forward to their quiet summer. But the war brings another person to the island, fifteen-year-old cousin Caroline who grew up in France with just her father. When he is sent to war-torn London, she comes to the island for safety. Caroline is beautiful and sophisticated. To her, the island is a prison, and the family is dull. She is determined to change it, and she does. Caroline divides the family, sets her own rules, takes over Mirabelle's room, and even tries to steal Mirabelle's maybe boyfriend. Mirabelle can't decide if she should just let Caroline hang herself, or hand her the rope. Mirabelle doesn't like what Caroline does, but she has to admit that she loves her style. This summer isn't going to be quiet and predictable for anyone. This summer, change is coming. This summer, like everybody else, Mirabelle has to make some big decisions because when Caroline shows up, this summer is truly the *Summer of the War.*

Get Involved

1. (Research) Mirabelle, her family, and the island could well represent the United States before World War II. Using your library resources, research the position of the United States in the world before and after the war. Be sure to consider the Puritan ethic and isolationist policies in your research. Act as a resource person during the discussion.

2. (React) On a scale of one to five, rate the title. Compare your rating with the ratings of others in the group. Use specifics from the text to defend your rating.

3. (React) Which girl, Mirabelle or Caroline, would you wish to have as a friend? Defend your answer with details from the text.

4. (Discuss) Is the grandmother or grandfather a better grandparent?

5. (Discuss) Why do you think Whelan removed the parents from the immediate story?

6. (Compare) Whelan writes about girls who make tough decisions in changing worlds. Read Related Works 4 and 5. Consider the types of decisions that are dealt with in each of her novels.

Related Works

1. Lisle, Janet Taylor. **The Art of Keeping Cool.** New York: Atheneum Books for Young Readers, 2000. 207p. $17.00. ISBN 0 689 83787 9. [fiction] MJ, CG with high interest for boys. A young man living with his grandparents during World War II finds himself in a family war when he discovers that his father left home because of the boy's controlling and abusive grandfather.

2. Lawrence, Iain. **B for Buster.** New York: Laurel-Leaf, 2004. 317p. $5.99pa. ISBN 0 440 23810 2. [fiction] MJS, CG with high interest for boys. Sixteen-year-old Kak enlists in the Canadian Air Force and learns compassion and the true meaning of bravery from an outcast labeled as a coward.

3. Weaver, Will. **Full Service.** New York: Farrar, Straus and Giroux, 2005. 232p. $17.00. ISBN 0 374 32485 9. [fiction] JS, CG with high interest for boys (See full booktalk in *Booktalks and Beyond,* 2007, pages 257 to 259.) Fifteen-year-old Paul Sutton takes a job in a gas station during the 1960s, and his experiences change his thinking and his relationship to his conservative religious family.

4. Whelan, Gloria. **Chu Ju's House.** New York: HarperCollins Publishers, 2004. 227p. $16.89. ISBN 0 06 050725 X. [fiction] MJS, G (See full booktalk in *Booktalks and Beyond,* 2007, pages 239 to 241.) To save her baby sister from being sent to an orphanage, fourteen-year-old Chu Ju runs away, and by the time she is eighteen reunites with her family as an independent landowner.

5. Whelan, Gloria. **Homeless Bird.** New York: HarperCollins Publishers, 2000. 216p. $15.95. ISBN 0 06 028454 4. [fiction] MJS, G (See full booktalk in *Booktalks and More,* 2003, pages 215 to 217.) Thirteen-year-old Koly marries into an abusive family. When her husband dies, her mother-in-law abandons her in the city of widows where she finds a new life and independence.

ር፝ጊ፝ን

Zusak, Markus. The Book Thief.

New York: Alfred A. Knopf, 2006. 552p. $21.90. ISBN 0 375 93100 7. [fiction]
JS, CG with high interest for girls

Themes/Topics: Germany, World War II, death, reading,
story-telling, Jews, blended families

Summary/Description

Death tells the story of Liesel Meminger, the daughter of a Communist in Hitler's Germany. While Liesel and her little brother are being taken to foster care by their mother, the brother dies. Her mother leaves a grieving and traumatized Leisel with the Hubermanns, her foster parents. Leisel becomes close to the gentle Mr. Hubermann and blustery Mrs. Hubermann, and forges deep friendships with her neighbor, the talented Rudy Steiner, and Max, the Jew whom Mr. Hubermann hides in the basement. Leisel steals books for comfort and reads them aloud to others in turmoil from war. Rudy helps her steal them. Mr. Hubermann helps her read them, and Max writes books for her. When the Allied bombing kills the Hubermanns and Rudy, Leisel is in the basement writing her life story. She survives, reunites with Max, and lives to old age in England. When she dies, Death returns to her the book she wrote, *The Book Thief*, from the basement.

Read Aloud/Reader Response

1. "Death and Chocolate," pages 3 to 5. Death introduces himself and the story.
2. "Hitler's Birthday," 1940," pages 104 to 105. Hans Hubermann and his son conflict over the definition of cowardice and the Nazi Party.
3. "The Aryan Shopkeeper," pages 154 to 156. The candy incident reveals the characters of Frau Diller as well as Rudy and Liesel.
4. "Pages from the Basement," pages 223 to 238. Max writes Liesel a book.
5. "The Floating Book, Part I," pages 250 to 251, beginning "For Max Vandenburg,..." and ending "Just Jew." Max imagines fighting Hitler and the entire German nation.
6. "The Word Shaker," pages 445 to 451, beginning "There was once a strange..." and ending with the chapter. Max writes a fairy tale for Liesel.

Booktalk

Liesel is only a little girl, nine years old, when she discovers her brother's dead body and knows that she will be left by her mother with a foster family. She is in Germany. The year is 1939. Her parents are Communists. In Hitler's Germany, being a Communist is a crime, and Leisel, with the rest of the family, suffers the consequences—losing the people and the things that she loves. But Liesel is a fighter, not a victim. If something is taken from her, she will take something back. At first, it is just an impulse to steal the graveyard manual from the boy who buries her brother. Then stealing becomes a release, a kind of blow for right and justice. She begins a barter system with life. It takes something from her, she takes something back. Sometimes it is food, but most of the time it is books, books that allow her to live in another world, another life, if only for a few moments. These worlds have heroes, great rulers, and even Jews: Jews who make human decisions, Jews who should have someone to defend them. The bold and sly Leisel becomes such a force in the universe that Death decides to tell her story. Even he can appreciate one brave, outstanding human. Even he can appreciate *The Book Thief.*

Get Involved

1. (Research) Using your library resources, continue to research the rise of Hitler in Germany. You may wish to start with Related Work 2.
2. (Research) When Max imagines his fight with Hitler, Goebbels is Hitler's trainer. (See Read Aloud/Reader Response 5.) Using your library resources, research the life and work of Goebbels. Share your information with the group during the discussion. Be sure to explain why Goebbels is an appropriate choice.
3. (React) Find the point in the story where each character is introduced. Discuss how that initial introduction affected you as a reader.
4. (Discuss) Examine the cover. How does it relate to the story?
5. (Discuss) Zusak presents good and evil throughout the story. Try to list the criteria you think that the author would require for an act or a person to be classified as either good or evil. Compare your list with the lists of others in the group. Be sure to support your list with specifics from the novel.
6. (Discuss) At the end of the story, both Liesel and Max are alive. What are the implications of Zusak's choice?

Related Works

1. Chotjewitz, David. Doris Orgel (trans.). **Daniel Half Human.** New York: Simon Pulse, 2004. 325p. $5.99pa. ISBN 9 780689 857485.

[fiction] JS, CG with high interest for boys (See full booktalk in *Booktalks and Beyond,* 2007, pages 191 to 194.) As an interpreter for the U.S. Army in 1945, Daniel, a Jew, returns to bombed-out Hamburg, Germany, and recalls the destruction of his friendship with Aryan and upwardly mobile Armin, a successful member of the Hitler Youth.

2. Giblin, James Cross. **The Life and Death of Adolf Hitler.** New York: Clarion Books, 2002. 246p. $21.00. ISBN 0 395 90371 8. [nonfiction] MJS, CG (See full booktalk in *Teen Genre Connections,* 2005, pages 250 to 252.) Giblin portrays a disturbed and dedicated individual who, with an exceptional gift for politics and speech making, appealed to the prejudices and fears of the German people after World War I.

3. Kuyper, Sjoerd. Patricia Crampton (trans.). Jan Jutte (illus.). **The Swan's Child.** New York: Holiday House, 2000. 122p. $16.95. ISBN 0 8234 1861 8. [fiction] MJS, CG This fairy tale tells about grief, love, and rebirth through the interaction of a little girl and the animals, with human traits, who adopt her.

4. Opdyke, Irene Gut, with Jennifer Armstrong. **In My Hands: Memories of a Holocaust Rescuer.** New York: Alfred A. Knopf, 1999. 276p. $18.00. ISBN 0 679 89181 1. [nonfiction] JS, G (See full booktalk in *Booktalks and More,* 2003, pages 255 to 257.) Opdyke describes how her family life and personal beliefs led her to help and hide Jews persecuted during the German occupation of Poland.

5. Roberts, Jeremy. **Joseph Goebbels: Nazi Propaganda Minister.** New York: The Rosen Publishing Group, 2000. 112p. (Holocaust Biographies). $19.95. ISBN 0 8239 3309 1. [nonfiction] MJS, CG Described as one of the most hate-filled members of Hitler's staff, Goebbels used half-truth, exaggeration, and omission rather than lies to push for Jewish extermination.

Shaping

ᘓᘔ

Bruchac, Joseph. Geronimo.
New York: Scholastic Press, 2006. 384p. $16.99. ISBN 0 439 35360 2. [fiction] MJS, CG with high interest for boys

Themes/Topics: Apache life, extended family, Geronimo

Summary/Description

Willie, Geronimo's "adopted" grandson, tells the story of the eighty-year-old Geronimo, the Apaches who followed him, and the white men who fought, supported, and betrayed him. On the train, Willie tells about the man who taught him to respect his heritage, develop physical and emotional toughness, maintain respect and fairness, and move beyond the tribal ways. Geronimo studied to become a medicine man and valued the tribe's children. He received the name *Geronimo* from the Mexicans he attacked after discovering that they massacred his entire family. He never understood why the white men did not join the Apaches against the Mexicans. Willie relates stories illustrating Geronimo's charisma, his willingness to adapt financially, and culturally, and his great pride in his own physical survival. The story also explores the Apache culture and the lies and misunderstandings from both the Native Americans and white men that led to conflict. An "Author's Afterword" explains the last days of Geronimo and the Apaches who followed him. "Geronimo Chronology" lists, with explanations, significant events in Geronimo's life, including his many wives. A "Bibliography" provides the author's main sources.

Read Aloud/Reader Response

1. "The Wagon Train," pages 34 to 40. Willie recounts why the Apaches believe that white men eat human flesh.
2. "Hungry Giant," pages 41 to 48. The chapter explains how story-telling inspires and defines the Apaches.
3. "Geronimo's Power," pages 122 to 138. In explaining Geronimo's power and weakness, Willie also explains the power and weakness of the Apache.
4. "Remembering Turkey Creek," pages 151 to 152, beginning "Of all the places..." and ending "...ridiculed by Apaches." Willie defines greatness in Apache terms.
5. "O, Ha Le," page 340, beginning "It was nearly..." and ending "...give a warning first." Willie compares the white man to a rattle-snake.

Booktalk

Ask how many people in the group ever heard of Geronimo. Share their perceptions.

To some people, the name *Geronimo* is a war cry. They think of attacks and killings and scalps. They would be surprised to learn that this fierce warrior was a healer, a medicine man. They might also be surprised to learn that he preferred to teach Apache children rather than to fight white men. But they would be most surprised to know that he believed that a warrior's best weapons were running away and hiding. Geronimo never understood his fight with the United States. He believed that the Apaches and the U.S. soldiers would unite against the Mexican army, the people who wiped out his entire family. Maybe misunderstandings about Geronimo started with those who told Geronimo's story—the white men and the Apaches who grew jealous of Geronimo's power. Now we can hear his story from another voice, a voice that Geronimo himself helped bring into the world, a voice who knew that the man called Clever One could never be conquered as other men are conquered. This story-teller shared Geronimo's battles as well as his journey into captivity. He knew all the triumphs and sorrows first-hand. Hear *his* story, the real story of *Geronimo.*

Get Involved

1. (Research) Choose one of the sources listed in the bibliography. After reading it, share the information that you feel is significant with the group.
2. (Research) Cochise is mentioned several times in the novel. Using your library resources, learn more about his life. Act as a resource person during the discussion.
3. (Research) Willie describes presidents in terms of their treatment of Native Americans. Using your library resources, continue to re-search legislation pertaining to Native Americans. Note the president serving at the time. Act as a resource person during the group discussion.
4. (React) After reading *Geronimo,* list three specifics about Native Americans that surprised you. Compare and share your list with others in the group.
5. (Discuss) Re-read the opening chapter. How does it introduce the story's facts and themes?
6. (Discuss) Consider what the "Author's Afterword" adds to the story.

Related Works

1. Calabro, Marian. **The Perilous Journey of the Donner Party.** New York: Clarion Books, 1999. 192p. $20.00. ISBN 0 395 86610 3. [nonfiction] MJS, CG (See full booktalk in *Booktalks and More,* 2003, pages 37 to 39.) Calabro describes the Donner Party journey from its hopeful and confident beginning of elaborate wagons and luxurious supplies through its bad habits of procrastination and mis-placed trust to a horrible deterioration of morale and health that resulted in cannibalism.

2. Carvell, Marlene. **Sweetgrass Basket.** New York: Dutton Children's Books, 2005. 243p. $16.99. ISBN 0 525 47547 8. [fiction, poetry] JS, G (See full booktalk in *Booktalks and Beyond,* 2007, pages 244 to 246.) Sent to an off-reservation school after their mother's death, Mattie and Sarah Tarbell find their Mohawk heritage and their own self-respect challenged by the white world's cruelty, prejudice, and ignorance.

3. Neihardt, John G. (text), and Standing Bear (illus.). **Black Elk Speaks: Being the Life Story of a Holy Man of the Oglala Sioux.** Lincoln, NE: University of Nebraska Press, 1979. 299p. $15.89. ISBN 0 8032 3301 9. [nonfiction] S/A, CG Black Elk tells the full story of his life and the failure he feels in not fulfilling his vision. The work was published originally in 1932.

4. Philip, Neil (ed.). **In a Sacred Manner I Live: Native American Wisdom.** New York: Clarion Books, 1997. 93p. $20.00. ISBN 0 395 84981 0. [nonfiction] JS, CG (See full booktalk in *Booktalks and More,* 2003, pages 44 to 46.) This collection of poems, songs, and speeches from 1609 to 1995 reflects a great respect for nature and language that allows Native Americans to live "in a sacred manner."

5. Stefoff, Rebecca. **Tecumseh and the Shawnee Confederation.** New York: Facts on File, 1998. 138p. (Library of American Indians). $25.00. ISBN 0 8160 3648 9. [nonfiction] JS, CG Tecumseh's story is told in the context of westward expansion. A central issue is each culture's perception of land and ownership and how the differences led to war and the destruction of the Native American world.

❧❧

Fradin, Judith Bloom, and Dennis Brindell Fradin.
Jane Addams: Champion of Democracy.

New York: Clarion Books, 2006. 216p. $21.00. ISBN-13: 978 0 618 50436 7.

[nonfiction] MJS, CG with high interest for girls

Themes/Topics: late nineteenth and early twentieth century,
Hull House, Chicago, settlement houses,
NAACP, peace movement

Summary/Description

The authors trace Addams's life, dedicated to social causes and social change, from her tragedy-marked childhood to her death in 1935. Losing her mother at two and suffering a deformed spine from tuberculosis, Addams flowers in higher education, but then succumbs to ill health and depression when she fails at medical school. After successful back surgery, she tours Europe and encounters the settlement house concept, which she transplants to Chicago. Addams enjoys overwhelming support from her clients and friends, takes on corrupt politicians, and as the first woman garbage inspector, cleans up the city and lowers the death rate. She becomes active in civil rights for both women and African-Americans, and with Ida B. Wells, founds the NAACP. Her peace crusades cause her to be labeled "the Most Dangerous Woman in America," but her continued devotion to the poor throughout the Depression eclipses the controversy. The authors also address the rumors of Addams's lesbian relationship. "Source Notes" and a "Bibliography" guide the reader to further information. An index with bold print indicating illustrations provides easy access to information.

Read Aloud/Reader Response

1. Chapter 2, page 14, beginning "I imagined..." and ending with the chapter. The passage describes how Addams's father helps her lose her self-consciousness about her appearance.
2. Chapter 13, page 159, beginning "Believing..." and ending "...of war." Addams declares her views on peace in her diary entry.
3. Chapter 13, page 162, beginning "Although we are..." and ending "...use in war's behalf." Addams addresses the issue of world peace at the Women's International League for Peace and Freedom in 1921.
4. Chapter 14, page 178, beginning "Twice I have..." and ending "...she now holds." Professor Halvdan Koht of the University of Oslo honors Addams when she is presented with the Nobel Peace Prize in 1931.
5. Chapter 15, pages 190 to 192, beginning "At least one newspaper..." and ending with the chapter. The excerpts note the honor given to Addams in death.

Booktalk

At twenty-one she was independently wealthy. Did she buy expensive clothes and jewelry, build a huge home, hire a staff of servants? No. She gave her money away. She didn't stand at the door and hand it out to anyone who asked. She did something better. She created a home where everyone could be welcome. She taught skills that would help others help themselves, and she fought corrupt governments that tried to keep the poor in their place. She thought everyone should have a chance and a voice in life. Her name was Jane Addams. She lived from 1860 to 1935. Her father was Abraham Lincoln's good friend. From her father, she learned much about Lincoln and thought that he was one of the most admirable people who ever lived. When she died, many in the world thought the same of her. Some didn't. She was often controversial but never dull. Read about one of the most influential women of the twentieth century, *Jane Addams, Champion of Democracy.*

Get Involved

1. (Research) Using your library resources, find out more about Hull House. Act as a resource person for the group.
2. (Research) Using your library resources, learn more about the NAACP. Act as a resource person for the group.
3. (Research) Learn more about one of the national or international events that influenced Jane Addams's life. Act as a resource person for the group.
4. (Research) List two other women during this time period who also achieved national prominence. Using your library resources, learn more about their lives. Compare their achievements with those of Jane Addams.
5. (Create and Follow-up) Organize a display that portrays the lives of significant women of that time.
6. (Create and Follow-up) List your own ideas for peace, and design a flag that represents the most important concept of your plan. With others in the group, arrange a flag display.

Related Works

1. Colman, Penny. **Adventurous Women: Eight True Stories about Women Who Made a Difference.** New York: Henry Holt and Company, 2006. 224p. $17.95. ISBN 0 8050 7744 8. [nonfiction] JS, G These eight brief biographical sketches include Louise Boyd, Arctic explorer; Mary Gibson Henry, plant hunter; Juana Briones, entrepreneur; Alice Hamilton, industrial detective; Mary McLeod Bethune, educator; Katharine Wormeley, nursing superintendent; Biddy Mason, emancipated slave; and Peggy Hull, reporter.
2. Fradin, Dennis Brindell, and Judith Bloom Fradin. **Fight On! Mary Church Terrell's Battle for Integration.** New York: Clarion Books, 2003. 181p. $17.00. ISBN 0 618 13349 6. [nonfiction] MJS, CG with high interest for girls. A lifelong friend of Ida B. Wells, Terrell was born in the middle of the Civil War, experienced the pain of her parents' divorce, excellent educational opportunities, and the sting of discrimination.
3. Fradin, Dennis Brindell, and Judith Bloom Fradin. **Ida B. Wells: Mother of the Civil Rights Movement.** New York: Clarion Books,

2000. 178p. $18.00. ISBN 0 395 89898 6. [nonfiction] MJS, CG with high interest for girls (See full booktalk in *Booktalks and More,* 2003, pages 249 to 252.) Born a slave in 1862, Wells came of age during Reconstruction and became a reporter, civil rights activist, and co-founder of the NAACP.

4. Freedman, Russell. **Eleanor Roosevelt: A Life of Discovery.** New York: Clarion Books, 1993. 208p. $17.95. ISBN 0 89919 862 7. [nonfiction] MJS, CG with high interest for girls. In this biography, Freedman relates the difficult challenges and victories in Eleanor Roosevelt's personal and professional lives.

5. Lawlor, Laurie. **Helen Keller: Rebellious Spirit.** New York: Holiday House, 2001. 168p. $22.95. ISBN 0 8234 1588 0. [nonfiction] MJS, CG with high interest for girls (See full booktalk in *Teen Genre Connections,* 2005, pages 40 to 42.) The story of this social activist is told in the context of post-Reconstruction South. Lawlor accents her activism rather than her handicap.

のめ

Murphy, Jim. **The Real Benedict Arnold.**

New York: Clarion Books, 2007. 264p. $20.00. ISBN-13: 978 0 395 77609 4.

[nonfiction] JS, CG with high interest for boys

Themes/Topics: Revolutionary War, U.S. history, Continental Army, politics, loyalty, betrayal

Summary/Description

Beginning with a view of the crucial Battle of Saratoga and the cryptic monument commemorating Benedict Arnold's part in it, Murphy examines the family background, social status, vicious rumors, political upheaval, jealousy, brilliant military sense, and personal relationships that shape Arnold and his final decision to side with the Loyalists in the American Revolution. Arnold's central roles at both Champlain and Ticonderoga are buried in politics, and he receives more recognition from the opposition than his peers and superiors. Although Washington supports him, he is regularly passed over for promotion, and although he uses his own funds to support his troops, he is additionally billed for his battle expenses. When Arnold saves the second battle of Saratoga, the more conservative warrior, Gates, takes the glory. Brooding while recovering from his painful leg wound, Arnold shifts his priorities from supporting a government he sees as growing tyrannical and corrupt, marries into a Loyalist family, and decides to provide for his dependents with loyalty to England, a government that he sees, along with other disillusioned Revolutionaries, as more stable. Washington finally secures him a promotion, but Arnold chooses to command West Point instead so that he can betray the colonial government. The plot fails, but Arnold leads British troops and eventually immigrates to England with his family. "Notes, Sources, and Related Asides" for each chapter provide additional comments as well as print and non-print sources of information. An extensive index allows easy access to the text.

Read Aloud/Reader Response

1. The introductory quotation by Bernard Bailyn. The quotation that appears on an unnumbered page preceding the table of contents raises the question of the person versus the story in history and news.
2. Chapter 1, pages 1 to 4. The chapter sets the stage for the contrasts of the Revolutionary War and Arnold himself.
3. Chapter 11, pages 102 to 105, beginning with the chapter and ending "...approaching British ships." The passage illustrates Arnold's military ability as well as his opposition.
4. Chapter 13, pages 131 to 132, beginning "These events..." and ending with the chapter. Overwhelmed by politics after proving his superior military skill, Arnold resigns.
5. Chapter 18, page 181, beginning "Twenty times..." and ending "...happiness depends." This is an excerpt from Arnold's love letter to Peggy Shippen.
6. Chapter 19, pages 191 to 193, beginning "But it is a mistake..." and ending "...clearer to Benedict." Murphy reviews the issues that influenced Arnold's decision.
7. Chapter 21, pages 215 to 218, beginning with the chapter and ending with "...was Benedict Arnold." The passage includes Arnold's letter to Washington and Washington's reaction to it.

Booktalk

Ask the group how they would feel about a military commander who would follow his men into battle, use his own money to pay for their food and medicine, and disregard his superior's orders so that he could win a battle and save lives.

In the late seventeen hundreds, America had such a commander, a man whom George Washington considered one of his best and most trusted officers. His name was Benedict Arnold. But Benedict Arnold decided to use his position as commander of West Point to help the British win their war against the colonies. If his plot had succeeded, we still would belong to England. Today, being called a Benedict Arnold means being called a traitor, someone who would sell out his country for just a few dollars. What happened to change this man whose brilliant military victories turned the Revolution to the colonies' favor? What happened to make him decide that England was his only friend? Was he an egomaniac and a liar manipulated by a beautiful young Loyalist woman? Or was he a true patriot who wanted to see his homeland preserved? You decide who was *The Real Benedict Arnold.*

Get Involved

1. (Research) Choose one of the sources listed in the section "Notes, Sources, and Related Asides." Examine it and share your evaluation of it or information from it with the rest of the group.
2. (Research) Murphy describes Arnold as an upwardly mobile businessman who was trying to break into an old and closed society. Choose another famous patriot of the period. Using your library resources, learn more about that person's background. Share the information with the group during the discussion. How could the differences in the background of the Revolutionary leaders have led to conflicts?
3. (Research) Using your library resources, research the position of the Loyalists versus the Revolutionaries in the colonies. Could the Revolution be considered the first American Civil War?
4. (Create) After completing Get Involved 2, construct a visual display that incorporates what you feel are the most appealing sources. You might also want to construct a visual display that illustrates the differences among the Founding Fathers.
5. (Discuss and Follow-up) Benedict Arnold's life and decisions teaches us about the problems of revolutions. List the things that surprised you about the American Revolution. Apply what you learned to events today.
6. (React and Follow-up) On page 233, Murphy includes Benedict Arnold's family mottoes. Discuss what you feel each reveals about Arnold. Then choose a motto for yourself or your family.

Related Works

1. Adler, David A. **B. Franklin, Printer.** New York: Holiday House, 2001. 126p. $19.95. ISBN 0 8234 1675 5. [nonfiction] MJS, CG (See full booktalk in *Teen Genre Connections,* 2003, pages 243 to 245.) In fifteen chapters, Adler describes Benjamin Franklin's working-class background, education, family, accomplishments, and death.

2. Allen, Thomas B. **George Washington, Spymaster: How the Americans Outspied the British and Won the Revolutionary War.** Washington, DC: National Geographic, 2004. 184p. $16.95. ISBN 0 7922 5126 1. [nonfiction] MJS, B (See full booktalk in *Booktalks and Beyond,* 2007, pages 215 to 218.) Beginning with Washington's early life and his gathering of intelligence for the French and Indian War, Allen portrays Washington as defeating the British with wit rather than might.

3. Aronson, Marc. **The Real Revolution: The Global Story of American Independence.** New York: Clarion Books, 2005. 238p. $21.00. ISBN 0 618 18179 2. [nonfiction] JS, CG (See full book-talk in *Booktalks and Beyond,* 2007, pages 218 to 221.) Framing the American Revolution in world events, Aronson begins with the sto-ries of three soldiers, Robert Clive, George Washington, and James Wolfe, and then expands to the challenges to eighteenth-century British expansionism that led to the developing American character and the eventual revolution.

4. Blackwood, Gary. **The Year of the Hangman.** New York: Dutton Books, 2002. 261p. $16.99. ISBN 0 525 46921 4. [fiction] MJS, B (See full booktalk in *Teen Genre Connections,* 2005, pages 142 to 144.) Set in 1777, the alternate history (uchronia) novel speculates what America would have been like if the British had prevailed. Benedict Arnold leads a band of pirates.

5. Sterman, Betsy. **Saratoga Secret.** New York: Dial Books for Young Readers, 1998. 249p. $16.99. ISBN 0 8037 2332 6. [fiction] MJS, G (See full booktalk in *Booktalks Plus,* 2001, pages 21 to 23.) In this coming-of-age novel, sixteen-year-old Amity Spencer must notify Benedict Arnold of Burgoyne's attack.

ᏨᏦ

Nelson, Kadir. We Are the Ship: The Story of Negro League Baseball.

New York: Hyperion/Jump at the Sun, 2008. 96p. $18.99.
ISBN-13: 978 0 7868 0832 8. [nonfiction] MJS/A, B

Themes/Topics: Negro League, baseball, discrimination

Summary/Description

Nine innings (chapters) explain the beginnings, development, style of play, travel and play schedule, gangster support and celebrity sup-port, all-stars, Latin circuit, differences between the Negro and white leagues, World War II popularity, and role of integration in ending the league. Nelson's spectacular oil paintings of league life, including a four-panel fold-out of the first Negro League World Series, take up at least half of the book. Quotations by central league figures cover the opening pages and introduce each chapter. Hank Aaron pens the foreword. An "Author's Note" explains the author's motivation. A bibliography, filmography, and source notes reveal the sources, and an index, with italicized references to illustrations, makes information easily accessible.

Read Aloud/Reader Response
Any of the pictures in the book are powerful sources for reader response.
1. The quotations arranged on the opening pages and the quotations introducing each chapter. Each is a signature comment that illustrates the confidence and optimism of the league.
2. 1st Inning, pages 1 to 2, beginning "In the mid-1860's..." and ending "...covering the base." The narrator describes the black man's position in baseball before blacks were banned from baseball altogether.
3. 2nd Inning, pages 17 to 18, beginning "Some guys would clown..." and ending "...up to the majors?" The narrator explains how clowning contradicted the image desired by the Negro Leaguers.
4. 5th Inning, pages 47 to 48, beginning "On the mound..." and ending "...was something else." The passage illustrates Satchel Paige's dedication, skill, and humor.
5. 9th Inning, pages 69 to 70, beginning "There is a story..." and ending "'...at that Cuban go!'" The anecdote illustrates the ridiculousness of the prejudice in the Major Leagues.

Booktalk
"Play ball!" signals the start of a baseball game. But before the 1940s, "Play ball!" in the Major Leagues was for white players only. Because African-Americans were banned from baseball by a so-called gentlemen's agreement of white owners, some other gentlemen formed their own league, the Negro League. Why? Because they liked to play ball too, and they knew that playing in their own league would show audiences that they could play the game just as well as whites. When the Majors were ready to play fair, the African-American players would be ready. The waiting ended when Jackie Robinson integrated the Majors. Robinson's efforts opened more doors than the one to baseball. If African-Americans could compete in sports, they could compete in other areas like education and medicine. But while the African-American

players waited for their chance, the Negro Leagues became a major part of American history. These fun-loving, dedicated young ballplayers often proved more skilled and determined than many of their white counterparts. They needed just one chance. (*Show the pictures.*) These are some of the faces. Read their stories, stories about the men who believed, as they navigated the stormy seas of injustice, neglect, and harassment, *We Are the Ship*.

Get Involved

1. (Research) Using your library resources, find out as much as possible about the Negro Leagues. Share your information with the group during the discussion.
2. (Research) Nelson also mentions discrimination in the service during World War II. Using your library resources, share the information that you find with the group during the discussion.
3. (Research) Using your library resources, examine discrimination against African-Americans in everyday life during that period. Share your information with the group during the discussion.
4. (Create and Follow-up) Find as many books about the Negro Leagues as you can. Then arrange a display in the library that will appeal to all ages of baseball fans.
5. (React) After reading *We Are the Ship*, list the information that you learned about the Negro Leagues and/or the time period that surprised you. Compare your list with the lists of other people in the group.

Related Works

1. Lynch, Chris. **Gold Dust.** New York: HarperCollins Publishers, 2000. 196p. $15.95. ISBN 0 06 028174 X. [fiction] MJ, CG with high interest for boys. Set in the 1970s, this story centers on the fantasy a young baseball player has about the Boston Red Sox rookies, the Gold Dust twins, and how that fantasy forces him to face some cruel facts about prejudice.
2. Myers, Walter Dean. **The Journal of Biddy Owens: The Negro Leagues.** New York: Scholastic, Inc., 2001. 144p. (My Name Is America). $10.95. ISBN 0 439 09503 4. [fiction] MJ, B Seventeen-year-old Biddy Owens travels with the Birmingham Black Barons in the 1948 season, the last big season of the Negro Leagues.
3. Robinson, Sharon. **Jackie's Nine: Jackie Robinson's Values to Live By.** New York: Scholastic, Inc., 2001. 192p. $15.95. ISBN 0 439 23764 5. [nonfiction] MJ, CG (See full booktalk in *Booktalks and More*, 2003, pages 123 to 125.) Sharon Robinson's articles illustrate the nine principles she feels guided her father's life—courage,

determination, teamwork, persistence, integrity, citizenship, justice, commitment, and excellence.

4. Russell, Nancy L. **So Long, Jackie Robinson.** Toronto, ON, Canada: Key Porter Books, 2007. 223p. $7.95pa. ISBN-13: 978 1 55263 863 7. [fiction] MJ, CG with high interest for boys. In the summer of 1946, twelve-year-old Matthew Parker lands a job selling concessions in the Montreal baseball park and follows the controversy and excitement surrounding Jackie Robinson as he struggles to become the first African-American player in the Majors.

5. Schmidt, Julie. **Satchel Paige.** New York: Rosen Central, 2002. 112p. (Baseball Hall of Famers of the Negro League). $31.99. ISBN 0 8239 3478 0. [nonfiction] MJ, CG with high interest for boys. Schmidt tells about the life of the flamboyant, determined Satchel Paige who refused to be ignored or underpaid. Other volumes in the series deal with Cool Papa Bell, Josh Gibson, Judy Johnson, and Buck Leonard.

🙣🙠

Sís, Peter. The Wall: Growing up behind the Iron Curtain.

New York: Farrar, Straus and Giroux/Frances Foster Books, 2007. 56p. $18.00.
ISBN-13: 978 0 374 34701 7. [graphic, nonfiction] MJS, CG

Themes/Topics: twentieth century, identity, Czechoslovakia (1945–1992), Cold War, illustrators

Summary/Description

In this illustrated memoir, Sís describes growing up in Soviet-controlled Czechoslovakia and how the brief glimpses of Western life changed his thinking and his life. The "Introduction" provides a historical context for the many illustrations that follow. Three double pages of journal entries about national events and the author's reactions to them complement the artwork, which reflects the author's growing interest in life beyond the Iron Curtain and the eventual destruction of the Berlin Wall. In the "Afterword" the author reflects on the difficulty he has communicating his own journey to his children.

Read Aloud/Reader Reaction

This entire book is a platform for sharing. The following are only suggestions for possible starting points.

1. The "Introduction," page 1, briefly describes the context of the Cold War.
2. The journal entries on pages 13 and 14, 21 and 22, 35 and 36 depict events and reactions that illustrate the decisions of the dictatorship and the author's reactions to them.
3. The "Afterword," page 47, describes the Cold War in the author's personal experience and his frustration in explaining this world to his now American family.
4. Pages 19 and 20, 27 and 28, 43 and 44, 45 and 46 are some of the more spectacular pages that will generate discussion about both the author's experiences and his technique in expressing them.

Booktalk

Ask how many in the group can explain the phrase, "The Cold War."
    Peter Sís lived through the Cold War, and he has difficulty explaining it himself. So he decided to use a medium with which he is most comfortable, pictures. (*As you speak, begin to turn the pages. Begin with the map of Czechoslovakia.*) He shows us where he lived. How he learned to think as the state wished him to. How the Western world began its artful "invasion." And how, finally, the dictatorship lost its grip physically and mentally. Take a closer look yourself, by yourself, and you will begin to understand that this experience, like every experience, is unique, and even when some stories are told, there still remains, between the teller and the listener, a bit of feeling or experience that can never come out from behind *The Wall.*

Get Involved

1. (Research) Using your library resources, research the period of the Cold War. Act as a resource person for your group during the discussion.
2. (Research) Using your library resources, find out more about people like Louis Armstrong who were sent as ambassadors. Act as a resource person for the group.
3. (Research) Find other works by Peter Sís and share them with the group.
4. (Discuss) Why do you think artists and performers were such a powerful influence in tearing down the wall?
5. (React) Choose your favorite picture from the book. Explain why it is your favorite.
6. (Create and Follow-up) Using pictures, words, or both, explain an experience of your own that you might feel is difficult for another person to understand.

Related Works

1. Durbin, William. **The Darkest Evening.** New York: Orchard Books, 2004. 240p. $15.95. ISBN 0 439 37307 7. [fiction] MJ, CG An American family in the Depression decides to relocate to Stalin's Russia and experiences the persecution and repression.

2. Grimberg, Tina. **Out of Line: Growing up Soviet.** Toronto, ON, Canada: Tundra Books, 2007. 128p. $22.95. ISBN-13: 978 0 88776 803 3. [nonfiction] JS, G Tina Grimberg's memoir combines her memories of personal relationships, the rules of a repressive government, and Ukraine's complicated relationship with its Jewish community.

3. Partridge, Elizabeth. **John Lennon: All I Want Is the Truth.** New York: Viking Press, 2005. 231p. $24.99. ISBN 0 670 05954 4. [nonfiction] JS, GC (See full booktalk in *Booktalks and Beyond*, 2007, pages 225 to 227.) Lennon's life from his birth during a bombing raid, through his tumultuous childhood, into his collaboration with the Beatles typifies the rebellious personality that finally destroyed the Cold War.

4. Tan, Shaun. **The Arrival.** New York: Scholastic, Inc./Arthur A. Levine Books, 2007. 128p. $19.99. ISBN-13: 978 0 439 89529 3. [wordless graphic] MJS, CG The story, told completely in pictures, communicates the joy of arrival and sharing.

5. Zindel, Paul. **The Gadget.** New York: HarperCollins Publishers, 2001. 184p. $15.99. ISBN 0 06 028255 X. [fiction] MJ, B (See full booktalk in *Teen Genre Connections*, 2005, pages 151 to 154.) Thirteen-year-old Stephen Orr, whose father works with other scientists to build an atom bomb, is befriended by an older Russian boy who is a spy. The story anticipates the conflict of the Cold War between East and West.

Multiple Cultures

Books that deal with multiple cultures let us see our own worlds through different windows. The girls' selections deal with women's often conflicting and conflicted roles within different cultures. The boys' selections focus more on young men discovering and protecting heritage.

Identity

ぐ゚ひ

Abdel-Fattah, Randa. **Does My Head Look Big in This?**

New York: Scholastic, Inc./Orchard Books, 2007. 352p. $16.99.
ISBN-13: 978 0 439 91947 0. [fiction] JS, G

Themes/Topics: Muslim life, spiritual journey, coming of age, conduct of life, prejudice

Summary/Description

Eleventh-grader Amal Mohamed Nasrullah Abdel-Hakim is an Australian-Muslim-Palestinian who decides to wear the *hijab*, the Muslim head scarf, full time. At her snobby prep school, she experiences prejudice, rejection, and crude jokes, even though her friends and family support her. The hijab symbolizes her dedication to her faith, and the close observation of her faith helps her deal with attackers, an obnoxious neighbor, a love interest, and the pressures of the most conservative and liberal Muslims. By the end of the novel, she realizes that the hijab is just the beginning of her faith journey, that she too holds prejudices, and that she has the ability to integrate positively her spiritual beliefs and intellect to form a positive and independent life. The story explains many facets of Islam, and, with humor, combines the faith journey with universal teen challenges.

Read Aloud/Reader Response

1. Chapter 7, page 79, beginning "What's happened to me?" and ending with the chapter. Amal questions her own dedication to her beliefs.
2. Chapter 8, pages 87 to 92, beginning "Our shopping spree…" and ending with the chapter. The passage describes a woman who embraces an Islam based on prejudice.
3. Chapter 11, pages 117 to 118, beginning with the chapter and ending "…off with Rita." Washing her feet before prayer, Amal encounters harassment.
4. Chapter 41, page 333, beginning "I feel guilty…" and ending with the chapter. Amal realizes her own arrogance and prejudice and decides that wearing the hijab is the beginning of the journey.
5. Chapter 45, page 359 to 360, beginning "Some people…" and ending with the chapter. Amal summarizes her experience and explains how it will help her move on.

Booktalk

Hold up a scarf that can be used as a hijab. Ask the group what they feel about it. Then fashion it as a hijab on your own head or on the head of a girl in the group. Discuss how their feelings about the piece of cloth have changed or failed to change.

Australian Amal Mohamed Nasrullah Abdel-Hakim is in the eleventh grade of a snobby Australian prep school. That kind of school could give a girl with a name like hers some problems. But Amal decides to complicate her life even more. She decides to wear the Muslim head scarf, the *hijab*. That decision means that she must also follow a devout Muslim life, which includes wearing clothes that cover her entire body except for her face and hands, praying several times per day, and washing her feet before prayer. All those things, combined with her name and skin color, should make her a real outcast. But Amal finds that putting on the veil really means taking off other things. She doesn't worry about fitting into the popular peer group. Being so different, she starts to see other different people differently. And, covered up, she pays more attention to what is inside her as well as what is inside others. But some people don't have that kind of revelation or insight. Suddenly they see a foreigner, a terrorist, a national threat. Suddenly they see someone that they don't want to see. And all that negative reaction forces Amal to one big question about her hijab, *Does My Head Look Big in This?* In fact, her head may look so big that it just frightens people from considering every other part of her. Join Amal on her journey. Then you decide.

Get Involved

1. (Research) Invite a priest, a rabbi, a minister, and an imam to discuss, in a panel format, the similarities among their beliefs.
2. (Research) Using your library resources, find out more about Arab/Israeli conflict. Share your information with the group in an oral and visual display.
3. (Research) Using your library resources, learn more about the beliefs of Islam. Act as a resource person for the group.
4. (React) Choose one character in the novel. Explain what that character reveals for you about Amal and about the Muslim experience.
5. (Create) Choose one symbol of your spiritual faith. Wear or display it. Record in a journal how that action affects you and those around you.

Related Works

1. Fama, Elizabeth. **Overboard.** Chicago, IL: Cricket Books, 2002. 158p. $15.95. ISBN 0 8126 2652 4. [fiction] MJS, G (See full booktalk in *Teen Genre Connections*, 2005, pages 109 to 111.) Fourteen-year-old Emily spends seventeen hours struggling for survival, reflecting on her priorities, and bonding with a nine-year-old Muslim boy after her boat, filled with Muslim pilgrims, sinks.
2. Fraustino, Lisa Rowe (ed.). **Soul Searching: Thirteen Stories about Faith and Belief.** New York: Simon & Schuster Books for Young Readers, 2002. 267p. $17.95. ISBN 0 689 83484 5. [fiction, short stories] MJS, CG The stories talk about the great faith required in all cultures to face life's problems and responsibilities.
3. Green, John. **An Abundance of Katherines.** (See full booktalk in "Contemporary"/"Learning about Love," pages 44 to 46.) Dumped by the nineteenth Katherine he has dated, Colin Singleton, a self-absorbed, has-been child prodigy, embarks on a road trip with his best friend, the humorous, overweight Hassan, who tries to stay loyal to his Islamic beliefs while fearing he will be mistaken for a terrorist.
4. Siddiqui, Haroon. **Being Muslim.** Toronto, ON, Canada: Anansi Press/Groundwood Books, 2006. 160p. (Groundwork Guide). $9.95pa. ISBN-13: 978 0 88899 786 9. [nonfiction] JS, CG Siddiqui explains the politics affecting the faithful, the situation of European Muslims, Muslim beliefs, women's role, the relationship between jihad and terrorism, and the future of the movement. He includes source notes, a list of readings, and an index.

5. Singer, Marilyn (ed.). **I Believe in Water: Twelve Brushes with Religion.** New York: HarperCollins Publishers, 2000. 280p. $24.89. ISBN 0 06 028398 X. [fiction, short stories] JS, CG In these dozen stories, the authors express the challenges of faith in religion and life.

ເ&ະ

Bastedo, Jamie. On Thin Ice.
Calgary, AB, Canada: Fitzhenry & Whiteside Company/Red Deer Press, 2006. 348p. $10.95pa. ISBN 0 88995 337 6. [fiction] JS, CG with high interest for girls

Themes/Topics: Inuit culture, polar bears, global warming, conduct of life, identity

Summary/Description

Sixteen-year-old Ashley, a mixture of Irish, French Canadian, and Inuk bloodlines, lives in a northern small town with her extended family, which includes ancient Uncle Jonah. She experiences dreams predicting imminent disasters that are tied to polar bears. As the family battles unusual storms and catastrophic environmental events caused by global warming, Ashley grows to accept the spiritual powers of her heritage and her affinity for the bear. Through art, her drawing and Jonah's carving, she learns that her Uncle Jonah, a shaman, holds similar powers. When Jonah dies, or vaporizes, she realizes that her uncle, her teacher, has become one with the bear. Now it is her job to accomplish the same blending of the world, dream, and spirit. The full song of the bear shaman and a "Glossary of Inuktitut Words" are at the back of the book. A companion Teacher's Guide is available through Red Deer Press or on-line at www. onthinice.ca.

Read Aloud/Reader Response

1. "Goodbye Nanurtalik," pages 14 to 16. This chapter, Ashley's first dream, anticipates the entire novel.
2. "Uitajuq," pages 16 to 22, beginning "It was the weirdest..." and ending with the chapter. This passage establishes Ashley's background and gifts.
3. "Uncle Jonah's Cup," pages 33 to 35, beginning "Uncle Jonah then..." and ending with the chapter. Uncle Jonah's unusual cup illustrates his talent and power.
4. "Bear Talk," page 75, beginning "I'm telling you..." and ending "...are for seals." The passage illustrates how both man and bear must depend on reading the ice for survival.

5. "The Bear Shaman's Song," pages 342 to 345. Each verse introduces a section of the novel. Together, the songs establish Ashley's growth into her native heritage.

Booktalk

A dead teenager on the ice. Mauled by a bear. No one can believe such a promising young man is dead. No one can believe that a polar bear, a bear that doesn't usually appear in that region, did it. Yet, another teenager, a seventeen-year-old named Ashley experiences the unbelievable each day. Ever since she and her family moved into a house with her Uncle Jonah, an ancient shaman, polar bears fill her disturbing dreams. The bears spill out her pencil and onto her sketchbook. To Ashley, they are pictures, even cartoons she is trying to figure out. To Uncle Jonah, they are important symbols that tie his people to the land. But Ashley sees more than bears in her dreams. She sees melting land, collapsing buildings, dying families. In this new and confusing shift in land and temperature, Ashley may be the only one with the vision to save her people. Her people? Ashley has what she calls "minestrone blood." Her grandfather was Irish. Her mother is French Canadian, and her father is Inuk. Yet she alone seems able to see the future of her Arctic community, a world that is disappearing rapidly, a world, like Ashley, hoping to find its balance *On Thin Ice*.

Get Involved

1. (Research) Using your library resources, learn more about global warming. Act as a resource person during the discussion.
2. (Research) Using your library resources, find out more about the Inuit culture and beliefs. Act as a resource person during the discussion or prepare a visual display for presentation to the group.
3. (Discuss) How do Ashley's dreams relate to her journey?
4. (React) Why do you think that Bastedo did not create Ashley as a pure-blood Native?
5. (React) Ask each person in the group to choose one or two characters that seemed to be central to Ashley's journey. Ask each person to explain the choices.

Related Works

1. Bledsoe, Lucy Jane. **How to Survive in Antarctica.** New York: Holiday House, 2006. 101p. $6.95. ISBN 0 8234 1890 1. [nonfiction] MJS, CG Bledsoe describes her exploratory trip to Antarctica and notes the efforts, in contrast to Arctic exploration, to preserve the land.

2. Evans, Kate. **Weird Weather: Everything You Didn't Want to Know about Climate Change but Probably Should Find Out.** Toronto, ON, Canada: Groundwood Books, 2007. 96p. $15.95. ISBN-13: 978 0 88899 838 5. [graphic, nonfiction] JS, CG Evans makes the case that we must act against global warming. She includes "Take Action" Web sites, Web sites with climate change news, "Interactive Online Games," and "Recommended Further Reading."

3. Newth, Mette. **The Transformation.** New York: Farrar, Straus and Giroux, 2000. 195p. $16.00. ISBN 0 374 37752 9. [fiction] JS, CG with high interest for girls (See full booktalk in *Booktalks and More,* 2003, pages 224 to 226.) Set in fifteenth-century Greenland, the story is about the journey of Navarana, a native of Greenland, and Brendan, an Augustine brother sent to convert the heathens. Navarana completes her shaman quest, and both realize their love and coming of age.

4. Pratt, Christina. **An Encyclopedia of Shamanism, Volumes One (A-Ma) and Two (N-Z).** New York: The Rosen Publishing Group, 2007. 316p. $433.50. ISBN-13: 978 1 4042 1040 0. [reference] JS, CG More than 750 cross-referenced entries listed alphabetically describe the major practices and beliefs of shamanism in multiple cultures. The introductory essays in Volume One provide excellent background information for *On Thin Ice.*

5. Sullivan, Paul. **Maata's Journal.** New York: Atheneum Books for Young Readers, 2003. 240p. $16.95. ISBN 0 689 83463 2. [fiction] JS, G Seventeen-year-old Maata, an Inuit, records her survival in an Arctic expedition from April to July of 1924. She reflects on two situations that brought her here: the resettlement of the Inuits by the Canadian government and the expedition's purpose of mapping and measuring nature rather than listening to the land.

☙❧

LAT. Kampung Boy.

New York: Roaring Brook Press/First Second, 2006. 142p. $16.95.
ISBN 1 59643 121 0. [graphic] MJS, CG

Themes/Topics: rural Malaysia, 1950s, Muslim life, rubber plantation, tin mining

Summary/Description

Starting with his parents' marriage and ending with his journey to school, *Kampung Boy* outlines the life of a Muslim boy within the customs of a disappearing rural family lifestyle. He explains birth, circumcision, and marriage customs, the rhythms of daily living, and family expectations. Like young boys of other nationalities, he deals with peer pressure, family duties, and school discipline. The simple and humorous graphics complement the text.

Read Aloud/Reader Response

1. Pages 4 to 8, beginning "I cannot truly recall..." and ending "...my folks had for them." The boy describes the birth ceremonies and customs.
2. Pages 15 to 18, beginning "At the age of four..." and ending "...Maimunah." The boy describes how he participates in the work of the village and home.
3. Pages 44 to 50, beginning "As I reached six..." and ending "Even that was all right." The boy explains his first school.
4. Pages 66 to 72, beginning "As far as I can..." and ending "...a very happy occasion." The boy describes a Muslim wedding.
5. Pages 95 to 107, beginning "Time traveled too fast,..." and ending "...Dad bought the tickets." The boy describes the circumcision ceremony.

Booktalk

As you can see, *Kampung Boy* is a little different. (*Show some of the pictures that illustrate the text.*) His creator, LAT, is sometimes considered the Charles Shultz of Malaysia. *Kampung Boy* grew up in a different culture and a very different time, the 1950s. In his village or *kampung*, everything that happens in life happens with a ceremony. There is a birth ceremony, a marriage ceremony, even a little ceremony for going to school. These rituals let people know what they are to do and how they are to act. But life and the world are changing. His family has rubber plantations, but the monster tin mines threaten to eat them. His village schools him in his Muslim religion as well as reading, writing, and arithmetic, but his father wants very much to see his son leave the village world and learn in a bigger school. One that will help him become an important man in a bigger world. Every day, life gets more serious and full of change. He tells you about that world, as he tells you about himself, the little *Kampung Boy*.

Get Involved

1. (Research) Learn more about Muslim ceremonies tied to life events. Act as a resource person for the group during the discussion.
2. (Research) The author talks about a way of life that is disappearing in Malaysia. Using your library resources, learn more about life in Malaysia in the 1950s and today. Act as a resource person for the group during the discussion.

3. (Create) Tell your own life story by using text and graphics.
4. (Research) Using your library resources, learn more about the history and manufacturing of rubber. Act as a resource person for the group during the discussion.
5. (Research) Using your library resources, learn more about the history and manufacturing of tin. Act as a resource person for the group.
6. (React) List one piece of new information that you learned from reading *Kampung Boy.* Explain how it related to your own experience.
7. (React) Do you see anything in the life of the Kampung Boy that is like your life?

Related Works

1. Cain, Timothy. **The Book of Rule: How the World Is Governed.** New York: DK Publishing, 2004. 320p. $30.00. ISBN 0 7894 9354 3. [reference] MJS, CG This reference discusses the governments of 193 countries and explains how power evolves in each. Malaysia is examined on page 111.
2. Lekuton, Joseph Lemasolai. **Facing the Lion: Growing up Maasai on the African Savanna.** Washington, DC: National Geographic, 2003. 123p. $15.95. ISBN 0 7822 5125 3. [nonfiction] MJS, CG with high interest for boys (See full booktalk in *Booktalks and Beyond,* 2007, pages 234 to 236.). Joseph Lekuton describes his nomadic life as a Maasai. In Chapter 1, he relates an unsuccessful lion encounter that teaches him to confront the other lions in his life.
3. Satrapi, Marjane. **Persepolis.** New York: Random House/Pantheon, 2003. 153p. $11.95pa. ISBN 0 375 71457 X. [graphic memoir] JS/A, CG with high interest for girls. The great-granddaughter of one of Iran's emperors, Satrapi recounts her life from age six to age fourteen that witnessed the overthrow of the Shah, the Islamic Revolution, and the war with Iraq.
4. Siddiqui, Haroon. **Being Muslim.** Toronto, ON, Canada: Anansi Press/Groundwood Books, 2006. 160p. (Groundwork Guide). $9.95pa. ISBN-13: 978 0 88899 786 9. [nonfiction] JS, CG Siddiqui explains the politics affecting the faithful, the situation of European Muslims, Muslim beliefs, women's role, the relationship between jihad and terrorism, and the future of the movement. He includes source notes, a list of readings, and an index.
5. Son, John. **Finding My Hat.** New York: Scholastic Press/Orchard Books, 2003. 185p. (First Person Fiction). $16.95. ISBN 0 439 43538 2. [fiction] MJS, CG (See full booktalk in *Booktalks and More,* 2007, pages 254 to 257.) In a series of essays, Jin-Han Park tells about his American life as a son of Korean immigrant parents.

ↂↂ

Myers, Walter Dean. Harlem Summer.

New York: Scholastic Press, 2007. 176p. $16.99. ISBN-13: 978 0 439 36843 8. [fiction]
MJ, CG with high interest for boys

Themes/Topics: Harlem, 1920s, conduct of life, self-determination, class distinction

Summary/Description

Sixteen-year-old Mark Purvis learns about the sunny side and shady sides of Harlem and life when he works for both Fats Waller and the newspaper, *The Crisis*, in his 1925 summer. Waller involves him in bootlegging, which connects him to white and black gangsters. W.E.B. Dubois's *Crisis* gives him a glimpse of the New Negro, a group of artists, intellectuals, and entertainers that include Langston Hughes and Miguel Covarrubias. After a summer of violence, snobbery, friendship, and new love, Mark decides that he loves all of Harlem. He won't be a gangster or a status seeker, but carve out a respectable, honorable, and happy life in Harlem.

Read Aloud/Reader Response

1. "A Registered Letter Brings Bad News from the South and I Start Looking for a Summer Job—Hopefully, Not in a Funeral Parlor," page 6, beginning "My brother, Matt..." and ending "...more crumby than crusty." Mark Purvis describes himself by comparing himself to his brother.

2. "How the Ruination of My Whole Summer Started and I Began to Be a New Negro When I Wasn't Really Through Being the Old Negro I Used to Be," page 12, beginning "Henry was my..." and ending "...friends ever since." Mark introduces his best friend, Henry.

3. "I Start Off Having a Bad Day, Miss Newsome Teaches Me What Uppity Really Means, and Then Things Get Much Worse As Henry and I Learn That We Are Doomed," pages 47 to 51, beginning "The job at *The Crisis*..." and ending "...answer that question." Mark learns the definition of the New Negro.

4. "I Meet Mr. Wallace Thurman and Decide That Being Strange Is All Right If You Are Strange in an Interesting Way," pages 78 to 79, beginning "Me and Daddy..." and ending with the chapter. After a basketball game, Mark's father reflects on segregation.

5. "I Am Taken to Jail Like a Common Thug, Given the Third Degree, But Am Saved by My Reputation as an International Gangster, Bad

Man, and the New Breed of Criminal," pages 138 to 139, beginning "Just then the door..." and ending "...the newest Negro of all." Mark marvels at how the talent and celebrity of Fats Waller give him privilege.

Booktalk

Sixteen-year-old Mark Purvis lives in Harlem. His mother's family is "uptown" respectable. His dad just works hard to keep them all going. When the family loses land, their nest egg, to back taxes, Mark decides to help out. In 1925, he has lots of choices, but his number one choice is becoming rich and famous by playing jazz. To get his break, he just has to connect with a rising Harlem star like Fats Waller. Fats has a job for him, but it's all about bootleg liquor, not jazz. Mark sees good money, short hours, and a way to break into the entertainment business. Even if it is a break in through the back door. What could go wrong? Everything he doesn't see when he says yes. But as those problems and complications start to appear, Mark gets a closer look than he wants. It all happens—fast and dangerous—in one short *Harlem Summer.*

Get Involved

1. (Research) Using library resources, find out more about one of the persons pictured in the back of the book. Act as a resource person during the discussion.
2. (Research) Using library resources, find out more about Prohibition and the Cotton Club. Act as a resource person during the discussion.
3. (Research) Using library resources, research black sports in both baseball and basketball. Act as a resource person during the discussion.
4. (React) Mark Purvis makes many choices that show what kind of person he is and will be. Cite one choice that you feel is most revealing. Share your opinion with the group. Be sure to consider how these choices move from the "sunny side" to the "shady side."
5. (Research) Using library resources, ask each group member to find one selection by Langston Hughes. Ask them to share the selection in relation to the story.

Related Works

1. Clinton, Catherine (prose text), and Stephen Alcorn (illus.). **I, Too, Sing America: Three Centuries of African American Poetry.** Boston, MA: Houghton Mifflin Company, 1998. 128p. $20.00. ISBN 0 395 89599 5. [poetry anthology] JS, CG (See full booktalk in

Booktalks Plus, 2001, pages 219 to 221.) The anthology includes thirty-six poems by twenty-five African-American poets, and spans three centuries. Each poet reflects the concerns of the time and the universality of poetry.

2. Giovanni, Nikki. **Shimmy Shimmy Shimmy Like My Sister Kate: Looking at the Harlem Renaissance through Poems.** New York: Henry Holt, 1996. 188p. $16.95. ISBN 0 8050 3494 3. [poetry] JS, CG (See full booktalk in *Booktalks Plus,* 2001, pages 236 to 238.) The collection celebrates the poets and spirit of the Harlem Renaissance, a period Giovanni sees as one of the first flowerings of African-American culture. Short essays explain the poets' place in African-American life and her reaction to the poets.

3. McKissack, Frederick. **Black Hoops: The History of African Americans in Basketball.** New York: Scholastic Press, 1999. 154p. $15.95. ISBN 0 590 48712 4. [nonfiction] MJS, CG with high interest for boys (See full booktalk in *Booktalks Plus,* 2001, pages 106 to 107.) *Black Hoops* tells the story of basketball in the larger context of race relations in America and American sports.

4. Myers, Walter Dean (poem), and Christopher Myers (illus.). **Harlem.** New York: Scholastic Press, 1997. 30p. $16.95. ISBN 0 590 54340 7. [illustrated poetry] MJS, CG with high interest for boys (See full booktalk in *Booktalks Plus,* 2001, pages 241 to 243.) In this celebration of the Harlem spirit, the pictures of Christopher Myers make a striking backdrop for the words of Walter Dean Myers.

5. Nelson, Kadir. **We Are the Ship: The Story of Negro League Baseball.** (See full booktalk in "History"/"Shaping," pages 252 to 255.) With beautiful full-color art and a folksy narrator, Nelson tells the story of the flash, humor, and grit that characterized the Negro Leagues.

Integration

෬෯

Alexie, Sherman, and Ellen Forney (illus.). The Absolutely True Diary of a Part-Time Indian.

New York: Little, Brown & Company, 2007. 228p. $16.99. ISBN-13: 978 0 316 01368 0.

[fiction] JS, CG with high interest for boys

Themes/Topics: Spokane Indians, reservations, race relations, diaries, family relationships, alcoholism

Summary/Description

Intellectually gifted, but physically challenged Arnold Spirit (a.k.a. Junior) decides to leave the reservation school and go to Reardan, a more prosperous white school. He tells his story in diary form. His best friend and neighbors turn into enemies. As the only Indian student in Reardan, he encounters prejudice but makes good friends and becomes a varsity basketball player. The Native American community shows its full resentment toward him when Reardan's team plays the reservation team. Even Arnold's former best friend seriously injures him. In the playoffs, Reardan defeats the reservation team. Arnold is the hero, but regrets the victory because he realizes how little the Native American team has.

Arnold chronically misses school because of his alcoholic father and a series of alcohol-related deaths in his family, but he still finishes the year with good grades. His reconnects with his best friend who concludes that Arnold is the old-style, nomadic Indian. Arnold believes he can continue at Reardan, avoid alcohol, and reach for success. The language and situations may be considered controversial.

Read Aloud/Reader Response

1. "Slouching Toward Thanksgiving," pages 82 to 88. Arnold enters Reardan and discovers that he is less than Indian and even less than human.
2. "Dance, Dance, Dance," pages 118 to 129. In this diary entry, Arnold takes Penelope to the dance and learns that his Reardan friends accept not only his race but also his poverty.
3. "Don't Trust Your Computer," pages 130 to 132. In this diary entry, Arnold reflects on the tribe's hostility toward him, and Gordy puts it all in the context of the individual versus the tribe.
4. "Red Versus White," pages 152 to 158. In this diary entry, Arnold reflects on the tolerance of his grandmother who is run over by a drunk Indian driver.
5. "Remembering," pages 216 to 218. In this diary entry, Arnold reflects on his year and what he has learned about himself.

Booktalk

Fourteen-year-old Arnold Spirit is one Indian who is ready to jump the reservation. He almost died when he was born. He has too many teeth. His hands, feet, and head are too big. And he has to wear huge glasses because his eyes are on the warpath with each other. Did I mention that he also has a speech impediment? He belongs to the reservation's Black-Eye-of-the-Month Club. Even the grown men get a kick out of kicking him, the resident loser, around. So what can a kid like Arnold do in his free time? Draw. (*Read pages 5 and 6, beginning with "I draw all the time." and ending with the chapter.*) Arnold also is smart enough to know that staying in reservation school means that he will never leave the reservation and never share his drawings with the rest of the world. So he decides to go to Reardan, a school of middle-class white kids. It has two things that the reservation school doesn't have: hope and competition. Arnold will be the only Indian besides that school mascot. But does that scare a warrior? You bet. How can Arnold live on an Indian reservation and compete both academically and socially in a white school? With great difficulty. Read all about it in *The Absolutely True Diary of a Part-Time Indian.*

Get Involved

1. (Research) Using your library resources, research the impact that casinos have had on Native American life. Act as a resource person in the group during the discussion.
2. (Research) Using your library resources, research one Native American custom or belief. Act as a resource person in the group during the discussion.
3. (Create) Arnold draws cartoons of people. Draw a cartoon of Arnold as a part-time Indian.
4. (Follow-up) Keep your own diary for a month. Illustrate it with cartoons or pictures. At the end of the month, take time to write an entry or draw a cartoon that communicates who you are.
5. (React) Do Arnold's experiences apply to more than Native Americans? Use specifics from the novel to support your opinions.
6. (Discuss) By the end of the novel, do you think that Arnold still feels that cartoons are a more trustworthy form of communication than words? Be sure to find specifics from the text to support your opinion.

Related Works

1. Bruchac, Joseph. **Code Talker: A Novel about the Navajo Marines of World War Two.** New York: Dial Books, 2005. 231p. $16.99. ISBN 0 8037 2921 9. [fiction] MJS, CG with high interest for boys. Ned Begay, as a grandfather, tells his grandchildren about the life that led him to a military medal in World War II.
2. Carvell, Marlene. **Sweetgrass Basket.** New York: Dutton Children's Books, 2005. 243p. $16.99. ISBN 0 525 47547 8. [fiction, poetry] JS, G (See full booktalk in *Booktalks and Beyond*, 2007, pages 244 to 246.) Sent to an off-reservation school after their mother's death,

Mattie and Sarah Tarbell find their Mohawk heritage and their own self-respect challenged by the white world's cruelty, prejudice, and ignorance.

3.   Noël, Michel. Shelley Tanaka (trans.). **Good for Nothing.** Toronto, ON, Canada: Groundwood Books, 2004. 322p. $18.95. ISBN 0 88899 478 8. [fiction] JS, CG with high interest for boys. In 1959, fifteen-year-old Nipishish, a Métis or half-breed, returns to the Indian reserve in northern Quebec after being thrown out of residential school and discovers the government's plots against his people.

4.   Olsen, Sylvia. **White Girl.** Winlaw, BC, Canada: Sononis Press, 2004. 235p. $9.95. ISBN 1 55039 147 X. [fiction] S, G When her mother marries an Indian, fifteen-year-old Josie Jessop moves to the reservation and discovers a new family, a new love, and her own prejudices. Some language may be considered controversial.

5.   Orenstein, Denise Gosliner. **Unseen Companion.** New York: Harper-Collins Publishers/Katherine Tegen Books, 2003. 357p. $16.89. ISBN 0 06 052057 4. [fiction] JS, CG In 1969 Bethel, Alaska, four teenagers tell their stories about a beaten half-breed teenage rebel, Dove Alexie, who, after being arrested, suddenly disappears.

ʚ̣ɞ

Cooney, Caroline B. **Diamonds in the Shadow.**

New York: Delacorte Press, 2007. 230p. $15.99. ISBN-13: 978 0 385 73261 1. [fiction] JS, CG with high interest for boys

Themes/Topics: refugees, Africans, civil war, family life, Connecticut, trust, redemption

Summary/Description

The Finch family, against the wishes of their teenage son Jared, agrees to sponsor the Amabo family, four refugees from a civil war in Africa. Under threat of death or maiming from a fifth refugee, the "family," made up of a married couple and two teenagers posing as their children, smuggles blood diamonds into the country. The "family" and the fifth refugee are separated at the airport. Jared and his younger sister begin to suspect the family's authenticity as its members adjust to American life. The fifth refugee, assigned to Texas, traces the Amabo family to their new Connecticut home. He enters the home and threatens to kill the daughters of both families if they don't give him the diamonds. The Amabo daughter, promising to give him the diamonds but knowing that he will kill them both, leads him to a supposed hiding place by the sea and then pulls him under. Jared, pursuing them with the Amabo son, saves her life. The Amabos are now a true family through adversity and plan a new life together.

Read Aloud/Reader Response

1. Chapter 1, pages 6 to 12, beginning "Kirk Crick launched..." and ending with the chapter. Kirk Crick tells about the family, and Jared reacts skeptically.
2. Chapter 3, page 32, beginning "The refugee officer..." and ending "...'shoe,' 'food.'" Andre Amabo explains losing his hands.
3. Chapter 5, pages 81 to 84, beginning "Neither Andre nor Celstine..." and ending with the chapter. The family travels to the supermarket.
4. Chapter 9, pages 138 to 141, beginning "A few classes later..." and ending "...without eating it." Alake reacts to all the positive feedback in America.
5. Chapter 11, pages 178 to 179, beginning "Jared listened..." and ending "What about me?" Jared reflects on faith and organized religion.
6. Chapter 12, pages 186 to 190, beginning "On Saturday..." and ending "Diamonds are money." Alake and Jared react to the service and hymns.

Booktalk

Ask how many people in the group would like to own a diamond. Let them explain why. In the remarks, ask them how much they expect to pay for a diamond.

Jared Finch doesn't know much about diamonds, but soon they will change his life. He lives in Connecticut. He has a great house, his own room, and an annoying little sister. He likes things just the way they are. He learns that he is going to have to share it all. Not the usual sharing with a family member or a friend but sharing with four African refugees, the Amabo family. They will be living in his house for a month. The Amabo's son will stay in Jared's room. Did anyone ask Jared? Jared's high-power, controlling mom, with the encouragement of their minister, is spearheading the effort. When the church committee gets together to tell the Finch family what to expect, Jared, with his questions and attitude, isn't the most popular person in the room. And when the family arrives at the airport, everyone gets a little more than they expect. The father of the African family has no arms. How will he ever support himself or his family? The son says he is carrying his grandparents' ashes in cardboard boxes. The daughter acts deaf, mute, and blind. The mother ignores her children. They wonder who permitted these people to immigrate. But there is an even bigger surprise, one they don't see. A fifth refugee. He killed to get here, and he will kill again. He knows about the Amabo family. He arranged to get them here. Now he is arranging to become a rich man in a rich country. How will he accomplish it all? With diamonds, not the love diamonds that Americans like the Finches connect with Valentine's Day, Christmas, and marriage, but blood diamonds that finance wars and take people's lives. The Amabos' world has no "good guys," just casualties and survivors. In their world, diamonds cost more than money, and they know that survival means keeping *Diamonds in the Shadow.*

Get Involved

1. (Research) Using your library resources, learn more about the Sudan. Act as a resource person for your group.
2. (Research) Cooney cites three sources about refugees in "A Note from the Author." Using those sources, find out as much as possible about the life of refugees. Act as a resource person for your group during the discussion.
3. (Discuss) What elements of the ending did you anticipate? Point to specific clues.
4. (React) How realistic are the American characters in the novel?
5. (Discuss) Why do you think that Cooney includes the theft within Jared's church?
6. (Follow-up) Decide in your discussion group what contribution you can make to this growing world problem and then craft your project according to your goal of informing, fund raising, or learning. You may wish to involve local churches.

Related Works

1. Cooney, Caroline B. **Code Orange.** New York: Delacorte Press, 2005. 200p. $15.95. ISBN 0 385 90277 8. [fiction] MJS, CG with high interest for boys (See full booktalk in *Booktalks and Beyond,* 2007, pages 116 to 118.) High school student Mitty Blake encounters smallpox scabs in an antique book, posts messages on the Internet, draws attention from the government and terrorists, and must save himself after being kidnapped.
2. Cooney, Caroline B. **The Terrorist.** New York: Scholastic Press, 1997. 198p. $15.95. ISBN 0 590 22853 6. [fiction] MJS, G (See full booktalk in *Booktalks Plus,* 2001, pages 135 to 138.) Unaware of political movements and motivations, Laura, living in London with her

family, seeks the terrorist responsible for her little brother's death and moves herself farther away from friends and closer to the actual killer.

3. Cross, Gillian. **Phoning a Dead Man.** New York: Holiday House, 2002. 252p. $16.95. ISBN 0 8234 1685 2. [fiction] MJS, CG (See full booktalk in *Teen Genre Connections*, 2005, pages 131 to 133.) When Hayley and her family learn that John, Hayley's older brother, died in a detonation accident, she and John's girlfriend refuse to believe the report and travel to Russia to find him. John is alive, and all three become embroiled in a conflict with the Russian Mafia.

4. Mankell, Henning. Anne Connie Stuksrud (trans.). **Secrets in the Fire.** Toronto, ON, Canada: Annick Press LATD, 2003. 166p. $17.95. ISBN 1 55037 801 5. [fiction] MJS, G Sophia, a young refugee from war-torn Mozambique, builds a new life after losing her sister and her legs in a land-mine explosion.

5. Miklowitz, Gloria. **The Enemy Has a Face.** Grand Rapids, MI: Eerdmans Books for Young Readers, 2003. 139p. $16.00. ISBN 0 8028 5243 2. [fiction] MJ, CG with high interest for girls (See full booktalk in *Teen Genre Connections*, 2007, pages 137 to 140.) When seventeen-year-old Adam disappears, the Hofmans, a Jewish family from Israel, now living in Los Angeles, suspect that Palestinian terrorists kidnapped or killed Adam but eventually discover that three American boys from good homes shot him in a random thrill killing.

෴

Hostetter, Joyce Moyer. **Healing Water: A Hawaiian Story.**
Honesdale, PA: Calkins Creek Books, 2008. 217p. $17.95.
ISBN-13: 978 1 59078 514 0. [fiction] MJS, CG

Themes/Topics: leprosy, conduct of life, Molokai (Hawaii), nineteenth-century history, family

Summary/Description

Thirteen-year-old Pia, feeling abandoned by Kamaka, his best friend and mentor, leaves his family to live in Molokai, as a leper. To survive physically, he becomes a slave to a man who controls the lawless island. Pia learns to steal from, intimidate, and exploit others. Eventually, Kamaka, with his wife who has leprosy, also comes to Molokai. Pia rejects Kamaka's attempts at reconciliation, but slowly pulls himself away from his evil master. He joins Kamaka's family in a mutual struggle for survival. They maintain their alliance without true friendship until Father Damien comes to the island, organizes it into a humane community, and demonstrates the difference between hate for evil deeds and love for the flawed people who commit them. Pia returns to the true Hawaiian custom of sharing and hospitality. He accepts the Christian forgiveness. Kamaka and he renew their friendship. The "Author's Note" explains the story's historical context. A "Timeline" traces the history of the disease in relation to Hawaii and Father Damien. "About Hawaiian" explains the pronunciation of the language. A "Glossary" defines Hawaiian words used in the story. "Resources" list relevant books, DVDs, audio, Web sites, and places of interest.

Read Aloud/Reader Response

1. Chapter 1, pages 13 to 14, beginning "My grief turned…" and ending with the chapter. Pia expresses his anger and frustration toward his disease and exile.
2. Chapter 4, pages 30 to 31. The two-page chapter explains the relationship between Pia and Kamaka. The last line of the chapter is repeated in Chapter 31, in the last sentence on page 199.
3. Chapter 12, pages 75 to 83. In this chapter, Pia receives his horse.
4. Chapter 30, page 198, beginning "Damien poured…" and ending with the chapter. Father Damien washes Pia's feet and begs Pia to keep emotional numbness from destroying him.
5. Chapter 31, pages 199 to 202. In this final chapter, Pia forgives Kamaka and finds renewal in his own life.

Booktalk

Ask how many in the group know about the disease leprosy or Hansen's disease. After members of the group contribute information, show pictures of people with the disease.

In the 1800s, leprosy was a death sentence. Victims who lived in Hawaii were torn from their families and sent to the island of Molokai. The government relied on the family and sharing traditions of the Hawaiian people to keep the island stable and patients of all ages safe. After all, Hawaiians believed in sharing. They took in the homeless and made them their own, but most of the people on this island were too sick to help anyone. Some were willing to kill and steal to survive. Thirteen-year-old Pia is sent to that world, a prison of disease and nature that he cannot escape. His family cries over him. His best friend abandons him. Grief and bitterness are his companions. He resolves to be strong, to do anything to survive. But as he destroys others, he is destroying himself. He is dying in both his body and his heart. In the middle of a lawless village on a remote island, where can he find the secret to staying alive? In the middle of the ocean, where can he find the *Healing Water?*

Get Involved

1. (Research) Using your library resources, continue to research the beliefs of the Hawaiian native population. Act as a resource person during the discussion.
2. (Research) Select one of the sources recommended by Hostetter. Examine it and share its information with the group during the discussion.
3. (React) Name one element or event of the novel that surprised you. Compare your reaction with that of others in the group.
4. (Discuss) Hostetter frames the illness of Pia in the friendship between him and Kamaka. Do you think this choice was more or less powerful than if Pia had been in conflict with a family member?
5. (Create) Pia describes the experience through his eyes. Choose one scene in the novel. Rewrite it from the point of view of another character.

Related Works

1. Bolognese, Don. **The Warhorse.** New York: Simon & Schuster Books for Young Readers, 2003. 165p. $16.95. ISBN 0 689 85458 7. [fiction] MJ, CG (See full booktalk in *Teen Genre Connections,* 2005, pages 228 to 230.) Against his father's wishes, fifteen-year-old Lorenzo Arrighi from the house of master armorers joins his duke in a war against a treacherous count. In his travels, he falls in love with the daughter of a leper family.
2. Cindrich, Lisa. **In the Shadow of the Pali: A Story of the Hawaiian Leper Colony.** New York: G. P. Putnam's Sons, 2002. 245p. $18.99. ISBN 0 399 23855 7. [fiction] MJS, G (See full booktalk in *Teen Genre Connections,* 2005, pages 90 to 92.) In the late nineteenth century, twelve-year-old Liliha, a leper, is sent to the newly formed lawless Hawaiian Leper Colony. After both fighting bullies and making alliances, she accepts her disease and resolves to make the colony her home.
3. Ellis, Deborah. **The Heaven Shop.** Narkham, ON, Canada: Fitzhenry & Whiteside, 2004. 192p. $16.95. ISBN 1 55041 908 0. [fiction] MJ, CG with high interest for girls (See full booktalk in *Booktalks and Beyond,* 2007, pages 229 to 231.) Thirteen-year-old Binti Phiri finds her family broken by AIDS.
4. Hostetter, Joyce Moyer. **Blue.** (See full booktalk in "History"/ "Struggling," pages 225 to 227.) Thirteen-year-old Ann Fay Honeycutt

becomes the man of the house when her father leaves to fight World War II, but soon finds herself battling polio.

5.   Talarigo, Jeff. **The Pearl Diver.** New York: Doubleday, 2004. 240p. $18.95. ISBN 0 385 51051 9. [fiction] S/A, CG with high interest for girls Shortly after Hiroshima, a young Japanese pearl diver discovers that she has leprosy, a disease that was perceived during the war as a block to expansionism. She is sent to an island for lepers, declared dead to her family, and given a new name.

ℭ ℜ
McDonald, Janet. Off-Color.
New York: Farrar, Straus and Giroux/Frances Foster Books, 2007. 163p. $16.00.
ISBN-13: 978 0 374 37196 8. [fiction] J, G

Themes/Topics: racially mixed people, mothers and daughters, single-parent families, interpersonal relationships, Brooklyn

Summary/Description

Rebellious fifteen-year-old Cameron and her single mother move to the projects when the mother loses her job and transfers to another nail salon for lower pay in an African-American neighborhood. In the move, Cameron discovers and comes to grips with the fact that her father is African-American. Now she meets and makes friends with some of the same people whom she challenged in shopping malls. The mother, a skilled technician, wins respect and friendship in her new job. An elderly lady in the projects befriends them, and Cameron is attracted to the woman's biracial grandson.

Read Aloud/Reader Response

1.   Chapter 3, pages 26 to 28, beginning "Patricia drained the last drops..." and ending "...class in no time." The passage illustrates how Cameron can get by with doing what she wants.
2.   Chapter 9, pages 88 to 98. In this chapter, Cameron discovers her father's identity.
3.   Chapter 11, pages 116 to 118, beginning "'Okay, guys,...'" and ending "...ending the year." The class talks about how skin color affects them.
4.   Chapter 12, pages 122 to 125, beginning "Patricia was showing..." and ending "'...white girl hair.'" Cameron faces the Project Girls who show her sympathy.
5.   Chapter 15, pages 155 to 163. This final chapter is Cameron's conclusion that her entire experience in moving to the projects is positive.

Booktalk

Fifteen-year-old Cameron has it made. She has good friends, goes in and out of school whenever she wants, and has her mother wrapped around her little finger. Now things are going to change big time. Mom is asking questions about Cameron's whereabouts. The guidance counselor at school isn't taking any more of Cameron's creative excuses. The salon where her mom works is closing down. Mom and Cameron are out of money and moving to the projects. The nightmare move unearths some old family pictures and documents that talk about Cameron's father, a topic Mom *never* talks about. Is that good news? Maybe and maybe not. Cameron is confused out of her mind. Suddenly, her bright and shining world with all its blue skies is starting to look just a little *Off-Color*.

Get Involved

1. (Research) Starting with those mentioned in *Off-Color*, use your library resources to research multi-racial couples, and celebrities with multi-racial heritage. Act as a resource person during the group discussion.
2. (Discuss) How realistic did you feel the story to be? Use specific details to support your answer.
3. (Compare) Read other novels about African-Americans. Compare the worlds described in those novels to the world that McDonald describes in her novel.
4. (Research) Using your library resources, learn how to trace your own family history.
5. (Follow-up) Use the information about your heritage to construct a family tree.
6. (Create) Write the most creative excuse that you can think of for not coming to school.

Related Works

1. Flake, Sharon G. **Begging for Change.** New York: Hyperion Books for Children/Jump at the Sun, 2003. 235p. $15.99. ISBN 0 786 80601 X. [fiction] MJS, G (See full booktalk in *Teen Genre Connections*, 2007, pages 286 to 289.) In this sequel to *Money Hungry*, Raspberry Hill steals from a friend and wonders whether she is as dishonest as her shiftless father. The novel also deals with racial identity and starting over in a new neighborhood.
2. Flake, Sharon G. **Money Hungry.** New York: Hyperion Books for Children/Jump at the Sun, 2001. 187p. $15.99. ISBN 0 786 80548 X. [fiction] MJS, G (See full booktalk in *Teen Genre Connections*,

2005, pages 285 to 289.) Thirteen-year-old Raspberry Hill becomes obsessed with money so that she and her mother will not end up being homeless again.

3. McDonald, Janet. **Chill Wind.** New York: Farrar, Straus and Giroux/ Frances Foster Books, 2002. 134p. $16.00. ISBN 0 374 39958 1. [fiction] MJS, G In this sequel to *Spellbound,* nineteen-year-old Aisha, mother of two, realizes that her welfare will be terminated in sixty days while her friend Raven is reaping the positive benefits of hard work and honesty.

4. McDonald, Janet. **Spellbound.** New York: Farrar, Straus and Giroux/Frances Foster Books, 2001. 138p. $16.00. ISBN 0 374 37140 7. [fiction] MJS, G Raven Jefferson faces the responsibility of her pregnancy and vows to finish high school, go to college, and become self-supporting in contrast to Aisha Ingram, her friend, who plans to lie and play the welfare system.

5. McDonald, Janet. **Twists and Turns.** New York: Farrar, Straus and Giroux/Frances Foster Books, 2003. 135p. $16.00. ISBN 0 374 39955 7. [fiction] MJS, G Keeba and Teesha, friends of Raven from *Spellbound* and *Chill Wind,* find success in the hair business after overcoming jealous friends, scheming politicians, and greedy landlords.

ርሻ ፕን

Yang, Gene Luen. American Born Chinese.
New York: Roaring Brook Press/First Second, 2006. 233p. $16.95.
ISBN-13: 978 1 59643 152 2. [graphic] MJS, CG with high interest for boys

Themes/Topics: prejudice, identity, schools, Chinese-Americans

Summary/Description

Yang blends three stories: fable of the monkey king; Jin Wang's attempt to fit in a Caucasian school; and a popular teenage boy's struggle with his stereotypical Chinese cousin who visits him each year. The monkey king, left out of the social life of the gods, wishes to shed his monkey form. Jin Wang, wanting to be Caucasian, tries to change his appearance so that he can fit in and be attractive to an American girl. Danny, popular and athletic, endures visits from his obnoxious Chinese cousin. When the frustrated Danny knocks his cousin's head off, he discovers the cousin was the monkey king in disguise. The monkey king counsels him about wanting to change his form and become Danny. Jin accepts his identity and reconciles with his true friend, a Chinese immigrant, whom the monkey king reveals to be his son, an emissary who is passing a test of virtue by living in the West for forty years. Although this story centers on Chinese-Americans, it speaks to anyone in an out-group.

Read Aloud/Reader Response

1. The frames appearing on pages 7 to 20. The monkey king reacts to being thrown out of the party for the gods.
2. The frames appearing on pages 23 and 24. The mother tells Jin the Chinese parable about neighborhoods.
3. The frames appearing on pages 27 to 29. The herbalist responds to Jin's desire to be a transformer.
4. The frames appearing on pages 163 to 198. Jin completes his transformation by selling his soul.
5. The frames appearing on pages 201 to the end of the novel. Jin confronts his cousin, and, in doing so, ultimately confronts his poor decisions.

Booktalk

Show a transformer to the group. Ask what they associate with it.

Jin Wang is the only Chinese-American student in his school. He wants to stop being beaten up. He wants to fit in. Solution? He will become a transformer. He will solve all his problems the all-American way. He will even date an all-American girl. It seems simple. A few changes to his thinking and appearance and all his problems will be solved. But the Chinese part of his life keeps pushing him back. His mother has her parables that remind him how he should live. His best friend who comes from China doesn't seem to want to join the all-American crowd. Even the Chinese gods seem to be taking an interest in his life, and messing it up. Getting through American high school is tough enough for an all-American, but it seems twice as tough when you're *American Born Chinese.*

Get Involved

1. (Research) Continue to find information about Chinese myths, especially the monkey king. Act as a resource person during the discussion.
2. (Discuss) After noting how Yang used the transformer as the center of his story, ask each person in the group to bring in or tell about a toy and how it influenced his or her life.
3. (Discuss) Does this story apply to more than people from Chinese-American culture?
4. (Research) Find a Western fable. Briefly summarize it, and tell how it applies to everyday living.

5. (Create) Compile a how-to book or speech based on the fables found in Get Involved 4. Share it with your peers through a student publication or Internet site.

Related Works

1. Bass, L. G. **Sign of the Qin: Book One.** New York: Hyperion Books for Children, 2004. 383p. (Outlaws of the Moonshadow Marsh). $17.99. ISBN 0 78681918 9. [fiction] MJS, CG with high interest for boys (See full booktalk in *Booktalks and Beyond,* 2007, pages 147 to 150.) In this combination of legend, history, and mythology, a young man marked to be Starlord begins his mission to save the earth with the guidance of a trickster monkey who hopes that this assignment will guarantee him immortality.

2. Giddens, Sandra, and Owen Giddens. **Chinese Mythology.** New York: Rosen Central, 2006. 64p. $29.95. ISBN 1 4042 0769 4. [nonfiction] MJS, CG with high interest for boys. The introduction defines myth and differentiates it from legends, folktales, and fables. It explains how myths have influenced Chinese culture, lists the main gods and deities, and gives examples of some major myths. The "Glossary" defines terms. "For More Information" lists addresses and Web sites. "For Further Reading" lists additional print sources, and a "Bibliography" lists the author's sources.

3. Nam, Vickie (ed.). **Yell-Oh Girls!** New York: HarperCollins/Quill, 2001. 249p. $13.00pa. ISBN 0 06 095944 4. [nonfiction] JS, G (See full booktalk in *Booktalks and More,* 2003, pages 262 to 264.) In essays and poetry, Asian-American females express their joy, frustration, and determination in relation to their ancestry.

4. Shone, Rob. Claudia Saraceni (illus.). **Chinese Myths.** New York: Rosen Central, 2006. 48p. (Graphic Mythology). $29.95. ISBN 1 4042 0799 6. [nonfiction] MJS, CG with high interest for boys. This graphic presentation includes three myths: "The Four Dragons," "Nu Wa Makes People and Mends a Hole in the Sky," and "The Ten Suns." "More Mythical Characters" lists the more well-known characters. The "Glossary" explains new terms, and "For More Information" lists addresses, Web sites, and print titles.

5. Son, John. **Finding My Hat.** New York: Scholastic Press/Orchard Books, 2003. 185p. (First Person Fiction). $16.95. ISBN 0 439 43538 2. [fiction] MJS, CG with high interest for boys (See full booktalk in *Booktalks and Beyond,* 2007, pages 254 to 257.) In a series of essays, Jin-Han tells about his integration into American life when coming from a Korean family.

Conflict

ଘ୨

Barakat, Ibtisam. Tasting the Sky: A Palestinian Childhood.

New York: Farrar, Straus and Giroux/Melamie Kroupa Books, 2007. 176p. $16.00.
ISBN-13: 978 0 374 35733 7. [nonfiction] JS, CG

Themes/Topics: Arab-Israeli conflict, family relationships, childhood

Summary/Description

In Parts I and III, the author speaks about her life, her frustration and hope, in 1981. Part II, the main story, extends from the first day of the Six Day War in 1967 to 1971 when the family finds a permanent home. At the beginning of the Six Day War, the author is three and a half years old, and in the panicked evacuation, she is swept away from her family. After their reunion, she experiences life in a shelter, her occupied hometown, towns new to her, an orphanage, and UN-provided schooling. Each description emphasizes the turmoil in her fragile family, their determination to survive, as well as the history and traditions that root them to the land. A map at the beginning of the book allows the reader to follow the events in the memoir, and a "Historical Note" explains the region's wars and conflicts. The "To Learn More" section in the back of the book suggests more books, a movie, and a Web site of related works.

Read Aloud/Reader Response

The entire book is an excellent and moving read aloud. The following are some specific sections for consideration.

1. Part I, pages 8 to 11, beginning, "Post Office Box 34..." and ending "...for their letters?" The author describes the importance of having her own post office box and communicating with her non-Palestinian pen pals.
2. Part II, pages 39 to 41, beginning "Crawling up the steps..." and ending "...less alarming." The author describes waiting with her swollen foot in the shelter and learning to cope with the pain and turmoil by imagining.
3. Part II, the entire section, "Return," pages 67 to 77. The author describes their return home after four months and thirteen days.

4. Part II, the entire section, *"Balad,"* pages 119 to 130. The visit reveals their culture and establishes their roots.
5. Part III, pages 170 to 171. The author explains that she can tell her story. "A Song for Alef," a poem that praises the first letter of the Arabic alphabet, implies that writing and telling the stories of war may be the answer to finding peace.

Booktalk

When she is three and a half years old, Ibtisam Barakat, a Palestinian, loses her home and almost her entire family. It is 1967, and Israel launches the Six Day War. Ibtisam, her mother, father, and two brothers are in its path. Her small hands cannot tie her shoe fast enough, and her family is swept away from her in the crowd of refugees. She finds them again, but will never find her old life. Her once happy and stable family now moves from town to town, fights poverty and hunger, and sees even their ties to each other threatened by violence and fear. And yet Ibtisam manages to find one friend, ever loyal Alef, the first letter of the Arabic alphabet. He can help her tell her story to the world and to move away from the desolation around her. He will show her how wonderful and how possible it is to be finally free, to be *Tasting the Sky*.

Get Involved

1. (Research) Using your library resources, learn more about the war of 1948. You may wish to start with Related Work 4. Act as a resource person during the discussion.
2. (Research) Using your library resources, learn more about the Six Day War. You may wish to start with Related Work 2. Act as a resource person during the discussion.
3. (Research) Using your library resources, learn more about the programs that the UN administers for children. Act as a resource person for your group during the discussion.
4. (React) Choose one fact or story that surprised you. Explain to the group what you learned from it. Ask each person in the group to share their choices also.
5. (Create) Compile a bibliography of stories or memoirs about families or young people whose lives are threatened or disrupted by war. Ask members of the group to choose one of the selections and then share their reactions in a discussion.
6. (Follow-up) In "To Learn More," the author provides a movie, Web site, and list of books. Ask each person in the group to read or examine one of the selections. Ask which selections they would

recommend to others. Be sure that each person supports the recommendation with specifics.

Related Works

1. Armstrong, Jennifer (ed.). **Shattered: Stories of Children and War.** New York: Alfred A. Knopf, 2002. 166p. $15.95. ISBN 0 375 91112 X. [short stories] JS, CG This collection includes stories about conflict in the Middle East, Vietnam, World War II, the Cold War, Russian/Afghanistan War, the American Civil War, and Bosnia. "The Second Day" by Ibtisam Barakat is an earlier version of the chapter "Shelter" in *Tasting the Sky.*

2. Broyles, Matthew. **The Six-Day War.** New York: The Rosen Publishing Group, Inc., 2004. 64p. (War and Conflict in the Middle East). $27.95. ISBN 0 8239 4549 9. [nonfiction] JS, CG Broyles explains the relationship between the Arabs and the Jews, the build-up to the war, the war, and the results.

3. Carmi, Daniella. **Samir and Yonatan.** New York: Arthur A. Levine Books, 2000. 192p. $15.95. ISBN 0 439 13504 4. [fiction] MJ, CG Samir, a Palestinian, and Yonatan, a Jew, supposedly enemies, bond while in a Jewish hospital. Only in an imaginary world created by Yonatan do they feel that they can live in peace.

4. Hayhurst, Chris. **Israel's War of Independence.** New York: The Rosen Publishing Group, Inc., 2004. 64p. (War and Conflict in the Middle East). $27.95. ISBN 0 8239 4548 0. [nonfiction] JS, CG Hayhurst explains the factors leading to the War of Independence and the impact it had on the Arab world.

5. Zenatti, Valérie. Adriana Hunter (trans.). **When I Was a Soldier: A Memoir.** New York: Bloomsbury Children's Books, 2005. 235p. $16.95. ISBN 1 58234 978 9. [nonfiction] JS, CG with high interest for girls (See full booktalk in *Booktalks and Beyond,* 2007, pages 241 to 244.) The author describes her compulsory military service in the Israeli army and the questions, pride, and maturity it brings to her.

Ellis, Deborah. I Am a Taxi.

Toronto, ON, Canada: House of Anansi Press/Groundwood Books, 2006. 204p.
(The Cocalero Novels). $16.95. ISBN-13: 978 0 88899 735 7. [fiction]
MJ, CG with high interest for boys

Themes/Topics: coca industry, Bolivia, child labor,
crime, protest

Summary/Description

Twelve-year-old Diego lives in San Sebastián Women's Prison in Cochabamba, Bolivia. He shares half a cell and one bed with his mother and three-year-old sister. His parents were given a sixteen-year prison sentence after being falsely accused of smuggling drugs during a trip into town to sell their coca crop. The father lives in the prison next door. Diego helps support his family by serving as a taxi for the inmates. He carries messages and runs errands for them. He also sells his mother's knitted goods, watches his little sister, and attends school. Mando, his friend, whose father also lives in prison, wants him to join him in a money scheme. Diego resists until he loses his taxi privileges for being negligent in watching his sister. Hoping to give his angry and desperate mother some money, he runs away with Mando to work for drug producers and dealers. Abused and drugged by the dealers, Diego persuades Mando to escape. Mando dies in the attempt. Recaptured, Diego manages to escape again and finds safety with a small farm family.

Read Aloud/Reader Response

1. Chapter 1, pages 9 to 23. The chapter describes the prison.
2. Chapter 2, pages 37 to 40, beginning "You are an honest boy?" and ending with the chapter. Diego visits the American consulate.
3. Chapter 5, pages 72 to 83. The chapter describes the mistake that causes Diego to run away.
4. Chapter 10, pages 138 to 139, beginning "I hope you're not…" and ending "…had a better life." Smith tells Diego about the positives of fear.
5. Chapter 11, pages 145 to 146, beginning with the chapter and ending "…watching television to care." Smith explains the power of drugs.

Booktalk

Twelve-year-old Diego has spent four years in a Bolivian prison. What did he do wrong? Nothing. Four years ago his parents were sentenced to sixteen years in prison for smuggling drugs. They didn't do it, but that doesn't make any difference. They were convicted. Now Diego lives in half of one cell with his mother and three-year-old sister. He helps pay for the cell and their food by delivering messages and running errands for the inmates. He is what is known as a taxi. It isn't a life anyone wants, but it is one that he knows. He is one of the best in the prison, and he helps his family get by. Then things change. His sister gets lost. Diego was supposed to be watching her. His mother is fined. Diego loses the right to be a taxi, and Diego's friend has an idea. The idea will make them lots of money. The money will give their families a more comfortable life. Diego and his friend will have to work just two weeks. Everything is right—until everything goes wrong. The new job may put Diego in prison for life or kill him. He left one prison for another, the jungle where no creature, man or beast, wants to listen to Diego's proud claim, *"I Am a Taxi."*

ᘓᘔ

Ellis, Deborah. Sacred Leaf.

Toronto, ON, Canada: House of Anansi Press/Groundwood Books, 2007. 206p.
(The Cocalero Novels). $16.95. ISBN-13: 978 088899 751 7. [fiction]
MJ, CG with high interest for boys

Summary/Description

Diego, sheltered by the Ricardo family who are, like his parents, poor coca farmers, finds himself protesting with the cocaleros against the army who has stolen and destroyed their coca crops. He earns the respect of both the protestors and the military when he stays and works with the protestors rather than return immediately to his family. The protestors are eventually removed from the bridge nonviolently, and both the protest organizer and the police captain offer Diego jobs when he reunites with his family in Cochabamba. At the end of the novel, Diego is helping the police captain apprehend the men who take boys like Diego and Mando to the jungle to process cocaine for foreigners.

Read Aloud/Reader Response

1. Chapter 5, pages 59 to 70. This chapter describes the confrontation between the soldiers and the protestors.
2. Chapter 7, pages 82 to 86, beginning "'There will be...'" and ending "'That's a very powerful job.'" Diego meets the team of runners.
3. Chapter 8, page 98, beginning "Diego saw a group..." and ending "...waved it in the air." Diego learns the meaning of Vargas's cowboy hat.
4. Chapter 14, pages 160 to 162, beginning "'What do you...'" and ending with the chapter. Diego tries to connect with Dario, but cannot move past the young man's immaturity.
5. Chapter 17, pages 182 to 189, beginning "Diego returned to..." and ending with the chapter. The ending of the blockade shows the character of the people on both sides.

Booktalk

Diego finds safety with the Ricardo family or does he? The Ricardo family, like other poor Bolivian families, grows coca. Bolivians have used and sold it for centuries. Other governments want that stopped. The coca can be turned into cocaine and sold on American streets. It helps Bolivian families and destroys North American ones. When the government soldiers arrive to seize the family's crop, Diego can't just stand by. These farmers have helped him, and he will help them. But a twelve-year-old boy is no match for the soldiers. Once again he is a prisoner. He could be thrown in prison like his parents, or he could be shot. Is Diego risking his future for just a deadly street drug or for his own people's *Sacred Leaf?*

Get Involved

1. (Research) Using your library resources, find out more about the production and sale of cocaine. Be sure to consider the role of the United States. Act as a resource person during the discussion.
2. (Research) Using your library resources, find out more about the government of Bolivia. Act as a resource person during the group discussion.
3. (Research) Using your library resources, find out the difference between an embassy and a consulate. Act as a resource person during the discussion.
4. (Discuss) How does Ellis depict the problem of coca and cocaine? Do you agree with her point of view? Be sure to support your opinion with specifics from the novels.
5. (React) Diego, at twelve years old, is considered to be almost a man. Compare his life and responsibilities with your own. In an essay or just in conversation, react to the similarities and differences that you find.

Related Works

1. Apel, Melanie. **Cocaine and Your Nose: The Incredibly Disgusting Story.** New York: Rosen Central, 2000. 48p. (Incredibly Disgusting Drugs). $26.50. ISBN 0 8239 3251 6. [nonfiction] MJ, CG with high interest for boys. Apel explains the effects of cocaine and its related drugs on the entire body, and provides possible support for keeping clean. Other titles in the series deal with alcohol, heroin, marijuana, speed, tobacco, oxycontin, crystal meth, depressants, prescription drugs, stimulants, and inhalants.
2. Cain, Timothy. **The Book of Rule: How the World Is Governed.** New York: DK Publishing, 2004. 320p. $30.00. ISBN 0 7894 9354

3. [reference] MJS, CG. This reference discusses the governments of 193 countries and explains how power evolves in each. The very poor and conflicted country of Bolivia is examined on page 254.

3. Ellis, Deborah. **The Breadwinner Trilogy.** Toronto, ON, Canada: Groundwood Books. [fiction] MJ, CG with high interest for girls.

    a. **The Breadwinner.** 2000. 170p. $5.95pa. ISBN 0 88899416 8. When the Taliban take eleven-year-old Parvana's father away, Parvana masquerades as a boy to support her family and discovers Shauzia, a classmate, doing the same.

    b. **Parvana's Journey.** 2002. 199p. $5.95pa. ISBN 0 88899 519 9. After her father's death, Parvana continues to search for her family, forms a new family with refugee children she finds along the way, and eventually reunites with her own mother in a refugee camp.

    c. **Mud City.** 2003. 164p. $5.95pa. ISBN 0 88899 542 3. Shauzia, Parvana's friend, gives up her dream to escape Afghanistan's devastation and realizes her responsibility to help people within the refugee camp.

4. Lunde, Paul. **Organized Crime: An Inside Guide to the World's Most Successful Industry.** New York: DK Publishing, 2004. 192p. $30.00. ISBN 0 7894 9648 8. [nonfiction] JS, CG with high interest for boys. Using full-color photographs, maps, and charts, the oversized volume deals with the history, development, and current statuses of organized crime groups all over the world. Pages 182 to 187 focus on the Colombian drug traffickers who collect cocaine from other South American countries and distribute cocaine world-wide.

ርʒ℞℧

Nanji, Shenaaz. **Child of Dandelions.**

Asheville, NC: Front Street, 2008. 214p. $17.95.
ISBN-13: 978 1 932425 93 2. [fiction] JS, G

Themes/Topics: Uganda (1971–1979), East Indians, family life, friendship, forced migration, ethnic group relations

Summary/Description

When President Idi Amin declares that all "foreign Indians" must be "weeded out of the country" in ninety days, fifteen-year-old Sabine, a Ugandan of Indian descent, agrees with her successful father that her family can remain safely in Uganda. As the ninety days progress, her uncle mysteriously disappears, her friendship with Zena, a native girl, deteriorates, and their household is threatened. Finally, a new law declares that *all* Indians must leave. Sabine and her family, with the help of her grandfather and the United Nations, weather the harsh treatment of Ugandan officials and flee the country. At the airport, she encounters Zena who is now engaged to Idi Amin. They understand each other's positions, and as Sabine leaves, she realizes that as a weed, a dandelion, she has the strength to extend tenacious new roots in a new land. The "Author's Note" explains the Indian history within Uganda. A map of Uganda appears at the front of the book.

Read Aloud/Reader Response

1. "The Dream," pages 9 to 11. The chapter depicts the tension produced by Idi Amin's dream.
2. "The Feather," pages 39 to 41, beginning "He always..." and ending with the chapter. Katana gives Sabine the feather to protect her, and the description explains why his magic is real and important.
3. "The Fight," pages 47 to 53. In this chapter, Sabine's mother and father fight over whether they should go or stay. The father explains to Sabine why they are a vital part of Uganda.
4. "At Zena's," pages 89 to 95. In this chapter, more high-profile people disappear, and Zena rejects Sabine as a "child of dandelions."
5. "Going, Going, Going," pages 204 to 210. In this final chapter, Sabine and Zena meet at the airport and renew their understanding. Sabine finds peace as she realizes that she is strong enough to start over.

Booktalk

Ask how many in the group have heard of Uganda or the former president of Uganda, Idi Amin. Have a map of the country and a picture of Idi Amin. Briefly explain Idi Amin's rule and his impact on Uganda.

Fifteen-year-old Sabine is a native-born citizen of Uganda, but she isn't black. She is brown, and her ancestry is Indian. Her family is wealthy. Her grandfather is a very successful farmer. Her father is a wealthy businessman. Her uncle is a famous race car driver who brings cheers from all Ugandans. So when the new president, Idi Amin, announces that all foreign Indians must be "weeded out" of Uganda, and that they must leave the country in ninety days, Sabine believes that he couldn't be talking about her, but as the days tick by she isn't so sure what she believes. Soldiers threaten her. Her famous uncle disappears. Zena, her best friend, doesn't want to be around her anymore. The family's loyal servant thinks she needs a magic charm for protection. Her mother begs the father to flee. And then another announcement: *All* Indians must leave the country. Sabine is no longer the child of a respected family or a beloved celebrity. She has been changed to someone who must be ripped from her roots and thrown away. She is now the *Child of Dandelions.*

Get Involved

1. (Research) Continue to find out more about Uganda. Act as a resource person during the discussion.
2. (Discuss) What event do you think effected the biggest change in Selene? Be sure to refer to specifics in the text for support.
3. (Discuss) Who are the good guys and who are the bad guys in the story? Be sure to refer to specifics in the text for support.
4. (Create) Sabine admires the sayings that Zena wears on her clothes. Select the sayings that you might wear on your own clothes. Explain your choices.
5. (Compare) Sabine and her family experience a forced migration because of political persecution. Read about experiences of other teenagers who have also been forced from their homes. Discuss the patterns that emerge among those persecutions. You may wish to start with the selections listed below.

Related Works

1. Bagdassarian, Adam. **Forgotten Fire.** New York: DK Publishing, Inc., 2000. 273p. $17.95. ISBN 0 7894 2627 7. [fiction] JS, CG with high interest for boys (See full booktalk in *Booktalks and More,* 2003, pages 49 to 51.) Based on fact, this novel tells the story of Vahan Kenderian, an Armenian boy who, between 1915 to 1918, suffered under the persecution of the Armenian holocaust.
2. Beah, Ishmael. **A Long Way Gone: Memoirs of a Boy Soldier.** (See full booktalk in "Adventure/Survival"/"Fight," pages 98 to 100.) In the upheaval of Sierra Leone, Ishmael becomes a boy soldier whose main focuses are killing and good drugs.
3. Mikaelsen, Ben. **Tree Girl.** New York: HarperCollins Children's Books, 2004. 240p. $16.99. ISBN 0 06 009004 9. [fiction] JS, CG with high interest for girls (See full booktalk in *Teen Genre Connections,* 2005, pages 94 to 96.) Fifteen-year-old Gabriela loses her teacher, classmates, and most of her family when government troops of Guatemala begin a systematic Indian massacre.
4. Müller, Melissa. Rita Kimber and Robert Kimber (trans.). **Anne Frank: The Biography.** New York: Henry Holt and Company, 1998. 330p. $14.00pa. ISBN 0 8050 5997 0. [nonfiction] S/A, CG This work places Anne Frank in a family, social, and political

context. It clearly describes the Jewish marginalization and eventual death.

5. Spalding, Frank. **Genocide in Rwanda.** New York: Rosen Publishing, 2009. 64p. (Genocide in Modern Times). $29.95. ISBN-13: 978 1 4042 1823 9. [nonfiction] MJS, CG This volume defines genocide and explains the one-hundred days of killing in Rwanda that the world ignored. On page 15, the author reveals a link between the genocide in Rwanda and the strife in Uganda. Other books in the series explain similar genocides in Armenia, Bosnia, Darfur, Rwanda, Germany, and Cambodia.

6. Ung, Loung. **First They Killed My Father: A Daughter of Cambodia Remembers.** New York: HarperCollins Publishers, 2000. 239p. $23.00. ISBN 0 06 019332 8. [nonfiction] JS, CG (See full booktalk in *Booktalks and More*, 2003, pages 54 to 56.) Loung describes the destruction of her family under the Khmer Rouge. She now works for Campaign for a Landmine Free World.

ᘓᘔ

Schmidt, Gary D. Trouble.
New York: Clarion Books, 2008. 297p. $16.00.
ISBN-13: 978 0 618 92766 1. [fiction] MJS, CG

Themes/Topics: Cambodian-Americans, Massachusetts, automobile accidents, grief, family life, refugees, prejudice, dogs, friendship

Summary/Description

On Henry Smith's fourteenth birthday, his older brother, Franklin, is fatally injured by a pickup truck supposedly driven by Chay Chouan, a Cambodian refugee who is also a student at the brother's exclusive preparatory school. As the brother lay dying, and Chay stands trial, the family learns that the athletic and much-celebrated Franklin cruelly bullied and harassed Chay. Accompanied by his best friend and an abused mongrel Henry saved from drowning, Henry decides to deal with the anger, fear, and grief from his brother's death by carrying out a plan that he and Franklin shared, climbing Mt. Katahdin. Chay, fleeing his own home, picks them up. At first, Henry conflicts with and beats up Chay, but gradually softens as he learns about Chay's Cambodian childhood, his harsh home life, and the prejudice he faces in America. After Chay risks his own life to save Henry's, Henry realizes that Franklin attacked Chay because Chay dated Louisa, their older sister, and that Louisa, not

Chay, was driving the truck that killed Franklin. Louisa confesses, and the family begins the healing process.

Read Aloud/Reader Response

1. Chapter 1, pages 1 to 9, beginning with the chapter and ending "...needing to say anything." The passage reveals Henry's establishment life, the accident, and Franklin's honored position.
2. Chapter 3, pages 36 to 40, beginning "During the rest..." and ending "...knows what it knows." Henry goes through a school day after the accident.
3. Chapter 5, pages 62, beginning "Louisa sat down..." and ending "...toward each other." Henry reminds Louisa of their camaraderie built on the *Wizard of Oz*.
4. Chapter 9, pages 121 to 122, beginning "Henry stretched his arms..." and ending "...ever leave him." Franklin dies.
5. Chapter 10, pages 138 to 139, beginning "His father took..." and ending "...never be fully decided." The father confides in Henry that his chief concern about Franklin's death is whether Franklin would have become a good man.

Booktalk

Let me read you just the opening sentence of this novel. (*Read aloud the opening sentence of the novel.*)

Henry Smith's house seems far away from trouble. It has kept the Smith family safe from storms and turmoil of the rugged Maine coastline for three-hundred years. It has assured them places in the best schools and the local Episcopal Church. It has been maintained by high-earning, well-educated fathers and stay-at-home mothers. But on Henry Smith's fourteenth birthday, Henry's older brother Franklin is hit by a careening truck driven by a boy who tried to build a house far from trouble too. His name is Chay Chouan, a Cambodian refugee who attends Franklin's preparatory school. Now trouble doesn't come just to the Smith family or the Chouan family, but to an entire town bubbling with grief, anger, and prejudice. Henry decides to move away from trouble again. He will take his stray dog and his best friend and climb the mountain that he and Franklin planned to climb together. But on the road the three meet Chay Chouan, also running. Chay has some grief, anger, and prejudice issues of his own. Henry and Chay discover that they share more trouble than anyone could have ever guessed. And when they decide to go to the mountain together, they find more of the unexpected, and of course, it's *Trouble.*

Get Involved

1. (Research) Find more information on the persecution by the Khmer Rouge that Chay Chouan describes. You may wish to start by reading *First They Killed My Father* (Related Work 5). Act as a resource person during the group discussion.
2. (Research) At the end of the novel, Schmidt says that Henry realizes that "The world is Trouble...and Grace. That is all there is." Continue to research the concept of grace in Christian belief. Act as a resource person during the discussion.
3. (Discuss) Fathers are an important part of the story. Compare all three fathers. Discuss the strengths and flaws of each man.
4. (React) Schmidt goes into great detail about the story's setting. Why do you think it is significant?
5. (Discuss) Why is the *Seaflower* important?
6. (React) Is any character in the story a hero? A villain?

Related Works

1. Blackman, Malorie. **Naughts & Crosses.** New York: Simon & Schuster Books for Young Readers, 2005. 387p. $15.95. ISBN 1 4169 0016 0. [fiction] JS, CG with high interest for boys (See full booktalk in *Booktalks and Beyond,* 2007, pages 16 to 19.) In this hypothetical society, two racially different young people fall in love and face the prejudice and destruction of their families and society.
2. Schmidt, Gary D. **Lizzie Bright and the Buckminster Boy.** New York: Clarion Books, 2004. 219p. $15.00. ISBN 0 618 43929 3. [fiction] MJS, CG (See full booktalk in *Booktalks and Beyond,* 2007, pages 251 to 254.) In the early 1900s, Turner Buckminster moves to Phippsburg, Maine, where he meets the smart and rebellious Lizzie Bright, the descendent of former slaves, and becomes embroiled in an attempt by the town to take her people's land.
3. Schmidt, Gary D. **The Wednesday Wars.** (See full booktalk in "Contemporary"/"Learning about Love," pages 56 to 59.) In the seventh grade during the Vietnam war, Holling Hoodhood discovers, through the teacher that he believes hates him, the meaning of faithfulness, true love, and open-mindedness.
4. Shea, Pegi Deitz. **Tangled Threads: A Hmong Girl's Story.** New York: Clarion Books, 2003. 236p. $15.00. ISBN 0 618 24748 3. [fiction] JS, G (See full booktalk in *Teen Genre Connections,* 2005, pages 264 to 267.) Chronically ill, thirteen-year-old Mai Yang lives in a Thailand refugee camp with her grandmother. When the refugees

are told that they must leave the camp, Mai Yang and her grandmother brave brutal soldiers and cultural misunderstandings.

5. Ung, Loung. **First They Killed My Father: A Daughter of
    Cambodia Remembers.** New York: HarperCollins Publishers, 2000.
    239p. $23.00. ISBN 0 06 019332 8. [nonfiction] S/A, CG Loung
    Ung's narrative begins when the Khmer Rouge take over her city.
    Driven from their homes, her family suffers beatings, humiliation,
    and starvation.

Index

About the Author

LUCY SCHALL, a former middle school English teacher, is a book reviewer for *VOYA*, and the author of four other acclaimed booktalking guides, including *Booktalks and Beyond* (Libraries Unlimited, 2007) and *Teen Genre Connections* (Libraries Unlimited, 2005).